Leadership and Information Processing

The study of executive leadership is critically important to understanding the workings and performance of organizations. Yet it is a topic that is usually ignored by mainstream leadership research. *Leadership and Information Processing* provides a much-needed analysis of this crucial element of organizational behavior.

Authors Robert G. Lord and Karen J. Maher use information processing and leadership perception processes to provide a theoretical and empirical basis for analyzing executive leadership. They focus on understanding how executives make decisions and how decision acceptance is constrained by the leadership perceptions of others. Specific concerns include leadership and social perceptions, perceptions of female leaders, dyadic leadership, organizational culture, effects of executive succession, and internal and external executive leadership.

Leadership and Information Processing offers crucial information for teachers, researchers and students of management, organizational behavior and organizational/social psychology. The authors apply state-of-the-art thinking in information processing in a way that is equally understandable to those with a non-cognitive background – for example, students of business, applied psychology and leadership.

Robert G. Lord is Professor of Industrial/Organizational Psychology at the University of Akron, Ohio. **Karen J. Maher** is Assistant Professor of Management at the University of Missouri, St. Louis.

D1255552

PEOPLE AND ORGANIZATIONS

Series Editor: Sheldon Zedeck, *Department of Psychology*
University of California, Berkeley

The study of organizations has increased significantly in recent years. In recognition of the growing importance of behavioral science research to our understanding of organizations, *People and Organizations* is a new series devoted to advanced research in industrial and organizational psychology, and organizational behavior.

The books in the series are derived from empirical programmatic research on topics related to organizations and the ways in which people interact, respond to, and cope with the organization. Topics of special interest include: organizational culture, work and family, high technology, organizational commitment, careers, and studies of organizations in international markets. Books in the series are theoretically grounded and include specific guidelines for future research.

Already available:

Volunteers
The Organizational Behavior of Unpaid Workers
Jone L. Pearce

Role Motivation Theories
John B. Miner

Leadership and Information Processing:

Linking Perceptions and Performance

Robert G. Lord
Karen J. Maher

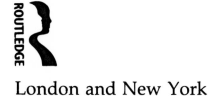

London and New York

First published in 1991
by Unwin Hyman Inc.

First published in paperback in 1993
by Routledge
11 New Fetter Lane, London EC4P 4EE

Transferred to Digital Printing 2003

Simultaneously published in the USA and Canada
by Routledge
29 West 35th Street, New York, NY 10001

© 1993 Routledge

Typeset in Palatino by Columns of Reading

British Library Cataloguing in Publication Data

A catalogue record for this book is available from the British Library.

Library of Congress Cataloging in Publication Data

Lord, Robert G. (Robert George), 1946–
  Leadership and information processing: linking perceptions and
performance/Robert G. Lord, Karen J. Maher.
  p. cm. – (People and organizations)
  "First published in 1991 by Unwin Hyman, Inc." – T.p. verso.
  Includes bibliographical references and index.
  1. Leadership. 2. Human information processing.
  3. Organizational effectiveness. I. Maher, Karen J. (Karen Jean),
  1962–. II. Title. III. Series: People and organizations
  (London, England)
  HD57.7.L67 1993;aa03 4–1–93
  303.3'6 – dc20   93–13076
                                                           CIP

ISBN 0–415–09901–3

Contents

Part I
Leadership and Information Processing

Part II
Perceptual and Social Processes

Part III
Leadership and Organizational Performance

Part IV————————————————————————————————
Stability, Change, and Information Processing

List of Tables

List of Figures

Acknowledgments

We would like to thank Terri Baumgardner, who was primarily responsible for chapter 6 and who also provided applications of our theory to female leaders. Such applications appear throughout this book.

Sheldon Zedeck provided many insightful comments on an earlier version of this book and extended to us the opportunity to write this book in the first place. We thank him for his input. We would also like to thank an anonymous reviewer for reading the entire manuscript and offering many useful suggestions. We acknowledge Lisa Freeman's patience, which was critical in helping us maintain our sanity throughout the process. Lisa also encouraged us to write the book we wanted to write.

We would like to thank the following colleagues who, patiently and without complaint, read and critiqued earlier versions of the manuscript: Carol Anderson, Jeff Bailey, Virginia Bartow, Larry Borodkin, Cathleen Callahan, Robert Depinet, Julia Gard, Jerilyn Lewter, Hal Hendrick, Lynn Kahney, Ken Kiernan, Arno Kolz, Mona Moths, Sandra Neal, Cindy Nordstrom, Matt O'Connell, Carol Oeth, Mike Polomsky, Michelle Rohrback, Scott Spera, and Sean Stevens. Their input was valuable in helping us clarify our thinking and writing.

We would also like to thank Dan Svyantek for his helpful comments and unique perspective on organizational evolution. Rosalie Hall willingly discussed several of the topics with us, and Ralph Alexander guided us through the cusp in catastrophe theory, making otherwise-inaccessible regions clear to us.

Finally, we sincerely acknowledge many of our colleagues who contributed to earlier theoretical development and empirical work in leadership and social information processing: Roseanne Foti, Jim Phillips, Dave Day, Mike Rush, Christy De Vader, Scott Fraser, Steve Cronshaw, Neal Hauenstein, Jay Thomas, Mary Kernan, Glenn Herbert, John Binning, Todd Maurer, George Alliger, Mike Campion, Paul Hanges, Sherry Hoy, Murray Barrick, Jonathan Smith, Ken Carson, Alicia Matthews, and Jan Walker.

Though the individuals mentioned above provided many valuable suggestions, any errors in analysis or logic remain the sole responsibility of the authors.

Series Editor's Introduction

The study of organizations has increased significantly in recent years as organizations and their human resources have realized the importance of sound practices and principles in achieving a competitive advantage. Though there is much that can be described as faddish in the arenas of industrial and organization psychology and organizational behavior, there is also a substantial body of research that has contributed significantly to our understanding of people and organizations. In recognition of the increasingly important role of behavioral science research in our understanding of organizations, the *People and Organizations* series was created to provide a forum for researchers to bring together their projects, data, results and theories. The books in the series are derived from empirical programmatic research on topics related to organizations and the ways in which people interact with, respond to, and operate within the organization. The purpose of the series is not only to provide a medium for describing advanced research in industrial and organizational psychology, but also to provide an opportunity for the researcher to discuss the implications of the findings in the context of the organization. In brief, the series will provide a thorough understanding of the results and direction of current research and at the same time act as a catalyst for further work.

The books in this series were chosen because they addressed issues that were timely, relevant, and sometimes controversial, but most importantly, of crucial significance for a better understanding of people and organizations. Although the series is of primary importance to the researcher, and to students of research, the books will also provide the practitioner with a deeper understanding of how the organization functions and why it functions in particular ways. The success of the series will be measured by the extent to which it acts as a stimulus for further inquiry, and, in the final analysis, by its success in contributing towards a better fit between people and organizations.

Sheldon Zedeck
Professor of Psychology and
Director, Institute of Industrial Relations

For their love and support
we dedicate this book to
Delma Lord and the memory of George Lord,
and to Bernard and Jerelyn Maher

Part I
Leadership and Information Processing

Chapter 1

Introduction

*W*ho *is Philip Caldwell?* Our guess is that most laypeople—and most leadership researchers—cannot answer this question. Yet most would immediately recognize the name of his counterpart in a competing organization. The question is interesting from a theoretical and a practical point of view. Philip Caldwell orchestrated one of the most dramatic corporate turnarounds in recent history, taking a company that lost $3.26 billion over three years (net losses of $1.54 billion in 1980, $1.06 billion in 1981, and $658 million in 1982) and turning it into a company that in 1986 outearned all its competitors with net profits of $3.29 billion, and that in 1987 set an all-time industry profit record of $4.62 billion (Halberstam 1986).

Philip Caldwell was the chairman and chief executive officer of Ford Motor Company. During his tenure as CEO, Caldwell and his management team, headed by Donald Peterson (who succeeded Caldwell as chairman and CEO of Ford in 1985), dramatically improved profits, product quality, sales, and stock prices. In the process Caldwell also changed the corporate culture, the nature of decision-making processes, and the strategic orientation of Ford Motor Company. Philip Caldwell created the prototypical American success story in one of America's most important industries.

Caldwell's more famous counterpart is Lee Iacocca. Fired from the presidency at Ford in July 1978, Iacocca went on to engineer the dramatic rescue of Chrysler, turning this near-bankrupt company into a profitable organization. There are many parallels between these two turnarounds, yet the more flamboyant and charismatic Iacocca achieved much greater recognition. His leadership qualities and reputation were so widely known that he went on to head the campaign to renovate the Statue of Liberty, wrote a best-selling autobiography, and was even seen as a potential candidate for president of the United States in 1988. Caldwell, on the other hand, achieved much more limited recognition, though his accomplishments at Ford were in many ways more impressive than those of Iacocca at Chrysler.

This contrast illustrates two of the major issues addressed in this

3

book—understanding leadership perceptions and understanding how CEOs can influence the performance of their organizations. Obviously, both Caldwell and Iacocca were very effective leaders, each engineering a dramatic turnaround at his respective organization. Yet their style of leadership and approaches to management were very different. A suitable theory of leadership should explain both the differences in the way these two individuals were perceived and how their alternative approaches to corporate leadership were successful. We address both these important issues in this book.

At this point we should distinguish between the constructs of leadership and management. We conceptualize leadership as resulting from a social-perceptual process—the essence of leadership is being seen as a leader by others. Management, in contrast, involves discharging a set of task activities associated with a specific organizational position. Leaders may or may not be good managers, and managers may or may not be viewed as leaders. Managers, though, can generally perform social tasks better if they are seen as leaders, and being perceived as a leader may be a significant determinant of recognition and promotion for managers. For these reasons, the theory of leadership perception developed in this book is relevant to managers as well as to top-level leaders. A discussion of managerial task activities, however, is beyond the scope of this book.

Who is Ann B. Hopkins? Again we expect that most readers will be unfamiliar with this individual's name. Yet her story is just as interesting and just as important as that of Philip Caldwell or Lee Iacocca. Ann B. Hopkins joined Price Waterhouse in 1978 and quickly became a successful manager and developer, bringing in more then $40 million in new business. She was the only woman out of 88 nominees for partnership in 1982, and she brought more business to the firm than any other nominee (Greenhouse 1989). But she was not made a partner, whereas 47 of the 87 men were granted this promotion. Her supporters described her as outspoken, independent, self-confident, assertive, and courageous. Opposition to Hopkins centered on her "interpersonal skills." Her detractors interpreted the same behavior as overbearing, arrogant, self-centered, and abrasive (American Psychological Association 1988, 15). In addition, many comments centered on the sex of Ann Hopkins and her "fit" with sex-related stereotypes. For example, one evaluator suggested that she take a "course at charm school," while another said the complaints about her use of profanity came up only because "she is a lady using foul language" (Bales 1988). Thus, the way Ann Hopkins was perceived by other partners was a key determinant in the decision to reject her bid for promotion. We suggest that her difficulties partially reflect the differential use of cognitive categories in the perception of men and women. Though

Ann Hopkins's interpersonal style could be interpreted as connoting leadership, we believe it was interpreted differently because Ann Hopkins is a woman and "leadership" is a categorization that is less likely to be applied to women than to men.

Ann B. Hopkins left Price Waterhouse and set up her own consulting firm. She also sued Price Waterhouse for sex discrimination under Title VII of the Civil Rights Act. She claimed that Price Waterhouse violated her civil rights by the discriminatory application of sex-role stereotypes in considering her request for promotion. Hopkins won at both the district and the appeals court levels. At the Supreme Court level, however, the Court acknowledged that sex-stereotype bias was discriminatory but remanded the case back to the appellate court to decide whether damages should be awarded (Greenhouse 1989). At the time of this writing, the appellate court has not yet ruled on damages.

LEADERSHIP AND FAILURE

Philip Caldwell, Lee Iacocca, and Ann B. Hopkins were all highly successful businesspeople but received varying degrees of recognition as leaders. Ironically, top executives of failed businesses (corporations filing for Chapter 11 bankruptcy) cannot escape receiving blame for the demise of their organizations (Sutton and Callahan 1987). Though executives play a role in organizational downturns, other factors, such as market conditions and technological innovations, also affect an organization's performance. Unfortunately for executives, these factors are often minimized by perceivers. Here, social and self-perceptions are critical, and a common issue is the perceived failure of such executives to exert sufficient leadership. For these individuals, corporate failure is interpreted as personal failure and their reputations are permanently tarnished. Such interpretations limit their future job opportunities and affect their personal lives. Moreover, these top managers often express considerable guilt over their corporations' performances, as quotations from presidents of bankrupt firms indicate: "I feel as if I committed some kind of sin"; "I think that it is the equivalent of having accidently [sic] killed your spouse and then having to live with it the rest of your life" (Sutton and Callahan 1987, 421). Thus, the attribution of business failures to top executives can have dire consequences for those involved.

LEADERSHIP PERCEPTIONS

Each of these examples highlights the importance of leadership perceptions. Being perceived as a leader affects social and self-evaluations, creates or limits future job opportunities, and enhances the ability of top leaders to garner the resources needed by their organizations. One of the major objectives of this book is to provide a detailed theory explaining leadership perceptions based on social-cognitive principles. We will do so by specifying both the features that distinguish leaders from nonleaders and the perceptual processes used by perceivers. These perceptual processes used by perceivers will be analyzed using the framework we developed in an earlier work (Lord and Maher 1990a). In that piece, we noted that leadership perceptions can be formed based on two alternative processes. Leadership can be *recognized* based on the fit of a person's characteristics with perceivers' implicit ideas of what leaders are—Lee Iacocca is recognized immediately as the prototypical leader, whereas Philip Caldwell and Ann B. Hopkins are not. Alternatively, leadership can be *inferred* based on outcomes of salient events. Business failures are usually attributed to executives, connoting a lack of leadership; dramatic successes, such as performance "turnarounds," usually cause top executives to be perceived as leaders. Similarly, in the political realm, favorable election outcomes can enhance leadership perceptions; unfavorable outcomes can detract from a candidate's perceived leadership qualities (Foti, Lord, and Dambrot, in press).

Our approach to understanding executive leadership is both social and cognitive. Leadership has long been recognized as a social process involving the mutual behavior (and perceptions) of both leaders and followers. Researchers concerned with behavior or perceptions have, however, increasingly turned to cognitive explanations of these processes. For example, behavior may be explained by the implicit theories that help a leader interpret a situation and generate appropriate responses. Similarly, perceptions may be explained by the cognitive categories (like leadership) that perceivers use to classify others. *Social-cognitive research*, which attempts to understand social processes in terms of the more fundamental cognitive processes that guide both parties in an interaction, has become very popular in the past decade. We apply this social-cognitive perspective to executive leadership, but it is also relevant to other areas of industrial/organizational psychology, such as performance appraisal and motivation.

This social-cognitive perspective will also be used to explain how leader-subordinate relationships develop and unfold over time. Dyadic relationships between superiors and subordinates will be interpreted in terms of the perceptual processes of both leaders and subordinates.

Such perceptual processes provide a context for the development and continuation of the leader-subordinate relationship. Leadership perceptions are also central to more abstract processes, such as symbolic management and the development and maintenance of organizational cultures. This basic information processing approach helps us to understand the processes of symbolic management and the important context for actions that is created by an organization's (or a nation's) culture.

Our approach to leadership is unique in two primary respects. First, much prior leadership research has focused on *motivational* processes pertinent to lower-level superior-subordinate interactions, such as path goal theory (Georgopolis, Mahoney, and Jones 1957; House 1971), reinforcement theory (Komaki 1986; Podsakoff 1982), supervisor feedback processes (Larson 1984, 1986), substitutes for leadership (Kerr and Jermier 1978), or self-leadership (Manz and Sims 1987). In contrast, our approach focuses on the *cognitive* processes of *subordinates and superiors.* This approach complements such theories by providing a broader theoretical base that helps to integrate much prior leadership research. It can be extended to upper- and lower-level leadership perceptions using the same basic social-cognitive principles. Moreover, the cognitive processes of superiors can be tied to many factors that influence *organizational* performance, in addition to the traditional focus on subordinates' performance. The second unique aspect of our approach is a focus on executive leadership and organizational performance. We will discuss this aspect below.

EXECUTIVE LEADERSHIP AND PERFORMANCE

In this book we will combine several perspectives to show how executive decisions are made, how they are accepted, and how they affect organizational performance. A cognitive perspective explains how executive decision making occurs using both logical and intuitive processes. For example, executives may use either rational processes or implicit theories to generate and evaluate alternatives in strategic decision making. Support for executive decisions can also be explained by the social-cognitive perspective. This approach helps clarify how executives are able to mobilize power to gain commitment and acceptance for their decisions, leveraging their impact on organizational performance. Executives can expand the latitude of managerial action (Hambrick and Finkelstein 1987) by appropriately managing the perceptual processes of key constituents.

Finally, we use work on systems and organizational theory to explain how executive-level actions can affect organizational performance. Our framework organizes both *internally* and *externally* oriented actions that may have either direct or indirect effects on performance. This comprehensive approach to executive actions and cognitions allows us to distinguish between executive *leadership* and the kind of executive decision making that is associated with routine management activities. For example, many decisions that top-level executives make on a day-to-day basis are not related to leadership activities.

We believe that theoretical and practical advancement requires a dual focus on leadership as a perceptual phenomenon and leadership as a determinant of performance. Yet these two foci must be integrated to develop an adequate theory of leadership. Some approaches underemphasize the effect of executive leaders on performance, while overemphasizing the importance of perceptual processes (Calder 1977; Meindl and Ehrlich 1987; Pfeffer 1977). Other approaches explain how executives can dramatically affect the performance of organizations, while underemphasizing the perceptual factors involved in leadership (Tushman and Romanelli 1985). Our approach addresses both the perceptual and the performance components of executive leadership, since perceptions and performance are reciprocally related in a process that unfolds over time. Different sets of theories are required to explain the perceptual and performance components crucial to executive leadership. Ultimately, however, these different theories should be integrated to create a useful theory of executive leadership. In separate sections of this book, we will develop a theory of leadership perception and a theory of executive performance. Then, in the final section of the book, we will combine these separate sets of theory into a more integrative theory of executive leadership—that is, we will explain when top-level executives need to be perceived as leaders to be effective and what processes produce leadership perceptions at that level of an organization. At the top level, leadership may be strongly associated with specific offices—for example, CEO or chairman of the board—but executive-level leadership may also be provided by other individuals who possess special qualities, such as expertise.

Returning to our examples of successful and unsuccessful business outcomes illustrates how the perceptual and performance aspects of leadership interrelate. Lee Iacocca had many highly visible successes at Ford Motor Company, such as his "Ford for $56 a month" in 1956 and his Ford Mustang in 1964. These successes helped establish his reputation as a leader, a crucial factor in his ability to marshal the resources needed to "rescue" Chrysler after he became CEO of that corporation. The success of Iacocca's effort at Chrysler in turn made additional resources available to buy companies like Lamborghini and American Motors. Lee Iacocca was even approached by disgruntled General Motors dealers who wanted to engineer an unfriendly takeover of General Motors by Chrysler (Iacocca and Kleinfield 1988, 121–22).

In contrast, Sutton and Callahan (1987) note that the failure of a CEO's company can dramatically reduce the capacity of that individual (and the organization) to garner needed resources: suppliers of bankrupt companies refuse to extend credit and may dump inferior products on struggling companies; bankers are unwilling to provide needed capital or to grant freedom of managerial action; consumers are hesitant to buy the company's products; and the most talented and mobile employees may leave for more secure positions in other companies. Moreover, the tarnished reputations of top executives in failed companies discredit any attempts to prevent such erosion of resources. Thus, successes enhance the leadership perceptions of CEOs, increasing CEOs' opportunities for further successes, whereas dramatic failures severely limit the potential actions of CEOs, diminishing their capacity to improve future organizational performance.

APPROACH TO LEADERSHIP THEORY

Our approach to understanding leadership is to develop a comprehensive theory addressing both leadership perceptions and organizational performance. Further, we support our theory by relying on our own empirical work, on the growing literature concerning decision making and social cognitions, and on work in organizational and economic theory. In drawing from this broad social science background we have been forced to ignore many traditional theories of leadership. (Yukl [1989] provides an excellent summary of such theories.) Our aim is to extend the theoretical basis and potential application of the leadership field, not to catalog past leadership theory. Yet when it is feasible to do so, we integrate more traditional theories with the framework we develop.

Two issues concerning our scientific philosophy should be briefly mentioned. First, we frequently use examples to illustrate the points we are making. We believe this approach makes a book more readable, more understandable, and more accessible to a broad audience of scholars, students, and/or practitioners. We acknowledge, however, that our examples do not prove the theories we propose. Theoretical support requires careful empirical work, which we will stress where it is available.

Second, we believe that theory in any scientific area is an ongoing social process. Theories develop and change as new data and perspectives are developed. Thus, a scholarly book on leadership theory should be as concerned with where the field should be going and how it should develop as it is with summarizing past research. It should attempt to go beyond empirical data to develop ideas that can be tested by future research. We propose ideas for future research, particularly in chapters 12 and 13, but we also tie these extensions to empirical and theoretical work whenever possible. Further, we will try to indicate clearly which theoretical ideas have been extensively investigated and which need additional empirical support. In short, we try to communicate both what we have found through research on leadership and what we as leadership researchers think about this topic.

ORGANIZATION OF THE BOOK

We have organized this book into four parts. The first part provides a basic introduction to leadership, describes a cognitive/ information processing approach, and shows how that approach can be applied to leadership. The second part focuses on perceptual processes associated with leadership, at both a dyadic and a more aggregate level. In this section we also examine the joint role of perceptual and performance processes relevant to female executives. Reciprocal influence in leader-subordinate dyads operates under a dual perceptual process involving both leader and subordinate perceptions of each other. At a more aggregate level, power, symbolic management, and organizational culture are shown to operate from a perceptual basis. The third part centers on explaining performance. In this section we briefly address the effects that lower-level leaders have on performance. Our primary focus, however, is on executive-level leadership and its relationship to organizational performance. Based on prior research, we will establish that executive-level leaders *do* have a substantial impact on organizational performance, either directly, through their effect on organizational strategy, or indirectly, through symbolic management and organizational culture. The fourth and final part integrates the two preceding sections into a more comprehensive theory of executive-level leadership. Readers with interests closely tied to social-cognitive work will find the second part to be especially relevant, while readers whose interests center on organizational performance may find the third part most relevant.

DEFINITION OF LEADERSHIP

Before proceeding, our definition of leadership should be clearly specified. According to Katz and Kahn (1978, 528), leadership involves an "influence increment" that goes beyond mechanically complying with one's role in an organization and routinely applying rewards or coercive power. A key argument we will make is that the ability to go beyond one's formal role depends on how a person is perceived by others. If a person is perceived as a "leader," he or she can exert more influence than if he or she is not labeled a leader by others. This influence increment can be traced directly to social perceptions.

Based on this logic, *we define leadership as the process of being perceived by others as a leader.* One of the aims of this book is to explain that process in terms of social-cognitive theory. Leadership at any level of an organization is defined in terms of the perception of relevant others, not merely by holding a specific organizational position. This definition implies that at the most fundamental level, leadership is an outcome of the social-cognitive processes we use to label others. The locus of leadership is not solely in a leader or solely in followers. Instead, it involves behaviors, traits, characteristics, and outcomes produced by leaders as these elements are interpreted by followers. Further, leadership processes are merely a specific example of more general social-cognitive processes that continually occur in everyday life. The content of leadership categories may be unique, and the consequences of being labeled a leader may be particularly dramatic when compared with the consequences of other social labels (for example, extrovert), especially as concerns top-level executives. The underlying cognitive and social processes involved, however, are quite general. Prior leadership research has emphasized the traits, behavioral style, and performance of leaders. These are certainly important factors associated with leadership, but the key issue is how these factors are used by perceivers to form or modify leadership perceptions and the organizational consequences of such perceptions. From our perspective, focusing only on such factors as leadership traits or behaviors misses a crucial aspect of leadership.

As noted by Katz and Kahn (1978), the influence increment associated with leadership is often (but not always) required in organizations because organizations cannot fully specify structures and procedures necessary for effective functioning. Yet leadership requirements can be very different at different hierarchical levels in organizations. At lower levels in organizational hierarchies, leadership involves administration utilizing existing structures and procedures. Such leadership usually involves face-to-face contact with subordinates, either individually (dyadic leadership) or in small groups. At this level, leadership perceptions are highly dependent on these face-to-face processes. Effective leadership depends not only on the adequate administration of rewards and technical abilities but also on how a supervisor's actions are interpreted by subordinates. We will not attempt to identify any behaviors or patterns of behavior that are appropriate for lower-level leaders. Rather, we will argue that the central issue is whether behaviors connote leadership to followers. That is, we will suggest that behavior builds a basis for future influence through its impact on subordinates' perceptions of leadership.

At upper levels of organizations, leaders change, create, or eliminate structures and procedures (Katz and Kahn 1978, 539). Such leadership goes beyond face-to-face contact with subordinates, relying on more formal means of communication, on indirect influence through association with significant organizational events, and on the development of appropriate organizational cultures. Like lower-level leaders, top-level leaders have to rely on influence tied to their perception as a leader. But this requirement is more complex at upper levels, since a variety of groups may be involved (organizational members, boards of directors, key external constituents). Perceivers interpret a variety of factors in assessing leadership at this level—formal communications, stories about leaders, assessments of organizational performance. In addition, a principal requirement of top-level leaders is that they be able to adopt a broad systems perspective, accurately perceiving both the internal and the external environments. Because leaders must effectively communicate to diverse audiences through varied means and must also accurately perceive different environments, top-level leadership is more cognitively demanding than lower-level leadership. We will therefore address some of the cognitive requirements of executive leaders that enable them to perceive and integrate multiple environments and issues.

The cognitive perspective has a dual application in understanding executive-level leadership. First, at top levels a cognitive perspective is useful in understanding how leaders manage the cognitive components in their jobs. Second, such a perspective also helps to explain how leaders are perceived by others. This cognitive perspective is developed in the next chapter.

Chapter 2 —————————————————————————

Human Information Processing

————————————————————————————————

A s noted in chapter 1, to understand leadership perceptions it is essential to understand how people process information. Information processing principles are central to understanding the *perceptions others hold of leaders*, including subordinates' perceptions of leaders; the nature of leader-subordinate interactions; the use of symbolism and indirect influence by upper-level leaders; and the amount of discretion afforded to leaders. Information processing principles are also important in interpreting the *perceptions held by leaders*, how these perceptions are related to decision making at both upper and lower levels of organizations, and how strategies are chosen and implemented by upper-level leaders. The purpose of this chapter is to provide the reader with a background of general cognitive processing principles. Subsequent chapters will expand on these principles and show how the model of leadership perception developed in this book differs from traditional work on this topic.

THE HUMAN INFORMATION PROCESSOR

The mind can be described as an information processing system, and human behavior is a consequence of such processing (Bourne, Dominowski, and Loftus 1979). This system is generally thought to consist of several components. An extensive discussion of those components is beyond the scope of this book. However, we will briefly discuss two issues that are important to understanding our approach to leadership perception: the different components of human memory and the allocation of attentional resources.

Memory Components and Attentional Resources
The different components of human memory have a temporal architecture that must be considered in attempting to understand information processing (Potter 1990). Humans have a very short-term sensory memory for visual information (often called iconic memory), one that holds information for up to 300 milliseconds. We also have a

very short-term conceptual memory, one that preserves information for less than 1 second. This latter type of memory is called conceptual because it retains symbolic information produced by matching sensory information to a relevant concept (for instance, the word *leadership* is preserved in terms of its underlying concept, rather than for its visual features, in very short-term conceptual memory).

We also have a more enduring and general short-term memory. Our short-term memory has only limited capacity: it can hold only about six or seven chunks of information for only 20 or so seconds. For example, when we look up a telephone number, remember it only long enough to dial the number, and then forget the number immediately, we are using our short-term memory. Here, the telephone number is held in memory for a very short time. Short-term memory serves as a kind of "buffer zone" in which information can either be retained for a minimal time (and then be forgotten) or be transferred to long-term memory if the information is rehearsed. If we were to dial the same telephone number repeatedly, the number would be committed to long-term memory and held there indefinitely. The reason we can generally recall the phone numbers of close friends and relatives without much effort is that these numbers are held in long-term memory—the final memory component in an information processing system and one that has unlimited capacity. The contents of long-term memory, however, depend on the information that passes through the short-term memory "buffer." Our focus in this book is primarily on the interplay between short-term and long-term memory.

The amount of attentional resources is also important, for these limited resources are used to process information. For example, when we encode information, we allocate attentional resources to sensory memory; when we remember information, we allocate attentional resources to search long-term memory; and when we solve problems or transform information, we allocate attentional resources primarily to short-term (working) memory (Anderson 1990). Our coverage of memory is based on a spatial metaphor; for instance, short-term memory is a work space in which only so many tasks can be performed. There is, however, an alternative way of thinking about memory, a view that emphasizes energy and the amount of energy required to perform a task. Using this latter metaphor, the number of tasks that can be performed concurrently is limited by the combined amount of energy the tasks consume (Anderson 1990; Kahneman 1973). The amount of energy required to perform a specific task depends on how well the task is practiced: novel tasks require substantial amounts of energy or attention (controlled processing), whereas well-rehearsed tasks require relatively small amounts of attention (automatic processing).

An analogy to computers (Lachman, Lachman, and Butterfield 1979) explains the operation of the information processing system in terms of a framework in which preexisting routines that function like computer programs guide information processing. These routines are stored in long-term memory but must be activated and executed by information in short-term (working) memory. Conscious, or *controlled*, processing places high demands on short-term memory (Shiffrin and Schneider 1977) and is generally thought to be serial. In other words, we cannot process multiple stimuli simultaneously in a controlled manner. *Automatic* processing of stimuli, however, can occur in parallel, often with little conscious awareness; we can process multiple stimuli at the same time using automatic processes. Automatic processes are highly dependent on preexisting programs (those held in long-term memory) and place little demand on short-term memory. When we dial a telephone number that is held in long-term memory, we often do not think about it—dialing is reflexive, or automatic. Normally, however, we do not process information in a purely controlled or purely automatic fashion; most processing is a mixture of the two.

We should emphasize that controlled processes place much greater demands on attentional resources and short-term (working) memory capacity than do automatic processes. Thus, task, social, or self-monitoring activities that use attentional resources interfere with controlled processing unless they can be done automatically. Automatic processing allows a person to do two things at the same time. For example, a person can automatically pay attention to nonverbal behavior while attending to the content of another's speech using controlled processes, can automatically self-regulate while interacting with others, or can monitor goal progress while automatically performing a well-learned task. Interestingly, many perceptual processes that are controlled (for example, attributional analysis) can be wiped out by concurrent attentional demands (Gilbert, Krull, and Pelham 1988; Gilbert, Pelham, and Krull 1988). When attentional demands prevent controlled processing, we often rely on simpler automatic processes, such as attributing causality to the salient factors.

The relative contribution of automatic and controlled processes depends on the nature of the task and the amount of experience in a specific context (Ackerman 1987; Anderson 1987). An experienced typist can type from text without consciously attending to the specific keys. The typist can probably attend to and process other environmental stimuli (for example, conversations of co-workers, supervisor requests) concurrently. Someone just learning to type, by contrast, devotes considerable effort to pressing the correct keys and may have substantial difficulty attending to other stimuli in the environment while typing. In short, the experienced typist processes task-relevant information in an automatic fashion, while the novice typist engages in controlled processing.

So far, we have identified several components of an information processing system and two different types of processing—automatic and controlled. We can also distinguish between certain *stages* of information processing. These different stages have implications for the transfer of information between short-term and long-term memories. Though there are several stages of information processing (see Lord 1985), two are of particular importance here. In the *encoding* stage, information is stored in memory while being transformed and simplified; encoding involves a transfer of the information from short-term memory to long-term memory. In the *retrieval* stage, information is recalled from long-term memory in order to make a judgment or decision. The manner in which information is encoded and retrieved has critical implications for our theory of leadership perception. For example, consider a typical board meeting. If the chairperson of the board exhibited certain traits (for instance, intelligence, effective communication skills), those qualities would likely be encoded as traits associated with leadership, given the context (board meeting). If, however, this individual were in a social context, such as a party, and exhibited the same qualities, they would not likely be encoded as leadership traits. Instead, the qualities might be encoded as traits associated with extroversion or some other social category. Whether the traits of this individual were associated with leadership or some other category at the time of retrieval would depend on whether they were initially encoded as leader traits (versus extrovert traits) in long-term memory.

Long-term memory has virtually limitless capacity, and information can be retained for many years; however, short-term memory processes limit encoding into long-term memory. Information must be retained in short-term memory while being encoded into long-term memory, where storage is relatively slow. Therefore, we cannot store every piece of information that we perceive in the environment; nor can we accurately retrieve every piece of information held in long-term memory. Retrieval often requires a cue, or cognitive set, that is consistent with the way information was initially encoded (Tulving and Thompson 1973). In short, the retrieval of information depends on the form in which it was encoded.

We cannot encode and store all incoming stimulus information as it exists in the environment, because short-term memory and limitations in attentional resources produce a "bottleneck" for inputting information into long-term memory. Therefore, we encode such information with the aid of *cognitive simplifying mechanisms*, and these same mechanisms operate at the time information is retrieved from long-term memory. Cognitive simplifying mechanisms—preexisting routines, in the computer analogy—help organize incoming information into more easily stored formats. For example, matching information to already-existing structures in long-term memory is much faster and more efficient than developing a unique encoding scheme for each new piece of information held in short-term memory. These simplifying mechanisms depend on *knowledge structures* (Galambos, Abelson, and Black 1986), which are held in long-term memory and are developed based on experience in particular domains. It is the nature of such knowledge structures and their role in the encoding and retrieval of information that is integral to our discussion of leadership perceptions. Knowledge structures also suggest ways in which problems can be solved, a factor that is particularly relevant to understanding how executive-level decisions are made.

Knowledge Structures and Labeling

The phrase *knowledge structures* is used here to refer to cognitive schemas that are otherwise known as scripts, plans, categories, implicit theories, prototypes, or heuristics. One of the most important characteristics of long-term memory is that it contains these knowledge structures, which allow people to select, interpret, simplify, and integrate environmental information. As noted, we cannot encode all information in the environment, because of memory and attentional limitations; we are limited-capacity processors. To help overcome these cognitive limitations, we develop hierarchically organized sets of information that enable us to process much more information than would be possible without these mental structures. The use of these schemas allows much more information to be held in short-term memory and encoded into long-term memory.

One very useful knowledge structure is a hierarchically organized collection of related categories. Categorization processes group non-identical stimuli into sets (categories) that are treated as being equivalent for encoding or retrieval purposes. Categorization processes can be applied to objects, people, and situations. According to Rosch's (1978) theory of categorization, most category structures organize a given domain into a three-level hierarchy of superordinate, basic, and subordinate categories. For example, the objects "chair" and "sofa" are basic-level categories that both fall under the superordinate category of "furniture." The basic-level category of "chairs" includes the subordinate categories "kitchen chair" and "desk chair." These category structures are hierarchically organized, mental representations that simplify information processing.

Information processors apply these same hierarchical structures in social contexts as well (Cantor and Mischel 1979). Specifically, we categorize leaders in the same hierarchical fashion as we do objects (Lord, Foti, and Phillips 1982). At the superordinate level, we distinguish between leaders and nonleaders. Moving down the hierarchy, basic-level leadership categories falling under the superordinate category of leader represent specific contexts—for example, political leader, religious leader, business leader, and so forth. Finally, at the lowest, or subordinate, level, we might categorize basic-level political leaders as liberal or conservative (Lord, Foti, and De Vader 1984).

How do we go about this process of categorization? According to Rosch (1978), we categorize objects based on their similarity or dissimilarity to abstractions, or *prototypes*, of category members. Cantor and Mischel (1979) suggest that we categorize people based on their similarity to prototypes derived from traits. A prototype of a leader is someone who is intelligent, goal oriented, and responsible. This prototype is held in long-term memory and is accessed when triggered by a stimulus in the environment. Knowledge of one's race, sex, physical appearance, or role can also evoke a category label. Categories of this sort are similar to commonly held racial and ethnic stereotypes, which guide perceptions, behavior, and emotional reactions. Further, when we label someone an extrovert, we conceive of other traits that are consistent with the label of extrovert. We imagine a prototype, or typical extrovert, and infer that the individual is someone who is friendly, outgoing, and gregarious.

We have mental constructions of prototypical events or situations that follow the same categorization model as traits (Cantor, Mischel, and Schwartz 1982). Knowledge structures are also organized in terms of how events occur sequentially in given situations. These knowledge structures are typically called scripts and specify appropriate behavior in certain circumstances (Gioia and Poole 1984; Schank and Abelson 1977). We also structure knowledge of nonsocial environmental events. Executives are thought to label environmental events as either threats or opportunities and to act differently depending on this label (Dutton and Jackson 1987).

One of the major points we want to make in this chapter is that the labeling process is powerful, for labeling matches unique stimulus configurations to existing, general knowledge structures. The label that is initially attached to a stimulus, be it an object, a person, or an event, guides subsequent information processing (Srull and Wyer 1989). Once a stimulus is categorized, much of the information encountered later that is relevant to the object, person, or event is processed in terms of that category. Information is encoded based on the category held in long-term memory, and information is retrieved based on that category. Recall our example from chapter 1. Labeling Ann B. Hopkins as a "macho" woman would influence how information about her interpersonal behavior was encoded and retrieved. Moreover, it is likely that different information would have been encoded and retrieved had she been labeled as a potential leader.

Although the labeling of others can have negative consequences for people who are unfairly or inaccurately labeled, the process also helps minimize social information processing demands. Existing structures (prototypes) provide generic and usually accurate means for representing the characteristics and *functions* of category members. Often it is this generic information that is retrieved when one tries to recall aspects of stimuli that were encoded through the category-matching process.

We can usually operate quite well with category-based processing, and we make correct responses and decisions as a result of categorization. Yet errors do occur as a result of the simplifying mechanisms. We commonly construct missing facts based on accumulated knowledge. Consider the following scenario:

A group of men and women are seated around a conference table. All are dressed conservatively in business suits. A few people sip coffee or glance periodically at their watches. At precisely 9:00 A.M., a man enters the conference room and strides purposefully to the head of the conference table. He then places several papers on the table and begins speaking to the others.

What is the role of the man who took the place at the head of the table? Most readers probably inferred that he was the supervisor or CEO or that he occupied some other leadership role. This information was not given in the scenario, yet it was inferred readily from the context. Here, the scenario was fleshed out based on our knowledge structure, or script, of a typical business meeting. Had the scenario described a woman entering the conference room, we might have drawn a completely different inference—that she was a secretary or administrative assistant. In normal situations, simplifying mechanisms help us encode and retrieve information. They also help us interpret situations and make predictions about what is likely to happen. Moreover, when participants share the same schema, these simplifying mechanisms provide frameworks that integrate and make sense of participants' actions. But as we have illustrated, sometimes schemas can provide us with faulty interpretations.

In most social situations, labeling based on simplifying schemas is not a static process; rather, it is modified over time, based on the nature of the interaction. Hastie and Park (1986) refer to this more dynamic view of social judgments as on-line processing, which they contrast to memory-based processing. Using on-line processing, judgments are made as information is encountered, and this information is encoded into long-term memory along with the judgment. On-line processing emphasizes continual updating of judgments; initial categorization processes do not need to be perfect if they are revised and updated as new information is encountered. Once we label someone an extrovert, subsequent information is processed in terms of the extrovert category. Because of the revision process, over time our perceptions of this person may become more like our image of the typical extrovert. Consider Lee Iacocca. With the turnaround of Chrysler, many labeled Iacocca a highly effective leader. As subsequent information was encountered (Iacocca's appearance in television ads and press coverage), this was processed in terms of an effective leader category. Most of this information encountered over time simply served to strengthen people's perception of Iacocca as an effective leader. It is, however, possible to classify a person incorrectly, because we focus on one category rather than another. For example, if a supervisor initially classifies an employee as a poor performer, subsequent performance information will be interpreted in terms of the poor performer label. This situation can be very damaging to an employee whose performance has improved over time but is still perceived to be ineffective. In this case, the revision process may be continually biased in the direction of the initial, incorrect classification.

This section of the chapter has presented a brief overview of basic principles and components of information processing and shown how they relate to leadership perceptions. We have seen that limited short-term memory (working memory) and slow input into and imperfect retrieval from long-term memory constrain the human information processing system. However, when highly organized and relevant knowledge structures exist in long-term memory, information processing becomes qualitatively different and much more efficient.

ALTERNATIVE MODELS OF INFORMATION PROCESSING

In this section, we present four alternative information processing models, which depict qualitatively different perspectives on how people process information. These models are important, since they include assumptions (often implicit) that guide scientific thinking and research. By delineating these models, we can provide a more comprehensive description of the potential range of cognitive processes that are commonly used. The alternative models all work within the short-term and long-term memory constraints we have just described;

however, they compensate for these constraints differently, producing qualitatively different types of information processing. The four information processing models we propose—rational, limited-capacity, expert, and cybernetic—acknowledge these differences in information processing requirements. (For a more detailed discussion of these models, see Lord and Maher [1990b].) We will discuss each of these models briefly below, with a summary description provided in table 2.1. The models will also be applied in later chapters in the book.

Rational

The optimal use of information in a deliberate, thoughtful manner is the hallmark of rational models. Attribution theory (Kelley 1973), which posits that perceivers operate like "naive scientists," is an example of a rational information processing approach that has been applied frequently to explain leadership and other social perceptions. The key assumption underlying rational models of information processing is that we have unlimited capacity to identify alternatives and to combine information in an objectively optimal manner. What rational models of behavior have in common is the requirement that extensive amounts of decision-relevant information be available in long-term memory. Moreover, these models assume that people can simultaneously access this information and optimally combine it to select the most desirable alternative, as defined in mathematical terms. This optimal combination implies that information processors use sophisticated computational algorithms stored in long-term memory and have extensive short-term memory capacity. Those requirements conflict with information processing limitations, as described in the preceding section. To overcome these limitations, people can rely on external memory aids (paper and pencil, computers, other people) and on logical processing systems, such as computer programs. These aids, however, are rarely used to make social judgments or to make intuitive decisions. Nevertheless, social scientists often mistakenly assume that rational models aptly describe how we process social information or make decisions.

When used to explain leadership perceptions, a rational model would assume that subordinates and other perceivers of a leader's behavior would be able to encode all relevant information in long-term memory without the use of simplification mechanisms or judgment processes. Subordinates would also be able to retrieve all information accurately and completely when a judgment was required. This type of processing describes Hastie and Park's (1986) memory-based processing. Questionnaire-based measures of leader behavior implicitly fit with this model; such measures assume accurate and independent encoding and retrieval of information concerning past leader behavior.

Certain leadership theories, too, reflect rational processing. The path goal theory of leadership (House 1971), for example, views subordinates as capable of assessing and combining expectancy, instrumentality, and valence information to form task perceptions.

As we have seen in the first part of this chapter, such processing is usually impossible, given the constraints of the human information processing system. Though rational models are *prescriptively* useful, in that they specify how optimal decisions could be reached, they are generally *descriptively* inaccurate: rational models do not describe how people actually process information in most situations. Because descriptive accuracy is crucial for developing a theory of leadership perception, other models of information processing are more applicable.

Limited-Capacity

We discussed several characteristics of limited-capacity models in the beginning of the chapter. These models acknowledge people's limited memory capacity and reliance on general cognitive simplification mechanisms. Much social and administrative science work attempts to integrate these limitations with theories of information processing (Cyert and March 1963; March and Simon 1958; Nisbett and Ross 1980). Such models also explain how people function effectively in familiar situations in spite of information processing limitations: by using less information, by relying on narrowly focused schemas, and by using minimal (satisficing) rather than exhaustive processing. Though generally useful, limited-capacity processing can result in biases and systematic errors.

Limited-capacity models are more congruent with short-term memory and attentional limitations than rational models are, because they require the use of less information at one time and simpler evaluation procedures. Limited-capacity models are also more congruent with long-term memory capacity, because of our use of general knowledge structures to organize information in long-term memory. Limited capacity models, then, are often descriptively accurate; however, they are prescriptively weak. In other words, though they do describe how people usually make judgments, they do not specify the best way to make judgments. In chapter 3 we present a limited-capacity model of leadership perception.

Expert

Expert models represent a third type of information processing. Experts are also limited-capacity, heuristic-driven processors, but the heuristic principles involved are likely to be different from those of novices (Chi, Glaser, and Farr 1988). That is, expertise supplements simple information processing. A key assumption of limited-capacity models is that people rely on general knowledge structures to process information. A key assumption of the expert model, on the other hand, is that people rely on very well organized or highly developed knowledge structures characteristic of a *specific content domain*. In other words, an expert is someone with a large knowledge base in a particular context or a particular task (for example, a chess grand master).

A growing body of literature suggests that experts and novices differ in the way they structure schema (Chi, Glaser, and Rees 1982; Lurigio and Carroll 1985) and in the way information is processed (Fiske, Kinder, and Larter 1983; McKeithan, Reitman, Rueter, and Hirtle 1981). More specifically, experts encode and retrieve information from long-term memory differently than novices do (Glaser 1982). The knowledge structures held in memory are larger and more easily accessed. Knowledge structures of experts are also useful in that they match situations to responses—that is, the knowledge structures of experts contain appropriate actions or behaviors that correspond to the problem representation. Novices typically do not have this advantage. Finally, the knowledge structures of experts may be organized so that complex procedures can be performed with fewer attentional demands. Glaser (1988) argues that experts' knowledge structures are organized in a manner that facilitates appropriate responses. This view is similar to Anderson's (1987) theory of learning, which posits that many separate problem-solving steps may be "compiled" into more integrated and easily used structures as we gain experience with a particular problem.

The result of this type of processing is that experts can process information or perform tasks in a qualitatively different manner from the way novices do. A grand master at chess can play against many novices (as many as 50) simultaneously, beating them all. In more typical situations, experts can often immediately recognize correct solutions to problems that novices must analyze very carefully to solve. Experts have this ability because their problem categorizations automatically evoke appropriate responses that have been stored in long-term memory. Experts can also store and retrieve more information because of their highly elaborate knowledge structures. This capacity for intuitive, automatic processing can, however, be applied only in one's limited domain of expertise. Moreover, this capability can produce inaccurate representations, descriptions, and responses to atypical stimuli.

In short, experts can be highly efficient processors of information but only in very specific social or task-related domains. In this sense, the expert model is descriptively limited. Experts are not superior information processors in general, only in the domains for which they have richly elaborated knowledge structures. In these specific domains, experts can perform tasks effortlessly and effectively; novices must devote much more effort to attain only mediocre levels of performance. Thus, when experts' knowledge structures are congruent with task demands, expert processing may be the preferred mode of information processing. In such situations, expert models are prescriptively appropriate. For example, top-level leaders with substantial experience in strategic decision making may formulate strategies intuitively through the use of expert processes, whereas leaders who lack such experience may instead depend on the advice of others who have substantial experience. Eisenhardt's (1989) research has shown that top-level strategists often used the advice of "counselors" experienced in a given domain.

Cybernetic

The final set of information processing models, cybernetic models, are much more dynamic than the other models. These models conceptualize information processing and actions as being interspersed over time. Cybernetic models are similar to limited-capacity models in their use of simple heuristic procedures, and they may involve situation-specific knowledge structures, as in the expert model. But in cybernetic models, interpretation of past social information is intermixed over time with planning future activities and executing current behaviors. Cybernetic models rely heavily on feedback from the task or social environment. Hastie and Park's (1986) on-line model of social judgment is a good example of cybernetic information processing. In their model, initial judgments about an individual are modified with additional experience. Thus, while cybernetic processing may be simple, it works well only when feedback is available and initial mistakes are not costly. In situations in which these two qualities are present, people can be described most accurately as cybernetic information processors. Under these circumstances, research has shown that cybernetic processing is often nearly optimal (Kleinmuntz and Thomas 1987). Hence, cybernetic models are both descriptively and prescriptively useful within a fairly narrow domain.

It should be noted that to this point we have dealt only with individual information processors. Many of the informational, short-term, and long-term memory limitations of people can be alleviated by having groups of individuals perform a task, such as using executive-level management teams to formulate strategy. Yet groups can also create additional information processing demands centered on communication, resolution of conflict, and social acceptance. These additional demands consume attentional resources, making it difficult to use rational processes in group situations. Such limitations can often be overcome if people have a specialized technical language for communicating, if they have shared cognitive structures for interpreting task and social requirements (Lord and Foti [1986, 38–43] illustrate the use of shared cognitive structures in group situations), or if group-related difficulties can be resolved through repeated interaction. These issues point to the importance of having communication mechanisms that are both formal (for instance, specialized technical language, standard communication channels and operating procedures) and informal (for example, generalized scripts for events, organizational culture). Such shared cognitive structures may help overcome information processing demands but may also serve to constrain the type and amount of information processing used by groups. Thus, expert and cybernetic models may be especially useful for understanding how groups can function effectively, whereas rational and limited-capacity models may be particularly useful for understanding the difficulties groups often encounter.

We have not conducted empirical research that contrasts these four information processing models, but in an extensive review (Lord and Maher 1990b) we have shown that each model is consistent with a substantial amount of empirical work. Moreover, in that article we have shown how each model can provide a unique perspective when applied to specific substantive issues, such as attribution theory, performance appraisal, decision making, and research methodology. In this book, we show that each model provides a unique perspective for understanding leadership.

SUMMARY

It should be emphasized that people are *flexible* information processors. We do not always process information in the same manner. Generally, information processing is characterized by a limited-capacity model; however in certain domains or contexts, alternative rational, expert, or cybernetic models better characterize our information processing. Therefore, each of the models we have briefly described above is important in understanding how people process information. Table 2.1 summarizes our coverage of these alternative models. It shows key memory demands of these models and where they stand on the criteria of descriptive accuracy and prescriptive value. Table 2.1 also highlights significant differences among these information processing models.

Like most people, leaders and followers are flexible information processors. Therefore, each model is relevant to how people perceive leaders and to how leaders perceive their environment and act upon it.

TABLE 2.1
Comparison of Alternative Information Processing Models

Model characteristics	Rational	Limited-Capacity	Expert	Cybernetic
Short-term memory demands	Extensive	Moderate	Low	Very low
Long-term memory demands	Extensive	Moderate	Extensive	Variable[a]
Descriptive accuracy	Weak	Strong	Limited[b]	Strong[c]
Prescriptive value	Strong	Weak	Strong[b]	Strong[c]

[a] Moderate for novel tasks, extensive for familiar tasks.
[b] Model limited to very familiar tasks or situations.
[c] Provided that feedback is available and that mistakes are not costly.

We will use these models to explain leader or follower information processing in various parts of this book. We turn now to a discussion of leadership categorization theory, a limited-capacity model.

Part II

Perceptual and Social Processes

Recognition-based Processes and Leadership Perceptions

*I*n this chapter we present a comprehensive and explicit theory of leadership perceptions that is derived from recent work in the social-cognitive area. This approach provides a more detailed view of leadership perceptions than work that typically focuses on the traits distinguishing leaders from nonleaders. We begin this chapter by examining trait views of leadership, showing how the emphasis has shifted from traits of leaders to leadership as a summary label used by perceivers. We then explain how these summary labels are formed from both *recognition-based* and *inferential* processes. In this theoretical model, recognition-based processes are analyzed in terms of categorization theory and inferential processes are tied to attributions about salient events. We assert that both these perceptual processes can involve either automatic or controlled modes of processing. Recognition-based processing is the topic of this chapter; inferential processing is covered in chapter 4.

TRAITS AND LEADERSHIP PERCEPTIONS

Traits of Leaders

Leadership perceptions are pervasive phenomena. By the first grade, children can clearly differentiate leaders from nonleaders and can articulate the factors that separate these two groups of people (Matthews, Lord, and Walker 1990). Younger children (grades 1 and 3), however, adopt a "bottom-up" (stimulus-based) definition of leadership that is egocentric and tied closely to specific exemplars (for example, identifying winners of spelling bees and track races as leaders). The leader-nonleader distinction becomes even more important for older students (grades 6, 9, and 12), who have developed a more general view of leadership consistent with "top-down" processing and prototype models of categories. Adults view leadership as having fundamental importance in many contexts (military, political, business, sports, religion, and so on). Much of the early work on leadership perceptions focused on such leader-nonleader distinctions, as many researchers searched for traits that universally distinguished leaders from followers.

Mann (1959) and Stogdill (1948) reviewed and organized much of this early work on leadership perceptions. They found that in small-group studies, some traits, such as intelligence, were consistently correlated with leadership perceptions or the emergence of leaders, although the strength of this relationship varied quite a bit from one study to another. Mann found several other traits (adjustment, sensitivity, masculinity, and extroversion) that were usually associated with leadership perception, but as with intelligence, these relationships varied considerably from study to study. This variability in results was discouraging for leadership researchers, who soon turned to contingency theories of leadership (for example, Fiedler 1964). Such theories attempted to explain how situational factors moderated the relationship of personality variables to leadership. Yet one methodological factor not widely understood at the time of these early reviews of trait research is that results will generally vary substantially from one study to another simply because of sampling error. Current meta-analytic techniques for quantitatively combining results from different studies can account for such variability (Hunter, Schmidt, and Jackson 1982) and can also correct for such factors as restriction of range, which can attenuate correlations between personality variables and leadership perceptions.

Lord, De Vader, and Alliger (1986) applied these meta-analytic statistical techniques to the data reviewed by Mann (1959), finding several results that conflicted with Mann's earlier conclusions. First, in examining the relationship of intelligence to leadership perceptions, they found that most of the variability from study to study could be explained by sampling error alone, implying that there was no need to search for variables that moderated this relationship. Further, when corrected for range restriction, the correlation across all studies between intelligence and leadership perceptions was substantial, $r = .52$. For other traits the pattern was similar, though the results were not quite so dramatic. For example, these researchers found the corrected relationship between masculinity and leadership perception to be .34 and almost 70 percent of the variability from study to study could be attributed to sampling error. Updating Mann's data with more current studies changed the results somewhat, but the basic conclusion of Lord and his colleagues was still supported: several traits (intelligence, masculinity, and dominance) were significantly associated with leadership perceptions, and most of the variability in these relationships could be attributed to sampling error alone. Thus, consistent with much of the earliest thinking on leadership, there are traits that are generally associated with leadership *perceptions*. This topic deserves further consideration, however, as there are fewer studies of leadership traits than is often thought. For example, there are 18 studies that look at intelligence and its relationship to leader emergence but only 4 studies that investigate the effects of masculinity/ femininity (Lord et al. 1986).

Traits as Perceiver Constructs

Two important theoretical articles help to clarify the relationship of leader traits to leadership perceptions. In a widely influential article, Mischel (1973) argued that an individual's traits are not very good predictors of behavior across situations; however, he argued that traits are important constructions of *perceivers*, helping them make sense of social situations. Following Mischel's logic, this point implies that while traits may not be potent *causes* of a leader's behavior, they are important summary labels that help perceivers understand and predict a leader's behavior. In other words, traits, like beauty, are in the eye of the beholder. Hollander and Julian (1969) provided a similar theoretical argument applied directly to leadership, suggesting that people emerge as group leaders by fitting the shared conceptions of followers. This view also emphasizes the role of *perceiver constructs* in explaining leadership perceptions. Thus, we see the emphasis shift from early work that focused on the traits of leaders as measured by standardized personality assessment techniques to more current work that centers on perceived traits used to form leadership perceptions.

This shift in emphasis from leaders' traits and behaviors to followers' perceptions is also illustrated by a laboratory study by Lord, Phillips, and Rush (1980) that examined ratee and rater effects in leadership perceptions. In this study, 96 undergraduates participated in four-person groups that solved four different problems. Groups solved problems for one to two hours, and their behavior was videotaped for later coding in terms of functional leadership behaviors (Lord 1977). After completing the group tasks, each subject rated the other group members on leadership and other social perceptions. A traditional, leader-oriented approach would explain these ratings in terms of leader traits and behaviors. Consistent with this perspective, the results showed that actual task behaviors explained almost 13 percent of the variance in ratings of leadership exhibited. In contrast, a perceiver-oriented perspective would focus on perceiver characteristics that might affect ratings of leadership. This approach found significant gender effects, which explained 12 percent of the variance in ratings of leadership exhibited, demonstrating that women gave higher leadership ratings than men.

To analyze the leader-perceiver question in more general terms,

Lord et al. (1980) partitioned variance in all ratings into three components—subjects' group, the ratee being rated, and the rater actually doing the ratings, with variance allocated in that order. Group effects, reflecting such factors as group performance, explained between 10 and 27 percent of the variance in ratings on measures of leadership and influence. As suggested by traditional trait theories, ratee effects were clearly important, explaining between 19 and 52 percent of the variance in social perceptions. But consistent with the perceiver construct view of traits, rater effects were also important, explaining between 17 and 44 percent of the variance in ratings. Such data plainly show that the task context (group), the potential leader, and the rater (perceiver) all have important effects on leadership perceptions.

Work on implicit personality theories has also emphasized the perceiver in explaining leadership perceptions. Extensive research in this area (Eden and Leviatan 1975; Rush, Thomas, and Lord 1977; Weiss and Adler 1981) has demonstrated widely shared beliefs about leader behaviors and traits. Such beliefs have affected the perception of leaders and the encoding, recall, and rating of leadership behaviors. Other researchers (Calder 1977) have identified both behaviors and events (performance on key organizational tasks) as evidence on which leadership perceptions are based. Thus, events, behaviors, and traits are crucial distinguishing features of leaders. Nevertheless, it is these features *as perceived and utilized by others*—not as they occur in any objective sense—that are crucial in explaining leadership perceptions (Hollander and Julian 1969; Lord et al. 1986). Though these features may be made salient by leaders, they must also be noticed by perceivers. Further, perceivers must encode these features in a way that is personally meaningful and must use them to differentiate others in terms of leadership. Such perceiver processes are the main focus of this chapter.

More recent theorizing on social perceptions (Brewer 1988) helps explain the leader-oriented and perceiver-oriented views of social perceptions. Brewer argues that perceptions can involve either of two modes of social perception. In the stimulus, or *person-based*, mode, which predominates under low cognitive load conditions, perceptions are based primarily on the features and behaviors of the person being perceived, and information is integrated to form a unified impression of that person. Such stimulus-based processing represents a leader-oriented view of perceptions; it also corresponds to a rational model of information processing described in chapter 2. The contrasting *categorical* mode of social perceptions predominates under higher cognitive load conditions, which could be expected when one interacts with others or observes an entire group interacting. Under this mode, the purposes and processing goals of the *perceiver* determine the relevance of perceptual categories, and these knowledge structures guide information processing. This mode corresponds to a perceiver-oriented model of leadership perceptions, and it fits with either a limited-capacity or an expert information processing model. Here information is processed in a top-down manner and is consistent with a "cognitive miser" perspective on social cognitions (Fiske and Taylor 1984); that is, perceivers resist moving down to a more specific processing level that requires elaboration or modification of existing cognitive structures. Category-based processing, then, proceeds from the global to the specific but tends to remain at fairly global levels, whereas person-based processing moves from the specific to the global (bottom-up processing) but tends to remain at fairly specific levels. Interestingly, classification using person-based processing emphasizes traits as continuous dimensions, whereas category-based processing focuses on those features which are evaluated only on a present/not present basis. Thus, these alternative modes of processing should also affect the type of leadership measurement (dimensional versus categorical) raters can provide.

In short, we have seen a shift in both leadership and social-cognitive areas, from a trait-oriented view of perceptions, which emphasizes stimulus characteristics, to a categorical view, which emphasizes the knowledge structures and information processes of perceivers. In the following section, we take a more detailed look at the cognitive processes related to leadership perceptions.

MODEL OF LEADERSHIP PERCEPTIONS

General Model
Although specifying the underlying process that produces leadership perceptions is difficult, much of the groundwork for this task has been provided by recent developments in cognitive and social-cognitive psychology. We rely extensively on the terminology, theories, and methods of these areas to develop our explanation of leadership perceptions.

Though people often think about or discuss leadership, sometimes it seems to emerge unintentionally through normal task-related activities in many different contexts. Leadership perceptions can be formed when people's attention and motivation are focused on task activities, suggesting that these perceptions involve what cognitive psychologists call *automatic processes*—processes that occur without awareness, without intent, without much effort, and without interference with other cognitive tasks. Our ability to think about or discuss leadership also involves *controlled processes*—processes that require awareness, intent, and effort and that do interfere with other activities. This distinction between automatic and controlled processes (Hasher and Zacks 1979; Shiffrin and Schneider 1977) is fundamental to understanding leadership perceptions.

Lord (1985) developed a social information processing model in which he asserted that leadership perceptions can be explained by two qualitatively different processes: either leadership can be *recognized* from the qualities and behaviors revealed through normal, day-to-day interactions with others, or it can be *inferred* from the outcomes of salient events. For example, someone who is intelligent, honest, outgoing, understanding, and verbally skilled is likely to be recognized as having strong leadership qualities. Alternatively, leadership is likely to be inferred when a person such as a CEO is seen as being directly responsible for a favorable performance outcome, such as increased profits.

Lord and Maher (1990a) explained how both inferential and recognition-based processes can be either automatic or controlled. They developed a two-by-two classification of leadership perception processes, summarized in table 3.1. This theoretical framework provides the basic structure for this chapter. A theory explaining recognition-based processes is developed in the following section.

Recognition-based Processes

Recognition-based perceptual processes help us form leadership perceptions from the normal flow of interpersonal activities. Because social interactions often place high processing demands on actors (Ostrom 1984), it makes sense to think of recognition-based processes as proceeding more automatically. Automatic processes compete less

TABLE 3.1
Alternative Types of Processes Used to Form Leadership Perceptions

Models of Perceptual Processes	Data	Mode of Cognitive Process	
		Automatic	Controlled
Recognition	Traits and behaviors	Prototype matching based on face-to-face contact	Prototype matching based on socially communicated information
Inferential	Events and outcomes	Perceptually guided, simplified causal analysis	Logically based, comprehensive causal analysis

with ongoing interactions than controlled processes do. Recognition-based processes also depend on exposure to the behaviors of others and on knowledge of their underlying traits. Thus, these processes involve the use of preexisting knowledge about leadership in a particular context. Such knowledge has been referred to as implicit leadership theories by academic researchers (for example, Lord et al. 1984). Yet because it relies on detailed, specific knowledge, it is also consistent with one of the four types of information processing discussed in chapter 2—expert information processing. In other words, through general, day-to-day experiences as well as through experience in a particular organizational context, people develop detailed knowledge structures pertinent to leadership. Perceivers then rely on these knowledge structures to simplify the processes required to recognize leadership in others. Consistent with our coverage of the expert information processing model, we would expect experts and novices to differ substantially in the amount and structure of underlying knowledge about leadership, as well as to exhibit qualitative differences in leadership perception processes.

Categorization Theory and Leadership. One theory about how recognition-based leadership perceptions are formed was suggested by Lord and his colleagues (1984). Their theory, based on Rosch's (1978) theory of cognitive categorization, jointly focused on the structure of knowledge used to classify leaders and the actual information processes used in perceptions. They viewed leadership as being a cognitive category (a type of knowledge structure) that was fundamentally important in many different situations. Leadership perceptions were equated with cognitive categorization, a process in which nonidentical stimuli are segmented into classifications (for example, leaders or nonleaders) that can be treated equivalently. Such categorization reduces the complexity of the external world, permits symbolic representations of the world in terms of the labels given to categories, and provides a system of shared names (category labels) by which people can communicate information about categorized entities (Cantor and Mischel 1979). Thus, a theory of leadership categorizations is more than just an explanation of leadership perceptions; it is also an explanation of how leadership schemas are organized in long-term memory and how people are likely to process information related to leadership.

Lord et al. (1984) argued that leadership categories are hierarchically organized. At the highest, most abstract level, leadership is a fairly general, superordinate category. The middle-range, or basic-level, categories refine the notion of leadership by incorporating situational (or contextual) information. In other words, leaders are differentiated into specific types of leaders, such as military, business, political, or educational leaders. Thus, basic-level leadership categories might simply consist of the traits and behaviors appropriate to a leadership role in a particular context. At the lowest, or subordinate, level, types of leaders within a context are differentiated. One general distinction is between lower- and upper-level leaders. Subordinate leadership categories might include hierarchical as well as contextual information: military leaders would be differentiated by rank; business leaders by their position in an organizational hierarchy; and political leaders by their role in political parties or whether they held local, city, state, or national offices.

According to this theory, categorizations are made based on the match of stimulus properties to abstractions or prototypes derived from characteristics common to category members. Essentially, perceivers use degree of match to this ready-made structure to form leadership perceptions. For example, in a business context, someone who is seen as well dressed, honest, outgoing, intelligent, and industrious would be labeled a leader, whereas in politics, someone seen as wanting peace, having strong convictions, being charismatic, and being a good administrator would be labeled a leader. Several laboratory studies now show that the fit of individuals' behavior to observers' prototypes of leadership affects leadership ratings (Cronshaw and Lord 1987; Fraser and Lord 1988; Lord et al. 1984). Such prototype matching can occur easily, perhaps automatically (Alba, Chromiak, Hasher, and Attig 1980), and this same basic process of leadership perception is used under conditions of high and low information load (Maurer and Lord 1988).

A typical study demonstrating the effects of prototype matching on leadership perceptions was also conducted by Lord and his colleagues (1984), who asked college students to read a short vignette about a hypothetical district manager named John Perry. The vignette was specially written so that key phrases could be changed to represent behaviors that were (a) very prototypical of leaders (provides information, emphasizes goals, talks frequently, and specifies problems), (b) neutral with respect to leadership (seeks information, seeks suggestions, explains actions, clarifies attitudes, and prevents conflict), or (c) antiprototypical of leaders (admits mistakes, withholds rewards, criticizes harshly, and neglects details). These three versions of the vignette, which were identical except for the four prototypical, neutral, or antiprototypical phrases, were shown to different groups of subjects, who then provided several ratings of John Perry. Consistent with categorization theory predictions, the ratings varied as a function of stimulus conditions. Perceptions that the stimulus person was a leader, as measured on a 5-point scale, were highest in the prototypical condition (M = 4.04), intermediate in the neutral condition (M = 3.84), and lowest in the antiprototypical condition (M = 2.62). This prototype-matching factor explained 53 percent of the variance in leadership perceptions. Causal attributions and responsibility attributions followed a similar pattern, although less variance was explained by this experimental factor (31 percent for each variable).

As shown in figure 3.1, taken from Lord et al. (1984), behavioral expectations were also affected by the prototype manipulation in this study, but here the relationship of the rated behavior to the category of leader must be considered to understand the results. For expected behaviors (judgments about behaviors not described in the vignette) that were very prototypical of leaders, ratings increased from antiprototypical to neutral to prototypical conditions; for neutral behaviors, there was little difference in expectations across experimental conditions; and for antiprototypical behaviors, expectations decreased from antiprototypical to neutral to prototypical conditions. All these results are consistent with a model in which at first a person is classified in terms of leadership based on his or her stimulus behaviors and then further inferences about the person are based on raters' implicit leadership theories (*general* knowledge associated with leadership categories), rather than on the person's actual behavior. In Brewer's (1988) terms, most processing is category based rather than person (stimulus) based.

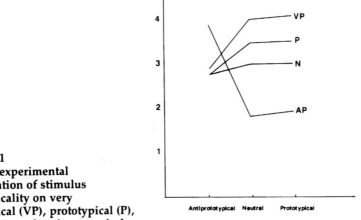

Figure 3.1
Effect of experimental manipulation of stimulus prototypicality on very prototypical (VP), prototypical (P), neutral (N), and antiprototypical (AP) behavior expectancy scales

This basic finding was followed up in several other studies with written or videotaped stimulus material. Fraser and Lord (1988) replicated the study just described, using a different vignette, different subjects, and several additional dependent variables. One noteworthy analysis they conducted clearly shows the importance of leadership categorization as a *mediating* process. This analysis is shown in table 3.2, which is reprinted from Fraser and Lord. As shown in this table, strong relationships were found between the prototypical, neutral, and antiprototypical stimulus conditions and several dependent variables. When, however, leadership perceptions were controlled using analysis of covariance, there was a substantial decrease in the variance explained for all dependent variables except for antiprototypical behavioral expectations. For example, the variance explained by the experimental factors in initiating structure ratings was 28 percent, but it was reduced to only 13 percent when leadership perceptions were controlled through analysis of covariance. Similarly, the explained variance in expectations for prototypical leadership behaviors was reduced from 42 to 22 percent by controlling for leadership perceptions. In general, about half the variance in dependent variables could be explained by statistically controlling for leadership perceptions—a finding that demonstrates the importance of leadership categorization processes in helping us organize, store, and retrieve information about potential leaders. These results suggest that many of the subjects in the Fraser and Lord study were using limited-capacity or expert information processes discussed in chapter 2; however, not all the variance in dependent variables was mediated by leadership labels, a finding that implies that some subjects were also using more rational information processes, consistent with the low processing demands and written stimulus material used in this study.

Two other studies of similar design used videotaped stimulus material. Both showed that the prototypicality of stimulus behaviors affected perceptions of leadership, although results were not as strong as when short, written vignettes were used. Cronshaw and Lord (1987) showed subjects 12-minute color videotapes of a simulated work group in which the focal person exhibited a large number (20) of prototypical behaviors (for example, he carefully planned what to do) or antiprototypical behaviors (for example, he was confused about an issue). Cronshaw and Lord also had subjects press a hand-held button while watching the videotape to identify behaviors they thought were meaningful. As expected, leadership ratings were significantly higher in the prototypical than in the antiprototypical condition, but only 3 percent of the variance was explained by this factor. *Encoded* leadership behaviors (as measured by button presses for meaningful behaviors) were, however, more strongly related to leadership ratings, explaining

TABLE 3.2
Effect of Stimulus Prototypicality on Social Perceptions and Behavioral
Expectations Scales

Dependent variables	Stimulus Prototypicality Condition			ANOVA	
	Prototypical	Neutral	Antitypical	F	eta²
Perceptions					
Leadership	4.32	4.02	3.00	15.128	.29
Effectiveness + performance	8.32	8.28	6.76	8.52*	.19
Influence + control	7.64	8.36	6.40	12.87*	.26
Initiating structure	38.76	39.64	32.56	13.78*	.28
Consideration	36.44	35.88	36.40	<1.00	.00
Behavioral expectations					
Prototypical	83.54	74.72	53.93	25.23*	.42
Neutral	68.57	71.32	56.99	5.64*	.17
Antiprototypical	49.03	45.91	56.66	7.04*	.17

* $p < .01$

15 percent of the variance in the high-prototypicality condition and 6 percent of the variance in the low-prototypicality condition.

In a second study, Maurer and Lord (1988) showed subjects videotapes of groups in which the target person's behavior varied on two dimensions: prototypicality of leadership behavior and frequency of leadership behavior. Both factors were significantly associated with leadership perceptions. This study is noteworthy in another respect, however. Maurer and Lord were also interested in how the peripheral cognitive demands placed on raters influenced the information processes used. They reasoned that frequency information was simpler to encode than prototypicality information, so that frequency information should have greater impact on leadership ratings under high cognitive demands and prototypicality information should have greater impact under low cognitive demands. The researchers manipulated the peripheral cognitive demands on raters during the videotape by having raters read background material and think of solutions to problems and by creating distractions from confederates in the high-demand conditions. These additional requirements were absent in the low-demand conditions. This cognitive demand factor was effective according to subjects' ratings of how they allocated attention during the experiment and also as indicated by subjects' memory for specific behaviors in the videotape. Contrary to predictions, however, the cognitive demand factor did not interact with either the frequency or the prototypicality factors in explaining leadership perceptions. Maurer and Lord's interpretation was that prototypicality information is encoded easily by subjects so that interference from other tasks is minimal. In other words, as we have asserted above, recognition processes based on category matching are fairly automatic, requiring minimal attentional capacity and little conscious intent. It should be noted that in all the studies described above, subjects were neither forewarned that they would be making leadership ratings nor told whom to watch in the stimulus videotape.

As shown in table 3.1, a more *controlled process* that is also critical in forming leadership perceptions is overt evaluation by others. In contexts in which leadership is important, leadership qualities are often directly discussed. For example, sports commentators and political analysts frequently comment on leadership qualities, and leadership may be formally evaluated through such procedures as are used in assessment centers. Although such procedures involve an explicit focus on leadership, they can still be considered a recognition-based process, since they use leader traits and behaviors rather than outcomes as a basis for leadership perceptions. In fact, we suspect that the same basic prototype-matching process is used to form leadership perceptions (to classify people as leaders or nonleaders) from either directly experienced (face-to-face contact) or indirectly experienced, socially communicated behavioral information.

Categorization and Political Leaders.   A general criticism of categorization theory as a model of leadership perceptions is that no real-world tests of the model have been conducted. Moreover, as previous studies have shown, in moving from written to videotaped stimulus material the amount of variance explained by prototypical behavioral factors declines substantially. This finding raises the question of whether prototypes would be important in real-world contexts as a basis for leadership perceptions. Generalization to real-world settings is difficult to assess, since correlations between prototypicality of traits and leadership ratings from organizational samples would be difficult to interpret. One would not know whether being perceived as a leader caused a person to be described in more prototypical terms or whether possessing more prototypical traits caused the person to be perceived as a leader. In spite of this caveat, there are nonlaboratory data, from studies done with political leaders, that do demonstrate a fairly strong relationship between prototypicality and leadership ratings.

Foti, Fraser, and Lord (1982) used Gallup survey data of political leaders' characteristics ("Phrase Portraits") to see whether leadership ratings and descriptions in terms of prototypical characteristics covaried. Gallup Phrase Portraits consist of 17 items that are worded first in positive and then in negative terms. Some examples of phrase pairs in the survey are "bright/not too bright"; "decisive, sure of himself/uncertain, indecisive, unsure"; and "has strong leadership qualities/lacks strong leadership qualities." In completing the Gallup poll survey, respondents select from each pair of opposites the item that best describes the person in question.

Foti and her colleagues (1982) had these Phrase Portrait items rated by college students in terms of their prototypicality to the category "effective political leader." The investigators then used these prototypicality ratings to predict which items would be rated differently as leadership ratings changed from one politician to another or from poll to poll. Using cross-sectional data from 1,509 respondents describing President Jimmy Carter, the researchers correlated each item with the Gallup poll item "has strong leadership qualities." These correlations were in turn correlated with the prototypicality ratings for items, to show whether the association of items with "has strong leadership qualities" depended on the prototypicality of the item. The analysis yielded a significant correlation of .35, showing that more prototypical items were more strongly associated with leadership ratings than less prototypical items were. These findings demonstrate the central role of leadership categories in accessing other behavioral information.

Foti et al. (1982) also investigated whether the prototypicality of Phrase Portrait items could predict longitudinal changes in endorsement rates for these items. For this task, the researchers computed changes in item endorsement rates from surveys of President Carter between the time he received his highest leadership rating (in September 1977, 69 percent of the sample thought he had strong leadership qualities) and periods during which his leadership ratings were lower (generally, only 20 to 30 percent of the sample thought Carter had strong leadership qualities). For two of these three comparisons, item prototypicality was significantly correlated (r = .57, in both cases) with changes in item endorsement from periods of high to low leadership ratings. Similar analyses were conducted using comparisons between President Carter and Senator Edward Kennedy, from an August 1979 poll in which Kennedy received a leadership endorsement of 64 percent and Carter 35 percent. Here again, item prototypicality predicted the differences in item endorsement between the two politicians (r = .48), showing that more prototypical items were more likely to be endorsed when high leadership ratings were given.

One alternative interpretation of these findings is that they reflect nothing more than changes in the favorability of political figures. This possibility was ruled out, however, in the Foti et al. study. Foti and her colleagues also measured the favorability of each Gallup poll item and found that it did not predict changes over time or across candidates as well as item prototypicality did.

As a whole, these data provide convincing evidence that leadership ratings and descriptions in prototypical terms are strongly associated. Yet the data do not tell us whether changes in leadership ratings caused changes in descriptions or whether changed descriptions caused changes in leadership ratings. Recall that laboratory studies have shown that both processes can operate. Nonetheless, the data do strongly suggest that the people responding to these Gallup poll surveys had a relatively general prototype of political leaders that guided their assessments of political candidates—an implication that is very consistent with categorization theory. In other words, leadership categories are important constructs that guided these perceivers' processing of information regarding potential leaders. The results are particularly impressive because the measures of item prototypicality came from samples different from those who actually completed the Gallup survey and because additional analyses suggested that item favorability could not explain these results.

In two subsequent studies that also focused on political leadership, the causal direction was more apparent. Based on the logic that winning or losing an election is an important outcome affecting the process of leader labeling, Foti, Lord, and Dambrot (in press) predicted that winners in political elections would be described in more prototypical terms, whereas losers would be described more antiprototypically. To test this prediction, Foti and her colleagues collected survey data one week before and one week after the 1982 Ohio gubernatorial election between Dick Celeste and Clarence Brown. For their sample of students, the researchers found a strong candidate effect, with the winner, Dick Celeste, being described in more prototypical terms both before and after the election. But for their sample of community members, who were more politically involved than the students, the investigators found the predicted time by candidate interaction for both prototypical and antiprototypical ratings. As predicted, ratings of Dick Celeste increased from the pre- to the postelection survey for prototypical items, but decreased for Clarence Brown. Exactly the opposite pattern occurred for antiprototypical items: Brown's ratings increased while Celeste's ratings decreased.

The second study, based on the Akron mayoral election in 1983, provided even clearer results, because the race was very close up to election day, with the underdog, Tom Sawyer, upsetting the incumbent, Roy Ray. In this election, the predicted interaction occurred for both prototypical and antiprototypical ratings; for the winning candidate, prototypical ratings increased and antiprototypical ratings decreased. As predicted, the opposite pattern held for the losing candidate. The reversal of the election outcome as predicted by polls suggests that the election changed the labels applied to both candidates and that this change in turn affected descriptions of the winners and losers. This pattern of changes is exactly what results showed. The second study provides strong evidence that labels of real individuals can significantly affect the way they are described. Again, these results provide support for a perceiver-based, categorical model of leadership perceptions.

These results show that once others are categorized as leaders, observers can rely on existing category structures to describe a leader's behaviors or form expectations about future behavior. Thus, a simple act of categorization may provide a powerful cognitive structure that shapes the nature of interactions among people. Information contained in such categories may also provide a self-standard that indicates to leaders themselves how they should behave (Carver 1979). Moreover, such effects seem to be independent of the means by which a person is categorized. Because categorization can affect perceptions of leaders *and* descriptions of their actual behavior, a more detailed examination of leadership categorization is warranted. The development, content, and structure of leadership categories is of both practical and theoretical importance. These topics are discussed at length in the following section.

Development of Leadership Categories. Rosch (1978) theorized that category prototypes develop from experience with examples of categories. Over time, people learn which attributes are both widely shared among category members (being high in family resemblance) and relatively rare among nonmembers of a category (being high in cue validity). These attributes become associated with each other and eventually form an integrated cognitive structure that is automatically accessed when the context, recent experience, stimulus attributes, or labels prime the category. This prototype is an abstract image, however, and is not based on any specific category member. Prior to the development of a category prototype, categories are often defined on the basis of exemplars—concrete examples of specific category members. For example, someone who has no experience with military leaders might define this category based on his or her knowledge of one salient military leader (for example, Eisenhower or Patton). But as experience with military leaders accumulates, a more general and representative composite of military leaders would define the category. Thus, as experience develops and relevant knowledge structures are created in long-term memory, perceivers develop the capacity to move from Brewer's (1988) person-based to category-based processes, which were discussed earlier.

Surprisingly, no published studies compare the basis for leadership perceptions across different age-groups. One unpublished study, however, by Matthews, Lord, and Walker (1990), did investigate principles based on Rosch's (1978) categorization theory for several different age-groups. These researchers predicted that younger subjects would use more data-driven, concrete, exemplar models for forming leadership perceptions, whereas older subjects would use more abstract, prototype-based categories. The investigators also expected that the complexity of categories would increase with age. Based on Rosch's work, they predicted that early categories would be formed around basic-level distinctions, with superordinate and subordinate categories developing as children gained more experience with leaders.

Matthews and her colleagues (1990) interviewed 160 subjects from five different grade levels (1, 3, 6, 9, and 12), asking subjects to answer such open-ended questions as "What is a leader?" "Name as many different kinds of leaders as you can," "Can you identify a leader in your age group?" and "List qualities and characteristics that you think make him/her a good leader." Responses to such questions were then content analyzed and compared across the different age-groups. The researchers found that, compared with older children, younger children made more egocentric comments, mentioned more specific actions of leaders, focused more narrowly on specific qualities, used fewer features and fewer dimensions to describe leaders, were more likely to use exemplar rather than prototype classification models, and mentioned different types of leaders. Younger children were also more likely than older subjects to indicate that high verbal activity characterized leaders. In short, younger children used more narrowly defined, data-based, bottom-up definitions of leadership; older children used more general, abstract, top-down definitions.

Matthews and her colleagues (1990) also posited that key changes in cognitive processes could be explained from a developmental perspective. Based on the developmental theories of Piaget, they expected critical differences between children younger than seven (Piaget's preoperational stage) and greater than seven (Piaget's operational stage). But nine years of age, rather than seven, turned out to be a critical difference in their sample. One of their explanations for this delayed critical age is quite consistent with the perspective on cognitive categorization offered in this chapter; that is, the researchers argued that the reason changes in social-cognitive categories and information processing lag changes in cognitive capacities is that it takes time for the relevant experiences and associations to accumulate. A shift from exemplar to prototype models of leadership perception may require considerable experience with leaders *after* the ability to use more abstract cognitive processes develops. Such experience takes time to occur. Moreover, use of a prototype model requires that abstract thinking become the *typical* rather than merely a *possible* mode of processing in forming social perceptions. Thus, developmental changes in typical processes may be "fuzzier" and slower than changes in possible processing.

It is also interesting to contrast the characteristics found by Matthews et al. (1990) to describe leaders with those found by Lord et al. (1984) in a study that used a similar open-ended methodology with college students. Intelligence was the only attribute found to be strongly associated with leadership in both studies. "Directing," "kind," and "helpful" were frequently mentioned as leadership traits by the students in grade school and high school, but those traits were not frequently mentioned by the college sample. In contrast, "aggressive" and "determined" were frequently mentioned by the college sample but used by less than 1 percent of the students in grade school and high school. These contrasts suggest that college students define, and perhaps encounter, qualitatively different leaders than children do.

Content and Structure of Leadership Categories. Lord et al. (1984) argue that leadership is a cognitive category that is hierarchically organized in a manner similar to that involving other object and person categories (Cantor and Mischel 1979; Rosch 1978). Leaders are distinguished from nonleaders at the highest, superordinate level based on an abstract but general prototype. Lord and his colleagues propose 11 different contexts that are used to specify types of leaders: military, educational, business, religious, sports, world political, national political, financial, minority, media, and labor.

Based on categorization theory, one would expect that those attributes which were most widely shared among these basic-level categories would define the superordinate-level leadership prototype. Widely shared attributes are high on what Rosch (1978) calls *family resemblance*. This principle of overlapping similarity distinguishes her view of how categories are structured from the classical view, which posits the existence of critical features that are shared by *all* members of one category but are absent in *all* members of contrasting categories.

Lord and his colleagues' (1984) findings, based on an extensive analysis of college students' leadership categories, supported both their own predictions and Rosch's (1978) theory of categorization. The most frequent attributes across the basic-level categories are listed in table 3.3. For example, intelligence was thought to characterize leaders in 10 of the 11 contexts (the sole exception being national political leader). Table 3.3 also contains prototypicality ratings for these same attributes. As predicted by Rosch's categorization theory, the most widely shared attributes (those highest in family resemblance) also tended to be rated as highly prototypical.

Data from other researchers are generally consistent with these

TABLE 3.3
Ratings of Leadership Traits

Trait	Prototypicality	Diagnosticity	Family Resemblance
1. Dedicated	4.65	.09	.27
2. Goal oriented	4.52	.09	.09
3. Informed	4.48	.18	.18
4. Charismatic	4.48	.09	.09
5. Decisive	4.44	.27	.27
6. Responsible	4.44	.0	.09
7. Intelligent	4.39	.27	.91
8. Determined	4.39	.18	.36
9. Organized	4.39	.0	.09
10. Verbal skills	4.30	.18	.45
11. Believable	4.30	.09	.09
12. Directing	4.30	.09	.09
13. Good administrator	4.30	.09	.09
14. Honest	4.26	.45	.64
15. Concerned	4.26	.09	.09
16. Disciplined	4.26	.0	.09
17. Trustworthy	4.26	.0	.09
18. Fair	4.22	.09	.18
19. Strong character	4.22	.18	.18
20. Open-minded	4.15	.09	.18
21. Persuasive	4.15	.09	.09
22. Interested	4.13	.09	.09
23. Insightful	4.04	.09	.09
24. Understanding	4.0	.36	.45
25. Competitive	4.0	.09	.09
26. Cooperative	4.0	.09	.09
27. Loyal	4.0	.0	.09
28. Educated	3.96	.09	.27
29. Industrious	3.83	.09	.36
30. Caring	3.74	.18	.27
31. Humanitarian	3.74	.09	.09
32. Persistent	3.70	.09	.09
33. Likeable	3.61	.09	.09
34. Well groomed	3.60	.18	.09
35. Healthy	3.52	.0	.09

Note: *Prototypicality* was rated on a 5-point scale: "fits my image of a leader not at all well" (1), "somewhat well" (2), "moderately well" (3), "very well" (4), and "extremely well" (5). *Diagnosticity* is the ratio of family resemblance values for "leader" categories as compared with "nonleader" categories. *Family resemblance* is that proportion of basic-level categories for which at least three of ten subjects mentioned a trait (range is 0 to 1).
Source: Lord, Foti, and De Vader (1984)

findings. For example, Offermann, Kennedy, and Wirtz (1989) investigated implicit leadership theories by having undergraduate subjects generate items that described leaders (as well as supervisors), using a free response format. The investigators then refined this list and developed a 57-item questionnaire that assessed how characteristic each item was of a particular type of category (for instance, leader, effective leader, supervisor). Their analysis indicated eight general factors (scales measuring a leader's intelligence, sensitivity, dedication, tyranny, charisma, attractiveness, masculinity, and strength) that generalized across the type of rater (males versus females) and the type of category being rated. They note that these factors are fairly consistent with the findings of Lord et al. (1984), as well as with topics commonly investigated by leadership researchers. Just as important, Offermann and her colleagues emphasized the value of investigating implicit leadership theories for what their content and structure can tell us about processes like leader-follower interactions.

Although both Lord et al. (1984) and Offermann et al. (1989) suggest that there are some fairly general aspects of leadership, Lord and his colleagues also found that many traits characterize leaders only in specific contexts. The fact that few of these attributes applied to all 11 basic-level categories is consistent with the principle of overlapping similarity among categories that Rosch (1978) labels as family resemblance. What this point means is that leaders in different contexts do not share exactly the same set of traits, even though they are all recognized as being leaders. This principle fits well with the frequently mentioned "situationally contingent" nature of leadership. It also suggests that leaders may have difficulty moving from some contexts to others. More specifically, if there is a high degree of overlap among the traits characterizing leaders in two contexts (for example, business and finance), leaders may be able to move from one context to the other without much difficulty. If, however, there is minimal overlap (for example, sports and finance), one would expect substantial problems for real-world leaders attempting to cross these contextual boundaries.

Because the structure of leadership categories is both theoretically interesting and practically important, it is necessary to explore alternatives to the context model of Lord et al. (1984). For example, rather than context being a basic-level distinction, a person's gender or hierarchical level in an organization might provide a more fundamental distinction among leadership categories. Baumgardner, Lord, and Foti (1990) addressed this issue in a study that contrasted context and hierarchical level as basic-level distinctions. Both experts (subjects with five or more years' experience in a context) and novices (undergraduate students) described the characteristics of high- or low-level leaders in seven specific contexts. Using the procedures of Lord and Maher

(1990a), Baumgardner and her colleagues examined the similarity of category prototypes, reasoning that if context was a basic-level distinction, then high- and low-level leaders within a context would be described more similarly than leaders at the same level but in different contexts would. This prediction was derived from categorization theory findings (Rosch 1978) that subordinate-level categories (leadership categories within the same context) share many common characteristics but that basic-level categories (which differ in terms of context) are highly distinctive. Alternatively, if hierarchical level was the more fundamental distinction, then prototypes at the same hierarchical level but from different contexts would be more similar than prototypes of high- and low-level leaders within the same context.

The results from two types of analyses clearly supported the context over the hierarchical model. For expert subjects, the average correlation (across their set of 70 traits) between low- and high-level leaders *within* contexts was .47, but the average correlation *across* contexts and within hierarchical level was only .21. That this difference was highly significant is consistent with context rather than hierarchical level being the more basic distinction among types of leaders. Cluster analyses also confirmed this pattern. Clusters should form first among high- and low-level leaders within contexts if a context model is correct, whereas different contexts at the same hierarchical level should be clustered first according to a hierarchical model. As shown in figure 3.2, for expert subjects, four of the first five clusters were between low and high hierarchical levels within the same context (for novice subjects, six of the first seven), which again strongly supports context as being the more fundamental distinction among leadership categories. Moreover, the larger clusters (for example, the cluster including the bottom nine categories in the top half of figure 3.2) were generally formed by linking smaller clusters that included both low and high hierarchical levels. A hierarchical model would predict larger clusters based on grouping all low- or all high-level categories.

Interestingly, this study also permitted comparing the results for experts experienced in a context with those for undergraduate subjects who had no experience in a context. Though by no means identical, the results for experts and novices yielded similar theoretical conclusions, strongly supported the context over the hierarchical model, and supported a family resemblance rather than a classical critical feature model of leadership categories. Moreover, as shown in table 3.4, expert and novice family resemblance values were significantly correlated with each other and with the family resemblance values from the study by Lord and his colleagues (1984).

In short, the study by Baumgardner et al. strongly corroborates the basic structure and conclusions of Lord et al. (1984), regardless of

EXPERT GROUP

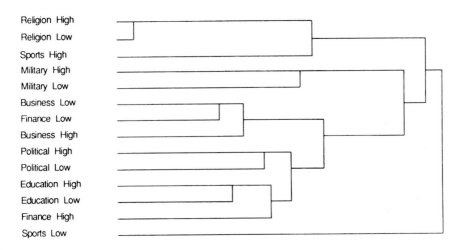

Religion High	
Religion Low	
Sports High	
Military High	
Military Low	
Business Low	
Finance Low	
Business High	
Political High	
Political Low	
Education High	
Education Low	
Finance High	
Sports Low	

NOVICE GROUP

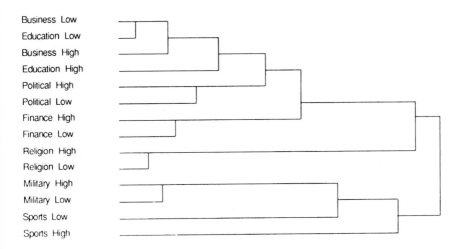

Business Low	
Education Low	
Business High	
Education High	
Political High	
Political Low	
Finance High	
Finance Low	
Religion High	
Religion Low	
Military High	
Military Low	
Sports Low	
Sports High	

Figure 3.2
Hierarchical Clustering of Leadership Categories by Level and Context

TABLE 3.4
Correlation of Family Resemblance Values from Different Samples

	1	2	3
1. Lord et al. (novice)	—		
2. Baumgardner et al. (expert)	.70**	—	
3. Baumgardner et al. (novice)	.69**	.57*	—

* $p < .05$
** $p < .005$

whether experts or novices are used as subjects. It should be noted, however, that part of this agreement may stem from common methodologies. The structure of leadership categories still needs to be investigated using different methodologies and larger samples. Nevertheless, this agreement among different samples and studies is encouraging. We think future research should extend this type of analysis to differences in the perceptions of male and female leaders, a topic we discuss in more detail in chapter 6.

Mobility of Leaders. Since the issue of moving across contextual boundaries (basic-level leadership categories) has never been directly addressed in the leadership literature, we will discuss it in a bit more depth and provide some illustrative data. Based on a *perceiver-oriented* view of leadership, we expect that leaders could function better in any context if they fit with the commonly held prototypes of followers. Under such circumstances, they would be categorized more easily as leaders, thereby enhancing their social power and ability to influence others. They would also conform more to subordinates' expectations, thereby allowing them to build up credit that permitted greater future deviations from group norms (Hollander 1958, 1964, 1985). For this reason, we predict that where prototypes are similar, common perceptual standards will make transitions across contextual boundaries easier for leaders than where prototypes are dissimilar.

Fortunately, the data to compare contexts in terms of prototype similarity are available from the previously discussed study of leadership categorization conducted by Lord, Foti, and De Vader (1984). We have compared the prototype similarity of the 11 basic-level leadership categories they identified. To do so, we simply used their data to create a context by trait matrix in which entries were 1 if a trait was found by Lord et al. to apply to a category and 0 if it was found not to apply. This procedure was done for the 35 most prototypical traits for the superordinate category of leader identified by Lord et al. and depicted in table 3.3. We then calculated measures of association for the 11 basic-level leadership categories across 35 traits. Chamber's r_e coefficients were calculated, as this measure of association gives the best approximation to the underlying correlation with dichotomous data (Alexander, Alliger, Carson, and Barrett 1985). The resulting matrix is shown in table 3.5. These indices reflect the degree of prototype similarity between contexts, and they imply an ease of transfer across some boundaries (business and finance or education and religion) but not others (military and business or sports and business). It should be noted, however, that there are additional factors (such as technical competence, style, source of power, and nature of subordinates) that would also affect ease of movement across these contextual boundaries and that are not reflected in table 3.5.

In spite of this caveat, table 3.5 shows some surprising findings. There were few high values, with only 8 of 55 associations reaching significance. There were many low values, however, and 13 pairs of contexts (24 percent) were actually negatively related. Together, these results indicate that there is not one homogeneous pattern of traits across contexts. Several contexts were generally not associated with other contextual prototypes—military, sports, national politics (which was significantly correlated only with world politics), labor, and media (which were significantly associated only with each other). This finding suggests that, contrary to popular myths, politics, sports, and the military may not be helpful contexts in which to learn *general* leadership skills. It is interesting to note the strong negative relationship between minority and national political leadership prototypes, a result indicating that minority leaders may have considerable difficulty moving into the political realm. Characteristics most prototypical of the category of minority leader are being humanitarian and being persistent, cooperative, and strong in character; those most prototypical for national political leaders are being a good administrator, wanting peace, having strong convictions, and being charismatic, goal oriented, and responsible.

To explore similarities further, we performed a cluster analysis on the data in table 3.5. This analysis indicated that there were only three general clusters: (a) business, finance, minority, religion, and education; (b) labor and media; and (c) national and world politics. The first cluster in figure 3.3 can be seen by looking at the triangle formed by the first five contexts in table 3.5. Many of these associations are significant, indicating substantial overlap of prototypical leadership traits across these settings.

Apart from these three clusters, prototypes were not very similar. Even within the main cluster, the relationships are only moderate. Thus, to move across even closely related contexts (for example, from religion to minority) requires careful planning and adjustment. To

TABLE 3.5
Similarity of Leadership Prototypes from Different Contexts

	B	F	Min.	E	R	S	NP	WP	L	Med.	Mil.
Business	—										
Finance	.83**	—									
Minority	.50	.67*	—								
Education	.57	.72*	.28	—							
Religion	.34	.54	.49	.80**	—						
Sports	.18	.32	.28	.36	.37	—					
National Politics	.20	-.06	-.47	.21	.06	-.07	—				
World Politics	.50	.67*	.20	.75**	.49	.28	.76**	—			
Labor	.57	.32	-.09	.36	.09	.36	-.07	-.09	—		
Media	.50	.25	-.16	.28	.00	-.09	.10	.47	.55*	—	
Military	.11	.25	-.16	-.09	-.34	.28	-.16	.20	.28	-.16	—

$N = 35$
* $p < .05$
** $p < .01$
Note: Significant values were obtained from a chi-square analysis for the 2×2 contingency tables from which Chamber's r_e statistics were calculated.
Source: Lord and Maher (1990a)

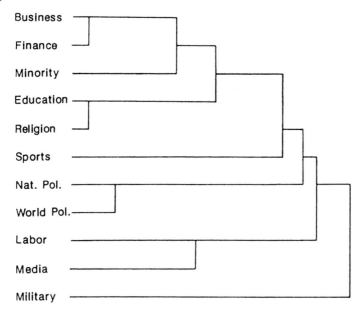

Figure 3.3
Hierarchical Clustering of Leadership Categories by Context Only

some extent, crossing any contextual boundary may require retraining or relearning of leadership skills, and for most transitions such relearning would have to be substantial for leaders to fit successfully the prototypes held by followers. For example, training might stress teaching leaders to emphasize those traits they possess which are consistent with prototypes in a new situation. Emphasizing a partial rather than a perfect fit is consistent with a family resemblance, as opposed to a critical feature, model of categorization. Without such training, commonly held prototypes within contexts could impede the movement of leadership talent across contexts. Yet even with successful training, moving across large perceptual boundaries would require that many leadership activities that had been done automatically, using expert information processing, would have to be carefully monitored, using more rational processes. This additional cognitive demand would compound the other information processing demands associated with new jobs.

We see the analysis of leadership contexts and their impact on leadership mobility as an exciting new area for the leadership field. Traditional work in this area, which has focused on leadership selection and training, has produced neither general theories of leadership nor broadly based training approaches. We suspect that what generally happens is that leaders, who are usually reasonably intelligent, learn a set of appropriate skills through experience. In other words, leadership is developed through on-the-job training and through more of an apprenticeship or mentoring model. We think it is crucial, however, that this experience be the "right" one: that leadership be learned in the context in which it will be applied, or in a fairly similar context. The former drill sergeant now serving in a leadership capacity for a creative advertising team is likely to experience some difficulty in acceptance if she or he does not alter behavior. Further, similarity in contexts can in part be defined and measured on the basis of perceivers' implicit theories of leadership, as we have shown in the above examples.

Future research should explore the effects of prototype similarity on both the effectiveness and the mobility of real leaders. This issue may be particularly important when leaders have to cross culturally defined perceptual boundaries. For example, as we show in chapter 15, prototypes of leaders are very different in the United States and Japan; nonetheless, the effects of these differences in multinational corporations have not yet been explored.

SUMMARY

In this chapter we have developed a categorization-based theory of leadership perceptions that emphasizes the role of perceiver knowledge structures. We proposed that perceivers can recognize leadership based on past experience with leaders. Recognition-based perception uses knowledge of underlying leadership traits and behaviors; this type of processing is usually assumed to proceed automatically. Categorization theory provides an explanation for how recognition-based leadership perceptions are formed and how leadership categories are structured. Briefly, classifying an individual as a leader involves matching certain stimulus properties (for example, traits and behaviors of the stimulus person) to a prototype of a leader held in memory. The prototype is an abstraction of features common to leaders that is developed through experience. Because experience with leaders is important in this process, recognition-based perceptions exemplify the expert information processing model discussed in chapter 2. Though primarily automatic, recognition-based perceptions can also be the result of more controlled processes. Here, leaders are not observed directly, but information relevant to leadership can be socially communicated (for instance, through the media or co-workers). In these instances, although controlled processing is required, the same prototype-matching process is used to form leadership perceptions. Empirical support for the development, content, and structure of leadership categories was also presented in this chapter.

Chapter 4

Inferential Processes and Leadership Perceptions

*I*nferential processes of leadership perception are different from recognition-based processes in that they emphasize the functional aspects of leadership, as opposed to specific traits or features. Function is still an important component of categorical information (Miller 1978; Rosch 1978), but the source of stimulus information is different. That is, people assume that a major function of leaders is to produce good performance outcomes, and they infer leadership from knowledge of successful task or organizational performance. Moreover, inferential processes are closely associated with attributional analyses. Classifications based on recognition processes, on the other hand, do not require causal analyses (Smith and Miller 1983; Winter and Uleman 1984).

In this chapter we explain inferential processes and their link with attribution theory, and we review extensive literature showing that performance feedback affects leadership perceptions. In addition, we consider the practical implications of both recognition-based and inferential leadership perceptions, for both lower and upper levels of the organizational hierarchy.

INFERENTIAL MODEL OF LEADERSHIP PERCEPTIONS

In the inferential mode, information on past performance is used to infer leadership. Once leadership perceptions are formed through *either* inferential or recognition-based processes, they provide a cognitive context that can affect future performance. For example, at lower levels leadership perceptions affect a supervisor's ability to motivate and socialize subordinates; at the highest organizational levels, leadership perceptions affect corporate culture and strategic decision making.

Performance and Causal Attributions

Inferential processes are used to link leadership perceptions to key organizational events. Performance outcomes for major organizational tasks (for example, producing corporate profit statements for businesses or winning championships in sports) are often key events, and many studies show that performance feedback does indeed affect leadership perceptions (Lord 1985). An example of such studies is an experiment done by Rush, Phillips, and Lord (1981). In this study, 15-minute color videotapes of group problem-solving sessions were shown to undergraduate subjects, who were then asked to make leadership ratings for the people in the videotape. After viewing the videotapes but before making leadership ratings, subjects were given bogus performance feedback indicating that the group they watched was either second best or second worst out of 24 groups performing the experimental task. This feedback manipulation significantly correlated with leadership ratings made immediately after viewing the videotape (r = .31) and with ratings made after a 48-hour delay (r = .40), even though subjects in both the "good" and the "poor" feedback conditions viewed the same leadership behaviors.

In short, success enhances the perception of leadership, while failure limits perceptions of leadership. Causal ascriptions to leaders are a basic part of this process. As traditional attribution theory implies (Kelley 1973), if people are seen as being more causal in determining favorable outcomes, then the perception that they are leaders is enhanced; if they are seen as being less causal for good performance, their leadership ratings are not as high. Similarly, causal ascriptions to actors produce lower leadership ratings than ascriptions to other factors do when outcomes are negative.

The effects of causal attributions on inferential leadership perceptions are readily illustrated by the experiences of real leaders. For example, one might expect that the favorable economic performance during Ronald Reagan's administration would translate into high leadership ratings for President Reagan because he would be seen as a key determinant of the policies producing a good economy. In contrast, former vice president George Bush (like many other vice presidents) would not be seen as a major cause of policy during the Reagan administration, and therefore his leadership ratings would not benefit as directly from the nation's favorable economic performance.

Causal attributions are also crucial in explaining observers' interpretations of poor performance. Sutton and Callahan (1987) point out that filing for bankruptcy under Chapter 11 of the Federal Bankruptcy Code stigmatizes both the organization and its management. One tactic for managing such stigmatization is for leaders to deny responsibility for poor organizational performance by attributing causality to the environment. Although this tactic often proves difficult to implement because top managers are expected to exercise control over their organizations and such control is expected to produce organizational success (Sutton and Callahan 1987, 406), its underlying logic can be readily seen in the attributional basis of inferential leadership perceptions. A less extreme but still important example of management's attempts to influence causal attributions can be found in the self-serving attributions (taking credit for successes but attributing failures to external sources) seen in corporate annual reports. Though such justifications may seem manipulative, they do have effects. For example, Staw, McKechnie, and Puffer (1983) found such attributions to be associated with subsequent changes in the stock prices of firms. Self-serving attributions may also be crucial to top management's ability to maintain favorable perceptions in terms of leadership; these perceptions are needed to maintain control over organizations. In other words, effective management at top levels of organizations requires some sensitivity to and control over the attributional processes of key constituencies.

Alternative Attributional Processes

Interestingly, the attributional component in inferential processes may involve either *automatic* or *controlled* processing (Lord and Smith 1983). People may think carefully about causality trying to assess the relative impact of facilitative or inhibiting factors. Such analysis is congruent with conceptualizing perceivers as rational information processors. Alternatively, causal attributions may unknowingly be influenced by factors in the situation that make some causal sources more salient than others. Taylor and Fiske (1978) list several properties of stimuli (movement, contrast, or novelty), situations (environmental cues), or perceivers (needs or self-schema) that affect salience. Salience can automatically affect causal attributions, with less salient factors being seen as having less causal impact. Such heuristics are easy to apply and are consistent with our discussion in chapter 2 of limited-capacity information processing models.

An experimental study by Phillips and Lord (1981) illustrates both automatic and controlled attributional processes. These researchers had subjects make leadership ratings after watching a specially developed videotape of a group problem-solving task and receiving bogus feedback on the performance of the videotaped group. As expected, even though all subjects viewed the same videotaped interaction, good performance feedback led to higher leadership ratings of the target person than poor performance feedback did. This effect, however, also depended on causal ascriptions. When other information given to subjects provided a plausible explanation for performance outcomes, this performance cue effect was diminished, as were causal ascriptions to the leader. For example, when subjects were told that groups in the stimulus tape performed *well* and that these groups were high in ability and motivation, or when subjects were told that groups performed *poorly* and that these groups were low in ability and motivation, the role of the leader was discounted. When information provided to subjects was inconsistent with the observed outcome (pairing low ability and motivation information with good performance feedback, or high ability and motivation information with poor performance feedback), the performance cue effect was strengthened, as were causal ascriptions to the leader. This logical integration of information, consistent with Kelley's (1973) augmenting and discounting configural factors, is suggestive of controlled, rational processing.

Yet causal attributions and leadership ratings were also affected by a less rational, more perceptually based causal factor in the Phillips and Lord study (1981). The videotapes shown to subjects were filmed from two alternative camera angles that made the target subject either more or less salient. Although these tapes were made *concurrently*, resulting in exactly the same behaviors being clearly visible on the videotapes, the salience manipulation affected causal attributions and leadership perceptions. Subjects shown the salient leader videotapes rated the leader as being more responsible for group outcomes and exhibited enhanced performance cue effects. Subjects shown the videotapes with the less salient leader rated the leader as being less causally responsible and exhibited weaker performance cue effects. This experimental factor seemed to involve more automatic processes, reflecting perceptually dominated, limited-capacity (Lowe and Kassin 1980) processes, rather than deliberate, reflective ones.

In interpreting this study, we should note that we are not arguing that each subject used both rational and limited-capacity processes to form causal attributions. Instead, some subjects probably emphasized rational processing based on augmenting and discounting, while others used more heuristic processes based on salience. Since the effects we discussed are for aggregations of subjects, these two types of processing cannot be separated. Nevertheless, separating the types of processing through measures of individual differences represents an interesting area for future research on leadership perceptions.

Much of the empirical support for an inferential model of leadership perceptions comes from experimental studies like that by Phillips and Lord (1981). These studies examine the effects of bogus performance feedback on leadership perceptions and questionnaire ratings of leader behavior. Lord (1985) reviewed 13 studies that demonstrate such performance cue effects on leadership ratings and descriptions of leader behavior. (These studies are covered in more detail in chapter 5.) Such effects generally explain a substantial proportion of the variance in ratings and are consistent over a number of differences in experimental stimuli and procedures. Several researchers (Binning and Lord 1980; Binning, Zaba and Whattam 1986;

McElroy and Downey 1982; Rush and Beauvais 1981) have explored potential boundary variables that might have an impact on performance cue effects, but these effects have proved to be quite robust.

To see how these experimental results might parallel real-world processes, consider the example of Lee Iacocca and Chrysler. When Iacocca became CEO, Chrysler had poor products and limited financial resources. Given these inhibiting factors, Chrysler's turnaround was naturally explained in terms of Iacocca's leadership. Such reasoning shows a logical integration of information and is consistent with controlled processing—that is, people might reason that some extraordinary quality of Iacocca (high leadership ability) allowed him to overcome these inhibiting factors. But Iacocca also made himself highly salient by testifying to Congress and by being personally featured in numerous television ads. This salience may have also triggered more automatic causal processes that supported his causal importance and enhanced leadership perceptions. Thus, both controlled and automatic attributional processes may have guided perceivers' inferences that Lee Iacocca had exerted substantial amounts of leadership at Chrysler. An inferential model would apply to observers' perceptions of Iacocca, since observers were judging leadership on the basis of the outcome of events—that is, Chrysler's turnaround—rather than on face-to-face contact. For people who interacted directly with Iacocca, recognition-based processes would also affect leadership perceptions.

Although Iacocca's self-promotion had a favorable impact on his perception as a leader, it had negative effects as well. Iacocca's increasing recognition as "the" leader of Ford Motor Company soured his long-standing relationship with Henry Ford (chairman of the board), a situation that was the major factor in Iacocca's dismissal as president of Ford Motor Company (Halberstam 1986, 374–75). Iacocca also took the lion's share of the credit for favorable outcomes at Chrysler when many others deserved substantial credit (Halberstam, 571).

It is worth contrasting Iacocca's management of attributions with those of Philip Caldwell, who succeeded him at Ford Motor Company. Caldwell's approach to leadership emphasized teamwork rather than individual prominence. He stressed the importance of everyone's (management's, union workers', and key suppliers') contribution to both the quality design and the production of automobiles. This approach resulted in Caldwell's receiving less credit for the dramatic turnaround of Ford that we described in chapter 1. Were the data available, we would also expect to find Caldwell's leadership ratings to be lower than Iacocca's, even though the performance of Caldwell's company was superior.

Recognizing that causal attributions can be made by either

automatic or controlled processes raises the question of which process will be used. One important limiting factor for controlled processing is the amount of processing capacity available. Logical integration of causal information from various sources is a form of rational information processing, which uses more processing capacity. One study showing the dependence of such processing on sufficient processing capacity was conducted by Gilbert, Pelham, and Krull (1988). These researchers argue that person perception involves three sequential processes: categorization of behavior (what is the actor doing?), characterization (what trait is implied by the action?), and correction (what situational constraints may have caused the action?). This last step corresponds to controlled attributional reasoning. Gilbert et al. found that correction is not performed effectively when perceivers are partially occupied with other cognitive tasks, that is, when they are "cognitively busy." Under such conditions, perceivers in this study attributed behavior to the traits of the actor when the behavior could easily be explained by situational factors. These effects demonstrate a deficiency in controlled processing. They are, however, explainable in terms of automatic processing, since causality would be automatically attributed to salient actors and such automatic effects would not be susceptible to interference from other tasks.

Extensions to Applied Settings

So far, we have described two perceptual processes—recognition based and inferential—by which people can be perceived as leaders. We expect that in most instances, perceptions are formed and modified over time, and that because of this time-distributed nature of perceptions, a mixture of processes is used. For example, initial impressions may be formed based on the recognition of prototypical behaviors, but these perceptions may later be revised, using inferential processes to integrate information on performance. This procedure relies on simple, automatic processes to confirm prior conclusions when new information is consistent with prior categorizations. It is likely that more controlled processes, however, are used to integrate information that is inconsistent with prior conceptualizations (Wong and Weiner 1981). In such cases, observers first carefully assess the causal role of leaders in producing inconsistent performance outcomes and then use performance to revise leadership ratings if the leader is seen as a cause. We believe that many leaders are not only aware of this phenomenon but do much to appropriately manage the "image" they have created. For example, a president of the United States may associate himself with successes, while letting subordinates (press secretaries, cabinet members) explain failures.

We should also note that such processing can be particularly troublesome for atypical leaders, such as minorities or females. (Recall the case of Ann B. Hopkins, discussed in chapter 1.) Because these individuals are rarely in leadership roles, they do not fit existing conceptualizations of typical leaders and therefore will not automatically receive credit for success, even though their unique status makes them salient. Instead, they will tend to receive closer scrutiny as perceivers consciously (but perhaps inappropriately) consider alternative situational causes for their success. Thus, minorities and women may have a particularly difficult time managing their impressions as leaders.

Here, let us summarize our earlier discussion of leadership perceptions. We explained that essentially four different types of processes are involved in forming leadership perceptions. These processes, shown in table 3.1, can be either inferential or recognition based and can involve either predominantly automatic or primarily controlled modes of processing information. The inferential/recognition dimension corresponds to the type of information used by perceivers—that is, to event or outcome information versus trait or behavioral information, respectively. The automatic/controlled dimension corresponds to the type of processes (and the amount of attentional resources they require) that are used to form perceptions.

We believe that most sources of information can be fit into the categories in table 3.1. Still, one important source of leadership information—that conveyed by television and similar media—does not fit very well. For example, viewing a political leader on television involves a complex, rich source of information similar to that which occurs in face-to-face contact, suggesting automatic processing. However, viewing television does not create the concurrent task and social information processing demands that normally occur during face-to-face contact in organizations—an aspect implying that television viewers would have sufficient spare processing capacity to utilize more controlled processes if they were motivated to do so. Thus, media such as television may be consistent with either automatic or controlled processing.

Empirical Limitations

Though the results of research on both recognition-based and inferential processing provide a compelling basis for theory and point to the important role of perceptions in leadership, such research has three general limitations. First, none of the studies has directly investigated how these processes operate during face-to-face contact between subordinates and leaders. Interacting directly with a leader invokes greater processing demands than receiving information about a leader from another source. For example, direct interaction may often require image management on the part of the subordinate, thereby increasing the processing demands of those involved in the interaction, as Gilbert, Krull, and Pelham (1988) have shown. (This issue is explored in more depth in chapter 7.) Then too, face-to-face interactions involve both verbally encoded and nonverbal components of behavior. Our research on leadership perceptions has emphasized the verbal component, but nonverbal behaviors (such as bearing) may also indicate leadership to many perceivers. Further, as suggested by the work of Gilbert and Krull (1988), people may be able to form impressions using nonverbal behaviors with less reliance on attentional resources. If so, nonverbal behavior would be particularly important in the kinds of high cognitive demand situations that characterize face-to-face interactions. In short, face-to-face interactions may operate quite differently from the way that passive observation, used in most social perception research, does.

Second, we have not investigated repeated perceptions of leadership. All the perceptual studies, with the exception of those investigating changes in perceptions of political leaders before and after elections, are cross-sectional. We think the issue of how perceivers change categories over time is important. Changes in evaluations of leadership are also the focus of a significant body of small-group literature that is reviewed by Stein and Heller (1979), who conclude that leaders emerge in groups through high participation rates—that is, people act, the acts are interpreted by members, leadership and social power perceptions change, and the cycle repeats. This process essentially reflects a cybernetic model. But it also has the advantage of showing how behavior, leadership, and social power interrelate over time. Future research should emphasize such cybernetic processing in forming leadership (and other social) perceptions. (This topic is covered in more detail in chapter 5.)

Third, research has not explained how inferential and recognition-based processes are combined. One possibility, relevant to Medin's (1989) recent theorizing about categories, is that performance is part of people's general knowledge about leaders (leaders cause good outcomes). That knowledge is accessed along with the "leader" category, and because of its strong association with this category, it provides an alternative basis for labeling someone as a leader. Another possibility is that most people see attaining good performance as a function of leaders and that they also include this function in their prototype of leaders. This possibility is congruent with some of Rosch's (1978) work and with the findings of Matthews, Lord, and Walker (1990) that young children name exemplars of leadership based on performance (spelling-bee winners). In other words, the ability to produce good performance outcomes is an aspect individuals use in categorization just as they use other characteristics, such as intelligence. But people may not mention functions when asked by experimenters to describe leader characteristics. This explanation suggests that the methodology typically used to operationalize prototypes may miss important aspects of leadership. This possibility should be examined in future research.

IMPLICATIONS OF PERCEPTUAL MODEL

In this section we address the implications of leadership perceptions for leadership theory and offer practical examples for both the recognition-based and the inferential models of leadership perceptions in business settings. We believe these models can be applied differentially to lower and upper levels of the corporate hierarchy. Lower-level leadership emphasizes automatic, recognition-based processes, because lower-level supervisors generally interact on a face-to-face basis with workers (see table 3.1). As a by-product of such interaction, leadership perceptions are formed by subordinates. Upper-level leadership emphasizes the remaining three processes depicted in table 3.1. Top-level executives must convey leadership through less direct means and to a much broader group than the co-workers with whom they interact directly. Thus, these executives are dependent on more controlled, recognition-based processes as well as on the inferences about leadership that are drawn from key organizational events. The implications of these two different types of leadership are discussed briefly below; they are covered in more detail in subsequent chapters.

Lower-level Leadership Perceptions
Most of the theoretical and applied work in the leadership field has focused on lower-level leaders. At this level, leadership theorists have been principally concerned with how supervisors motivate and train subordinates and with the decision-making style of leaders. Unfortunately, much of this research has focused on the supervision of workers, rather than on how leadership occurs at lower levels of organizations. An advantage of the perceptual viewpoint we have developed is that it can explain how leadership occurs in conjunction with these normal work activities. In other words, we assert that leadership perceptions are a normal *by-product* of a worker's interactions with his or her boss. Neither the supervisor nor the subordinate gives much thought to the formation of leadership perceptions while his or her attention is channeled toward specific work tasks. However, leadership perceptions do develop based on such processes, and these perceptions provide an important social

context that has a broad impact on subordinates. For these reasons, in chapter 7 we will focus on automatic, recognition-based perceptual processes at lower hierarchical levels, showing how such processes can help explain both a leader's impact on subordinates and a subordinate's impact on leaders.

Thus far, we have suggested that subordinates use prototypes to understand and predict the behavior of their superiors. Interestingly, because these leadership prototypes are widely held and understood, leaders themselves may also be aware of these prototypical leader behaviors and traits, and they may make use of this knowledge to guide their own behavior. Thus, managers compare their own behavior with self-generated behavioral standards (Carver 1979) derived from leader prototypes. If managers have a clear idea of the appropriate leader prototype, such a comparison could provide a means of self-evaluation and feedback. Prototype matching can therefore provide information as to the appropriateness of a manager's behavior and can directly guide behavior generation through behavioral scripts (Lord and Kernan 1987). Strict adherence to a prototypical set of behaviors, however, may be an overly restrictive way to behave and could be inappropriate in certain instances. But the point we wish to make is that prototypes help subordinates understand and form behavioral expectations of leaders, while managers use these same prototypes to help guide their own behavior and self-presentations.

Given that recognition-based leadership perceptions are pervasive in organizations, some prescriptive statements can be made regarding managerial behavior. The category of an effective leader may be widely held by subordinates in a given context. Therefore, it may benefit the manager to learn what traits and behaviors are prototypical of effective leadership and to make an effort to behave in congruence with this prototype when feasible. As such, leadership training programs should aim toward identifying subordinates' perceptions of effective leadership in particular contexts. Although behaviors and traits associated with effective leadership are thought to be consistent across situations by popular writers (for example, Peters and Waterman 1982), there may be important differences across organizations, among different levels of the same organization, across different task domains (Lord and Alliger 1985), or even among different subordinates in a given work unit. Thus, managers new to an organization, those transferring to different departments within an organization, or those with heterogeneous work groups should be sensitive to different prototypes that affect subordinates' perceptions of effective leadership in these domains.

Executive-level Leadership Perceptions

Executive-level leadership perceptions emphasize the processes in the remaining quadrants of table 3.1. For the most part, executives do not interact on a face-to-face basis with organizational members other than their immediate team of managers. Here, automatic, recognition-based processes would also be important, although top executives often have only indirect influence, through symbolism, images, and policies that affect the organization as a whole. Nevertheless, executive-level leadership can have a significant impact on the performance of an organization, as we show in chapter 10 (see also Day and Lord 1988). Though how top executives can have such a broad impact is the major focus of the third part of this book, three key factors are closely tied to perceptual processes: Hambrick and Finkelstein's (1987) notion of managerial discretion; power and political processes (discussed in chapters 10–12); and organizational culture (covered in chapter 8). We will briefly comment on managerial discretion below.

Hambrick and Finkelstein (1987) argued that the degree of managerial discretion determines the impact a CEO can have on an organization. One of our main points is that leadership perceptions play a large role in determining managerial discretion. To be effective, executive leaders *must* make use of perceptually derived power to substantially influence factors that affect organizational performance, either directly or indirectly. Perceptions create power by expanding what Hambrick and Finkelstein call the zone of acceptance of powerful constituencies in organizations. If the outcome of actions within the zone of acceptance is favorable, executive influence will be enhanced; if the outcome is unfavorable, the influence of the leader will eventually decline.

The processes shown in table 3.1 help explain how an executive's zone of acceptance may be expanded or contracted. Recognition-based processes and inferential processes are both important. If an executive fits an effective leader prototype held by members of powerful constituencies, then the leader's zone of acceptance will expand through *automatic*, recognition-based perceptual processes. Moreover, if socially communicated information about the leader's behaviors is compared with a leader prototype, a recognition-based, *controlled* mode of processing may be used. Once categorized in terms of leadership, subsequent actions and their associated outcomes may be interpreted in light of these perceptions through inferential processes. If leaders are seen as being responsible for events, leadership perceptions will be affected substantially by good or bad outcomes. Responsibility may be assessed *automatically*, if the leader is saliently associated with an event. Alternatively, a more *controlled* process may operate if it is inferred that the leader caused the event or outcome because of his or her level of discretion. We have already explained the way in which both automatic and controlled attributional processes affect leadership perceptions and have provided examples showing how leaders can enhance or minimize such causal attributions. An important implication is that top executives need to manage such perceptual processes to expand their zone of acceptance and maximize managerial discretion. This kind of image management is often necessary to maintaining one's position as a top executive.

Let us return to our example of Philip Caldwell. His personality, being much more conservative, indecisive, and aloof (Halberstam 1986), did not fit well with expectations for typical leaders. Further, he appeared to have poorly understood the recognition processes that affect leadership perceptions. Halberstam (1986) reports that Caldwell had poor relations with the press and did not give much priority to this aspect of his job. In commenting on Caldwell's media relations, Halberstam states: "When journalists tried to ask him [Caldwell] questions about himself, he immediately expressed not only impatience but disrespect for what they did: What he *was* was not important, he said, lecturing them; what he *did* was. That there might be some connection between the two was not something he considered relevant" (661). Caldwell's use of inferential bases for leadership perceptions was also ineffective, and his emphasis on teamwork did not enhance his perceived causal importance.

In short, unlike his counterpart Lee Iacocca, Caldwell did little to appropriately manage his image as an effective leader. The personal consequences were substantial. Caldwell was due to retire in January 1985 after a five-year term as president of Ford, but it was well known within the company that he hoped to continue as president. Yet despite the impressive turnaround Caldwell had managed, Henry Ford quickly dismissed this possibility. He named the quicker, more innovative, and more decisive Donald Peterson as the new chairman. On February 1, 1985, Peterson replaced Caldwell as chairman of Ford (Halberstam 1986, 667).

Our comments on how a leader's zone of acceptance is expanded or contracted is of practical importance for it pertains to both substantive and symbolic actions. Leadership perceptions affect the amount of discretion executives are allowed in several substantive domains (for example, resource allocation, administrative choice, market selection) and several symbolic domains (for example, language and other actions used to affect organizational values). We suggest that substantive, direct actions are associated with perceptions of power and leadership, whereas symbolic, indirect actions are principally associated with perceptions related to organizational culture.

Questionnaire-based Measurement of Leader Behavior

A final implication concerns what is measured by questionnaires commonly used to assess leader behavior. The reason this issue is noteworthy is that during the past 25 years, the primary approach to investigating leadership has been to try to differentiate effective from ineffective leaders in terms of their behavior vis-à-vis subordinates. Leader behavior was usually measured by questionnaires given to subordinates, who then rated the past behavior of their leader. This methodology and the constructs it produced defined the leadership field during the 1960s and 1970s. Such scales as Consideration and Initiation of Structure of the Leader Behavior Description Questionnaire (LBDQ) (Stogdill 1963) provided the major constructs in theories about leadership. For example, House's (1971) path goal theory of leadership attempted to explain whether leaders should emphasize consideration or initiation of structure in clarifying paths to goals valued by subordinates, thereby ensuring adequate motivation.

Difficulties with this approach occur on two levels, both of which are closely related to the perspective developed in this book. First, although the logic of this measurement approach is tied directly to a bottom-up, stimulus-based, rational model of social perceptions, categorical-based, top-down processing is probably more common. As we have seen, behavioral information is not simply preserved by raters for later use by researchers; it is also actively transformed into more general and useful (for the subordinate) constructs that allow the classification of others and the prediction of their behavior. Such transformations involve integration of behavioral information to form leadership perceptions, and these perceptions (along with underlying knowledge structures in memory) *mediate* between much of the behavioral information to which subordinates are exposed and their responses on descriptive questionnaires (Fraser and Lord 1988; Rush et al. 1981). Thus, leadership questionnaires measure much more than just leader behavior: they are affected substantially by the perceptual processes of raters, as well as by the behavior of the leader being rated.

Second, perceptions of leadership can be based on inferential procedures, as well as on the more behaviorally based recognition procedures we have discussed in this chapter. As many laboratory studies have shown, leader "behavior" ratings reflect both behavior-based recognition processes and performance-related inferential processes (see Lord 1985 for a review of this literature). Thus, ratings based in part on the effects of prior leader performance provide a biased and somewhat circular means of explaining that performance. Correlations between behavioral ratings could reflect either actual behavior/performance relations or the effects of past performance on *ratings* of leader behavior. In chapter 5 we provide more detailed coverage of questionnaire-based ratings of leader behavior.

SUMMARY

In the last two chapters, we have presented a theory of leadership based on a perceptual view of leaders. Leadership perceptions are formed through two perceptual processes: recognition based and inferential. Both processes are often used in leadership perception, but the distinction between them is important for understanding how leadership perceptions are developed and maintained.

In this chapter, we have discussed how leadership perceptions can be formed through inferential processes. Rather than relying on observed traits and behaviors, leadership perceptions are formed through linkages to organizational outcomes. Such perceptions are formed primarily through assessments of causality for outcomes or events. If leaders are seen as causes of outcomes and if outcomes are successful or favorable, leadership perceptions of individuals linked with those outcomes will be enhanced. Outcomes that are unsuccessful, however, may limit leadership perceptions of individuals linked to those failures. As with recognition-based processes, inferential leadership perception may use either automatic or controlled processes. Automatic inferential processes occur when causal linkages are made based on salience and proximity. For example, leaders can make themselves highly salient with respect to favorable organizational events; here, perceptions of leadership are more likely to occur. Controlled inferential processes reflect a more careful, deliberate analysis of likely causal agents for organizational outcomes. Automatic processes may be more likely when perceivers' available processing capacity is limited. Such may be the case when perceivers are operating under strong task demands or other forms of information overload.

Our discussion of recognition-based and inferential processes of leadership perception point to some important implications for leaders. First, we suggest that the two processes are differentially emphasized at different levels of an organization. Lower-level leadership perceptions emphasize automatic, recognition-based processes of leadership, particularly in the development of dyadic relationships between leaders and subordinates, a topic discussed in chapter 7. Executive-level leadership perceptions place greater emphasis on inferential processes. Leadership perceptions of this nature largely determine the degree of discretion an executive holds in various domains of the organization, issues that are discussed at length in chapters 9–12.

A final implication of a perceptual view of leadership pertains to the use of questionnaire-based measures of leader behavior. Rarely is leader behavior information retained in memory without being transformed through integrations with raters' implicit leadership theories. These knowledge structures in part determine how leader behavior information is encoded and recalled. Therefore, questionnaire-based measures of leader behavior (such as the LBDQ) are likely to tap these knowledge structures held in memory, as well as actual leader behavior.

Chapter 5 ———————————————————

Social Perceptions, Information Processing, and Change

———————————————————————————

Understanding how individuals are labeled as leaders is only a first step in understanding how we process information about other people in work situations. In this chapter we take a brief but more detailed look at social information processing. This topic is interesting for three reasons. First, being limited information processors, we take many shortcuts in forming expectations about other people's traits and behaviors. We rely on only part of the information to which we are exposed when we form assessments of others. Nevertheless, these expectations provide a cognitive context that affects future actions with individuals. Second, as we noted in our discussion of limited-capacity information processing models, many biases in information processing can be traced to perceivers' use of cognitive simplifications. For example, gender-based biases in social perceptions may be related to using gender as a salient category for encoding and retrieving social information, rather than to using alternative categories, such as "potential leaders." Third, as noted in the last chapter, the primary methodology used to study leadership (and many other types of social perceptions, such as performance evaluations) is questionnaire-based descriptions of behavior, provided by organizational members. Understanding how we process information related to questionnaires may help us see the limitations of this methodology as well as indicate ways such limitations can be overcome. As we take a more microscopic view of social information processing, we will comment on each of these three areas, but our emphasis will be on assessing traits and measuring behavior. The impact of expectations on superior-subordinate exchanges and gender-related biases will be addressed in subsequent chapters.

TRAIT ASSESSMENTS AND BEHAVIORAL EXPECTATIONS

In the preceding chapter we explained how leadership perceptions can be formed by both recognition-based and inferential processes in either an automatic or a controlled fashion. In figure 5.1 we extend this

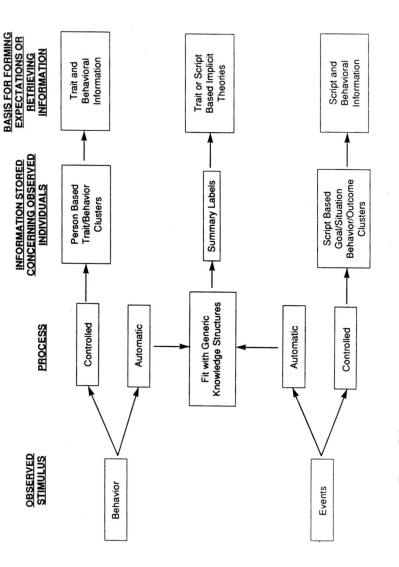

Figure 5.1
Model of Social Information Processing Based on Behavior and Event Schema

thinking to provide a more general model in which social perceptions are formed on the basis of either behavioral stimuli, involving recognition-based processes, or knowledge of events and their outcomes, involving inferential processes. Further, both behavior and events can be processed using *either* automatic processes or controlled processes. As we show in the figure, the type of process used has consequences for the information that is encoded and stored in memory, which in turn affects the information that can be used to form behavioral expectations or to complete questionnaires. In fact, some questionnaires, like the Behavioral Expectations Scales (Smith and Kendall 1963), are completed with expectations in mind.

In figure 5.1 we assert that in work situations, perceivers are usually exposed to both behavioral and event information, since most social interactions involve people performing work tasks. Further, observers usually have both person- and event-related knowledge structures in memory. Therefore, observed information can be interpreted and stored by reference to either person- or event-related knowledge structures. But since perceivers are limited-capacity processors with limited attentional resources, at a given time only one knowledge structure will predominate. Consequently, only minimal amounts of information (general evaluations of fit and summary labels) will be processed in relation to another knowledge structure. Person-based processing, as compared with event-based processing, should result in different information being stored in memory and in a different organization of that information.

Person-based processing usually involves classifying people in terms of traits, such as leadership, and many relevant traits exist as knowledge structures held by perceivers. *Event-based processing* often involves an analogous type of schema called scripts. Scripts are goal-based, hierarchical structures that can be used either to help make sense of perceived events or to help generate actions required to attain goals (Lord and Kernan 1987). The use of these alternative types of schemas by perceivers was contrasted in a laboratory study by Foti and Lord (1987) that used videotapes of a group meeting as the stimulus. They found that under conditions that elicited use of a script structure (informing subjects about group goals and asking them to try to remember as much behavioral information as possible), a greater proportion of script- than leader-relevant items was remembered and that recalled information was clustered in an order that paralleled the script organization. Alternatively, in conditions that fostered the use of person-based schemas (asking subjects to form an impression of the chairman in the meeting and providing no information on goals), leader-relevant information was more likely to be recalled than script-related information was. Thus, there is direct experimental evidence for our assertion that person- versus event-related processing involves organization around different schemas, producing different memory for leader versus script information and a different organization of that information.

Before taking a closer look at person- and event-related processing, we should first note an important qualification that applies to most social perceptions in applied settings—namely, that these evaluations of others are made repeatedly, being updated in a manner that fits closely with chapter 2's description of cybernetic processing. Hastie and Park (1986) assert that most trait judgments are made spontaneously (without intention) during the course of social interactions using *on-line processing*. Such processing relies on immediately available information (information in working memory or in the stimulus environment) in making social judgments, minimizing the role of information retrieved from memory. When long-term memory is accessed, what we usually retrieve are prior judgments about an individual, not the original evidence on which that judgment was based (Lingle, Dukerich, and Ostrom 1983; Lingle and Ostrom 1979). In other words, when revising a judgment about a superior, subordinates may recall prior judgments about his or her leadership ability, but not the original behaviors or performance episodes on which those leadership judgments were based. On-line processing may be very efficient in zeroing in on an appropriate trait judgment while minimizing social information processing demands, but only for those traits which are likely to be evaluated. Information not relevant to traits being evaluated may never be incorporated into a trait judgment (Srull and Wyer 1989). In organizations, most formal processing (written communications, such as résumés and memorandums) is likely to elicit encoding in terms of work-related traits, such as ability. Face-to-face communications, however, may automatically elicit the use of more socially based traits. For example, individuals may be evaluated on task-related traits, such as "competence," at certain times but then be evaluated on sociability when we interact with them.

Person-based Processing

Person-based processing is particularly interesting, since there are usually many traits that could be used to make sense of a person's behavior. Which traits are chosen to guide processing depends on which traits are suggested by the context, which traits have been recently used (are more available), which traits are suggested by salient features of the person being perceived (males over six feet, four inches tall are often evaluated as potential basketball players), and which trait schemas are possessed by perceivers (people concerned with obesity may tend to label others as thin or fat more often than other perceivers do). Choice of traits is generally unintentional but does have significant consequences in terms of what information is noticed or elaborated on using controlled processing. Choice of traits also determines what summary labels are formed (or revised) on the basis of behavioral information and what types of knowledge structures can be applied to forming expectations about the person being perceived.

The importance of which traits are selected is illustrated by the following example. Consider a female employee who is a potential leader or manager. If females are in the minority, so that gender is a salient attribute, then many types of on-line judgments may be made concerning traits closely tied to gender—friendly or unfriendly, attractive or unattractive. Gender-related processing makes evaluations that are more related to work (for example, intelligence, motivation, or dependability) less likely to be formed. While gender-related processing is occurring, other information related to potential management ability may never be incorporated into perceivers' judgments. Further, rather than being independently stored in memory, information relevant to management potential is simply lost when attention is focused on gender-related trait judgments. Therefore, if the potential female manager in this example is subsequently considered for promotion to manager, evaluators may have no clear assessment of her management potential, because this judgment has not been made repeatedly and updated based on prior interactions. It also follows that were researchers to come into the organization and ask these same evaluators to rate the management-related behavior of the potential female manager, the evaluators would not be very accurate in describing either behavior or management potential. Thus, both managers and researchers may inaccurately evaluate females if gender-related traits are typically more salient than traits that are more closely related to potential work activities. Perceivers simply lack the relevant data base (prior judgments or related behaviors) to form accurate judgments.

What Is Stored in Memory. We distinguish among three types of information that may be stored in memory: summary labels, trait-behavior clusters, and specific behavioral content. *Summary labels* reflect the end result of repeated cybernetic processing with respect to some relevant trait. Behaviors or characteristics are compared with a relevant trait prototype, and if a sufficient degree of matching occurs, a trait label is applied to the person being evaluated. Consistent with Rosch's (1978) work on categorization theory, matching is based on a family resemblance process, meaning that all prototypical features or behaviors need not be present for a trait label to be applied. As shown in the middle part of figure 5.1, these labels may be formed through automatic processing, while controlled processing capacity is focused elsewhere. In such cases, little behavioral information specific to the labeled person is connected with these labels. Nevertheless, the labels can easily be related to general knowledge traits (generic trait information). Connection to such generic structures has two important consequences. First, it makes behavior meaningful and allows us to form expectations about the labeled individual, even when we can accurately remember little about his or her past behavior. This point is particularly significant, since, as noted earlier, cybernetic processes are future oriented. Thus, the ability to label individuals helps us see how they fit with our own objectives. Labeling also reduces uncertainty by suggesting how the other person is likely to behave. Second, ratings of past behavior are unlikely to be very accurate when labels are formed solely through automatic processes. In fact, we assert that in most real-world situations, accuracy in remembering the past behaviors of others is much less important than forming comprehensive expectations.

Trait-behavior clusters are formed when more controlled processes are used to evaluate the observed behavior of another in terms of some relevant trait. These clusters connect behaviors to trait labels through an associative memory network. Srull and Wyer (1989) suggest that there are two different types of clusters that may contain behavioral information. The first, which is shown in figure 5.2a, merely attaches behavioral information to trait labels. We expect that such clusters are very similar structurally to generic implicit theories, which also connect behavioral information to categorical labels. Hence, the behavior encoded on such structures may be easily confused with information in generic trait structures. The second type of trait-behavior cluster, shown in figure 5.2b, is quite similar, but it also has associative paths that connect different behaviors. Importantly, the behavioral information contained in these clusters can be accessed in memory both from other behavioral nodes and from a trait node (that is, both the top and the bottom of figure 5.2b).

The specific behavioral content that is stored in memory depends on how thoroughly information was encoded. For information that is consistent with trait schemas (the current evaluation of a person), information can be encoded generically, that is, by merely matching the behavior to an already-existing code contained in one's general trait structures. Such encoding contains little information specific to that person or situation.

Opinions differ regarding the way in which information about inconsistent behaviors is stored. Information that is inconsistent with a prior evaluation may be processed more thoroughly (Srull and Wyer 1989), unless multiple dimensions are being evaluated (Hamilton, Driscoll, and Worth 1989). Inconsistent behaviors are generally

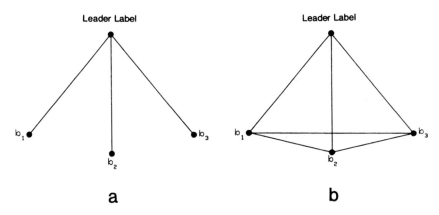

Figure 5.2
Two Alternative Models of Trait-Behavior Clusters

evaluated in relation to other behaviors, as shown in figure 5.2b. Elaborations concerning inconsistent behavior are tagged onto generic structures (Woll and Graesser 1982). Alternatively, causal attributions may be made for the behavior, and behaviors attributed to external sources may be discounted and not associated with a trait cluster. Causal ascriptions affect the use of inconsistent information in revising trait assessments (Crocker, Hanna, and Weber 1983).

Forming Behavioral Expectations and Retrieving Information. We have posited that updating trait labels is a main consequence of cybernetic processing; such updating allows revision of expectations for the future behaviors of the person being perceived. In forming these expectations, we see little advantage to more elaborate encoding of behavioral information. Implicit theories may be just as useful as recall of specific behaviors, *once appropriate trait labels have been applied to a person.* In some respects, implicit theories may be superior because they allow the formation of expectations for behaviors that have not yet been observed. In such cases, perceivers can rely on general knowledge gained through experience with many people. In this respect, experts may have advantages over novices. We have argued that expert information processors are especially good at recognizing meaningful patterns. Applying this view to a social context, we would expect experts to be especially adept at seeing the match between behaviors and relevant trait categories. Further, because experts' categorical structures are more detailed and more highly organized, we would expect experts to be much better at using these structures to make predictions about future behavior. For example, Zalesny and Highhouse (in press) found that after viewing a small videotaped segment of a teacher's classroom behavior, experienced school administrators could predict subsequent teacher behavior better than novice student teachers could. We posit that experienced assessment center raters would be able to classify ratees more quickly and easily and would also be able to make better predictions about future behavior or performance.

Interestingly, if we define *behavioral-level accuracy* as the ability to distinguish observed from unobserved behavior (see Lord 1985), then experts may be at a *disadvantage* compared with novices. Experts' quicker recognition of patterns of behavior and their greater ability to make matches to existing knowledge structures should yield a more categorically based encoding of information. Experts would encode schema-consistent information more similarly to figure 5.2a's depiction than to figure 5.2b's (Hauenstein [1987] provides data that support this assertion), thereby reducing their ability to distinguish observed from unobserved behaviors. But experts are also highly sensitive to schema-inconsistent behavior. Thus, while novices may be better at accurately assessing behaviors that are consistent with a relevant trait schema, experts are likely to be better at evaluating inconsistent behaviors. We also suggest that experts would be better at accurately making overall trait judgments, which has been labeled *classification-level accuracy* (Lord 1985).

Event-based Processing

Whereas person-based processing relates behaviors to the perceived internal aspects of actors, event-based processing relates behaviors to the accomplishment of goals and to features of the situation. Thus, person- and event-based processing provide alternative ways of interpreting and understanding behavior. Nevertheless, many aspects of event-based processing are analogous to person-based processing. For example, as with person-based processing, summary labels serve to identify and access relevant knowledge structures. Labels for events consist of goals or goal-related phrases—preparing a report, having a meeting. These labels usually also incorporate information about the outcome of such events. More complex event-related structures also exist and are analogous to trait-behavior clusters. Usually called scripts, these hierarchical structures link goals to necessary behaviors (or subgoals), often specifying the order in which behaviors must be performed. Finally, the behavioral content of these structures may be generic or expected behavior, but unexpected or unusual behavior may be explicitly "tagged" (Woll and Graesser 1982).

Since our focus is on person-based processing, our coverage of event-based processing is brief. But we should stress that it is an important alternative type of processing that may affect what information is noticed and encoded and how it is organized. Event-based processing may also affect behavioral expectations and causal attributions in certain situations. Interestingly, individuals with more task experience (experts) may rely more on event-based processing, compared with individuals who lack task experience (novices). This factor may lead people to assess causality differently and to produce different reactions to poor performance. For example, Mitchell and Kalb (1982) found that supervisors with experience in the subordinate's task gave more situational attributions to subordinates' poor performance than supervisors without such experience did.

The model shown in figure 5.1 implies dual encoding of behavior in terms of person- and event-based schemas. Each type of schema, however, is not fully utilized *at the same time*. Focusing on people minimizes the use of event-related schemas and vice versa. Yet we would expect that inconsistent behaviors could lead a person to focus on alternative schemas as a way of making sense of this inconsistency. One may consider script-based schemas for explanations of behaviors that are inconsistent with the person-based schemas being used to understand behavior. We think the use of script-based cognitive structures to understand behaviors inconsistent with prior trait ascriptions is an unexplored topic that warrants future research.

CHANGES IN PERSON EVALUATIONS

We have asserted that evaluations of people are modified over time through cybernetic processes. In this section we comment briefly on how these processes work to update overall evaluations or trait ascriptions. This topic is obviously relevant to leadership perceptions, but it is equally relevant to other work-related perceptions, such as performance appraisals. Updating perceptions is particularly important to understanding social cognitions in work settings, in which the same people are encountered day after day. Interestingly, researchers concerned with social cognitions have given little attention to this issue, perhaps because it is more difficult to investigate experimentally than initial impression formation. We can form some tentative propositions as to how the impression-updating process works, based on the theoretical framework we have developed; however, we think this issue should be investigated more extensively in future research.

Updating Using Controlled Processes

Perhaps the most important prediction we can make is that updating perceptions should work differently when controlled, as compared with automatic, processes are emphasized. When controlled processes are used, more information should be stored in memory and thus be used in revising impressions. We would expect this process to produce gradual changes in the way an individual is evaluated. Based on our discussion in chapter 3, controlled, recognition-based ratings of leadership should change gradually as new information is accumulated. We would also expect controlled processing to be important in inferential revisions of leadership perceptions. Events attributed to an actor may cause substantial revisions in leadership evaluations, whereas those attributed to situational factors may cause less change in such perceptions.

The top panel of figure 5.1 suggests that repeated evaluations using controlled processing would result in modification of trait-behavior clusters and in changes in the overall evaluation of a person. We would expect that as more information is encountered, more information would be attached to the clusters that characterize a particular person. But because an impression develops over time, there should be an increasing tendency to pay attention mainly to inconsistent information, which would receive more careful encoding. Srull and Wyer (1989) posit that this process would result in more behavior-to-behavior linkages for inconsistent behavior (see figure 5.2b). There are, however, at least two other possibilities that deserve mention. One, which is suggested by the work of Crocker et al. (1983), is that raters first analyze whether the behavior was caused by the person or the situation. If situationally caused, the information is discounted and may not be processed further; that is, it may not be stored in long-term memory and may not result in a changed perception. A second possibility is suggested by our model in figure 5.1—namely, that information inconsistent with a person-based schema may be evaluated for consistency with an event-based schema. Such analysis may involve a quick check to see whether behavior is consistent with scripts that characterize the situation. This process may be part of the correction phase in Gilbert's model of social perceptions, discussed earlier (Gilbert, Pelham, and Krull 1988). If behavior fits relevant scripts, then situational rather than dispositional attributions may be made (see Read 1987 for a further discussion of this process) and behavioral information may not be processed further. That is, such information would be tagged onto an event cluster, rather than onto a trait-behavior cluster, and no revision in overall leadership ratings would occur. Such possibilities need to be integrated with a more comprehensive model that can be examined empirically.

Updating Using Automatic Processes

Impression revision using more automatic processes should also be discussed. Here we think the process works differently. Since only summary information, rather than specific behavioral information, is stored, we would expect no gradual changes in ratings. Instead, changes should be discontinuous, corresponding to large changes in perceptions associated with the recognition that an entirely different category may be more appropriate for perceiving an individual. Such changes may involve shifts from "poor leader" to "good leader" categories. They may also represent shifts from one trait category to another. For example, shifts from encoding information using gender-based distinctions to encoding in terms of leadership should produce discontinuous changes in the way female managers are evaluated.

We think these changes can be so dramatic that they cannot be modeled by ordinary analytic techniques using linear relationships or continuous monotonic relationships. A special type of mathematics called catastrophe theory, based on the work of Thom (1975), develops elementary forms of discontinuous change that are useful in understanding changes in social perceptions. One of the simplest forms of catastrophe models, the fold catastrophe, is shown by the solid line in figure 5.3. This graph shows differences in evaluations of an individual as one proceeds from different starting points at either end of the figure. For example, the evaluation of an individual at a given level of objective performance may be very different depending on whether he or she is initially thought to be a good or a poor performer.

The unusual characteristic of this graph is that it folds back on itself. The fold in the figure illustrates that the history of evaluations is important; history determines the underlying schema used to assimilate new information. One's initial evaluation can be thought of as a source of "cognitive inertia" that must be overcome before one's evaluation will shift. If one begins with an unfavorable impression, as shown on the extreme left of this figure, and then encounters more and more favorable behaviors, one may still be reluctant to shift to a positive evaluation, and the unfavorable evaluation persists well past the midpoint of the scale. On the other hand, if one begins with a very favorable impression and encounters behaviors that are less favorable, one may be reluctant to shift to a negative evaluation, and these favorable evaluations again persist well past the midpoint of the scale. Thus, as shown in figure 5.3, how intermediate levels of performance are evaluated depends considerably on whether performance is initially categorized as either good or poor.

This model has several implications. First, the difference in evaluations for identical performance levels (the center of the figure) can be thought of as an index of bias in social evaluations associated with automatic processing. For example, if a female manager's work activities are initially evaluated with respect to gender, perceivers may evaluate her management potential much lower than if she was

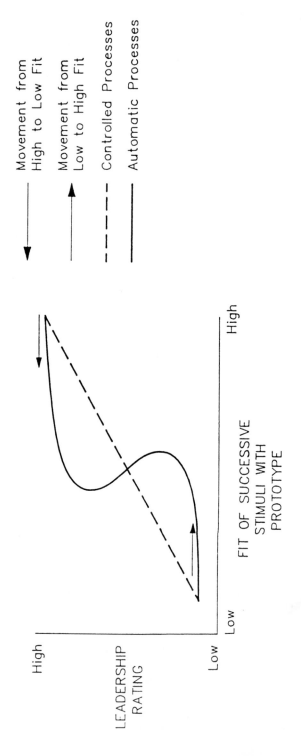

Movement from
High to Low Fit

Movement from
Low to High Fit

Controlled Processes

Automatic Processes

High

LEADERSHIP
RATING

Low

Low

FIT OF SUCCESSIVE
STIMULI WITH
PROTOTYPE

High

Figure 5.3
Revision of Initial Leadership Rating When Prototypical Leadership
Information Is Repeatedly Encountered

initially evaluated in terms of leadership. In this case, switching from a gender-based to a leadership-based impression involves a substantial amount of cognitive reorganization and reinterpretation of past behaviors. Such extra processing is the source of this cognitive inertia. Thus, initial labeling processes can be very powerful.

Second, when different perceivers evaluate the same individual but apply different schemas, their evaluations may be very different. The use of different schemas implies a high degree of variability across perceivers in evaluating intermediate levels of behavior (behaviors within the fold region). A practical implication is that one will have consistency in evaluations based on automatic processes only when perceivers are operating from the same underlying schema. A means of increasing agreement may be to train perceivers to develop a common prototype or standard (Hauenstein and Foti 1989).

Because history is reflected in the direction from which one approaches the fold region, fold catastrophe models are a useful way of thinking about changes in social perceptions. The link between contrasting initial impressions (for instance, a good or a poor employee) and the use of contrasting cognitive schemas (for example, an in-group or an out-group member) is another key advantage of this model.

Both theoretical and empirical work support this model of change. Theoretically, Stewart and Peregoy (1983, 340–44) suggest that this type of discontinuous change can be represented by a fold catastrophe model (which we show in figure 5.3 as a solid line), and some of their principal examples involve changes in social schemas (for instance, male-female). Stewart and Peregoy's example of a switch from male to female categories is shown in figure 5.4. In this figure, as we move from left to right we encounter information that is increasingly inconsistent with our initial impression that the figure is a male. Little change in evaluations is made until the information is so inconsistent that an entirely different category (the figure is a female) is more appropriate. Such models are in contrast with the more gradual changes in evaluations that we would expect when controlled processes are used. (See the dashed line in figure 5.3.)

An additional feature of catastrophe models is that they explain movement along the fold in terms of underlying control variables. We posit that in the area of social perceptions, these underlying control variables can be equated with cognitive processes directly related to cognitive categorization. Initial classification depends on the salient features of (a) the person being classified, which may suggest appropriate schemas; (b) which schemas are chronically available to perceivers (which schemas predominate in one's self-schema); and (c) which schemas are primed by the situation. Any of these factors can

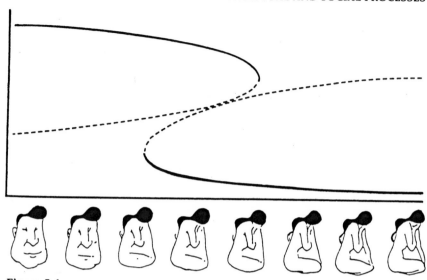

Figure 5.4
Two-fold Catastrophes Developed by Beginning the Experiment at the Two Different Ends of the Stimulus Sequence (Hysteresis is illustrated, since the predicted catastrophe points occur at different places in the sequence.)

make a particular schema more (or less) available in memory and increase (or decrease) its likelihood of being used to classify a stimulus person.

Movement along the horizontal dimension in figure 5.3 depends on how well subsequent stimuli fit the prototypes of the initial categories applied to stimuli. Much work on categorization theory indicates that differences in how well stimuli fit a prototype form a gradient of goodness of fit with a category that is meaningful to perceivers (Rosch 1978). It seems reasonable to extend this same principle to explain changes in subsequent judgments, as Fiske and Neuberg (1990) have done.

Exactly what processes produce the sudden shift to another category requires further research. One possibility is that perceivers momentarily shift to controlled processing to resolve inconsistencies, but when these inconsistencies become so numerous or extreme that they cannot be discounted, more appropriate alternative categories are accessed and used to form different judgments.

This explanation suggests that the availability to perceivers of specific categories can have a dramatic impact on perceptions, either through initial classifications or by affecting reclassification. This conclusion has important applied implications. It may be quite easy for leaders to affect the relative availability of alternative categories that might be used to make sense of the same stimulus information. Both the explicit statements made by leaders and factors more typically associated with culture (artifacts, stories, and so on) may affect category accessibility and thereby substantially affect how behavioral information is interpreted. For example, in an organization in which both top leaders and the culture imply that women will function effectively as leaders, the leadership category might be highly available for perceivers evaluating the management potential of women. Availability would be especially high if there were also many examples of female executives in that organization. In another organization, one in which women are discouraged from attaining leadership positions and in which examples of female executives are few, the leadership category may be much less available for interpreting the behavior and characteristics of women. We would expect that a woman exhibiting the same behaviors and performance levels would be evaluated differently in these two organizations. In the latter organization, initial judgments would be less likely to be made with respect to leadership. Moreover, even if in both organizations initial judgments were made with respect to gender rather than leadership, the switch to encoding in terms of leadership should come much earlier in the first than in the second organization. In other words, the bias associated with using the wrong categories would be much less in the first organization.

Determinants of Automatic and Controlled Processing

The difference between the folded and the unfolded lines in figure 5.3 is that the straight line involves piecemeal integration of information, whereas the folded surface reflects integration with respect to different cognitive categories. Fiske and Neuberg (1990) discuss similar processes in explaining continua of impression formation. They argue that categorization requires minimal amounts of cognitive resources and therefore has priority over controlled processing. Further, they assert that perceivers attempt to use new information mainly to confirm prior categories. But if this confirmation is unsuccessful (that is, if information is highly inconsistent with prior categories), recategorization is possible. Recategorization requires, however, the use of more cognitive resources, a point that is consistent with our explanation for cognitive inertia. Fiske and Neuberg equate piecemeal processing with controlled processes that place high demands on perceivers' attentional resources. In short, their perspective is quite consistent with our treatment of changes in social perceptions, but our treatment goes beyond their model, in postulating a folded region of discontinuous change when categorization changes.

One way to integrate impression formation by automatic and controlled processes is to add an additional control variable to our catastrophe theory framework, a variable that specifies the type of processing used in forming (or revising) social perceptions. Addition of this second control variable, called a bifurcating variable in catastrophe theory, produces a three-dimensional model of social perception, as shown in figure 5.5. This model has continuous change on the back surface but the discontinuous change of our fold catastrophe model on the front surface. The model makes the most sense if one conceptualizes the distinction between automatic and controlled processing as involving a continuum pertaining to the relative amount of automatic and controlled processing used by perceivers.

Several factors should increase the likelihood that controlled processes are used in forming social judgments. Perceiver factors, such as high motivation and spare cognitive resources, should be important in making controlled processing more likely. Novel stimuli and stimuli inconsistent with prior impressions should also increase the likelihood of controlled processing. Finally, the role of culture may again be significant, as it may include norms that emphasize rational information processing or such values as concern for evaluating people fairly. Each of these factors would increase the likelihood of controlled processing in forming social judgments; all of them may be involved in specifying the bifurcating control variable shown in figure 5.5.

Our previous discussion suggests that automatic versus controlled processing may help determine bias in social judgments. Although this suggestion implies that controlled processing may be preferred, we should remember that people are limited-capacity processors. Cognitive resources allocated to social perceptions may often come at the expense of task performance. Therefore, in most instances social perceptions formed during work activities will be based on automatic processing.

While speculative, our cusp catastrophe model provides a mathematical formulation for revision in social judgments, with the controlled versus automatic processing distinction serving as a bifurcating variable in catastrophe theory terms. The work of Hanges, Braverman, and Rentch (1989) on the revision of performance evaluation ratings over time supports a cusp catastrophe model of revision in social judgments, but this model has yet to be applied to the leadership domain. We also need to explore the effect of automatic processing on the revision of such social judgments as leadership.

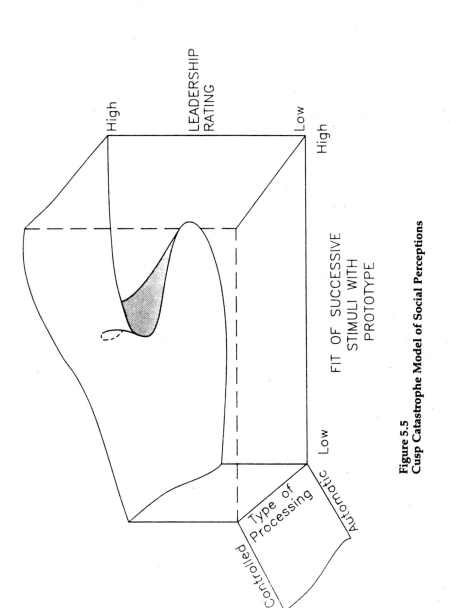

Figure 5.5
Cusp Catastrophe Model of Social Perceptions

RELATIONSHIP OF AUTOMATIC AND CONTROLLED
PROCESSING TO MEASURES OF LEADER BEHAVIOR

The cusp catastrophe model we have explained suggests very different functional forms for social perceptions, depending on the type of cognitive processes used. These alternative types of information processing also have profound implications for the accuracy of questionnaire measures of leadership behavior. In general, we think behavioral accuracy in person perception will be much higher when controlled, as opposed to automatic, processing is used.

The model of perception and information processing that we have presented can also be used to explain three important findings concerning questionnaire measures of leadership behavior. We will discuss these findings as follows: first, we will show how inferential modes of leadership perceptions affect ratings of leadership behavior; second, we will demonstrate that a key determinant of leadership ratings is the relationship of rated behavior to underlying categories, *not necessarily to the behavior of the target person*; and third, we will show how the constructs assessed by questionnaire measures can be tied to the implicit theories of raters.

Inferential Perceptions and Rated Behavior. The effects of inferential processes on questionnaire ratings are best illustrated by studies showing that bogus performance feedback affects leadership perceptions and ratings of leadership behavior; an example is the study by Rush, Phillips, and Lord (1981) that was described earlier. When subjects were told that a leader's group performed well, they rated the behavior they had just observed differently from the way similar subjects, told that the leader's group performed poorly, did. Lord (1985) reviewed 13 studies that have demonstrated such performance cue effects on descriptions of leader behavior. Such effects generally explain 5 to 25 percent of the variance in ratings and are consistent over a number of different experimental stimuli and procedures. Several researchers have explored potential boundary variables that might have an impact on performance cue effects, but these effects have proved to be quite robust. Rush and Beauvais (1981) found such effects to occur for items both with *and without* clear behavioral referents; Binning, Zaba, and Whattam (1986) showed that performance cue effects occur for both specific observable behaviors and global evaluations; and McElroy and Downey (1982) found that performance cue effects occur for both involved and uninvolved observers. One powerful moderator of such effects, however, was the causal attributions formed by raters, as indicated in the article by Phillips and Lord

(1981) that was discussed earlier, when we explained inferential leadership perceptions.

Mediating Role of Categories. As we have suggested, one explanation for performance cue effects centers on the mediating role of rater knowledge structures and leadership categorization. We have shown that inferential processing affects leader labeling, or categorization. Such categorization then makes available generic structures (figure 5.2a) that link labels to likely behaviors. Further, since alternative trait-related structures and associated behaviors would not be available simultaneously (Srull and Wyer 1989), inferential labeling would selectively access generically encoded behaviors or actually observed behaviors that were related to such structures. Subsequent ratings would then be derived or inferred from the way the stimulus was categorized and from the relationship of a rated item to the cognitive categories held by raters.

Three types of evidence support this interpretation of leader behavior ratings. First, the mediating role of global ratings has been demonstrated by two studies. Fraser and Lord (1988) showed that the effects of performance feedback on leadership ratings could be greatly reduced by controlling for a global leadership rating. Similarly, Rush, Phillips, and Lord (1981) showed that controlling for global leadership ratings could eliminate performance cue effects on leadership ratings as well as eliminate the effects of manipulations of stimulus behavior.

Second, the degree of association of an item to the category label "leader" should explain the extent to which that item is affected by bogus performance feedback; these performance cue effects reflect top-down processing, as shown in figure 5.2a, and the strength of association between a behavior and a trait node should correspond to the prototypicality of that behavior for the category in question. Lord (1981) investigated this issue using data from four previous studies demonstrating performance cue effects. He correlated the size of performance cue effects (means for items in "good" feedback conditions minus means under "poor" feedback conditions) with ratings of the prototypicality of items. These correlations were quite high, ranging from .72 to .88, indicating a very high dependence of performance cue effects on the prototypicality of items. Similar but weaker effects were found for manipulations of actual stimulus behaviors. We suggest that behavior is integrated with a leadership impression through recognition-based processes, and performance information through inferential-based processes. But after a leadership perception is formed, both sources seem to have the same impact on leadership behavior ratings. The reader will recall that highly similar results were previously discussed with respect to ratings of real political leaders (Foti et al. 1982; Foti et al. in press), adding generality to such effects.

In a laboratory study specifically designed to investigate how information is accessed when questionnaire ratings are made, Maher, Lord, and Scheiwe (1990) had subjects rate the prototypicality of a number of leadership items that were presented on a computer monitor so reaction time data could be collected. The researchers then had subjects view a videotape of a small-group task *after* having received bogus performance information on how well that group did. In combination, these two procedures should have made leadership salient and induced subjects to encode the behavior they saw in terms of leadership. Maher et al. then had subjects rate the behaviors of one of the people on the videotape they had just seen.

The results showed that subjects' behavioral ratings used the category structure and content of their leadership categories. Though all subjects saw the same behaviors, Maher and her colleagues (1990) found that the target person was seen as being more typical of a leader in the good than in the poor performance feedback condition. They also found the well-replicated performance cue effect showing that leadership behaviors, whether present or not present on the videotape, were more likely to be recognized after receiving good performance feedback than after receiving poor performance feedback. More importantly, they tied this performance cue effect directly to category-based processing by showing that (a) performance cue–based distortions (average ratings for an *item* in the good minus the poor performance feedback conditions) were significantly correlated with an item's prototypicality to the category "leader" ($r = .56$, $p < .001$), and (b) this relationship was stronger for those questionnaire items which followed an item that was neutral with respect to the category "leader." This latter result is consistent with Srull and Wyer's (1989) theory, which posits that neutral items (items with a clear relation to categories) are encoded as items in figure 5.2a are shown to be. Hence, subjects must return to the category label node in memory (the top node in figure 5.2a) before they can search for other information within a category. These two findings tie performance cue effects directly to top-down processing within leadership categories. When behavioral associations can also be used as a retrieval route, which is possible when prior questionnaire items are not neutral with respect to leadership (for example, when the horizontal linkages in figure 5.2b can be used to retrieve information), some subjects may be using bottom-up, behavior-based processing. This type of processing should minimize distortions tied to category labels and structures.

Using reaction times for rating items as indicators of search processes, Maher et al. (1990) also found a large set of items for which a subject's reaction time in making behavioral ratings was highly correlated with the same subject's reaction time for making proto-typicality ratings, a finding that again implicates category structures in memory search and behavioral ratings.

Still another experimental finding supports the importance of item prototypicality in determining performance cue effects. Phillips and Lord (1982), Phillips (1984), and Binning, Zaba, and Whattam (1986) all found interactions between item prototypicality in the category "leader" and performance cue effects. These effects occurred for prototypical and antiprototypical items but not for neutral items. According to Srull and Wyer (1989), neutral items will not be associated with trait schemas. Therefore, such items should not be affected by changing trait labels through inferential processes.

Third, performance cue effects are greater when there are limited amounts of behavioral information (Rush, Thomas, and Lord 1977) than when actual behavioral information is available (Lord, Binning, Rush, and Thomas 1978). The former case corresponds to figure 5.2a when behavior can be accessed only through those trait nodes which access schema-consistent behaviors. But when multiple behaviors have been observed and integrated with a leadership label, the encoding would correspond more to figure 5.2b. Here, when completing behavioral ratings, raters can access behaviors from behavior-to-behavior linkages when strength of association is independent of an item's prototypicality. Moreover, schema-inconsistent as well as schema-consistent behaviors may be incorporated into such structures.

In short, subjects tend to rely on leader labels and the degree of prototypicality of questionnaire items when making ratings. Subjects can be more accurate processors for unrelated items, but such items do not form scales that are psychometrically adequate (Phillips and Lord 1982). Such rating is fully consistent with the use of trait-behavior structures, such as are shown in figure 5.2a.

Underlying Constructs Assessed by Measures. An important issue related to questionnaire-based measures of leader behavior concerns the constructs they are purported to measure. These scales are generally developed through factor analytic techniques, which tradi-tionally were thought to capture dimensions in the behavior of leaders. Research by Rush and his colleagues (1977), however, questions this interpretation. They had subjects rate leadership using Stogdill's (1963) Leader Behavior Description Questionnaire (LBDQ) under what they called a limited information condition. That is, subjects rated a fictitious company leader about whom they had no behavioral information at all. The investigators reasoned that if factors were stimulus based, factor analyzing such data should produce no clear factors, since subjects' responses would merely be random errors. Alternatively, if factors were perceiver based, then factor analyzing such data should produce factors that were very similar to other factor analytic studies of the LBDQ. They found the factor structures from such limited information condition ratings to be highly congruent with those based on ratings of real leaders. The factor structures were also quite congruent with ratings from different samples of subjects rating ideal leaders, with observer ratings of leaders shown in laboratory videotapes, and with leadership ratings made by subjects participating in group problem-solving sessions. Similar findings have been reported by Eden and Leviatan (1975), using a similar approach but a different leadership questionnaire.

The most parsimonious explanation for such effects is that the factor structure for the LBDQ in all these situations was *perceiver rather than stimulus based*. That is, the process that produces covariances among rated behaviors was *primarily*, but not entirely, the relationship of behavioral items to common constructs of perceivers. Observed behaviors that are not related to constructs salient to perceivers will be either ignored or attached to general evaluative schemas rather than to leadership schemas (Srull and Wyer 1989). Alternatively, observed behaviors may have been encoded in terms of event- rather than person-based schemata. These alternative types of encoding would be less available when subjects completed leadership questionnaires. But items that relate to common constructs will be encoded using the same trait-behavior clusters, and because of this common linkage they will tend to be recalled together.

This explanation of factor structures does not mean that factor analytic dimensions are unimportant in terms of leadership, since they probably are quite important to perceivers in guiding their reactions to and expectations of leaders. The explanation does, however, suggest that the most immediate source of these behavioral constructs is in the categorical systems of perceivers, rather than in the actual behaviors of leaders. Along with others (especially Calder 1977), we question whether behavior ratings should be the primary source of constructs investigated by leadership researchers.

SUMMARY

We have shown that social perceptions are formed using cybernetic processes that repeatedly update relevant schemas that are either person based or event based. Which schemas are used and the amount of elaborative encoding affect the labels that are formed, the structure of trait-behavior clusters, and the amount of specific behavioral content that is stored in memory. Thus, the nature of the encoding has critical implications for the expectations we form of others. This process creates a cognitive context that structures our future interactions and perceptions.

We have also explained how automatic processing and controlled processing can each lead to different means of updating new information related to a stimulus person. Presented was a cusp catastrophe model that showed (a) how discontinuous changes are produced by recategorization and (b) how automatic and controlled processes can be combined into a more comprehensive model that depicts both continuous and discontinuous changes in impression formation.

The catastrophe model also explains many of the distortions in measures of leader behavior. These issues are important to the leadership area, but they also apply to other types of measurement based on social descriptions (such as performance appraisals). We think the implication for more general theories of measurement using social cognitions as raw data is a key area for future research.

Chapter 6

Perceptions of Women in Management

Terri L. Baumgardner
Robert G. Lord
Karen J. Maher

*I*n this chapter we apply the framework developed in this book to an issue of general importance—leadership perceptions of women managers and the consequences of those perceptions for performance. We show how an information processing perspective is helpful in understanding a diverse array of empirical findings. We also suggest new theoretical explanations for past research and new areas for future research.

The role of women in management and how they are perceived as leaders are certainly important enough to warrant a separate chapter. We should point out, however, that many of the issues we examine also apply to other groups that must overcome stereotypical perceptions arising from being included in convenient categories. Age, race, and national origin are also salient bases for forming social categories, and managers who are so categorized may face many of the same problems experienced by women managers. Further, white males may experience similar problems when operating in a management culture in which prototypes of leaders are nontraditional. For example, based on the comparison of prototypes for American and Japanese leaders that is covered in chapter 15, we expect that American males working in Japanese firms in the United States may have difficulty being perceived as leaders by Japanese top management. Thus, while we focus in this chapter on perceptions of women managers, the underlying issues are more general.

CURRENT STATUS OF WOMEN IN MANAGEMENT

The outlook for women moving up the corporate ladder is both encouraging and discouraging. The percentage of women in management has increased from less than 6 percent to more than 39 percent during the period from 1960 to 1988 (Bureau of Labor Statistics 1988), but women tend to be concentrated in lower ranks and are underrepresented in relatively powerful managerial positions (Brown 1981; DeVanna 1987; Dipboye 1987; Morrison and Von Glinow 1990; Terborg 1977; White, De Sanctis, and Crino 1981). By some estimates, women hold 15 percent of entry-level management positions but only 5 percent of middle-management positions and only 1 to 2 percent of top management positions (Brown 1979; U.S. Department of Commerce 1984; White et al. 1981). Women seldom reach top-level positions in organizations (Raynolds 1987; Tsui and Gutek 1984), and they do not appear to move up the hierarchy as rapidly as their male counterparts (Olson and Becker 1983; Smith 1979; Stewart and Gudykunst 1982; White et al. 1981).

A common finding is that promotion requirements are more stringent for women than men. For example, Olson and Becker (1983) compared the earnings and promotion experience of a large sample of men and women over the period 1973 to 1977. After controlling for job level and ability, they found that women in their sample were held to higher promotion standards than men and therefore received fewer promotions than men with equal measured ability. Similarly, using a matched cohort of men and women MBAs with continuous work histories, DeVanna (1984, 1987) found that men and women experienced different rates of success. She concluded that women had to prove their ability to handle the next assignment beyond a shadow of a doubt, whereas men were presumed capable of handling the next assignment unless they had blundered at the current level. Morrison, White, Van Velsor, and the Center for Creative Leadership (1987) reached a similar conclusion based on their three year study of the top female executives in Fortune 100-sized companies. In their words, ". . . it appears that in order to approach the highest levels, women are expected to have more strengths and fewer faults than their male counterparts" (44). We suggest that these extra requirements are needed to overcome the biases against women managers that stem from the way people normally process information in forming social perceptions.

Before continuing, we should briefly mention some other explanations for the underrepresentation of women in top levels of management. Many explanations for the seemingly disadvantaged position of women in management have emerged in the literature. Researchers have examined male-female differences in managerial style or behavior, with some researchers concluding that men and women differ in the traits and behaviors necessary for successful management (e.g., Hennig and Jardim 1977; Schwartz and Waetjen 1976). But, most often only modest, if any, sex differences on these key characteristics have been found (e.g., Bass 1981; Day and Stogdill 1972; Harlan and Weiss 1982). Alternatively, researchers have proposed: 1) that women simply have not been in the workforce long enough to occupy top-level management positions (Brown 1981), 2) that there is a "pro-male bias" in evaluation (Nieva and Gutek 1980; Pazy 1986; Tsui and Gutek 1984) which benefits men but impedes the career progress of women, or 3) that women are excluded from the informal relationships (e.g., mentor-protege relationships, networks) critical to the acquisition of power and influence in organizations (Farris and Ragan 1981; Fernandez 1981; Morrison et al. 1987; Ragan 1984; Rosen, Templeton, and Kechline 1981). Researchers have also proposed that the structural characteristics of organizations serve to block the upward aspirations of women (Brass 1985; Kanter 1977, 1982). There is mixed support for each of these explanations of the underrepresentation of women in management (Dipboye [1987], and Morrison and Von Glinow [1990] provide reviews of many of these explanations.)

We believe it is more useful to apply the theoretical perspective developed in this book to help understand the biases that may be encountered by female managers (or by managers classified in terms of age, race, or national origin). This approach is needed because it ties biases to underlying social-cognitive processes involved in perceptions. In addition, we explain how such biases may affect women's performance as top-level leaders. These biases occur because of widespread sex-related stereotypes that define those attributes which typically characterize men and women. Stereotypes also provide expectations for the behavior of men and women. We posit that the operation of stereotypes and the subsequent biases that occur with respect to leadership perceptions are likely to vary throughout a woman's career progression.

To help understand how sex-role stereotypes may affect leadership perceptions, we will first review briefly the differential perceptual processes, discussed in chapters 3 and 4, that normally operate to establish leadership perceptions. Here, a career progression framework is used to integrate the literature on leadership perception with that on women in management. This framework accomplishes two purposes. First, it explicitly acknowledges that perceptions are not static phenomena but, rather, are formed and modified over time. Second, the perceptual processes that operate with respect to leaders are very likely to involve quite different considerations at upper versus lower hierarchical levels. The literature on women in management fails to recognize that stereotypes may not consistently influence leadership perceptions over time or over the stages of a woman's career progression.

LEADERSHIP PERCEPTIONS

While perceptions may not be reality, they are used by perceivers to evaluate and subsequently distinguish leaders from nonleaders. They also provide a basis for social power and influence. In this respect, it becomes extremely important for women (as well as men) to understand how leadership perceptions occur. As discussed in chapters 3 and 4, leadership perceptions can be explained by two qualitatively different processes (Lord 1985). First, recognition-based processes help us to form leadership perceptions from the normal flow of interpersonal activities, using either automatic or controlled processes. Automatic recognition-based processes depend on a prototype-matching process based on face-to-face contact; controlled recognition-based processes depend on the use of preexisting knowledge about what traits and behaviors are important to leader success and emergence in a particular situation. In the ideal sense, these processes work effectively to label leaders and nonleaders by comparing an individual's characteristics with those defining the category of leadership.

Inferential processes, on the other hand, are used to link leadership perceptions to outcomes of key organizational events. These inferences, too, may be guided by automatic or controlled processes. Automatic inferential processes use perceptually guided, simplified causal analyses, whereas controlled inferential processes operate according to logical, comprehensive causal analyses. Causal ascriptions to leaders are a basic part of this process—success enhances the perception of leadership, while failure can limit perceptions of leadership.

Both recognition and inferential processes are important to women aspiring to key managerial positions; however, as is explained in the next section, recognition and inferential processes are likely to be complicated by the presence of gender-related stereotypes, which may bias leadership perceptions. Three types of cognitive processes may be involved. First, much information may be encoded in terms of gender, rather than leadership, categories, particularly for females. This situation produces extensive gender-related knowledge but little knowledge related to leadership for specific individuals. Second, because gender is such a major category for social classifications, much of our social knowledge may be related to it. Medin (1989) has suggested that categories are defined in part by our world knowledge; thus, general social knowledge related to gender may help us define leadership. Third, because gender is associated with clear pictorial images, we may use what Brewer (1988) has described as "pictoliteral" categories based on gender as an initial social classification. Leadership categories may develop *within* these general classifications. In other words, we may develop separate categorical structures and prototypes of leadership for males and females. Leadership within a female category may be less available, because of the smaller number of female leaders, or it may be defined in terms of different prototypes, in comparison with leadership within a male category. Any of these cognitive processes, individually or in combination, could be responsible for the effects discussed in the following section.

A STAGE MODEL OF LEADERSHIP PERCEPTIONS

In this section we explain how stereotypes can bias observers' perceptual processes throughout each stage of a woman's career. Though we depict the stage model as sequential, it also depends on the level at which a woman enters an organization and on her qualifications. For convenience, we assume entry into an organization at a lower-level management position and proceed through the career stages until a woman gains access to dominant coalition membership within the organization and assumes a top-level leadership role.

Lower-level Management

Recognition-based Processes. For women in entry-level management positions, sex-related stereotypes are likely to bias observers' perceptual processes. At this level, observers have little information with which to evaluate women beyond their gender and the stereotypes often associated with gender. Thus, in many instances initial exposure to a female manager results in the immediate categorization of her into a female category, as opposed to a manager or leader category. This type of schema-driven, limited-capacity framework for processing information is often useful to observers. It provides a simple means of "categorizing" a person when little is known about her or him, and it serves to guide observers' expectations and interactions with others. Yet this type of processing may also be a source of bias. The vast research base coined "stereotype-fit" research (Dipboye 1985) makes explicit the problems associated with such categorization.

Such research supports the claim that male trait stereotypes are equated with "successful manager" trait stereotypes in samples involving both students (for example, Powell and Butterfield [1979]; Rosenkrantz, Vogel, Bee, Broverman, and Broverman [1968]; Schein, Mueller, and Jacobson [1989]) and managers (for example, Brenner, Tomkiewicz, and Schein [1989]; Schein [1973, 1975]). Conversely, female trait stereotypes are noted to differ significantly from both male trait stereotypes and successful manager trait stereotypes. For example, with regard to achievement-oriented traits, men are thought to be competent, strong, independent, active, and competitive, whereas women are thought to be incompetent, weak, dependent, passive, uncompetitive, and unconfident (for instance, Dubno 1985; Heilman 1983). These pervasive perceptual effects consistently appear in the literature comparing typical male, typical female, and successful manager trait prototypes. Further, despite dramatic changes in the role of women in several aspects of society (such as family and work), these prototypes have not changed much in the past fifteen years (Brenner et al. 1989; Powell and Butterfield 1988; Schein et al. 1989).

What this research suggests from an information processing perspective is that when processing proceeds in an automatic, schema-driven fashion, categorization into a "female" category, as opposed to a "leadership" category, often occurs. As we noted in chapter 5, Srull and Wyer (1989) assert that information encoded with respect to one category (that is, female) is not available when an alternative category (that is, leader) is accessed. Further, when sex-related stereotypes guide information processing, information relevant to the leadership category (but irrelevant to sex-related stereotypes) may not be encoded at all. One consequence of encoding many behaviors with respect to gender rather than leadership may be that perceivers are less certain of leadership classifications. Thus, people would not have clear expectations about the leadership capabilities of women. This use of different encoding categories for men and women may subtly bias the subsequent evaluation of leadership. As a result of such processing, equally qualified males and females may not be evaluated similarly. Promotion to jobs for which leadership is a key requirement may favor men because evaluators are more certain of men's leadership capabilities. Here, we must emphasize that this bias is not intentional discrimination; rather, the evaluation is biased because of information processing limitations.

Given time, the initial perceptions that are formed on the basis of sex-related stereotypes are likely to be revised. Revision may involve either tagging the original category with inconsistent information (Woll and Graesser 1982) or switching to a more appropriate category. As noted in the previous chapter, however, cognitive inertia may delay this switch long past the time when it is appropriate, producing biased perceptions and a "folded" perceptual function. Further, because female categories and leadership categories differ dramatically from each other, switching to the "more appropriate" leadership category may not be the first change in categories that occurs. Perceivers may first use categories more closely related to the female category, such as "aggressive, dominant female," rather than "leader." Yet categorization into an "aggressive, dominant female" category is highly likely to result in a negative evaluation for the woman manager, because those behaviors are inconsistent with traditional sex-related stereotypes—as chapter 1's example of Ann B. Hopkins illustrates.

In summary, recall from chapter 5 that perceivers use cybernetic, on-line processes to revise initial judgments. But when evaluating women, perceivers will, we posit, have difficulty shifting from initial gender-related classifications to leader classifications. This factor is particularly problematic for women in lower-level positions in which sex stereotypes are prominent. Consistent with our coverage in chapter 5, we would expect discontinuous changes in perceived management potential when perceivers switch from a gender to a leadership schema. But even if classified as leaders, females, as we noted earlier, may be evaluated differently because people temper classifications using their world knowledge or because they use different categorical structures for males and females.

Inferential Processes. Fortunately for women at this level, there is a second way in which initial perceptions based on sex-related stereotypes may be revised. Inferential processes may be used by perceivers to integrate information on performance. As discussed in chapter 4, inferential processes may be either automatic or controlled. For example, when observers encounter performance information that is inconsistent with their initial categorization of a woman into a nonleader category, controlled inferential processes may come into play as perceivers carefully assess the causal role of the woman in producing performance outcomes. Alternatively, salient or strong associations with successful outcomes may automatically result in causal ascriptions to leaders. Observers may then use performance to revise leadership ratings if the leader is seen as a cause. Thus, if a woman in a lower-level management position is seen as responsible for successful performance outcomes, initial perceptions of her may be revised.

Inferential processes are probably more easily used by perceivers to establish leadership perceptions for low-level management positions. As we will discuss in chapter 9, there are two means—direct and indirect—by which leaders at this level can affect performance and consequently be perceived as leaders through controlled inferential processes. Direct means are those situations in which leaders influence subordinates, decisions, or policies in ways that change subordinates' task (or social) behaviors and have a substantial impact on performance. Thus, the source of a leader's effects on subordinates can be localized in his or her specific behaviors. Indirect means by which leaders affect subordinates (or organizations) involve the creation of ongoing conditions that then have an impact on subordinates, organizational decisions, or policies. Thus, there is an important intervening mechanism (for example, subordinate socialization) that is not present in direct means, and this mechanism often has diffuse linkages both to the leader and to performance.

It is quite likely that direct means may be successfully employed by women managers to affect performance. For example, women at this level can successfully influence subordinates' motivation through such techniques as feedback or goal setting. Further, women are as qualified as men to raise successfully the levels of subordinates' skills through such approaches as training. (See figure 9.1, which illustrates the way in which these direct effects, as well as indirect effects, operate to influence task performance.)

One caveat must be noted here. There is some evidence that women will have to accomplish these goals differently from the way men do. These types of concerns are exemplified in a line of research proposing that women who exhibit sex-role-congruent behaviors are more favorably evaluated than those who exhibit sex-role-incongruent behaviors. For example, Jago and Vroom (1982) used a sample of male and female managers to describe their affective responses to participative versus autocratic behavior on the part of male and female managers in mixed-sex training groups. These researchers found that females perceived to be autocratic were negatively evaluated, whereas males perceived to be autocratic were positively evaluated. Both males and females perceived to be participative were rated equally favorably. In short, direct means of influence may be used by women at lower levels to enhance leadership perceptions, but these women may have to make use of more participative methods than men do.

Indirect means of influencing performance are somewhat more complicated. Indirect means to influence subordinates' motivation and subsequently task performance involve such processes as socialization and dyadic exchanges. We will discuss indirect means of managing performance more explicitly in relation to top-level women managers. Inferential leadership perception, however, will not work well when indirect means are emphasized, because leaders will not be perceived as direct causes of subordinate behavior. Thus, for lower-level women managers with limited access to recognition-based models of leadership perception, it may be crucial to rely more extensively on direct means of influencing subordinates' performance. While this process may not result in the long-term results achieved by using indirect means to influence performance, it may be the most efficient route for women in lower-level positions to establish perceptions as leaders. Once these perceptions are made, women in middle-level management positions can rely more equally on both direct and indirect means of influencing subordinate performance.

One further complication should be noted. While the evidence is scarce in relation to managerial samples, some researchers posit that performance by men tends to be attributed to causes that are favorable to them, whereas performance by women tends to be attributed to less favorable causes. Terborg and Ilgen (1975) postulated an attributional basis for the differential evaluation of male and female performance in which a woman's success is attributed to factors other than ability, such as effort, task ease, or luck. One study is particularly interesting in this regard. Pazy (1986) had 48 managers review performance appraisal information about fictitious male and female employees whose work success was attributed to the same causes. Even after controlling for attributions, pro-male bias in treatment and evaluation persisted. Though the evidence for Terborg and Ilgen's hypothesis is weak when managerial samples are used, the issue should be one that women consider. If a woman's success is attributed to luck, for example, inferential models of leadership perception are unlikely to apply.

To create more favorable evaluations in terms of leadership, women may therefore consider emphasizing direct rather than indirect leadership activities or influencing automatic attributional processes by being more salient or more closely associated with successful outcomes. In pursuing these tactics, however, women run the risk of violating traditional sex-related stereotypes and of thereby being evaluated negatively. They must operate within a narrow band of acceptable behavior. This is exactly the process that Morrison and her colleagues (1987) discuss in their popular book *Breaking the Glass Ceiling*.

Figure 6.1 provides a more specific illustration of the way in which both recognition-based and inferential models of leadership perception are likely to operate for lower-level women managers. As figure 5.3 shows, for women the process is complicated by the operation of sex-related stereotypes, which often serve as an alternative to explaining behaviors or events in terms of leadership. Many of these same processes operate for women in other stages of their careers. Likewise, the same type of bias may operate for other social categories based on age, race, or national origin.

Middle-level Management

We believe middle-level management to be the least problematic stage of a woman's career in terms of the perceptual barriers that may occur to influence leadership perceptions. With the passage of time, the initial categorization made in reference to the woman manager (that is, "female") has most likely been modified through inferential processes, and increased information and familiarity make recognition-based processes less biased. Thus, both recognition-based and inferential processes may be more likely to establish leadership perceptions for women in middle management.

Recognition-based Processes. At middle levels, recognition-based perceptual processes may be less biased than at lower levels, perhaps because at this level, perceivers simply have more relevant trait and behavioral information about a particular woman manager (Heilman and Martell 1986). In addition, observers at this level may utilize more expert modes of processing information (see chapter 2) in relation to the woman manager. With increased experience, they have become more familiar with the traits or behaviors characterizing successful managers and have a better-developed categorical system for making such classifications.

One study that is particularly indicative of the way in which categories or schemas are modified with more specific information was conducted by Heilman, Block, Martell, and Simon (1989). These authors replicated and extended the earlier research on sex-related stereotypes that was done by Schein (1973), wherein trait adjectives were rated as to the extent they characterized certain social categories. Heilman and her colleagues' results closely paralleled those of Schein's earlier study, indicating that men in general are described as being more similar to successful managers than women *in general* are, even after 16 years of more open attitudes toward the role of women in society. Illustrating the effect of more specific categories, these investigators found that the correspondence between descriptions of women and successful managers increased dramatically when women were depicted as managers. But women managers were still seen as being more different from successful managers than men were. Some of the specific descriptors that were applied to women managers but not to male managers or successful managers were as follows: bitter, hasty, quarrelsome, selfish, less understanding, independent, high need for power, and high need for achievement. When the category "successful woman manager" was used, however, many of these differences were eliminated.

These results are consistent with the notion that global, "typical women" kinds of stereotypes are inappropriate for characterizing women in management (Dipboye 1987), and that rather than there being one global and homogeneous stereotype of women, people have subcategories of women, each with its own stereotypic association (Ashmore 1981; Noseworthy and Lott 1984). Still, the results of Heilman and her colleagues (1989) do provide evidence of stereotypical

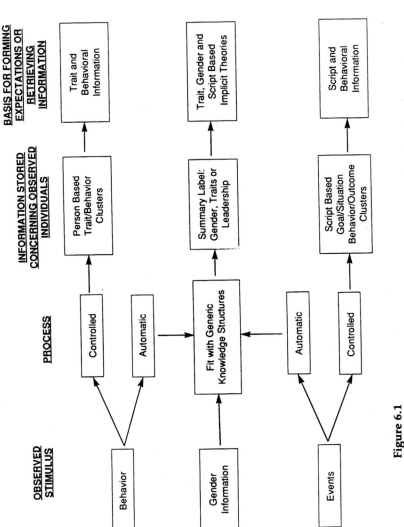

Figure 6.1
Model of Social Information Processing Based on Behavior, Gender, and Event Schema

perceptual barriers that women in middle-management positions must overcome. Further, the content of the "successful women managers" category also reveals the presence of some stereotypes; however, because the category content of "successful women managers" also reveals many similarities to that of "successful managers," one can argue that recognition-based categorization processes may establish the perception of leadership for many women in these positions.

There is also a theoretically interesting possibility suggested by the recent work of Medin (1989). Rather than having separate categories for men and women managers, raters asked to describe a woman manager may use general world knowledge (gender-related stereotypes) to make appropriate adjustments in the content of general (or male) manager categories. Thus, the data of Heilman et al. (1989) may reveal the effects of on-the-spot adjustments, as well as the content of more specific cognitive categories. These alternative interpretations have very different implications (for example, how effective training to eliminate bias is likely to be), and they should be compared in future research.

Inferential Processes. Observers are likely to have increased information about performance in relation to women who have established a track record within an organization. At least one field study conducted with a multicompany corporation sample of middle-level male and female managers (with tenure of 9.2 and 12.3 years for men and women, respectively) suggested that increased performance information about the female manager results in less biased evaluation. In other words, a pro-male bias may not prevail in middle management (Tsui and Gutek 1984). The results of this study were particularly interesting. Women managers were evaluated more favorably than male managers and had better affective relationships with others than male managers did. Women managers were also more successful in their careers than male managers were, as measured by promotion rate and merit increase, and were more satisfied with their jobs than male managers were. Eighteen months after the main study, all the focal managers were contacted for a follow-up survey. In the follow-up study, women were evaluated similarly to (not more favorably than) and promoted as rapidly as (not more rapidly than) men. Nevertheless, consistent with the results of the first study, women, on average, received a higher percentage of merit increase than men did.

Tsui and Gutek's (1984) results supported Nieva and Gutek's (1980) assertion that pro-male bias in evaluation is less likely to occur when the level of inference about performance or other job-related information is low. Thus, women who have advanced to the middle level usually have some accumulated record of achievement, and in the case of Tsui and Gutek's study (as in our stage model), the achievements have been made, in large part, within the same organization. Therefore, raters who are more certain of past performance information should be less reliant on gender information in assessing leadership.

Heilman (1984) supports the assertion that the more information available to an evaluator, the less influence will stereotypes and bias have on performance evaluation. Heilman's study was conducted with MBA students, who reviewed an employment application form in which the sex and information type were varied and who then determined whether or not to interview the target individual. Heilman found no significant difference between male and female stimulus persons in the condition of high relevancy of job information. Tosi and Einbender (1985) conducted a meta-analysis of the research on pro-male evaluation bias and found that the mean amount of gender-salient information was significantly greater for the studies showing discrimination. Conversely, more job-relevant information was related to findings of less discrimination.

We believe this limited research base to be indicative of the fewer perceptual barriers that women in middle-level management positions are likely to face. With increased information concerning a woman's ability to affect performance outcomes and with more controlled, expert processing on the part of observers, both inferential and recognition-based models of leader perception are likely to operate more fairly. Thus, for aspiring women in middle-management positions, there appears to be hope for establishing the perception of leadership. The above discussion should make clear, however, that women in these positions must still face substantial perceptual barriers; this fact may help explain the results of studies revealing women's relatively slow movement up the organizational hierarchy (for example, Olson and Becker 1983; Stewart and Gudykunst 1982).

Upper-level Management

As encouraging as this picture may seem for middle-level female managers, we think it is more pessimistic for women in top-level management. There are several reasons for this conclusion. First, as discussed previously, the work on leadership perceptions makes a distinction between upper- and lower-level leaders. Thus, a substantial *recategorization* may be required prior to moving from middle- to upper-level management. In addition, leaders at different organizational levels will often have to manage observers' perceptions of leadership quite differently. Second, because women are underrepresented in top-level management positions, their gender often becomes quite salient. Third, women at this level are now in a situation in which they not only must manage the perceptual processes of their immediate subordinates and supervisors but also, to be effective, must be able to manage the perceptions of constituencies outside the organization. Such women also serve as a symbol to individuals throughout all levels of the organizational hierarchy. Since nonorganizational members and individuals at lower levels of that hierarchy have limited exposure to top-level leaders, they may again rely on general stereotypes. These perceivers may also lack highly refined categories for classifying female leaders. In other words, they are likely to be limited-capacity rather than expert processors. Below we elaborate on each of these considerations, as well as exploring some of the organizational consequences that may result from observers' perceptual processes.

The difference between leadership at upper and lower levels is substantial. At upper levels of organizations, leaders change, create, or eliminate structure and processes (Katz and Kahn 1978, 539). Such leadership goes beyond face-to-face contact with subordinates, relying on more formal means of communication, indirect influence through association with significant organizational events, and the development of appropriate cultures. Like lower-level leaders, top-level leaders have to rely on influence tied to their perception as a leader. As discussed in chapter 1, however, this process is more complex at upper levels, since a variety of groups may be involved (such as organizational members, boards of directors, any key constituents external to the organization). Further, perceivers interpret a variety of factors in assessing leadership at this level (for instance, formal communications, stories about leaders, or assessments of organizational performance). In addition, a key requirement of top-level leaders is that they be able to adopt a broad systems perspective and accurately perceive both the internal and the external environments. Each of these factors may be difficult for leaders to manage. But for the woman executive, such difficulties are compounded by the presence of stereotypical ideas that may function to bias both recognition-based and inferential perceptual processes.

Recognition-based Processes. As discussed in chapters 3 and 4, because executives do not normally interact on a face-to-face basis with most organizational members, executive-level leadership emphasizes controlled recognition-based processes and both controlled and automatic inferential processes, as opposed to automatic recognition-based processes. We will expand on how these processes are likely to occur for top-level women managers.

First, in contrast to middle-level management positions, very few women occupy top-level positions. Therefore, constituents typically will have limited experience with women in general in these positions, and their refined schemas may not be applicable to female executives.

Consequently, sex-related stereotypes may serve to "fill in the blanks" for observers—that is, observers are likely to rely on stereotypes to develop expectations of these women and to guide their interactions with them.

While perceivers are unlikely to utilize a general, "typical woman" stereotype to process information about women executives, they may still hold stereotypical ideas about what a "successful *woman* manager" —as compared with a "successful male manager"—is like. Recall the study by Heilman et al. (1989). Here, the vast majority of differences in the characterizations of women and successful managers were attenuated when raters were given an explicit statement of a woman's success as a manager. Thus, "successful women managers" were characterized very similarly to the way in which "successful managers" were. But the qualities of "leadership ability" and "skill in business matters" were seen to characterize "male managers", "successful male managers," and "successful managers" more than "women managers" or "successful women managers." Ironically, both those qualities are central to effective managerial performance (Mintzberg 1973). Even when a "successful woman manager" label is applied to women, the label is lacking favorable qualities that would likely be applied to a man.

Thus, even a successful woman manager may not be seen as possessing the behaviors and attributes necessary for effective top-level leadership. Further, she may again be the victim of double-bind situations, in that if she does exhibit many of the traits characteristic of successful leaders, often she is also violating sex-related stereotypes, as was illustrated by the Jago and Vroom (1982) study and by the Ann B. Hopkins case (see chapter 1). For example, suggestions that Ann B. Hopkins take a "course at charm school" and complaints about her use of profanity occurred only because she was a "lady" using foul language (Bales 1988). Her behavior was seen as incongruent with traditional sex-related stereotypes, and this incongruent behavior was viewed by some as at least partially responsible for the denial of her partnership at Price Waterhouse.

What the foregoing discussion suggests is that stereotypes are likely to have detrimental effects for women in top-level management, impeding recognition-based processes of leadership perception. Men entering the executive suite are subject to the same critical evaluation by both internal (organizational) constituencies and external constituencies, but we think the process is likely to be more complicated for women because of the presence of sex stereotypes.

Inferential Processes. Most often, perceptions about upper-level leaders emphasize inferential rather than recognition-based processes.

A number of factors are likely to limit the extent to which top-level women executives will be perceived as leaders. First, to the extent that the majority of individual interactions in which a woman executive is involved are characterized by stereotypes, she is likely to be less firmly connected to the dominant coalition and her leadership activities will be less salient. Second, even though a woman may have objective control of organizational resources or rewards and the power associated with this control, the extent of influence she wields may not be perceived by others. This distinction between objective and perceived power (Kaplowitz 1978) is important, because gender-related stereotypes may lead people to perceive women as having less power than they actually have (Broverman et al. 1972).

Thus, we suggest that women in top-level management have extensive perceptual barriers to overcome. Although this point is true of most top-level executives who are males, female leaders have more severe problems because they must also deal with sex-related stereotypes. These stereotypes can lead to misperceptions, differential expectations, and negative evaluations of behaviors necessary to effective top-level leadership. We expect that many top-level female leaders can effectively handle these additional demands. Yet those demands add another source of cognitive and emotional complexity to a job that, we assert (see chapter 14), is already high on these dimensions. The additional demands may not have an impact on organizational performance during stable convergent periods, but their effect during reorientation periods may be dramatic.

An additional complication concerning role-related inferences should be mentioned. An individual (male or female) who fills an executive role may receive expanded leadership perceptions by virtue of that role. In other words, it may be *assumed* that prior performance was successful, even though no direct knowledge of performance is available. Likewise, knowledge of a leadership role may trigger leadership rather than gender-related schemas, again increasing leadership perceptions for the female executive. In the case of female executives, however, other processes may serve to undercut role-based, inferential, and recognition-based leadership perceptions. For example, given the widespread existence of equal opportunity and affirmative action programs and the threat of litigation, a common assumption is that females (or minorities) have achieved a particular position because of gender (or race). In these instances, leadership perceptions of female executives are likely to suffer because perceivers may assume the executive holds the position only by virtue of her gender. Thus, previous performance may be ignored. This process may also undercut recognition-based perceptions of leadership. If perceivers think a woman holds a position only because of her gender, sex-related categories and labels will be more easily accessed than leadership categories will. In short, we think assumptions about how women attain managerial roles have the potential to further undermine leadership perceptions for women.

The above discussion reflects controlled processing on the part of perceivers, whereby various reasons for women's presence in executive roles are carefully evaluated. We must stress, though, that the operation of sex-related stereotypes and their relationship to leadership perceptions may be largely an automatic process. The implication is that any bias resulting from the process of accessing gender-related rather than leadership categories is not intentional. In contrast, many explanations for why there are relatively few women in management assume there is a controlled, intentional bias operating to obstruct women from these positions.

Our perspective suggests it is an automatic, unintentional process that weakens leadership perceptions for women. Gender is highly salient, perhaps the most salient, aspect of an individual. Therefore, attempts at minimizing this bias by instructing perceivers to ignore gender will fail. Further, gender-related research that emphasizes controlled processes (whether in laboratory or field situations) may dramatically underestimate the effects of gender on leadership perceptions. This issue presents an interesting topic for future research on sources of gender-related bias.

We concur with Dipboye (1985) that there is a long-overdue need within the literature on women in management to move away from the narrowness of "stereotype-fit" research that dominates the field. Research should also focus on the problem of managing perceptions and managing organizational performance that top-level women executives are likely to face. For years it has been recognized that men in leadership positions need proactively to manage the perception of leadership. Women, too, must acquire the skills necessary to do so. This task is more complex for women, however, because they must simultaneously anticipate and manage the stereotypical impressions that appear to be common. But we should emphasize that many of the difficulties originate in unfavorable organizational cultures that complicate internally oriented leadership and in broader societal cultures that limit top-level female leaders' attempts to manage external environments. Thus, changes that go far beyond the actions of a single top-level female leader are required.

Longitudinal empirical studies such as that conducted by Tsui and Gutek (1984) provide excellent frameworks within which to investigate the process of acquiring leadership. Such studies offer a comparison not only of the problems women face in different career stages but also of these problems as relevant to men in similar positions. One possibility consistent with this recommendation and with the general model of change developed at the end of chapter 13 is to conceptualize career progression as involving a recategorization process. For superiors making promotion decisions, recategorization would have to occur prior to promotion; for most other perceivers, recategorization would occur after promotion. In either instance, recategorization may involve a shift in the type of information processing used by perceivers and in the particular category they apply to an individual. As discussed in the preceding chapter, there are many sources of cognitive inertia that resist such recategorization. Understanding what facilitates or inhibits such shifts may be crucial to developing a fuller model of leadership perceptions for females or of other salient social categories pertaining to race, age, or national origin.

SUMMARY

Despite the increase in women in the work force as a whole, women are underrepresented in management positions. A variety of explanations exist for the dearth of female managers in organizations, but we offer an alternative explanation based on the perceptual approach of this book. We suggest that sex-related stereotypes operate throughout a woman's career progression to impede leadership perceptions; however, at certain stages of career progression, these stereotypes are likely to be less problematic than at other stages.

In lower-level management positions, we posit that sex-related stereotypes weaken recognition-based leadership processes because gender-related categories are more readily accessed by perceivers than leadership categories are. Inferential processes, however, may be used to revise initial stereotyped categorizations. Women can utilize both direct and indirect means to increase inferential perceptions of leadership. When using direct means, such as behaviors intended to increase subordinates' skill or motivation, women may have to be particularly aware of using participative leadership. Yet inferential processes may still be weak, because women at this level are likely to have no performance history on which inferential processes can be based.

At middle-level management positions, both inferential and recognition-based processes are more likely to establish leadership perceptions for women. Recognition-based leadership perceptions may be improved, because perceivers at this level have more experience (are expert processors) with recognizing the traits and behaviors of effective leaders. Thus, expert processors may access leadership categories more readily than they do gender-related categories. Inferential processes also increase leadership perceptions, in that perceivers at this level are more familiar with women managers and their past performance records. Though the chances for women to establish leadership perceptions are greater at middle hierarchical levels, difficult perceptual barriers remain.

Women at executive management levels may still suffer from weak leadership perceptions. Observers in the immediate environment may be considered expert processors, but external constituents may rely more on general stereotypes and on limited-capacity processes. Further, gender is highly salient because women executives are relatively rare. Therefore, gender-related categories may be used for processing information. Inferential processes are emphasized at upper levels of organizations for both men and women, but several factors can limit leadership perceptions for women. Moreover, in addition to handling the cognitive demands required of all executives, women also have to manage stereotype-based perceptions that may affect their performance.

In conclusion, women at all levels of an organization are likely to experience some problems in establishing perceptions of leadership. The problems may be unique at each level of the organizational hierarchy; however, the consequences are not. The perceptual biases that women encounter are likely to affect many of the processes we discuss in subsequent chapters. As a result, these biases may also limit women's ability to influence organizational effectiveness and performance.

Chapter 7 ─────────────────────────

Dyadic-level Perceptions and Reciprocal Influence

─────────────────────────────────────

*T*he focus of this chapter is on dyadic relations between leaders and subordinates, drawing on both the alternative information processing models presented in chapter 2 and the leadership perception model presented in chapter 3. A discussion of dyadic relationships also provides a natural extension of the impression formation literature from chapter 5. Perceptions of actors in dyads have significant consequences, not only for impression formation but also for the continuing relationship between the two parties and on relevant organizational outcomes.

Explaining the perceptual and behavioral processes operating in leader-subordinate dyads is important for several reasons. First, leader-subordinate dyads essentially constitute the understructure of organizations; all levels of the corporate hierarchy consist of leader-subordinate relationships, forming a chain of command such that dyadic relations at one level can affect those at higher and lower levels of the organization (Graen, Cashman, Ginsburg, and Schiemann 1977). We suggest that perceptual processes play a role as critical as overt leader activities in this process.

Second, an emphasis on leader-subordinate relationships highlights the importance of leadership perceptions within an interactive, social context. Superior-subordinate relationships are a specific example of the more general cognitive/behavioral processes that guide social interactions, as described in chapter 5. Leadership perceptions develop based on social processes, and these perceptions provide an important "cognitive" context that has a broad impact on subordinates and leaders; however, the cognitive context created by subordinate traits and behaviors is equally important. Chapters 3 and 4 presented a more one-sided view of the perception process, focusing solely on observers' formation of leadership perceptions. Yet leaders as well use these processes to form perceptions of subordinates. Some behavioral and relational consequences of these perceptions are discussed in this chapter.

Third, explaining the perceptual processes of dyads provides new insights into the cybernetic nature of interactions and how relationships unfold over time. For both parties in a dyad, expectations are confirmed behaviorally through the use of "on-line" (Hastie and Park 1986) cybernetic processing. We show how our model of leadership perception provides an explanation for the development of expectancies, how they are translated into behavior, and how they are related to the categories and scripts of both parties.

Finally, perceptual processes at the dyadic level also have implications for understanding the generation of leader and subordinate behavior, self-leadership phenomena, and organizational culture. The same processes that allow us to form perceptions of others can also serve as guides for our own behavior. If these behavioral guides are transferred to the other party, they can serve as a powerful and enduring form of indirect influence. For example, when subordinates learn superiors' standards and incorporate them into their own cognitive schemas, a leader's influence may become a form of self-leadership. Culture, too, is tied to available behavioral or perceptual schemas: when culture provides sets of categories and scripts, perceptual and leadership processes work more efficiently but they may also be restrictive. We expand on each of these topics in the final section of this chapter.

IMPORTANCE OF PERCEPTIONS IN DYADS

Previously, we argued that primarily recognition-based processing occurs at lower levels. Thus, recognition-based processes form the basis for our discussion of dyadic relations. Much of the theoretical and applied work in the leadership field focuses on the activities of lower-level leaders. At this level, the major concerns of leadership theorists are with how supervisors motivate subordinates (for example, House 1971), with the decision-making styles of leaders (Vroom 1964; Vroom and Jago 1988; Vroom and Yetton 1973), or with the needs of leaders and the degree of situational control (Fiedler 1964). Other lines of research focus on leadership behavioral styles and their impact on leader effectiveness (that is, the Ohio State and Michigan State studies; see Stogdill 1974). The factors identified by these theories as being important—leader behaviors, decision-making style—have clear intuitive linkages to task performance at lower levels of organizations. Since these leadership factors are thought to affect performance, the performance-related activities of supervisors provide a natural focus for the development of leadership theories. These behaviorally focused leadership theories are depicted in the upper panel of figure 7.1, where leader behaviors are thought to have a direct impact on subordinate skill and motivation. The perceptual perspective presented in this book, however, offers a departure from this position.

A perceptual perspective highlights the important distinction between supervisory behaviors and leadership perceptions, a distinction that parallels the difference in emphasis between traditional theories of leadership and the recognition-based model developed further in this chapter. Though not explicitly addressing dyadic relationships, other theorists have acknowledged the role of perceptual processes. For example, French and Raven's (1959) work on power and influence approaches our perspective with the idea that power depends on how one is perceived; perceptions of power lie within the observer. Hollander and Offermann (1990) discuss the significance of subordinate perceptions, or "followership" in dyadic power relations. Hollander (1958) also addresses the central role of subordinate perceptions in allowing the leader "credits" to engage in task-related activities.

Consistent with these perspectives, our view is that perceptions of leadership lie within the observer. Expectations, implicit theories, and cybernetic processes are important in determining leadership perceptions. Much of the research mentioned above that emphasizes behavioral styles has focused on influence processes or the supervision of workers, rather than on how leadership perceptions develop and affect performance. The perceptual viewpoint goes beyond observable leader behaviors by acknowledging that the perceptions of supervisors as leaders can affect subordinate performance. An advantage of this position is that it can explain how leadership occurs in conjunction with normal work activities, which are the focus of traditional leadership theories. Social perceptions are an unavoidable by-product of a worker's interactions with his or her supervisor. Often neither the supervisor nor the subordinate gives much conscious thought to the formation of leadership (or subordinate) perceptions while his or her attention is focused on specific work tasks. These perceptions do, however, develop based on such processes, and they can affect task performance and the relationship between leader and subordinate. We will focus on mutual perceptual processes in leader-subordinate dyads at lower hierarchical levels. Of course, we acknowledge that the same processes apply at upper levels with top executives and their immediate subordinates, but we suggest that inferential leadership perception processes are more important for the leadership perceptions of executives. (These ideas are expanded in the third part of this book.) At lower levels, the opportunity for leadership perceptions to develop through inferential processes is less likely than through recognition-based processes.

The upper panel of figure 7.1 shows the assumptions of

contemporary theories of leadership, wherein leader behaviors have a direct linkage to subordinate behaviors, and subordinate behaviors directly affect leader behaviors. Early theories of leadership initially assumed unidirectional influence: leaders' behaviors were thought to have an impact on subordinates' behaviors. But it is now acknowledged that dyadic leader-subordinate relationships have bidirectional influence. For example, Farris and Lim (1969) and Lowin and Craig (1968) have shown that subordinate performance affects subsequent leader behavior and have thereby demonstrated subordinate influence on dyadic processes.

Thus, leader-subordinate dyadic relationships are best conceptualized as a mutual influence process (Herold 1977). The dyadic exchange relationship has also been viewed as a reciprocal influence process in a Vertical Dyad Linkage theory framework (Dienesch and Liden 1986) and in an attribution theory framework (Martinko and Gardner 1987). A mutual influence model of leader-subordinate dyadic relations acknowledges that leader behavior influences subordinates' reactions, while subordinate behavior influences leaders' responses. This process is depicted in the upper panel of figure 7.1 by both arrows.

This research aptly recognizes that reciprocal influence processes operate in leader-subordinate dyads; however, we have added subordinate and leader perceptions as mediators of behavior in the

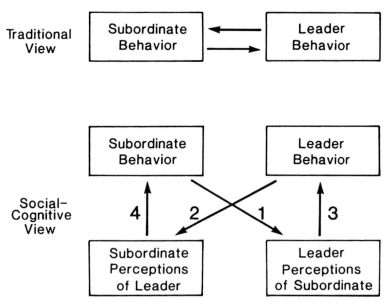

Figure 7.1
Views of Leader-Subordinate Reciprocal Influence Processes

lower panel of figure 7.1. In the following sections we will first discuss the mediating processes of perceptions and their role in dyadic relationships (the lower boxes of figure 7.1). Then, in a later section of this chapter, we will discuss the reciprocal influence process as a whole, depicted by the entire lower panel of figure 7.1 (labeled "Social-Cognitive View"). This figure shows how the leader-subordinate dyadic exchange is cyclical, repeating itself over time, while also including the critical role of leader and subordinate perceptions.

PERCEPTIONS AS MEDIATORS OF BEHAVIOR

Subordinate Perceptions of Leaders

The key mediating factor of leader and subordinate perceptual processes is depicted in the lower panel of figure 7.1. In chapter 3 we argued that recognition-based processes operate in situations in which considerable face-to-face contact provides opportunities to observe leader behavior and infer leader traits. Typical leader-subordinate interactions provide such a context. Most subordinates have significant amounts of direct contact and daily interaction with their managers. Recognition-based processes are particularly important in these situations.

For recognition-based processing to occur, organizational members are thought to have preexisting knowledge of the traits and behaviors that constitute effective leadership. Some of this knowledge is likely to be common across members of a societal culture; intelligence, for example, is seen as a characteristic of leaders in most contexts. The impact of organizational culture also contributes to the leadership perceptions held by subordinates. Cultural influence reflects limited-capacity processing because culture provides a general framework for interpreting leader behavior and traits by matching them to leadership categories. Culture serves as a filter whereby leader activities and characteristics are understood in broad terms defined by that culture.

In addition to broader cultural constraints, leadership-related knowledge is developed through experience in specific organizational contexts, exemplifying expert processing. Here, relevant knowledge is connected to appropriate behaviors for both leaders and perceivers. These categories are much more refined than the general limited-capacity categories and are likely to apply to specific people or specific types of people. For example, a participatory decision-making style might reflect effective leadership in some organizations or departments, whereas an autocratic style might be perceived as effective in others. Such knowledge becomes stored in the long-term memories of organizational members, and appropriate behaviors consistent with this knowledge are automatically elicited. In other words, with experience, rules about appropriate means of approaching tasks can become proceduralized into systems of hierarchical goal structures (Anderson 1987). The entire goal structure is accessed from long-term memory, and behaviors associated with the knowledge structure are elicited automatically in appropriate situations.

From the perspective of categorization theory, organizational members develop a prototype of a leader through experience within the organization. Such experience can include forms of vicarious learning—for example, role modeling. Members also develop prototypes through formal and informal socialization processes of the organization and, in some cases, through standards of specific professions. When subordinates interact with supervisors, the traits and behaviors of the supervisor are compared with this prototype. To the extent that the supervisor's behaviors match the prototype held in the subordinate's memory, the supervisor will be perceived as having leadership qualities. One of the main points to be made in this chapter is that the same type of recognition-based processes occur with leaders' perceptions of subordinates. Whereas managers may be categorized as leaders or nonleaders, we suggest that subordinates are categorized as "good" or "poor" employees. Though the content of the categories differs, the same basic processes underlie both types of perceptions. The interaction of these perceptual processes results in unique dyadic exchanges between leader and subordinate.

Leader Perceptions of Subordinates
Support for the importance of leaders' perceptions of subordinates comes from several research streams. Work based in attribution theory provides a considerable contribution. In addition, research in performance appraisal suggests that leaders, as well as subordinates, use categorization processes to make sense of the interaction. Finally, the work of Graen and his associates on Vertical Dyad Linkage theory (later research refers to this research as "Leader-Member Exchange" theory) illustrates some of the effects of leaders' perceptions of subordinates on dyadic exchanges. Each of these sets of research is relevant to our perspective and summarized briefly below.

Attribution Theory. A substantial body of literature by Mitchell and his associates addresses leaders' attributions of subordinate behavior. Green and Mitchell (1979) developed a cognitive theory of leader-member interactions based on Kelley's (1973) attribution theory principles. According to Green and Mitchell's model, leaders engage in careful causal analyses that mediate between subordinate behavior and superior responses to that behavior. This theory has received much empirical support. Ilgen and Knowlton (1980) found that superiors in ad hoc laboratory groups altered their feedback to subordinates as a function of attributions and performance level. Mitchell and Wood (1980) showed that nursing supervisors reacted to written case histories in a manner consistent with attribution theory predictions: a history of poor performance produced greater assessments of subordinate causality and a tendency to direct responses at the nurses, rather than at situational constraints. Mitchell and Kalb (1982) found that supervisors with experience at the subordinate's job were more likely to attribute causality for poor performance to environmental factors.

The programmatic line of research initiated by Green and Mitchell (1979) provides a good example of how cognitive approaches enable an understanding of dyadic processes. Although the conceptual model developed by Green and Mitchell does provide evidence for the impact of leader perceptions on leader behavior (arrow 3 in figure 7.1), the model is overly restrictive as a general model for superior-subordinate interaction. The type of processing needed to form attributions of subordinates reflects rational information processing that requires considerable cognitive capacity, which, we have noted, is not descriptively accurate in most cases.

Other attribution models, however, describe simpler limited-capacity processing, wherein explicit causal analyses do not serve as mediators between perceptions and behavior. Lord and Smith (1983), for example, argue that automatic attribution processes based on salience and proximity occur. Smith and Miller (1983) also provide evidence for schema-based attributional processes. They found that trait judgments could be made more quickly than causality judgments, implying that attributions to person or situation are not the first judgments perceivers make. This work illustrates the importance of automatic, schema-guided processes that are more consistent with our recognition-based perspective than with the controlled, causal attribution analyses described by Green and Mitchell (1979).

There is some evidence that managers tend to ask subordinates to make causal attributions for them instead of making them automatically (Gioia and Sims 1986), reflecting a more controlled type of activity. It is also possible that causal analyses follow superior reactions to subordinates as a means of rationalizing those reactions. In other words, supervisors may make sense of their behavior, after the fact, through the use of controlled attributional processes. We suggest that attribution processes of the kind described by Green and Mitchell (1979) are rarely used; rather, attributional processes are linked to more schema-driven processes.

In general, then, supervisors form perceptions of subordinates using the same recognition-based processes that perceivers use when forming leadership perceptions—limited-capacity or expert processing. Recognition-based processing is illustrated by categorization processes wherein supervisors develop prototypes of effective subordinates and use the degree of prototype match to interpret subordinate behaviors. As with perceptions of supervisors, we maintain that these perceptions occur relatively automatically through daily interaction with subordinates. A categorization model of leaders' perceptions of subordinates that investigates the content and structure of such categories has not received direct empirical investigation, but results consistent with such a model can be found in the performance appraisal literature.

Performance Appraisal Literature. Theoretical work by Feldman (1981) on performance appraisal suggests that raters use both automatic and controlled categorization processes to categorize subordinates. Processing is assumed to proceed automatically if subordinate behavior is consistent with expectations (or matches the perceiver's prototype). Once the subordinate is categorized, further information about him or her will be automatically interpreted in terms of the category. Controlled processing will occur only if information is inconsistent with expectations. Thus, categorization processes serve as a powerful determinant of performance appraisal rating outcomes. We suggest that such processes do much more than affect performance appraisal ratings: categorization processes affect the development and nature of leader-subordinate interactions from the very beginning of the relationship, with performance appraisal ratings serving as an indirect outcome of more fundamental, on-line recognition-based processes.

Empirical research is also consistent with a recognition-based view of subordinate perceptions. Borman (1987) found that supervisors use "folk theories" to make judgments about subordinates' effectiveness on the job. Folk theories are a form of schema used by individuals who are very familiar with the job in question. Borman found that army officers with significant knowledge about a subordinate's job could articulate categories of subordinate effectiveness on that job. Moreover, these schemas were found to be common across officers in the military setting. The officers in Borman's sample were relatively experienced, with a range of from 2 to 20 years as an officer ($M = 8.2$ years). Borman's results are consistent with expert information processing. Leaders having substantial experience within a given context can develop knowledge structures highly specific to that context—schemas that are related to subordinate performance.

Vertical Dyad Linkage Theory. The work of George Graen and his colleagues on Vertical Dyad Linkage (VDL) theory focuses on the dyad and the development of dyadic exchange as an important determinant of organizational outcomes (Dansereau, Graen, and Haga 1975; Graen and Cashman 1975). VDL does not address the cognitive processes used by leaders and subordinates but does provide evidence that categorization at the initial stages of leader-subordinate interaction can determine the quality of the interaction throughout the relationship. Thus, VDL research illustrates some of the significant outcomes of recognition-based processing. Moreover, the VDL model can be advanced by incorporating what we know about recognition-based perceptual processes.

Dansereau and his colleagues (1975) assert that traditional leadership research operated under two assumptions: (a) that members of work groups are homogeneous in many characteristics; and (b) that the supervisor behaves in the same manner to all subordinates. VDL research has demonstrated that these assumptions are erroneous by showing that supervisors behave differently toward different subordinates within the same work units. It is our view that recognition-based processing and unique categorization of subordinates form the basis for different leader behavior with different subordinates.

Dansereau et al. (1975) identified the "negotiating latitude" construct—the extent to which a leader allows subordinates to influence their own role development—as central to the evolution of the quality of the leader-member exchange. Based on the degree of negotiating latitude offered to a subordinate, he or she is categorized into in-group (high negotiating latitude) or out-group (low negotiating latitude) status. The results of the study by Dansereau et al. indicated that in-group members reported higher leadership attention and job satisfaction than out-group members did. Interestingly, the negotiating latitude construct relies heavily on measures of summary perceptions that classify the nature of the exchange, much like the categorization process we propose. In short, Dansereau et al. concluded that the degree of negotiating latitude offered to subordinates early in the dyadic relationship led to differential leader behavior throughout the relationship. This interpretation is consistent with our discussion of "cognitive inertia" (see figure 5.5).

Leader-member exchange quality has important implications for dyadic relationships. Members of the in-group tend to show higher agreement with their leader about job-related events, such as job problems, than out-group members do (Graen and Schiemann 1978). The quality of the exchange also has implications that extend beyond routine interactions and perceptions of leaders and subordinates. For example, it has been shown that exchange quality can predict subordinate turnover (Graen, Liden, and Hoel 1982). In-group and out-group status of certain members is also observable to other members of the work unit (Duchon, Green, and Taber 1986), thus extending the effects of leader-subordinate exchange beyond the particular dyad, with implications for group performance and other group-related outcomes. Finally, exchange quality is thought to have significant consequences for employees' career development (Graen and Scandura 1987). Clearly, the results of this research indicate that the nature of the leader-subordinate relationship has far-reaching organizational implications. For this reason, we think a precise specification of the cognitive processes involved in the development of exchange quality is crucial to a thorough understanding of the nature of the relationship.

The theoretical framework of VDL characterizes the leader-subordinate exchange process as being a socialization process that focuses on behaviors. The VDL model evolved from role theory (Katz and Kahn 1978), in which interactions between subordinate and supervisor are thought to take place within the context of a role episode—a sequence of role communication and expectations (Graen and Scandura 1987). Development of the relationship between supervisors and subordinates consists of three phases. In the role-taking phase, the supervisor communicates to the subordinate a "sent-role," or desired role. In this phase, the subordinate is thought to play a relatively passive role, receiving communication from the supervisor but not reciprocating in any significant manner. In the role-making phase, the supervisor-subordinate relationship continues to develop and its nature becomes increasingly defined for both parties. Finally, in the role routinization phase, the nature of the exchange becomes routinized and established. In sum, the nature of the exchange is related to the role-taking, role-making, and role routinization phases of the interaction.

This role episode as described above is primarily a controlled process, whereby roles (task expectations and so on) are consciously and intentionally transmitted to the subordinate in the form of overt leader activities. At the same time, the subordinate consciously attends to the sent-role to engage in appropriate job behavior. In other words, the focus is on supervisory behaviors rather than the perceptual component of the process. Automatic processes, however, are also important in the development of the dyadic relationship. For example, Dienesch and Liden (1986) offer a model of leader-member exchange development in which both controlled attributional processes and relatively automatic categorization processes are thought to operate in exchange development. These authors also offer a process-oriented model of exchange development in which exchange processes begin with initial interaction and proceed through leader delegation and leader and member attributions and behaviors. Thus, Dienesch and Liden acknowledge the important role of limited-capacity processing in the development of dyadic interaction, in addition to controlled, more rational forms of processing.

It is also likely that expert processes develop within the VDL framework to guide perceptions and behavior. Because expert processing ties well-developed schemas to specific behaviors, it follows that categorization into in-group or out-group status leads to differential cognitive patterns and behaviors. For example, there is evidence that categorization leads to different types of attributions for in-group and out-group members. Heneman, Greenberger, and Anonyuo (1989) found that when subordinate performance was effective, supervisors' internal attributions for ability and effort were higher for in-group as opposed to out-group members. When performance was ineffective, supervisors gave more internal attributions to out-group members than to in-group members. Yet Heneman et al. found no differences in external attributions based on group membership and differing levels of performance. Thus, we suggest that internal attributions proceed automatically and are directly tied to knowledge structures related to in- or out-group status. In other words, causal attributions are part of the category of in-group or out-group, with different types of attributions connected to each. Others have made similar arguments (Cronshaw and Lord 1987; Phillips and Lord 1981). Because this type of internal attribution occurs automatically for in-group and out-group members, a more extensive controlled search for likely external causes is never undertaken by supervisors. Perceivers may use attributions to confirm a person's membership in a category, rather than comprehensively assessing causality for performance or behavior. Attributions for the behavior of in-group members, for example, may be used to support the perceiver's expectations of good performance or appropriate behavior. If in-group performance is poor, supervisors may attribute causality to situational constraints. In this way, the subordinate is still perceived to belong to the in-group category.

Other research also suggests that attributions are tied to schemas that guide behavior. Dugan (1989) found that managers' internal attributions for subordinates' poor performance led to different roles being taken by managers. When managers attributed poor performance to lack of effort, subsequent communication with subordinates was characterized more by problem-solving techniques. On the other hand, when managers attributed poor performance to lack of ability, they controlled subsequent interaction with subordinates more so than when they made attributions concerning effort. Thus, attributions are closely tied to scripts for appropriate behavior. It is also likely that there are different scripts for behavior associated with in-group versus out-group members.

The implementation of scripts may provide another basis for

inferences about subordinates. Utilizing different scripts for in-group and out-group members causes different leader behaviors for these two groups. Because responses are tied to subsequent perceptions, it is also possible that we use behavior to infer attributions. That is, initial categorization can dispose us to behave in certain ways toward individuals; our behavior then colors our subsequent perceptions, instead of behavior following *from* perceptions. Behavior of a supervisor toward an in-group subordinate grants more negotiating latitude and participation. Out-group behavior may include more direct influence on the part of the supervisor. Supervisors themselves may believe they are personally responsible for the out-group subordinate compliance because of their controlling behavior exhibited to out-group members. Associated with the belief that the supervisor is personally responsible for member compliance is a tendency to devalue the subordinate and to maintain social distance (Kipnis, Castell, Gergen, and Mauch 1976). There is also evidence that more trust exists in the relationship when supervisors attribute a type of "self-oriented" motivation to subordinates (Strickland 1958); this type of motivation attribution is more likely for in-group than out-group members. These effects are dramatic illustrations of the powerful influence of categorization on a supervisor's behavior and thought patterns. These findings also demonstrate how a supervisor's behavior following categorization can perpetuate the initial status of the subordinate.

In-group or out-group status and its associated scripts can affect subordinate perceptions in another way as well. Supervisors may enable in-group members to pursue learning goals while emphasizing performance goals (Elliot and Dweck 1988) for out-group members. The high degree of supportiveness typically found for in-group members may allow these subordinates to improve their competence by pursuing mastery-oriented, or learning, goals. On the other hand, the less supportive style of supervisors in dealing with out-group members may lead such subordinates to adopt performance goals, wherein their focus is on avoiding negative feedback. Over time, an emphasis on performance goals can lead to a situation of learned helplessness for the subordinate involved (Elliot and Dweck 1988).

It is suggested that automatic, recognition-based processes deserve more attention in the development of leader-member exchange quality. Instead of the controlled, social influence process characterizing the role episode, relatively automatic processes are also appropriate to describe the development of leader-subordinate interaction, particularly after initial periods of interaction. Interestingly, supervisors may have little insight into how such automatic processes affect different interaction patterns for in-group and out-group members. An important implication is that supervisors may also be unaware of the unintended negative consequences of classifying subordinates as out-group members—consequences such as learned helplessness. Another implication of the operation of automatic processes in dyadic interaction is that it may be difficult for supervisors to change their classifications of subordinates and alter the scripts associated with a given classification. This conclusion is consistent with our discussion of "cognitive inertia," or automatic on-line processing, which is summarized in figure 5.5. It implies that some form of intervention, such as training, may be necessary for supervisors to understand how their categorizations can affect the nature of the interaction and performance.

In addition to understanding the significance of how automatic processes affect supervisor-subordinate relationships, it is also important to understand how cybernetic processes characterize the development of the nature of the exchange. Cybernetic processing is illustrated by the entire lower panel in figure 7.1, where behaviors and perceptions of those behaviors for both leaders and subordinates continue over time. In the next section, we present an example of how such cybernetic processing operates using a behavioral confirmation model of social interaction. This model of leader-subordinate interaction highlights the importance of automatic, recognition-based categorization processes at initial stages of the relationship. Moreover, a behavioral confirmation perspective acknowledges that the leader-subordinate relationship is one of reciprocal influence, with both leaders and subordinates affecting the perceptions and behaviors of the other.

In this section we have focused primarily on the processes affecting leader perceptions of subordinates. We would argue, however, that very similar processes operate for subordinate perceptions of leaders. Though the content of categories is different, the perceptual processes are the same. (This research was covered extensively in chapters 3 and 4.)

RECIPROCAL INFLUENCE THROUGH BEHAVIORAL CONFIRMATION

Much of the research and theorizing on reciprocal influence in the leadership literature has assumed a behavioral orientation. That is, the reciprocal process focuses on behaviors, on the part of either the leader or the subordinate, while ignoring the mediating role of perceptions. We think, though, that leader and subordinate recognition-based perceptual processes operate at the core of the dyadic exchange. We suggest that the cybernetic reciprocal influence process (the lower panel of figure 7.1) can be conceptualized within the behavioral confirmation framework.

The behavioral confirmation model of dyadic interaction is based on the general social interaction sequence outlined by Darley and Fazio (1980). This model serves as a framework for the reciprocal influence behaviors of leaders and subordinates. The idea of behavioral confirmation and reciprocity in interaction is similar to Weick's (1979) concept of the double interact, wherein the behaviors of one individual are contingent on the behaviors of another. We attempt to explicate this process more precisely with an emphasis on the perceptual processes that mediate behaviors. Behavioral confirmation is similar to the "self-fulfilling prophecy" notion commonly investigated in classroom settings. More recent research extends this thinking to work settings, where a supervisor's expectancy that an employee will perform well can cause that employee to perform well (Sutton and Woodman 1990). Snyder (1984) provides a review of behavioral confirmation processes and suggests that the behavioral confirmation process is one of reality testing, which then becomes reality construction. In general terms, expectancy confirmation describes the process by which an individual's expectancies about another's behavior can cause the other to behave in ways consistent with those expectancies. We define expectancies as perceptions of likely future behavior that are tied to categories. Script-based expectancies can develop for others' behavior and one's own behavior, and they are not necessarily conscious. Our definition is not the same as the way the term *expectancy* is used in motivation theory, wherein it refers to one's expected performance outcome and is generally thought to be a conscious process. This consistency between expectancies and behavior may be either real (that is, the individual's expectancies alter the behavior of the other) or perceived (that is, the individual interprets the other's behavior as consistent with expectancies). The behavior confirmation process begins to operate at the initial interaction between two persons, and it provides a source of consistency in the relationship over time. We maintain that limited-capacity processes determine the nature of the initial interaction between leader and subordinate; the initial interaction forms the basis of the behavioral confirmation phenomenon.

Nevertheless, since this process occurs over time, the behavioral confirmation model reflects cybernetic information processing, discussed in chapter 2. Perceptions of one's own behavior, perceptions of another's behavior, and actions are interspersed over time, with perceptions revising actions and actions revising perceptions in a cyclical manner. The behavioral confirmation model reflects the true dynamic nature of dyadic interchange, rather than a static view of the process typical of most leadership research. Such a behavioral confirmation process has also been suggested by Feldman (1986) within

TABLE 7.1
Stages of Behavioral Confirmation and Social Cognition

Darley and Fazio (1980)	Social-Cognitive View
1. Perceiver forms expectancy	Lower boxes
2. Perceiver acts	Arrows 3 or 4
3. Target interprets perceiver's act	Arrows 1 or 2
4. Target responds	Arrows 3 or 4
5. Perceiver interprets target's act	Arrows 1 or 2
6. Target perceives own act	

the context of performance appraisal. Feldman suggests that perceivers form categorization-expectation-behavior links, which are then used to form performance appraisal ratings. The process starts with the supervisor categorizing the subordinate, a process that gives rise to expectations of subordinate behavior, thereby affecting the quality of the interaction (for example, in-group versus out-group). In the following section we will break down this process into its constituent stages, illustrating how it unfolds over time.

The social interaction sequence outlined by Darley and Fazio (1980) can be used as a framework to describe the manner in which behavioral confirmation processes occur. Darley and Fazio's steps are listed in the left-hand column of table 7.1. The right-hand column of this table shows the correspondence between Darley and Fazio's steps and our social-cognitive view from figure 7.1. In the following discussion, we begin the interaction sequence with leaders' perceptions of subordinates, but the word *subordinate* may be substituted for the word *leader* at any point in the sequence, because the same processes occur for both dyad members.

In the first stage of the process, the leader (subordinate) develops a set of expectancies about a subordinate (leader) based on prior observations and on categorization processes that are likely to be culture based. Recall from chapter 5 that behavioral expectancies follow from categorization processes. In a VDL framework, having categorized a subordinate as a member of the in-group, the leader may have different sets of expectancies for this member as opposed to those for out-group members. Similarly, the subordinate may have categorized the supervisor as an effective leader, thereby expecting the leader to behave in ways consistent with this category in the future. These assumptions, too, may be culturally based or follow from extensive experience. The lower boxes of the social-cognitive view in figure 7.1 correspond to this stage (see table 7.1).

At this stage, limited-capacity or expert processes are very important. A supervisor with experience on the job has developed a prototype of an effective subordinate and, during initial interaction, matches the behaviors of the subordinate to this knowledge structure held in memory. On a more controlled level, the supervisor may have expectancies about the subordinate based on socially communicated information—for instance, verbal reports about the subordinate's performance or written material like résumés and letters of recommendation. The subordinate can also recognize leadership on the part of the supervisor by comparing the supervisor's behavior with a leadership prototype held in memory. These categorization processes lead to the development of expectancies about the behavior of the other person in the dyad. A supervisor who perceives a subordinate as having potential will expect behaviors consistent with those perceptions. As Darley and Fazio (1980) report, it is difficult to change expectancies, even in the face of disconfirming evidence. Thus, expectancies for another's behavior provide a powerful determinant of the nature of continuing interaction between the members of a dyad.

In the second stage of behavioral confirmation, the leader acts toward the subordinate in a way congruent with his or her own expectancies. This behavior is referred to as the expectancy-action link (Darley and Fazio 1980) and corresponds to arrows 3 or 4 in figure 7.1. We assert that at this stage, categorizing a person as an in-group or an out-group member integrates the stimulus person with different cognitive systems for accomplishing activities. Here, managers with experience supervising a given position have developed knowledge structures of effective performers (for example, Borman 1987)—they are expert information processors. As we noted in chapter 2, expert information processors have appropriate behavioral responses, and scripts stored in memory that are linked to category structures (Lord and Kernan 1987). For example, leaders may structure actions differently with in- and out-group members, or they may vary in the participativeness of their decision-making style. These behavioral responses are thought to be elicited automatically when the relevant knowledge structure is activated. At a general level, if the subordinate is perceived as an ineffective performer, a low degree of negotiating latitude behavior (in VDL terms) may be elicited on the part of the supervisor. If, however, the subordinate is perceived as effective and is expected to behave in this manner, a high degree of negotiating latitude behaviors may be evoked. Such scripts may be common across supervisors in a given organization. For example, some scripts may involve authoritarian leadership behaviors, while others involve participatory supervisory behaviors.

Thus, the simple act of categorization may elicit different behaviors by accessing different scripts. An analogous process may operate for subordinates. With experience within a given organization or profession, subordinates may recognize effective leadership and automatically link appropriate responses to this categorization structure. Moreover, it is possible that alternative categorizations lead to different metascripts (Gioia and Poole 1984), which can uniquely structure entire relationships. Behaviors elicited from such metascripts go beyond a single role episode and may affect the ensuing relationship and perhaps a subordinate's career development process (Graen and Scandura 1987). For example, as noted earlier, "learning" versus "performance" metascripts may be differentially applied to in-group and out-group members by both supervisors *and* subordinates.

Research showing that subordinate behavior affects leader behavior (for example, Farris and Lim 1969; Lowin and Craig 1968) is also consistent with this interpretation. Subordinate behavior can influence subsequent leader behavior by affecting supervisor categorization processes and expectancies for subordinate behavior. Sims and Manz (1984) found that supervisors provided a greater number of verbal rewards for those subordinates who were perceived as high performers. Because alternative category structures are linked to different behaviors, supervisor behaviors are different for subordinates who are associated with distinct categories.

In the third stage of the behavioral confirmation model, the subordinate interprets the meaning of the leader's actions (arrows 1 or 2 in figure 7.1). If the leader has categorized the subordinate as effective and has engaged in behaviors linked through scripts with this categorization (such as high negotiating latitude), then the subordinate will perceive these behaviors differently from the way a subordinate whose supervisor engaged in behaviors linked to an ineffective subordinate categorization (low negotiating latitude) would. Some empirical research on leader-subordinate behavioral confirmation processes provides support for this stage of the process. Eden and Shani (1982) found that increasing supervisor expectancies for subordinate performance evoked more positive perceptions of leadership on the part of subordinates. The results of this study illustrate that supervisor expectancies may lead to differential behavior on the part of the supervisor, as perceived by the subordinate. At this stage, the subordinate not only interprets the leader's behavior in terms of leader perceptions but also interprets the leader's behavior in terms of the subordinate's own self-perceptions. Eden and Ravid (1982) showed that supervisors instilled higher self-expectations in subordinates of whom they expected more, demonstrating the powerful effects of expectancies in dyadic exchanges. These results are also consistent with the distinction made by Elliot and Dweck (1988), illustrating how supervisors can affect subordinate self-perceptions by differential emphasis on performance or learning goals.

In the fourth stage of the process (arrows 3 or 4, figure 7.1), the subordinate responds to the leader based on his or her interpretations of the leader's previous actions. For example, if the subordinate perceives that he or she is not to engage in participatory decision-making behaviors on the job, he or she will not ask to participate. Thus, perceptions of leader's behavior may affect the subordinate's motivation levels, thereby increasing or decreasing work performance (Eden 1984). Eden and Ravid (1982) found that subordinates in a high-expectancy condition performed better than subordinates in a control group. Thus, the response made by the subordinate at this point in the interaction process is directly related to how the leader's behaviors are perceived.

The fifth stage of the process is simply the reverse of the third stage, wherein the perceiver interprets the target's acts. Though the role of the perceiver is reversed, the same cognitive processes operate as in the third stage. Arrows 1 or 2 depict this process in figure 7.1.

Darley and Fazio (1980) add a sixth step in their behavioral confirmation model that does not correspond to our figure 7.1, yet it is nevertheless important (see table 7.1). In this step of the social interaction sequence, the leader or subordinate interprets the meaning of his or her own actions. We suggest that prototype-matching processes occur here, as well as in the initial stages of the interaction. In terms of leadership perceptions, it is thought that a leader's knowledge of an effective leader prototype provides a self-standard about how the leader should behave in a given situation. Prototypes may also be thought of as self-schemas of a sort (Brickner 1989), in which behaviors reflect attempts at validating these schemas. In this sense, the categorization process may help individuals interpret their own behavior. Similar processes may operate on the part of the subordinate if he or she is aware of effective or ineffective subordinate prototypes within the work context. Because the process of categorization serves as a filter for incoming information, interpretations of one's own behavior may be biased toward the prototype. Thus, if a subordinate has a prototype of effective behavior in the work context, his or her behavior may be interpreted in ways consistent with the prototype, even if the behavior was inconsistent or ambiguous. The idea that prototypes serve as sources of behavior generation is an important one, and we will discuss this issue further at a later point in this chapter.

It must be emphasized that this process is a cybernetic one that continues in a cyclical manner. For example, the leader interprets the actions of the subordinate and the social interaction sequence begins anew. This cyclical process occurs whenever there is any interaction between leader and subordinate. Again, the interpretation of behaviors is affected by prior categorization processes. Because of most people's bias to interpret information as being consistent with their prototypes, subsequent social interaction cycles may perpetuate and strengthen initial interpretations. Over time, associations between classifications of people and relevant scripts become strengthened through use. In this way, the presence of a stimulus person can prime the category and its associated script. Thus, initial categorizations of subordinates into in-groups or out-groups are likely to determine the nature of the leader-subordinate relationship over time and carry implications for members of the dyad far beyond initial social contact between leader and subordinate (Graen et al. 1977; Graen and Scandura 1987).

The social interaction sequence presented above highlights the reciprocal nature of the influence in dyads and its source in perceiver cognitions. Categorizations and expectancies by both leader and subordinate are formed simultaneously, and perceptions are revised simultaneously based on altered expectations and the other member's behavior. Thus, the relationship is mutually influencing. Both leaders and subordinates operate within the constraints of the process; both members recognize the behaviors of the other member as consistent or inconsistent with a category prototype and form expectancies of the other member based on these perceptions. Expectancies are then associated with certain behaviors. The cycle continues over time, perpetuating initial perceptions and expectancies. Because the process is cyclical and interactive, members continually receive feedback from each other.

This model also acknowledges that subordinates have an equal part in influencing the dyadic exchange. Research conducted by Gioia and Sims (1986) illustrates the effects of such a process. In their study, managers and subordinates interacted with each other following subordinates' performance. After the interaction, managers changed their attributions for subordinates' performance from those made prior to the interaction. After face-to-face contact with the subordinate, managers were more likely to make more favorable attributions to the subordinate (such as attributing failure to external sources). Thus, subordinates played a strong role in influencing the nature of the exchange. Both members come to the dyad with expectancies and pattern their behavior after these expectancies. The behavioral con-firmation model acknowledges that the sequence of events that occurs at the beginning stages of the interaction is crucial in determining the nature of the continuing relationship. Thus, recognition-based processes operate as a primary determinant of the nature of the leader-subordinate relationship.

Changing Perceptions in Social Interaction

We have argued extensively that initial categorizations color subsequent interactions and influence the nature of the dyadic relationship as well as factors beyond the dyad. Often, these processes operate to categorize individuals correctly and lead to accurate expectancies and assessments of behavior. Yet sometimes categorizations are incorrect and can be changed or updated. Because the process we have described in this chapter is cybernetic, the principles of updating and changing perceptions that were discussed in chapter 5 are easily applied.

The locus of attributions may be crucial in such an updating process. There is evidence that when performance is effective, supervisors' internal attributions to subordinates' ability and effort are higher for in-group members. When performance is poor, supervisors give more internal attributions to out-group members than to in-group members (Heneman et al. 1989). Crocker et al. (1983) found that causal analyses for inconsistent behaviors were much more likely to occur than for consistent behaviors. Further, these causal attributions based on inconsistent behaviors were much more likely to be *external* attributions. Given external attributions, however, internal causes are discounted and impressions are not revised. Following the logic of Crocker and her colleagues, episodes that are inconsistent are forgotten, thus perpetuating initial categorizations. The findings of Crocker et al. illustrate a failure of controlled processing to produce change in impressions over time.

Not only is the locus of causal attributions important, but there is evidence that cognitive demands may cause perceivers to eliminate the attribution process entirely and fail to identify the situational constraints on individuals' actions. Gilbert, Pelham, and Krull (1988) found that those subjects who were given an extra task when forming judgments about target individuals were less likely to correct their judgments based on situational constraints than perceivers who were less "busy." Gilbert and his colleagues argue that the correction process uses a great deal of cognitive resources; if these resources are unavailable, perceivers will not make use of situational information to form attributions. The effects of restricted cognitive resources are fairly pervasive; perceivers can correct their impressions if given the opportunity to do so but are unable to correct subsequent inferences that have been biased by the initial categorization (Gilbert and Osborne 1989). Thus, even when it may be appropriate to use contextual information in forming judgments, perceivers do not necessarily make use of this information, because doing so requires more cognitive resources than they have available. Resources may be especially scarce during face-to-face interaction between leaders and subordinates. In these situations, the effects of initial impressions may be particularly potent.

One important implication of this discussion is that the process of image management may drain cognitive resources in face-to-face dyadic contact. For example, a subordinate who is very concerned about presenting himself or herself in a positive light to a supervisor may be unable to use all available resources to assess the supervisor's behaviors accurately. This idea suggests that attempts at image management may fail more often than they are successful, because subordinates may not have the cognitive capacity to monitor accurately their own behavior and the supervisor's behavior simultaneously.

We suggest that automatic processes are more likely to operate when initial categorizations are changed, resulting in a switch to a different category, though this process is also difficult. As described in chapter 5, inconsistent information can cause individuals to switch categories, but we suggest that it may take repeated instances of information inconsistent with initial categorization for this switching to occur. Moreover, if metascripts are operating for individuals and behaviors are thereby strongly linked to perceptual processes, updating may require the use of an entirely different system of behaviors. This process requires more than simply changing labels, thus further limiting changes in categorization. A change in behavior patterns may also be resisted by the other member of the dyad. Still, revision of categorization can occur, though more probably through automatic than controlled processes, when inconsistent attributions are simply discounted. This idea can be graphically illustrated with the cusp surface in figure 5.5. Discounting inconsistent attributions may serve to reinforce the process depicted by the fold on the front surface of the figure. At the fold region, the very same behaviors or performance may be interpreted differently, based on whether a dyadic partner is operating from an in-group or an out-group script. This model again shows the potent effects of categorization on subsequent impressions.

In sum, we have described leader and subordinate perceptions of each other that reflect recognition-based processes. We have also described the reciprocal, cybernetic process of behavioral confirmation. In the final section of this chapter, we present some implications of the perceptual processes operating at the level of the dyad.

IMPLICATIONS

Shared Schemas

Each member of the supervisor-subordinate dyad brings certain expectancies and assumptions to the dyadic interaction. Thus, each member's perceptions and actions are constrained by these expectancies and assumptions. One may then ask how reciprocal influence processes can operate successfully to accomplish task performance and motivation. We suggest that the extent to which schemas are shared between leader and subordinate governs the degree to which the exchange is characterized by trust, motivation, and performance, and limits the degree to which misperceptions will occur. Thus, schema congruence can have affective as well as cognitive consequences. Shared schemas may provide a basis for tacit understanding and reliance on "intuition" during interaction. Much of the literature on perceptual congruence supports these suggestions.

Tsui and O'Reilly (1989) found that decreases in demographic similarity between manager and subordinate were associated with increased role ambiguity of subordinates and lower perceived subordinate performance. Pulakos and Wexley (1983) found that managers and subordinates who perceived greater similarity between each other evaluated each other more favorably than was the case when perceptual dissimilarity existed. Those with perceptual dissimilarity were suggested to have weak, or out-group, exchange relationships. Interestingly, Pulakos and Wexley point out that as long as subordinates feel they are similar to managers, they give high performance ratings to managers, regardless of managers' perceived similarity to subordinates. These findings also suggest the role of reciprocal influence. Subordinates' perceptions can affect the nature of the relationship even when managers' perceptions are not congruent. Similar findings were obtained by Turban and Jones (1988), who found that perceived similarity between dyad members was strongly associated with satisfaction, pay, and performance. Meglino, Ravlin, and Adkins (1989) found that congruence of values between supervisor and subordinate was associated with greater satisfaction and organizational commitment. These findings, taken together, illustrate the powerful effect of shared schemas on dyadic relationships. To the extent that dyadic members perceive similarity, they are likely to have similar schemas about job- and work-relevant factors.

Recognition-based Processes in the Generation of Behavior

Prototypes not only serve as filters for the perception of others' behavior but also serve to generate one's own behavior, as we noted in the discussion of the sixth stage of the behavioral confirmation sequence. We have suggested that subordinates use leadership prototypes to understand and predict the behavior of their superiors. Interestingly, because these prototypes are widely held and understood within specific organizational contexts, leaders themselves may be aware of these prototypical leader behaviors and traits and may use this knowledge to guide their own behavior. Thus, supervisors compare their own behavior with self-generated behavioral standards (Carver 1979) derived from prototypes. If managers have a clear idea of the appropriate leader prototype, such a comparison could provide a means of self-evaluation and feedback. Prototype matching can therefore provide information as to the appropriateness of a manager's behavior and can directly guide behavior generation through links to behavioral scripts (Lord and Kernan 1987).

Given that recognition-based leadership perceptions are pervasive in organizations and that they can be used to guide behavior, some prescriptive statements can be made regarding managerial behavior. If the category of an effective leader is widely held by subordinates in a given organization, it would benefit the manager to learn what traits and behaviors are prototypical of effective leadership and to make an effort to behave in congruence with this prototype when feasible. As such, leadership training programs should aim toward identifying subordinates' perceptions of effective leadership in particular contexts. Although behaviors and traits associated with effective leadership are thought to be consistent across situations by popular writers (for example, Peters and Waterman 1982), there may be important differences across organizations, among different levels of organizations, or across different task domains (Lord and Alliger 1985). Research should compare prototypes across contexts to see how they differ (preliminary research of this nature is described in chapter 3). Thus, managers new to an organization or those transferring to different departments within an organization should be sensitive to different prototypes that affect subordinates' perceptions of effective leadership in these domains.

Just as supervisors are aware of leadership prototypes and can use them to generate behavior, subordinates, too, are likely to make use of prototypes in the same manner. We suggest, however, that subordinates would need considerable experience within an organization or industry to make effective use of such constructs for behavior generation. Newcomers to organizations are unlikely to be aware of such prototypes. Here, the role of socialization processes is critical in transmitting prototypes and perceptual standards to new employees. Our discussion of shared schemas as being key determinants of successful dyadic relationships suggests that such schemas may be important in self-leadership as well. If leaders' prototypes of effective subordinates are similar to subordinates' self-schemas used to guide behavior, the subordinate may be highly successful at initiating appropriate task-related behavior, and the affective responses of leaders and subordinates are also likely to be congruent.

Self-Leadership

Self-leadership can be defined as the ability of a subordinate to motivate himself or herself. Self-leadership could be interpreted as a "substitute" for leadership; however, we think a more appropriate interpretation is to link it with prior dyadic-level perceptual processes. It has been suggested that certain characteristics of the subordinate, the task, and the organization may serve as substitutes for formal leadership behaviors (Kerr and Jermier 1978; Manz 1986; Manz and Sims 1980). Manz and Sims (1980, 1987) have noted that leader-subordinate interactions are integral in promoting self-leadership among subordinates through modeling and reinforcement. We believe leadership perceptions may be as important in the formation and maintenance of self-leadership behaviors as modeling and reinforcement are. There is evidence that members of in-groups receive more latitude in defining their work activities (Dansereau et al. 1975). Thus, self-leadership might be considered a component of an in-group script. The social categorization process may prime and strengthen self-leadership scripts for in-group members, thereby allowing better management of activities for these individuals. We have already argued that a perceptual perspective offers a departure from the traditional theories of leadership with their emphasis on formal, task-directed behaviors. We think the perceptual view also offers an alternative explanation for the phenomenon of self-leadership.

A self-leadership perspective implies that leader traits and behaviors have less impact on subordinate behavior to the extent that self-leadership is present. If one accepts the idea that employees can be motivated through self-leadership, then traditional theories of leadership are not directly relevant, because those leader behaviors which usually serve to direct subordinates (for example, initiating structure) are internalized by subordinates. Mentor-protégé relationships are characterized by this process. Over time, the protégé typically develops an internal model of the mentor's thought processes and can identify what the mentor would do in certain situations. When protégés begin to rely on this internal model rather than consulting their mentor, self-leadership can be said to substitute for the traditional, task-directed behaviors of leaders.

Yet when self-leadership is interpreted in social-cognitive terms, it can be seen that leadership still has an influence over the subordinate. This influence does not occur directly, through overt leader behavior, but *indirectly*, through perceptions of leadership that have been internalized by the subordinate, thereby affecting the degree to which the subordinate engages in self-leadership. Cognitive similarity may play an important role in the internalization process because similarity increases identification with the leader. This internalization process can be further understood by returning to the behavioral confirmation model. Within this framework, self-leadership can be viewed as a result of this social interaction sequence. Though the model consists of only a single episode, it can have cumulative effects that influence identification with the leader. Recall the fourth stage of the behavioral confirmation model. It was suggested that perceptions of a leader's behavior can affect the subordinate's motivation levels (Eden 1984). Increased levels of motivation may be related to what is typically termed self-leadership and may replace task-related manager directives. Thus, the manner in which the subordinate interprets the meaning of the leader's behavior (the third stage) can affect levels of motivation.

The Effect of Culture on Dyadic Interaction

An organization's culture can affect dyadic perceptions in two primary ways. First, we view culture as having an effect on the types of relationships that develop between leader and subordinate. Managers with experience in a particular context are likely to have developed prototypes of effective subordinates, prototypes that are probably a partial result of the particular culture of the organization. Some organizations, for example, assume participatory decision-making styles; others assume autocratic decision-making styles. Culture also suggests scripts that are appropriate for good or poor performance and suggests ways of processing information. For example, norms for equity and fairness may influence the nature of prototypes. These basic assumptions of a particular organization's culture determine the prototypes held by managers. Through behavioral confirmation processes, then, these assumptions become ingrained in the relationship between leader and subordinate. Kozlowski and Doherty (1989) suggest that leadership processes help in the formation of climate perceptions in an organization. In a field study, they found that high degrees of negotiating latitude by supervisors were related to positive climate perceptions. Thus, culture may be one of the primary determinants of the work-related prototypes that are developed in the organization.

Culture can be maintained through dyadic relationships in another way, as well. As we mentioned at the beginning of this chapter, the effects of dyadic relationships extend far beyond the particular leader-subordinate dyad. Dyads can be thought of as linking pins (Graen et al. 1977), wherein the type of relationship in one dyad can cascade upward or downward to other dyads. In this sense, dyadic relationships established through behavioral confirmation processes can be considered one means by which organizational cultures are perpetuated and maintained throughout an organization. Chapter 8 will continue the discussion of leadership perceptions and culture.

Future Research

There are several suggestions for continued research based on our discussion in this chapter. First, with the exception of much of the work by Graen and his colleagues, relatively few studies have taken a longitudinal perspective on dyadic development between leaders and subordinates. We think leadership researchers could benefit from more longitudinal field research assessing how perceptions change over time. We suggest, however, that well-controlled laboratory studies may be most effective at studying the behavioral confirmation process in manager-subordinate dyads.

Second, more research is needed on the content and structure of leaders' categories of subordinates. It would be useful, for example, to identify what the categories of in-group and out-group members consist of in specific contexts. Another area for research is the investigation of category-script linkages, with an analysis of behaviors associated with categories. The research investigating leadership perceptions (see chapter 3) provides a model of how this research might proceed. Recent research on performance appraisal seems to be taking this approach; however, when viewed from our perspective, the implications of dyadic exchange extend far beyond biannual performance appraisals: the organization as a whole is influenced by types of dyadic relationships, and thus the implications are much broader than performance appraisal. It would also be interesting to investigate how attributional processes are tied to categorization processes. Researchers should investigate whether internal or external attributions are contained within certain categories and whether they are made automatically.

A third area for future research deals with the role of affect in leader-subordinate dyadic relationships. Wayne and Ferris (1989), in a field sample, found that performance and ingratiation behaviors operated through liking to affect exchange quality. Interestingly, Srull and Wyer (1989) suggest that affectively based global evaluations are always made in evaluating others and serve as default values when no specific trait ratings have been made. Affectively based associations can also strengthen linkages in information processing (Bower 1981).

The hedonic-relevance perspective discussed by Hogan (1987) is also compelling. Hogan's findings suggest that people react negatively to a disconfirmation of expectations. In this study, performance appraisal ratings were lower than actual performance when performance disconfirmed prior expectations. Ratings decreased when present performance was better than as well as when it was worse than expectations. Disconfirming information may be uncomfortable to perceivers, and they may attempt to avoid it. The operation of such affect-driven processes suggests an even more powerful effect of initial impressions; perceivers may be reluctant to change categories or alter perceptions, so as to avoid the negative affect associated with disconfirming information. Recall the example of Ann B. Hopkins (see chapter 1) who acted "macho" and thus was perceived to be inconsistent with a traditional female category. Behaviors that are inconsistent with a prior categorization (for example, a woman acting aggressively, a man displaying effeminate behavior) may trigger strong negative affective reactions. In sum, though our model explicitly acknowledges cognitive factors in exchange quality, it does not address the relationship of affect to exchange development. We think further research should investigate how affect mediates labeling and categorization processes.

SUMMARY

In this chapter we have analyzed the leader-subordinate dyad in terms of social information processing. The dyad as the unit of analysis highlights the importance of dyadic relationships to other aspects of organizational life. We described recognition-based processes of both leaders and subordinates and suggested that these processes are crucial to the development and maintenance of the leader-subordinate relationship. Much of the work related to subordinates' perceptions of leaders is summarized in chapter 3.

In this chapter we expanded our coverage to include leaders' perceptions of subordinates and the role of these perceptions in the dyadic relationship. Here, we suggested that recognition-based processes are also used to form perceptions of subordinates, and we briefly summarized relevant work from the literature on attribution theory, performance appraisal, and Vertical Dyad Linkage theory.

We also explained how perceptual processes of both members operate in a cybernetic manner to characterize the dyadic relationship as a reciprocal influence process. A behavioral confirmation model was presented as an example of how these processes operate over time to determine the nature of the relationship. In this framework, both leaders and subordinates form expectancies and act based on those expectancies. The cycle proceeds over time, with continual updating and feedback.

Finally, several implications of our behavioral confirmation framework were presented. One notable implication is the manner in which categorization processes and prototype matching can lead to the generation of behavior. Also discussed were the importance of shared schemas to successful exchanges, how the model can explain self-leadership, and how culture can shape the nature of the exchange. In addition, several suggestions for future research on leader-member dyads were set forth.

Chapter 8 ───────────────────

Culture, Information Processing, and Leadership

───────────────────────────────

*I*n this chapter we discuss the role played by leadership and information processing in the development, maintenance, and change of organizational culture. The importance of culture to organizational performance, attitudes, strategic choices, and other variables of interest is exemplified by the number of books, articles, and presentations on this topic in the past decade. The popularity of this topic, however, belies the lack of an intelligible theoretical grounding that characterizes much of the literature. This chapter will present an information processing approach to organizational culture in an effort to align the topic more closely with a theoretical base. We will also address the role of leadership in this approach.

Ott (1989) proposes that an organizational culture perspective be used as a framework for studying organizations, as opposed to the traditional systems and structural perspectives discussed in the management literature. Ott (1989, 2) suggests that "organization behaviors and decisions are almost predetermined" by the basic assumptions of a given culture. Other authors also identify the importance of culture to organizational functioning (for example, Gordon 1985; Peters and Waterman 1982; Wilkins and Ouchi 1983). Weick (1985), for instance, equates culture with strategy, illustrating the impact of culture on an organization's interaction with the environment. Culture, then, is seen as a critical factor in organizational functioning. Moreover, leadership is thought to be a critical factor in the management of culture (Schein 1985). Focusing on the information processing aspects of culture can aid our understanding of how leadership affects culture and how culture, in turn, influences leadership.

There is a wide variety of definitions of culture, reflecting varying levels of abstractness (Ott 1989). Our purpose is not simply to add to this lengthy list of definitions but to integrate the more widely accepted definitions of culture with information processing concepts. By viewing culture from an information processing perspective, we can take a general approach that we think "demystifies" the study of culture. Culture can be a powerful determinant of behavior; an information processing perspective can explain why culture is powerful. Moreover, in taking this approach, we believe the impact of leadership on culture can be more clearly articulated.

We propose that three primary facets of organizational culture affect culture perpetuation and change: (a) values and beliefs, (b) schemas, and (c) the type of information processing (rational, limited-capacity, expert, cybernetic) used by members. Each of these facets reflects an emphasis on different aspects of information processing. Although the facets are interrelated, highlighting these distinctions helps to illustrate how culture change may occur and shows how leaders' activities maintain or change culture. In the following section we discuss the three facets of culture in our conceptualization, as well as the primary components of Schein's (1985) taxonomy. We show how both these conceptual frameworks can be organized and understood in terms of information processing.

CULTURE FROM A THEORETICAL PERSPECTIVE

Schein's Model of Culture

Schein (1985) proposes a three-level definition of culture—artifacts, values, basic assumptions—with elements that correspond closely to our conceptualization. Schein's three levels increase in the extent to which organization members are aware of them and in their influence on behavior. (Ott [1989] also provides a thorough discussion of levels of culture). According to Schein, the first level of culture is artifacts, which include those elements of the organizational environment which are tangible reflections of the culture, such as physical layout, language, stories, ceremonies, and behavior patterns. Artifacts, though the most easily observed aspects of a culture, are the most difficult elements from which to derive meaningful insights into the true nature of the culture. We propose that artifacts result from organizational members' information processing (either controlled or automatic) applied to context-specific knowledge structures. For example, organizational members may frequently enact widely shared scripts. Consistency in cultural artifacts reflects stable underlying knowledge structures coupled with consistency in processing information using those knowledge structures. Richer information about culture, then, may be obtained through knowledge of organization members' categories and scripts, rather than artifacts.

While artifacts provide a source of interesting examples for culture researchers (for example, Deal and Kennedy 1982), they do not explain how values are formed, nor do they tell us how behavior is produced. Moreover, the study of artifacts provides us with no theoretical linkages; the bulk of the literature is anecdotal. Artifacts can provide insight into the nature of the culture, but altering the artifacts does not imply that the culture is altered. Artifacts are important in one respect: they can provide organization members with new ways of looking at things in the environment, thereby triggering (priming) alternative schemas. We look more closely at this issue in the section on culture change; however, we suggest that other aspects of culture are more worthy of investigation because they directly address the schemas used to perceive the organizational world. In the following sections, we integrate the other components of Schein's (1985) taxonomy with our framework.

Values and Beliefs

The first aspects of culture in our model are values and beliefs. Most discussions define culture as shared values (for example, Deal and Kennedy 1982; Weiner 1988) or beliefs (for example, Sapienza 1985), corresponding to Schein's (1985) second level of culture. Values and beliefs reflect organization members' sense of what should be and what is, respectively. They provide the justifications for organizational members to behave as they do at work. These aspects of culture are conscious and are used to articulate reasons for behavior. Values and beliefs have an impact when used either before behavior, as a way of generating behavior using rational information processes, or after behavior, as part of a rationalization process. Researchers need to proceed cautiously when investigating values; articulated values as rationalizations may not correspond to the processes that generated behavior. For example, people could generate behavior using automatic processes (for instance, modeling, categories, and scripts) that are not tied to the culture's espoused values but later may rely on espoused values to rationalize such behavior. Thus, values used to rationalize behavior may differ from those which produced the behavior in the first place, or initial behavior may have been generated by different types of information processes that were not directly tied to conscious values.

Schemas

The second aspect of culture in our conceptualization is schemas—knowledge structures that exist in long-term memory. These structures guide information processing in several domains, such as problem solving, and are used to generate skilled behavior, form social perceptions, and guide social interactions. Schemas related to problem solving and behavior are labeled scripts, implicit theories, or heuristics; those related to social perceptions and interactions are labeled categories, stereotypes, or implicit personality theories. Distinguishing between these two types of schemas is important to an understanding of how culture affects organizational functioning.

In Schein's (1985) conceptualization, the third level of culture consists of basic assumptions, that is, taken-for-granted perspectives of viewing the world that guide behavior. In our conceptualization, *assumptions are schemas*. Whereas values and beliefs provide justifications for behavior, assumptions actually drive behavior. Because schema-guided assumptions are automatic and most behavior is generated by limited-capacity or expert modes of information processing, stated values and beliefs may be either consistent or inconsistent with underlying assumptions, which remain unconscious. People are generally unaware of these assumptions, but they offer the greatest insight into the nature of culture. For Schein, these basic assumptions *are* the culture. Basic assumptions are "preconscious" (Schein, 14) perceptions that have become so ingrained they have fallen out of the awareness of organizational members. Ott (1989) provides several examples of how organization members have expressed surprise and even denial at the existence of some of the basic assumptions "discovered" by interventionists. Organizational members are usually aware of espoused values in contrast to assumptions, and can link values to behavior when required.

An example may further illustrate the distinction between values and assumptions. An organization may espouse an open-door policy that is explicitly stated in company documents or through employee communications. The articulated value associated with an open-door policy might be "Employee input is valued and encouraged." The unarticulated basic assumption that guides most behavior, however, may be "The open door policy is a waste of time; if you take advantage of it, it might hurt you because you will annoy your boss." Thus, the basic assumption and the espoused value are incongruent. But since the assumptions serve to guide behavior, in this example, employees may not make use of the open-door policy and management may not value employee input if the open-door policy is used. Similarly, a culture could espouse equality in the perceptions and treatment of men and women managers, but if underlying schemas are not consistent, women may be perceived and treated differently from the way men are. Of course, values and assumptions are not always at odds, but the point is that only the unspoken assumptions are true indicators of the culture and can explain behavior.

An interesting situation occurs when schemas guide the generation of behavior that is then rationalized through linkages to existing organizational values. In information processing terms, values and beliefs may serve as controlled rationalizations of behavior that was generated by more automatic processes. This situation may ensue as much from the need for political support of behavior as from the need to rationalize behavior for oneself. Limited-capacity processes often generate behavior, whereas behavior is often rationalized after the fact using controlled processing. The articulation of values may often characterize a controlled type of information processing that evokes socially desirable responses. Particularly when espoused values are solicited, basic assumptions may be incongruent with values and beliefs. As stated earlier, basic assumptions reflect automatic processing and consist of schemas that guide information processing and behavior. From this perspective, assumptions serve as cognitive filters, or primes, that predispose people to think and act in certain ways. Thus, the basic assumptions of a culture can be considered sets of cognitive schemas or knowledge structures that guide organizational behavior. Values do not always directly tap into the schemas of organizational members. Values and beliefs are nevertheless important, because they often form the basis for assumptions and can provide key mechanisms for change. Yet when viewing assumptions as the schemas possessed by those within a culture, the study of culture becomes simply the study of these schemas and how they relate to values and to type of information processing. Accordingly, we can apply the perspectives developed in chapters 2 and 5 to cultural issues.

As we noted in prior chapters, schemas affect how information is interpreted and acted upon. A considerable body of literature addresses how knowledge structures color social perceptions (for example, Lord et al. 1984), strategic management decisions (for example, Dutton and Jackson 1987; Porac and Thomas, in press), and/or serve as guides to behavior (Gioia and Poole 1984). We think the content of these types of schemas defines the organizational culture. Schema content can refer to cognitive categories that guide the interpretation of people and problems, or content can refer to scripts that are used to generate familiar behaviors. From our perspective, it is difficult to discuss strategic orientation or social perception as distinct from culture to the extent that strategic and social assumptions are unconscious guides of behavior.

Types of Information Processing

In our conceptualization of culture, we include values and beliefs, and schemas (assumptions). We add a third aspect to culture—namely, the type of information processing engaged in by organizational members. Here, we go beyond the content of the schemas and focus on the way in which information is processed irrespective of its content. Recall from chapter 2 that there are four alternative information processing models: rational, limited-capacity, expert, and cybernetic. We suggest that culture is characterized as much by the model of information processing emphasized as by the basic assumptions or schemas held by members.

Limited-capacity processes are most often used to guide culturally based behavior. Cultural assumptions are based on schemas, and information is filtered through these schemas to be interpreted, generally in ways that are shared by organizational members. The limitations of schema-based processing are well documented (for example, Nisbett and Ross 1980); therefore, the basic assumptions in a given culture can have the same limiting effect as does limited-capacity processing in other domains. Particularly in familiar situations, and because of cognitive demands in organizational settings, information is automatically filtered through existing schemas. These constraints are equally likely to occur for social perceptions, such as leadership, as they are for problem solving.

Other types of information processing also are related to culture. For experts, schemas are linked directly to behaviors or may even be organized around familiar responses. Culture can specify what behaviors are appropriate or inappropriate, thereby constraining the kinds of expert schemas that develop. While we have argued that expert processing can reduce the information processing demands associated with generating behavior, it can also substantially limit the kinds of behaviors that are considered or tested. This problem is a common criticism of culture (for example, Wilkins and Dyer [1988] suggest that the less "fluid" a culture, the less it is amenable to change). Such processing may emphasize fit within an individual or cultural context rather than fit with external environments, either inside or outside an organization. Thus, expert processing may minimize social friction within a group but may not be appropriate for reacting to novel or changing environments. These limitations can be especially severe when coupled with group processes, such as groupthink (Janis 1982), that are also limiting.

The relationship between culture and rational information processing is especially interesting. Ideally, the values of a culture would be incorporated into rational models of information processing prior to generating behavior. Thus, strategy, social actions, and interpersonal perceptions should be closely tied to cultural values. We have argued elsewhere (Lord and Maher 1990b), however, that most organizational behavior is not generated by rational processes; rather, it is more likely to involve schema-guided, limited-capacity or expert processing. In other words, it is often assumed that people weigh all alternatives before acting. This is not the case in most situations. Though we use values to explain behavior (for example, values espoused by other workers, supervisors, and leaders), we may base our behavior more on other factors (such as role modeling), and so our explanations for behavior may not be at all related to the schemas that guide behavior. One implication is that espoused values may be related to behavior only as a means of rationalizing behavior, whereas most people assume the source of behavior to be cultural values. Thus, changing values does not necessarily change behaviors in organizations. Where behavior is schema based, one would need to identify and change assumptions and schemas to produce behavioral changes. The same values may be used to describe different types of behavior. Instead of attempting to increase product quality by stressing values associated with high quality, one should instead attempt to change the knowledge structures used by workers to generate task activities.

Cybernetic processes are particularly interesting because of their role in learning and change; they are based on feedback and on comparison with relevant standards, and so discrepant feedback suggests a need for changing behavior or adjusting standards. Thus, both task behavior and social perceptions can be guided by cybernetic processing. Key determinants of how well cybernetic processing works are speed of feedback and how receptive people are to updating behaviors or standards. Some cultures tend to emphasize this type of processing, while others emphasize more rationally based approaches. Organizations that constantly deal with changing environments, such as those in the financial, fashion, and entertainment industries, should stress cybernetic processes. In these situations, cultures that emphasize cybernetic processing and learning should be especially effective. Entrepreneurial activities on the part of members would be expected and rewarded in these types of organizations. Moreover, effective leadership might be more of a source of change than a source of stability.

Our point is that behavior can be generated through entirely different types of information processing that are related to different facets of organizational culture. Consequently, the study of organizational culture and how it relates to individual or organizational functioning can be confusing. Previous research on organizational culture has focused on some of the processes we just discussed without developing a systematic understanding of how culture and information processing are interrelated. People need to be aware of what type of information processing organizational members are using so as to understand how culture is likely to affect behavior. Values are important when behavior is generated by rational, controlled processes; schemas (assumptions) are important when expert or limited-capacity processes produce behavior.

For example, one can assert that socialization is related to the culture of an organization. Nevertheless, one needs a more fine-grained understanding to gain much insight. Especially for new employees or veteran employees in unfamiliar situations, behavior may occur through rational processes based on the values of a culture in order to understand their surroundings. In this sense, commonly articulated values and beliefs are very important. Cybernetic processing is also important at this stage to enable employees to adjust standards and behavior based on task and social feedback. Over time, values and beliefs become cognitively reorganized into simplifying schemas. Coupled with limited-capacity or expert processing, such schemas can automatically generate behavior that is consistent with cultural expectations and most task demands.

Recognizing that culture can operate through different types of information processing also helps us understand why culture is resistant to change. Change attempts based on rational processing and associated with cultural values generally will not produce the intended results, because most behavior is produced by alternative types of information processing that operate on schemas that may not be linked to underlying values. Further, limited-capacity or expert processing may be highly resistant to culture change. Behavior is not readily questioned or modified without some external stimulus. With these types of information processing, it is difficult to assimilate new information into existing schemas to produce behavioral change. Information that is schema-inconsistent may even be discounted or ignored. Moreover, changes in expert processing require more than a switch in schemas; such switches require changes in the compiled procedural knowledge (Anderson 1987) that underlies skill in task behavior or social interactions.

LEADERS' IMPACT ON ORGANIZATIONAL CULTURE

Most scholars of culture have either implicitly assumed that leaders can affect culture or have tried to identify specific leader behaviors that can affect culture. Others, however, have argued that leaders are constrained by culture (for example, Pfeffer 1977). We suggest that leaders can affect some aspects of culture but are constrained by others, particularly those having an impact on processes that affect leadership perceptions. We discuss each of these issues in the following sections.

Leaders as Sources of Culture

Leaders can have an impact on organizational functioning through both direct and indirect means (Day and Lord 1988). Direct means generally reflect political influence and overt strategic decisions. In a cultural context, leaders can directly influence culture through speeches, stories, and other mechanisms intended to affect values and beliefs directly. Indirect means reflect symbolic management and the effects of leaders' schemas and labeling processes. Leaders specify strategies, make decisions, advocate values, and define acceptable approaches to problem solving. Other organization members work within this framework and over time develop scripts and categories that are consistent with leaders' strategies, values, and so forth. Thus, indirectly, leaders can create and maintain an organizational culture. Leader behavior may simply be an artifact of culture; it may be necessary to determine leaders' schemas to understand culture. These indirect means are of primary concern in this chapter.

The effects of leaders are especially apparent when considering the role of company founders in articulating a culture. Founders play a dominant role in shaping the culture in the early stages of a company's growth cycle (Schein 1985; Weiner 1988). Brief and Downey (1983) provide an interesting example of how two different founders, Henry Ford and William C. Durant, both formed automobile companies under the same market conditions and ran them under two strikingly different strategic orientations. Ford valued manufacturing efficiency, leading him to develop a vertically integrated manufacturing complex; Durant, on the other hand, focused on acquiring existing plants by buying out competitors. Vestiges of these implicit theories of organizing (Brief and Downey 1983) are still apparent in these companies today. Such differences in underlying schemas can determine differences in the way organization members interpret organizational phenomena.

Thus, the values and assumptions of company founders can continue to be reflected in the organizational culture even after the founder withdraws from the organization. One method by which a leader's personality continues to shape culture is suggested by the work of Schneider (1987). Over time, organizations tend to attract and retain those individuals who are similar to one another, while those who do not fit the culture leave. People who belong to the same organization actually are alike. Thus, because of attraction-selection-attrition cycles, early cultural forms may be perpetuated. In our terms, organizational members share the same schemas, thereby sharing and perpetuating a common culture. Here, the source of values and assumptions lies in tradition, with the same values being passed down through the years to company employees (Weiner 1988) and common experiences creating shared schemas. Thus, the values, personality, and assumptions of founders can potentially affect culture beyond the initial stages of a company's existence. Though other factors can affect the culture as the organization grows (Martin, Sitkin, and Boehm 1985), the founder's attributes can be significant in shaping culture.

Leaders as Constrained by Culture

After the initial growth period, one of the new leader's primary tasks may be the maintenance of the culture. Here, the objective is to perpetuate the culture over time, unless there are forces for change. The application of the perceptual framework developed in chapters 3 and 4 provides some interesting proposals for leadership perception during times of cultural stability. During times of stability, recognition-based and inferential processes of leadership perception may often conflict with each other. Behaviors and activities that lead to recognition as a leader may undercut attributions that a leader is responsible for the success of the organization.

Inferential leadership perceptions may be particularly limited by cultural prescriptions. Under circumstances in which the environment is relatively stable, leaders may not be perceived as engaging in leadership activities, especially those of a substantive nature. Because of the predictability of the situation, events and leaders' responses to those events are likely to be highly congruent with cultural expectations and norms. In these cases, members may attribute causality to the organization, instead of to the leader. Such reasoning is consistent with Calder's (1977) theory of leadership perception and with Jones and Davis's (1965) correspondent inference model of causal attributions. In other words, the leader may simply be perceived as operating as expected, given cultural constraints. Unless organizational phenomena deviate from cultural expectations, those phenomena are likely not to be attributed to leadership.

The extent to which recognition-based processes operate to form leadership perceptions during times of cultural stability is more complex. Here, leadership perceptions depend much more on cultural assumptions about appropriate leader behavior. Behaviors and traits that trigger leadership labels are closely tied to the cultural assumptions (categorical schemas) regarding leadership. Established organizations are likely to have shared assumptions about the type of leadership that is effective in the organization. Different cultures have unique definitions of leadership. For example, executives at General Motors were of a certain "type" (Yates 1983), and those who conformed to GM's definition of an executive were those who were promoted. In this way, culture can determine the type of leaders in an organization (Schein 1985).

During stable and predictable periods in an organization's growth cycle, leaders who conform to leadership schemas are likely to be perceived as leaders, thus expanding their latitude of discretion and power. As long as leaders conform to cultural expectations of appropriate behavior, they will continue to be perceived as leaders. Perceptions of leadership held by constituencies can affect the degree of latitude afforded to executives to make changes in the organization (Lord and Maher 1990a). Since perceptions of leadership are influenced by the culture of the organization, the change-related activities of top managers must be congruent with the leadership perceptions held by members. If not, leaders' attempts at change may fail. Members' perceptions of leadership must be altered concurrently with executive changes in symbolic activities to afford the executive with enough discretion to succeed at changing the nature of the organization's culture. Likewise, if perceivers acknowledge changes in environmental contingencies that require different strategies, they may change their prototypes of effective leaders to fit the environment. Leaders may also have to engage in different activities simply to reinforce an existing culture (Martin 1985). If leaders do not alter behavior or traits to achieve alignment with the environment, discretion is likely to be decreased (Boal, Hunt, and Sorenson 1988).

This reasoning creates a paradoxical situation for leaders. They gain social power by behaving in a way that is consistent with followers' expectations, yet deviations from those expectations, which may be necessary, limit perceptions, discretion, and power. Creating significant change may be difficult for leaders, particularly in cultures that emphasize efficiency, rational processing, and the avoidance of mistakes and conflict. Change may be much easier to manage in cultures that emphasize more cybernetic processing, wherein innovation and learning are highly valued. In these latter situations, leaders might be expected to deviate because cultural norms support proactive, innovative behaviors. We would expect the prototypes for effective leaders to be quite different in these two types of cultures. Moreover, as we suggested in chapter 3, leaders who are skilled in operating in one culture would have difficulty operating in a very different context. Cultural specificity of leadership skills is one way that culture promotes stability, even when stability may lead to misalignment with the environment. Our information processing perspective is especially important for understanding culture change, which we address in the next section.

Another key source of cultural constraint is the schemas leaders use to guide their own strategy, problem solving, and social perceptions. Here, the source of the constraint lies within the leader, not in the perceptions of organization members. This type of constraint has been mentioned frequently in the literature on strategic decision making (Hambrick and Mason 1984; Schwenk 1988; Walsh 1989). These researchers see strategic decision making as being highly dependent on the schematic orientations of executives. This view is quite similar to our argument that schemas and limited-capacity or expert processing are critical aspects of culture.

CULTURE CHANGE

Can Leaders Change Culture?

There is some debate in the literature on culture as to whether culture can be changed at all and whether culture change can be managed. We argue that leaders can manage culture change, and we suggest alternative means of change that follow from our definition of culture. Three factors can determine the extent to which leaders can affect culture: periods of crisis, latitude of discretion, and strength of culture. We discuss each of these factors below.

Periods of Crisis. The best time for culture change may be during a crisis period (Dyer 1985; Lundberg 1985) or time of organizational transition (Siehl 1985). Lundberg (1985) identifies five types of crises that can lead to change through organizational learning: environmental calamities, environmental opportunities, internal revolutions, external revolutions, and managerial crises. This learning may provide the basis for subsequent change in culture. For example, AT&T experienced an environmental calamity when the federal government restructured the long-distance telephone industry by breaking it into competing companies. (Ott [1989] provides an extended discussion of AT&T and its culture.) Similarly, models of organizational evolution (for example, Tushman and Romanelli 1985) suggest that major change occurs when external factors upset the fit of an organization with its environment. Such factors can signal a need for change and provide new information. Crisis periods may also disrupt stable political or social structures and enhance the discretion of leaders to manage change.

Discretion. During times of organizational stability, deviations from cultural assumptions regarding appropriate leadership may weaken discretion. During crisis periods, however, such deviations on the part of executives may be expected. Leaders must be able to recognize these changing expectations and assume a more proactive role when the need for change is indicated by environmental factors. Simultaneously, other organizational members may perceive changes in the environment and recognize that different types of leadership are required to respond to such changes (Boal et al. 1988). Thus, crises may elicit slightly different leadership prototypes. Crisis prototypes support more innovative, proactive leadership than prototypes compatible with stable situations do. In short, the recognition-based processes described in chapter 3 may limit discretion during stable periods but enhance discretion during crises.

While changed definitions of leadership are important, discretion also depends on the cumulative effect of past leadership perceptions, as implied by our discussion of "cognitive inertia" in chapter 5. Prior classifications based on leaders' traits, behaviors, and performance persist during periods of crisis affecting levels of discretion. Moreover, perceivers may be reluctant or incapable of switching schemas. During times of stress, members tend to rely on well-learned, schema-guided behavior and cognitive patterns. Thus, the cumulative effects of the recognition-based and inferential processes described in chapters 3 and 4 affect a leader's discretion. Perceptions summarized over time reflect both the characteristics of leaders and the various determinants of important prior events. They also reflect how well the leader has managed perceptual processes in the past.

In short, perceptual processes operate much like Hollander's (1958) notion of idiosyncratic credit. Here, leaders accumulate "perceptual credits" by conforming to expectations of what typical leaders should do as defined by the culture and can draw on these credits as a basis for exceptional leadership activities during periods of crisis. Thus, conformity to cultural norms may expand discretion to deviate from those norms when necessary.

Strength of Culture. The third key factor in the extent to which leaders can effectively change culture centers on the strength of the culture. (Saffold [1988] discusses several means of measuring culture strength.) We define culture strength as the extent to which schemas and type of information processing are shared by organizational members. The importance of culture strength is also closely tied to the evolutionary period of the organization. During times of stability, strong cultures can provide a substitute for leadership at all hierarchical levels. Culture provides values, schemas, and ways of processing information that generate appropriate individual and collective responses. Supervision is needed to make organizations function, but leadership may only be required to maintain the culture.

Still, the same processes that operate to maintain a culture can also limit the capacity of the organization to adapt to change. Strong cultures can increase the chance of organizational obsolescence (Deal and Kennedy 1982). Stereotypical interpretations of environmental situations and stereotypical responses may also result from strong cultures, since the widely shared schemas in strong cultures guide limited-capacity or expert types of processing in predictable and routinized ways. Similarly, stereotypical responses may occur from applying rational processes to values that are widely shared in a strong culture. Moreover, when environmental change requires the use of alternative schemas or values, strong cultures can inhibit the extent to which other schemas may be identified and transmitted throughout the organization.

Specific examples of such limitations can be seen in terms of the skill required by leaders to manage heterogeneous ideas. In weak cultures, or those without widely shared schemas, differences in opinion or values must be routinely managed by leaders. This experience develops skills in managing conflict and uncertainty, skills that involve developing appropriate conceptual schemas and linking them to script-guided responses. Such skills are needed by leaders during times of crisis, but they should be developed before a problem occurs, if leaders are to effectively manage such crises. Weak cultures provide leaders with a "cognitive inoculation" that increases their ability to handle crisis.

Strength of culture also interacts with discretion. In strong cultures, leaders may have discretion only within a narrow conceptualization of effective leadership, thus placing them at great risk of appearing inconsistent (Deal and Kennedy 1982). In weak cultures, however, members' ideas of what constitutes effective leadership may vary considerably across the organization. Leaders may have greater discretion in various domains, making it more effective for leaders to manage change when necessary. Thus, weak cultures are easier to change than strong cultures are.

In brief, we suggest that the management and change of culture is one activity in which leaders can and do engage. The extent to which leaders can initiate and successfully accomplish culture change depends, however, on the precipitating situational factors, such as a period of crisis, the amount of discretion, and the strength of the culture. In the following section we provide suggestions on how culture might be changed following our three-level definition of culture.

How Is Culture Changed?

We suggest that our framework can provide new insight into possible processes and mechanisms for culture change. Change can be achieved through changes in types of information processing, changes in schemas, and changes in values. Many discussions of culture change focus on changing values or beliefs through systematic, rational processes. Our perspective suggests that there are alternative means of changing an organization's culture, means that are more congruent with the ways in which people process information. We think that changing schemas is necessary for enduring culture change but, perhaps more importantly, that changing the type of information processing engaged in by organizational members is central to effective culture change.

Changing Values. Researchers concerned with transformational leadership (Bass 1985; Burns 1978; Kuhnert and Lewis 1987) emphasize the role of leaders in changing values. In fact, these researchers define transformational leadership as change that occurs through changing followers' values and goals. Yet changing the values associated with an organizational culture may not produce the intended behavioral changes, because those values may not be linked to behavior-generating scripts. When behavioral changes are desired, changing the schemas or type of information processing that produces behavior may be more effective. Simply espousing alternative values or spreading new stories and myths is not sufficient. New values and schemas derived from them must have linkages to appropriate behavioral responses and must be related to the type of information processing used by organization members.

Changing Schemas. To change people's behavior and cognitive patterns, one can change the schemas from which thoughts and behavior are derived. One factor crucial to changing schemas is the extent to which alternative schemas are available (Wilkins and Dyer 1988; Wilkins and Ouchi 1983). This idea suggests that alternative schemas must be created or identified; there must be linkages to alternative frames within an existing individual (a top-management team member or CEO), within a new individual, or through a subcultural group.

One way to change culture is for leaders to identify alternative schemas in others or to develop them within themselves. This view suggests that leaders may look to the immediate environment as a source of change or themselves serve as such a source. Leaders may make use of others' schemas through the identification of "hybrids," individuals who are accepted by the culture but whose assumptions are somewhat different from those of the mainstream (Schein 1985). Similarly, Deal and Kennedy (1982) propose that the presence of "outlaws"—individuals who violate cultural norms but can still identify with the cultural values of the organization—can provide one means of identifying alternative schemas.

To incorporate these alternative views and integrate them with the culture, leaders must have enough discretion to place those individuals in key positions. More importantly, however, leaders must be aware of the need for alternative frames, which can occur in part through changes in types of information processing. Obviously, one additional means of integrating alternative schemas at top levels of an organization is leadership succession (Dyer 1985; Schein 1985). Dyer (1985) suggests that both leadership succession and a crisis are necessary to change culture.

Leaders can also develop their own alternative schemas. We suggest, however, that this step may require shifts in types of information processing in order to be effective. Some management training techniques are designed to accomplish this objective; an example is double-loop learning (Argyris 1976). In general, though, changing from schema-guided to rational processing may be very difficult, and severe environmental constraints may be necessary for leaders to switch modes of information processing.

Another important role of leaders interested in culture change involves influencing others to adopt new schemas. Dandridge (1985) provides an interesting illustration of how change in schemas might occur at an individual level. Dandridge describes four stages of belief in a symbol. In the first stage, there is unquestioning belief in the symbol. Schema-driven processing characterizes those at this stage. At the second stage, perceivers acknowledge the possibility that there may be an alternative belief, and they may recognize that others do not believe in the symbol. In the third stage, the individual ceases to believe in the symbol. At the fourth stage, there is disbelief, but the perceiver is able to act as if he or she believes in the symbol (for example, leaders may act as if they believe in order to espouse certain values or assumptions). The potential for change may be enhanced or diminished as it relates to each of the stages. For change to occur, organizational members should be in the second or third stages. In the second stage, they acknowledge that there are other ways of viewing situations, thus beginning to acknowledge alternative schemas. At the third stage, members realize that there are alternative schemas and they may adopt them. Those at the fourth stage may be considered rational processors, consciously articulating values to influence organizational members. Thus, according to Dandridge, the extent of schema change is affected by the stage of both the influencer and the respondent.

Another means of tapping alternative schemas is through subcultures. As we have suggested, this element is more likely to be a source of change in organizations having relatively weak cultures or in those having many distinct subcultures. Subcultures that are more congruent with organizational contingencies may be identified if alternative schemas exist in an organization. Many authors assume that organizational subcultures exist (Louis 1985; Saffold 1988; Wilkins and Ouchi 1983), and strongly homogeneous cultures are rare. Subcultures may exist in "vertical slices" of an organization, such as divisions, or in "horizontal slices" of an organization, such as particular hierarchical levels or jobs (Louis 1985). Occupational communities (Van Maanen and Barley 1984) may also have distinctive subcultures. It is important that subcultures have schemas in common with the culture as a whole, in addition to having alternative schemas (Deal and Kennedy 1982; Schneider 1987). If not, these individuals or groups may be discounted or alternative frames may never be accessed by dominant subgroups.

Changing Types of Information Processing. We suggest that changing the types of information processing engaged in by organizational members is a significant means of changing culture. It is often necessary to change the type of information processing in order to access or develop new schemas. Limited-capacity or expert processing that is schema guided can significantly constrain an organization's ability to adapt to changing contingencies. Thus, cultures that automatically operate from basic assumptions are likely to continue to base behavior on these assumptions, even when doing so is inappropriate. Strong cultures are likely to function in this fashion. To change culture, then, it is necessary both to "break down" schemas that are strongly tied to responses and to question existing schemas. The schema-response linkage can be broken down by changing the type of information processing; questioning existing schemas often results from switching to cybernetic or rational modes of processing information.

Morgan (1986) stresses the importance of learning to learn—of questioning the appropriateness of actions and modifying them through cybernetic processes. New information processing capacities can lead to new organizational forms. Morgan's discussion of information processing capacities focuses on electronic forms of information processing and their effects on structure and strategic issues. We argue, however, that this logic can be extended to human information processing systems. To use an analogy, it is possible to create new organizational forms, or change the organization's culture, by changing the nature of information processes within an organization. A switch to more cybernetic forms can therefore aid in the identification or creation of alternative schemas.

One of the main points we wish to make is that it may be necessary to switch modes of information processing, moving from limited-capacity (or expert) to rational (identifying new schemas) to cybernetic (promoting organizational learning and creating a new climate for change). But these changes may not be permanent. Change may involve a shift from automatic to controlled and then back to automatic processing again, with new schemas guiding interpretations and actions. Interestingly, if organizations follow this pattern, the new culture may be inappropriately constraining because of reliance on schema-guided processes, albeit operating with new schemas. It may then be desirable for organizations to maintain a culture that emphasizes cybernetic processing (Morgan 1986), thereby making the culture more amenable to change in the future, creating what Wilkins and Dyer (1988) call a "fluid" frame.

Changing organizational goals may be one way to emphasize cybernetic processing. Goals and feedback define the "discrepancies" that are detected and corrected by cybernetic processes. Thus, by changing current goals or emphasizing new ones, leaders can trigger cybernetic processing on the part of others. Encouraging feedback-seeking behavior may also elicit more cybernetic processing. If new goals or alternative means to goals are emphasized, then feedback-seeking may be incorporated and accepted as a cultural norm. Similarly, new values can lead to cybernetic processing if leaders link them to clear standards.

SUMMARY

In this chapter we have extended our information processing framework to organizational culture and have discussed the role of leadership perceptions in perpetuating or changing a culture. We defined culture as consisting of values, schemas (categories and scripts), and type of information processing (rational, limited-capacity, expert, and cybernetic). Each of these facets of culture can lead to unique types of behavior generation.

Leaders are important in maintaining and changing cultures. Company founders can play a large part in developing a culture, through their personalities, strategic orientations, and social perceptual processes. At the same time, however, culture constrains the type of leadership that is accepted and the kinds of actions leaders can take to make needed changes, because leaders who deviate from cultural norms may be afforded less discretion to act.

Both information processing and leadership are important in instituting cultural changes in organizations. Leaders can change culture, but their ability to do so is influenced by such precipitating situational factors as crisis, the amount of discretion offered by constituents, and the strength of the culture. Finally, this chapter discussed ways in which leaders can change culture, integrating the information processing principles developed in this book. For culture change to occur, changes can be made in values, schemas, or type of information processing used. We suggest, however, that changes in schemas and information processing are necessary for culture change to produce substantially different behavior (artifacts).

Part III

Leadership and Organizational Performance

Chapter 9 ———————————————————————————

Direct and Indirect Effects of Leadership on Performance

Much of the fascination with the topic of leadership stems from its assumed impact on performance. This assumption is supported by research on inferential models of leadership perceptions, which we have already examined. Moreover, leadership as a determinant of performance has been the central focus of leadership research for several decades, with interest shifting from trait to behavioral to contingency to reciprocal influence to social-cognitive theories of leadership. The main thesis of this chapter is that much of the extant leadership literature can be better understood by distinguishing between direct and indirect means by which leaders affect performance. The distinction between direct and indirect effects on organizational outcomes has been made by other leadership researchers (Hunt et al., in press) and is equally applicable to upper- and lower-level leadership.

By *direct* means, we denote situations in which leaders influence subordinates, decisions, or policies in ways that change subordinates' task or social behaviors and have a substantial impact on performance. For example, first-line leaders may set goals or provide feedback to subordinates as a means of increasing their motivation; alternatively, such leaders may instruct or train subordinates as a means of increasing their job skills. For direct means, the source of a leader's effects on subordinates can be localized in *specific leader behaviors*. Most "behavioral" theories of leadership imply that lower-level leaders will use direct means to affect a subordinate's performance. This type of leadership process is illustrated in the top panel of figure 9.1.

Top-level leaders can also directly affect the performance of an entire organization. Rather than changing the work behavior of subordinates, however, at this level a leader's impact usually involves changing general aspects of an organization that are closely related to performance. For example, decisions to adopt new production technologies can have a dramatic effect on an organization's performance (Tushman and Anderson 1986). So, too, can decisions to reduce or expand the number of employees in an organization. Here, the

DIRECT EFFECTS

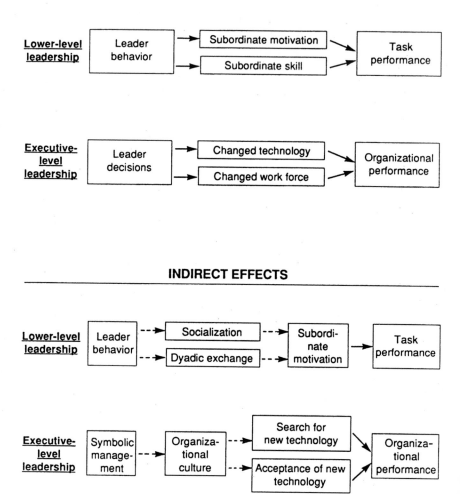

Figure 9.1
Examples of Direct and Indirect Effects of Leadership on Performance

source of impact is the nature, or substance, of top management's decision, not the manner in which the decision was reached or the decision-making style. This type of effect is shown in the second panel of figure 9.1.

Indirect means by which leaders affect subordinates (or organizations) involve the creation of ongoing conditions that then have an impact on subordinates, organizational decisions, or policies. In other words, as shown in the third panel in figure 9.1, there is an important intervening mechanism (such as subordinate socialization or culture) that transmits the influence of leaders. This intervening mechanism is not present in direct means, and it often has diffuse linkages to both the leader and performance. To illustrate such processes at lower levels of an organization, recall our analysis from chapter 7 of the development of dyadic relationships between superiors and subordinates. Graen's early VDL model (Graen and Cashman 1975) reflects a behavioral orientation in its investigation of lower-level leadership, focusing directly on leader behavior as an explanation of the type of dyadic linkage that develops. The emphasis on overt leader behavior exemplifies direct means of leadership. We argue, however, that a social-cognitive approach, acknowledging indirect means, would also be appropriate. According to this approach, dyadic relations develop over time through repeated leader-subordinate interactions, which have a lasting impact on subordinates. The development of these relationships is based on categorization processes and the expectations of the dyad members. Explaining the impact leaders have on these cognitive intervening mechanisms is a theoretically and methodologically challenging topic. We assert, however, that these indirect cognitive processes, as well as more direct leader behaviors, affect subordinate performance.

At the level of top executives, indirect means by which leaders affect organizations involve such mediating mechanisms as corporate culture, the cognitive schemas of executive teams, and management's strategic orientation. These mechanisms have diffuse causes and effects, which are spread over substantial time periods. Moreover, they are generally of a social-cognitive nature, with their causal locus considered to be distinct from the direct behavior of a CEO or top manager. For example, we saw in chapter 8 that founders' personalities can have important influences on a corporation's culture. Such means are graphically represented by the bottom panel in figure 9.1. The simplicity of this graphic representation should not, however, mislead the reader into assuming that these mechanisms are easy for organizational participants to perceive; nor are they easy for top leaders to manage. Indeed, as we will discuss later, these mechanisms have often been overlooked by leaders and leadership researchers alike.

In the following sections we will take a closer look at direct and indirect means of affecting performance at both lower and upper levels of leadership, considering the nature of each of these types of leadership.

LOWER-LEVEL LEADERSHIP

Direct Means

Direct means by which superiors affect the performance of subordinates have been one of the most central concerns of leadership theory. Leader behaviors can directly affect both the motivation and the skill levels of subordinates. It is generally thought that leaders can have a direct impact on subordinate motivation through a number of means: setting goals, providing feedback on performance, clarifying paths to goals, and contingently rewarding workers, to name a few. Some of the work on leader motivating behavior follows from the operant reinforcement tradition, examining the reinforcement activities of leaders (Komaki 1986; Podsakoff 1982; Sims 1977). For example, Komaki (1986) and her associates found that compared with ineffective supervisors, effective supervisors monitor subordinate behavior more frequently. Other research explains the effects of leader behaviors on subordinates through the impact of leader activity on specific subordinate expectancy and instrumentality perceptions (House 1971). Still other research spans both learning theory and cognitive approaches (for example, Ashour 1982; Larson 1984, 1986). Though the theoretical emphasis varies, all of this work examines the motivational impact of specific types of leadership behaviors.

As suggested by Ashour (1982), leaders can also directly affect the skill levels of subordinates through such processes as modeling. Implementation of training programs is another direct means of improving employee skill levels. Other complex skills may be refined in part through an apprenticeship or residency model, wherein direct feedback from superiors is an integral component of skill development. Finally, direct effects of leaders are often attributed to their decision-making skill (Vroom and Jago 1988; Vroom and Yetton 1973) and their ability to manage group processes.

The basic premise of this work on leadership is that leaders do something (make decisions, moderate conflict) that either directly affects performance or influences (motivates) subordinates, which in turn affects performance. Leaders are initiators who produce favorable performance outcomes, as implied by an inferential model of leadership perceptions or implicit theories about leadership.

Indirect Means

Less direct means by which lower-level leaders affect performance generally change the cognitive structures, needs, or values of subordinates. These elements take longer to change, but they may have more lasting and powerful effects on subordinate performance. Moreover, changes in these factors and their causes are difficult to pinpoint. The contrast between transformational leadership and transactional leadership provides a good illustration of the difference between indirect and direct means. Kuhnert and Lewis (1987) explain that *transformational* leaders are able both to unite followers and to change followers' goals and beliefs through articulating their own underlying values, such as justice and integrity. We classify this instance as an indirect means, because leaders create an ongoing and sustaining change in subordinates. Moreover, this change need not involve explicit influence attempts by superiors; instead, the key process is subordinate identification with leadership values. In contrast to transformational leaders, Kuhnert and Lewis describe *transactional* leaders as operating on a narrower, more concrete level, exchanging valued resources with subordinates. Such resources may be goods or rights (low-quality transactions) or interpersonal bonds (high-quality transactions), but in either case, the exchanges must occur regularly to maintain transactional leadership. Transactional leadership involves direct effects, because specific, intentional actions of leaders result in short-run effects on subordinates. Transformational leadership, in contrast, can have a lasting but indirect impact on followers.

There are many other means by which lower-level leaders can have enduring but indirect effects on subordinates. Leaders and subordinates reciprocally influence each other through normal activities, and as we explained in chapter 7, this arrangement directly affects leader and subordinate perceptions of each other as well as self-perceptions. Yet such activities also eventually differentiate subordinates into in-group and out-group status, and this classification in turn affects subordinates' activities, responsibilities, and rewards. Thus, the formation of in- and out-groups is an important indirect means by which leaders influence subordinates. Self-motivation (self-leadership), socialization, and social networks are also affected by the nature of the dyadic relationship that develops. These latter factors, too, reflect indirect leadership effects.

Some leader activities can have similar indirect effects on both in-group and out-group members. For example, participative leaders have a decision-making style that involves subordinates, thereby creating opportunities for growth and commitment to decisions that are reached (as well as creating better decisions, which can be categorized as a direct effect). More autocratic leaders may routinely exclude subordinates from decisions, thereby limiting subordinate growth or commitment. Leaders can also be a powerful source of group norms that affect the interaction of one subordinate with another. Some leaders encourage a cooperative, team-based approach, while others foster competition among subordinates. For example, at Pepsico in the early 1980s, competition between managers was advocated and expected as a means of increasing Pepsico's market share and profit. In contrast, J. C. Penney promoted a different approach, emphasizing management cooperation and loyalty to customers ("Corporate Culture" 1980). Such norms can be a powerful means of influencing interaction among management teams.

Two aspects of indirect leadership are both practically and theoretically important, although, with the exception of Graen's work (VDL), these aspects are often ignored in leadership research. First, because indirect means of leadership often have a lasting effect on subordinates and because this impact may be very general (cooperative versus competitive orientations affect many task activities), indirect effects may have a substantial influence on performance, which makes them practically important. Such effects are usually complex as well, making them theoretically interesting. Second, indirect effects are easy to overlook or misunderstand, because of their diffuse link to both superior activities and subordinate responses. These effects are difficult to identify because they may operate automatically, outside the conscious awareness of both leaders and subordinates. This tendency is accentuated because indirect effects may accumulate slowly over time. Thus, appropriate indirect means are particularly challenging for leaders to master—they are difficult to learn, and because relevant feedback is often slow, they are difficult to manage. Moreover, leaders who emphasize indirect rather than direct factors may not be perceived as having much impact. Inferential models of leadership perception will not work well when indirect means are emphasized, because leaders will not be perceived as direct causes of subordinate behavior. For similar reasons, indirect approaches may not be incorporated into widely held prototypes of leadership. Thus, while indirect leadership may work well in terms of creating good performance, it may not work well for a superior interested in creating the perception that he or she is an effective leader.

Direct and indirect means do, of course, occur simultaneously, with supervisors engaging in direct activities (such as goal setting) while those activities are also serving as the source of socialization processes that indirectly affect subordinate performance. Typical mentoring processes provide a good example of how both direct and indirect means can affect performance at the dyadic level. The mentoring process can have a direct impact on the skill leve.s of subordinates through, for example, teaching. For some skills, such as political sophistication, mentoring may be preferred to other forms of learning. Nonetheless, the mentoring relationship also serves as an indirect means of affecting performance. Quite often, the protégé adopts the values and beliefs of the mentor as part of the mentoring process. In fact, this indirect method may be one of the primary purposes of establishing a mentoring relationship. Still, changes in protégés brought about by indirect means of influence emerge slowly and are difficult to identify.

Thus far, we have discussed the difficulties associated with identifying indirect means of influence at lower levels of the hierarchy; however, these difficulties become even more problematic at upper levels of the organization. Cognitive factors (appropriate experience and insight, the ability to assimilate or analyze information, the use of an appropriate information processing style) are likely to be much more important at upper levels than factors associated with how leaders behave vis-à-vis their immediate subordinates. Cognitive factors are less observable, often making the impact of a top-level leader more ambiguous than that of lower-level leaders, particularly when assessments of a leader's influence are perceptually based. In the next section, we expand these ideas in our discussion of direct and indirect means of upper-level leadership.

UPPER-LEVEL LEADERSHIP

Direct Means

Top-level executives, such as CEOs, have a variety of means to affect organizational outcomes directly. Day and Lord (1988) classified these means ("tactics," in their terms) into three types. First, executive-level leaders *initiate internal changes* that alter organizational structures and systems. For example, two of the more dramatic changes Alfred Sloan made at General Motors in the 1920s were the creation of a multidivisional (M-form) structure and the institution of cost accounting systems (Chandler 1962). Armour and Teece (1978) document the importance of such changes by showing that M-form organizations exhibited superior performance during the early adoption period (1955–68) of this now-common organizational form. Internally focused changes also include acquiring capital (new plants or technologies), making major reductions in personnel costs (which is often the focus of internal restructuring), and increasing quality control. Second, executive leaders may directly change an organization's *capacity to adapt to external environments*. Perhaps the most frequently discussed adaptive factor concerns the effects of executive leaders on strategic planning. Yet organizational design is also important, for it affects the ability of an organization not only to coordinate internally but also to adapt to the external environment, particularly in areas where markets and competition are global rather than national. Third, executives can often directly *influence external environments*, and controlling the environment can dramatically affect performance (Hirsch 1975). Horizontal and vertical integration are two well-known techniques for altering the nature of environments. Moreover, direct political influence through government can affect regulatory environments, taxation, or trade policies, and organizations frequently engage in lobbying activities to promote their interests. As noted before, our use of the term *direct* in these examples simply means that the executive leader is the source of influence and that this influence can be associated with specific activities and a relatively short time frame. Such means are frequently discussed in the management literature as applications of power, but indirect means are often ignored.

Indirect Means

These same three classifications of Day and Lord (1988) can be used to organize indirect means by which executive-level leaders affect performance. Such means often have less specific ties to executive activities, occur slowly, and affect many different outcomes. They may also reflect cognitive changes in others induced by the activities (both intentional and unintentional) of executive-level leaders.

Indirect means of influence can be very effective at initiating internal change. Indirect effects having an impact on internal aspects of an organization include the creation or maintenance of an organizational culture, the strengthening of norms for quality or productivity, the symbolic use of information as a means of legitimizing activities (for example, reference to rational types of information processing, even though other information processing models may be more descriptive of decision processes), and the use of analogies or metaphors to facilitate communication and identification with the organization.

Indirect leadership can also be effective in building commitment to organizational objectives. For example, Westley and Mintzberg (1988) illustrate how effectively Lee Iacocca used war metaphors to guide his own thinking and to create the appropriate interpretations for the difficult actions he took when he arrived at Chrysler. During 1979 and 1980, Chrysler laid off thousands of workers. Iacocca justified this metaphorically: "But our struggle also had its dark side. To cut expenses we had to fire a lot of people. It's like a war—we won, but my son didn't come back" (Westley and Mintzberg 1988, 192). Westley and Mintzberg note that such images concealed the culpability of

Chrysler in its own financial difficulties while emphasizing the need for loyalty and joint actions.

Further, executive leaders can indirectly affect the capability of an organization to adapt to changing environments. They can, for example, influence the way environmental events are labeled. Dutton and Jackson (1987) posited that labeling (for example, threat versus opportunity) can profoundly affect the way managers think about environmental events, their communications about events, and the actions management eventually adopts. On a more detailed level, the development of schemas relevant to specific problems can also have dramatic indirect effects. For example, as noted by Schwenk (1988, 51–52), John DeLorean's difficulties in starting his own automobile manufacturing company illustrate how managers' labeling and implicit theories of the environment can affect organizational performance. John DeLorean learned at General Motors that mass production and large sales volume were the marks of a successful company. When DeLorean started his own company, he maintained this perspective and pushed production far beyond what was appropriate for his intended market. Clearly, DeLorean's belief that large sales volume was necessary was incongruent with the capacity of the market to absorb his much more expensive product. That DeLorean was unable to adapt to a different consumer market than that of GM was one of the factors leading to the demise of the DeLorean Motor Company.

Indirect leadership can also influence external environments. For example, top leaders can do much to enhance the image of their organization through civic and philanthropic activities. They can also indirectly influence government through many constituent groups (suppliers, unions). It is common for organizations to promote trade associations that then lobby for their interests in Washington.

Such indirect means of leadership are important for top-level executives, because these means may have broad effects that pertain to most members of an organization (such as culture) and because their effects may endure for a long time. We suspect, though, that these means of leadership are very difficult to manage effectively, and they are very difficult for others to correctly assess. As with lower-level leadership, indirect means are less salient, are less likely to be noticed, and therefore may not be incorporated into common leadership prototypes, particularly prototypes learned through experience with lower-level leadership. Thus, leaders may not have readily available prototypes to help guide indirect leadership actions. Further, observers (both inside and outside an organization) may not interpret these indirect activities as conveying leadership. Though the indirect effects of lower-level leaders are manifest through a small group of subordinates, the comparable effects of CEOs may be organizationwide. Thus, both the causal actions of CEOs and the specific group affected may be difficult for observers to pin down with much certainty. Correctly assessing the impact of leaders is closely related to an inferential approach to leadership, implying that *indirect* leadership activities are not likely to produce perceptions of leadership. Since we argue that inferential models are particularly important for upper-level leadership, we expect that CEOs who are especially skilled at indirect types of leadership may not be perceived as exerting as much leadership as equally effective CEOs who emphasize more direct leadership activities.

Consider again the contrast between Lee Iacocca and Philip Caldwell, noted at the outset of this book. Iacocca was directly involved in developing the highly visible, government-backed plan to rescue Chrysler; in dramatically cutting costs at Chrysler; in making such key acquisitions as Lamborghini and American Motors; in deciding to offer extended warranties for Chrysler products (Halberstam 1986, 568); and in advertising many of the Chrysler products. Such activities exemplify direct leadership. Of course, Philip Caldwell was also involved in many direct leadership actions at Ford, such as extensive cost cutting and the decision to "bet the company" (Doody and Bingaman 1988, 34) on the Taurus program. But Caldwell also changed many factors at Ford that had more indirect effects on performance. He created a fundamentally different approach to automotive design that was outwardly rather than inwardly focused, relying extensively on incorporating marketing research into the design process. He also dramatically changed the corporate culture by developing a consumer- and product-oriented design and production process (as opposed to the production-oriented approach of General Motors); emphasizing teamwork, coordination, and extensive involvement of production workers (and suppliers) in the design and production process; instituting employee involvement programs that were supported by top management; and developing a profit sharing program for hourly workers (average bonuses for 1987 were $3,700 per worker) (Doody and Bingaman 1988). In other words, Caldwell changed basic values and the basic schemas for management at Ford. Such changes were far-reaching and had a lasting impact on the company, its products, and its workers, but perceivers did not credit Caldwell for these successes at Ford.

We assert that Iacocca and Caldwell were perceived quite differently in part because of their fundamentally different approaches to leadership: Iacocca emphasized more direct means of affecting performance, and Caldwell emphasized more indirect means. These differences made Iacocca's actions an obvious explanation for the turnaround at Chrysler, whereas the causal impact of Caldwell's changes was less obvious. Thus, casual observers could more easily apply inferential models of leadership perception to Iacocca than to Caldwell.

ASSESSING LEADER CAUSALITY

Since we have previously argued that inferential modes of leadership perception are crucial to top-level executives, in this section we will integrate the ideas developed so far in this chapter with the perceptual viewpoint developed in chapters 3 and 4. In those chapters we explained that perceptions of followers are crucial for executive-level leadership because at that level, leaders generally cannot rely on formal rewards and sanctions to buttress their influence. Being perceived as an effective leader affords a wider range of activities that are accepted by key constituents. The previous discussion implies, however, that many important activities of executive-level leaders will not be translated into leadership perceptions through either prototype matching or inferential processes, because they are indirect. This issue can be explored in more depth by analyzing probable causal ascriptions for both direct and indirect means by which lower- and upper-level leadership occurs.

In chapter 2 we discussed alternative models of information processing, illustrating how each could be applied to the issue of explaining causal attributions. Such analyses can involve controlled, rational processes, but we asserted that observers are more likely to use limited-capacity or expert models. Expert models may be used by perceivers who frequently assess the leadership qualities of top executives (for instance, assessment center raters, management analysts), but for most observers, we expect that limited-capacity models would provide the best descriptions of their cognitive processes in assessing leadership at the executive level. A perceiver using limited-capacity processes might assess causality by looking for explanations that are closely associated with an outcome, in terms of either time or space. Such a perceiver would also rely on salience and would conduct a very limited causal evaluation, stopping with the first satisfactory explanation for an event (Lord and Smith 1983; Taylor and Fiske 1978).

Consider first the issue of assessing causality for lower-level leaders. We maintain that much of these leaders' impact on subordinates results from directly observable behaviors of the leader vis-à-vis the subordinate. In addition, the behavior of one's boss is highly salient to a subordinate or other observers. We assert that many important effects occur through changes in subordinate motivation or ability. Such effects occur within a relatively short time span and often in the context in which task performance occurs. For example, in a nationally televised Monday-night football game in December 1989, a member of the Chicago Bears was penalized for running into the punt kicker. Immediately, Coach Mike Ditka forcefully yelled at the offending player. Our point is that salient leader behavior such as this should be noticed and associated with changed subordinate behavior, because it is contiguous in both time and space. The next time the player was required to attempt a punt block, he did not make the same mistake. In situations like these, perceivers should be able to see a clear causal chain from leader behavior to subordinate reactions to improved performance; leaders who set difficult goals have subordinates who work hard and perform well.

At lower hierarchical levels, indirect leadership (such as the socialization of subordinates) may still be salient, but it is the cumulative effect of such behaviors, rather than any single event, that is significant. The association between leader behavior and its impact on subordinates would be lower. In addition, the relationship between changes in subordinates and performance would also be lower. Thus, we expect that leaders would be less likely to be seen as being causally important for indirect effects occurring through changes in the cognitive structures, needs, or values of subordinates.

At upper levels of an organization, the causal role of leaders is even less clear. As explained earlier, top-level leaders can directly affect organizational performance by changing those general aspects of an organization which have a broad impact on performance. For example, such leaders may institute technological change. This type of change would undoubtedly be salient, but its impact might take time to occur and the performance effects could be uneven—unlearning old skills and relearning new ones might be required before technological change translated into improved performance. Hence, the temporal association between leader activities and improved performance could be low, attenuating perceptions of the leader's causal impact.

Indirect means used by top-level leaders may be even less clearly associated with a leader's activities. Such factors as corporate culture, the cognitive schemas of executive teams, and the strategic orientation of management have multiple and diffuse linkages with both the activities of top-level leaders and the performance of organizations. Such linkages may involve comparatively long periods of time. Thus, perceivers do not expect strong associations between such factors and either leadership or performance. Further, we posit that a leader's role in affecting such factors is low in salience. Thus, a limited-capacity model would predict that perceivers would not see leadership as causing performance when it operated through such indirect processes.

Our assessment of causal ascriptions that are likely to be made to leaders is summarized in table 9.1, which illustrates the main effects that both leadership level and type of leadership tactic have on such ascriptions. This table shows that lower-level leaders should be perceived as having a moderately high impact on the performance of their subordinates, whereas top-level leaders may be perceived as having a moderately low impact on organizational performance. Whether top-level leaders do in fact have a critical effect on performance will be addressed in the next chapter.

Implications

Perhaps the most important implication of this chapter is that executives need to be aware of the existence of indirect means for affecting performance. Such means can have long-lasting and pervasive effects on organizational outcomes, but they can be easily overlooked and misunderstood by perceivers.

Three problems derive from our assertions that perceivers will have difficulty assessing the causal role of executive-level leaders and that reliance on typical heuristics (association, salience) will produce low assessments of an executive's causal impact on organizational performance. First, if we are correct in asserting that inferential models of leadership perception are emphasized at the top level, then top-level executives may have difficulty being perceived as leaders. This difficulty seems especially likely if a leader's traits and activities do not match widely held prototypes of effective leaders. Thus, top-level leaders may experience hardship in developing the type of perceptually based power they need to manage their organizations effectively. These problems are compounded when top leaders must influence activities outside as well as inside their organization.

Image management activities are one way executives can affect the credit they receive for indirect means of influence. Even factors that many executives might view as trivial can affect perceivers' leadership attributions. As we saw in the Phillips and Lord (1981) study discussed in chapter 4, camera angles have been found to affect perceptual salience, which in turn were found to affect causal attributions. Thus,

TABLE 9.1
Causal Ascription to Leaders

Means of Influencing Performance	Organizational Level	
	Low	High
Direct	High	Moderate
Indirect	Moderate	Low

the positions leaders occupy while sitting at tables or standing at ceremonies could affect whether they are perceived as leaders. Ronald Reagan, with his acting background, was knowledgeable of the importance of "camera angle" effects and how they affected perceptions. Many executives, however, are probably unaware of the impact such factors can have. Thus, it is crucial for executive leaders to understand the processes involved in causally assessing both direct and indirect means of influence and to appreciate the limitations they may face in being perceived as a strong leader. As we saw in chapter 6, these issues are particularly critical for female executives: women have the additional problem of being perceived as leaders when widely held stereotypes work against that perception.

The second problem occurs when perceivers (and leaders), experiencing difficulty in accurately assessing causality, substitute culturally based assumptions for precise causal assessments. Here, limited-capacity rather than more rational information processing predominates. It is easy to assert that leaders can (or should be able to) control all factors that may affect the performance of an organization. This myth is comforting to people dependent on an organization, and it may be perpetuated by leaders as a means of enhancing their power. For leaders, this myth has benefits when organizations are performing well, because leaders are given more credit than they may deserve; when performance is poor, however, leadership is seen as the principal cause of problems. As Sutton and Callahan (1987) have documented, this myth of *sufficient* leader control can stigmatize leaders of corporations that fail dramatically. Because CEOs personally accept responsibility for failure, stigmatization is often accompanied by extreme guilt and personal anguish on their part.

Third, effective learning is undercut by the difficulty in easily assessing top executives' causal impact on an organization. Organizations have difficulty learning what types of leaders and what types of leader activities produce effective performance. Without such information, cultural beliefs are likely to exert too strong an influence on the selection and grooming of leaders. We have already noted Yates's (1983) descriptions of the problems at General Motors created by reliance on what he calls the "Detroit mind" in selecting executives. Overcompliance with this restrictive stereotype kept innovative leadership out of GM at a time when innovation was sorely needed.

Leaders, too, have difficulty learning from their own actions when it is hard to assess causality. We argued in chapter 2 that cybernetic models of information processing were both effective and cognitively easy to apply. These models may yield accurate judgments when more rational models are difficult to use. Yet in situations in which feedback is slow and multiple factors affect performance, cybernetic information processing would not work so well. Instead, to supplement rational information processing, leaders are forced to rely on their own expertise, often gained through years of experience in a particular culture. Compliance with the "default values" provided by an organizational culture reflects leaders' limited ability to process information. Expert information processing models may work well in periods of stability (as the 1950s were for GM) but may be quite limiting when situations change dramatically and new approaches are required (GM in the 1980s).

SUMMARY

In this chapter we have explained the difference between direct and indirect means of leadership. Direct means refer to those leadership activities which explicitly influence the behavior of subordinates or the strategies of organizations. Direct means form the basis for most existing leadership and management theory. Indirect means, however, are often ignored in the literature, yet they also form a powerful mode of affecting subordinate and organizational performance. Indirect means involve establishing certain conditions, such as socialization processes or culture, which then affect subordinate and organizational performance. Indirect means are more diffuse and abstract than direct means but are just as important in determining organizational outcomes. This problem in identifying and assessing indirect means of influence makes our social-cognitive approach particularly relevant.

Indirect and direct means of leadership can be distinguished at both lower hierarchical levels and executive levels of an organization. At lower levels, direct means of leadership reflect explicit methods of securing subordinate performance, such as goal setting, feedback, and reward contingencies. Indirect means of leadership at lower levels involve altering the values, needs, and schemas of subordinates. Indirect leadership may operate through the quality of the dyadic relationship or through socialization processes. At upper levels, leaders can have a direct impact on organizational performance by affecting technology and organizational structure or by adopting certain strategies for interacting with the environment. Executives can also indirectly affect an organization's performance through culture and norms.

In the final section of this chapter we noted that indirect means of leadership are difficult to identify and to associate with either specific leaders or organizational performance, particularly at executive levels. At upper levels, the length of time between leader behaviors or decisions and outcomes related to those behaviors or decisions is often considerable, perhaps spanning several years. Moreover, often specific leader behaviors cannot be identified. In short, top-level executives may have difficulty being perceived as leaders.

Chapter 10

Leadership Succession

LEADERSHIP PARADOX

*P*opular writers like Peters and his associates (Peters and Austin 1985; Peters and Waterman 1982) emphasize the importance of executive leadership in creating "excellent" organizations. Others see executive leadership as a solution to crucial problems. For example, Yates (1983, 213), after an extensive critique of the American automobile industry, concludes that we need new leadership, not more resources. Similarly, Kotter (1988) argues that more leadership is needed for organizations to successfully adjust to greater worldwide competition and increased complexity. Such thinking is consistent with the popular belief that effective leadership *causes* organizations to perform effectively.

In contrast to such thinking, academic researchers have challenged the importance of leadership (Calder 1977; Pfeffer 1977; Salancik and Pfeffer 1977). This line of reasoning has been extended by Meindl, Ehrlich, and Dukerich (1985, 79), who assert that laypeople have developed highly romanticized, heroic views of what leaders do and what they can accomplish. These researchers argue that leadership is a perception through which people provide a simple causal explanation for organizational events that actually have complex causes. Further, Meindl and his colleagues suggest that such perceptions are *biased* in attributing causality to leadership in the absence of direct, unambiguous information that permits one rationally to infer the locus of causality. Although this romanticized conception of leadership is comforting to those who prefer to see causality in other people rather than in complex organizational and environmental phenomena, it is not necessarily accurate. Thus, this academic group asserts that leadership is best conceptualized as an *explanatory category* with an ambiguous relationship to performance.

Academic interest in leadership as a romantic but impotent cause of performance can be traced to three sources. First, as we explain in this book, leadership is a perceptual phenomenon, one that has an important symbolic component. Building on the early work of Staw (1975), Calder (1977), and Pfeffer (1977), this perceptual view of leadership has gained increased attention by academic researchers. (We have already examined most of this work.) Second, Pfeffer (1977) has persuasively argued that there are several reasons leaders have little impact on organizational outcomes—leaders are a rather homogeneous group, due to restrictive selection processes that favor only certain, limited styles of behavior; the actual discretion of leaders is constrained by a number of organizational factors; and leaders can typically affect only a few of the variables that have an impact on organizational performance. Third, empirical studies of leadership succession have generally been interpreted as showing a minimal impact of leadership on performance. For example, Brown states, "Once other factors influencing effectiveness are accounted for, it is likely that leadership will have little bearing on organizational performance" (1982, 1).

In short, most laypeople think leadership is a significant determinant of performance. Paradoxically, many scientists have recently questioned the impact of leadership on performance, but they see leadership as an important perceptual construct. Resolving this paradox is the central concern of this chapter.

Perceptions and Performance

These alternative views of leadership seem paradoxical, but in large part they merely reflect the complex processes that have already been discussed in this book. Four perspectives crucial to understanding this area are depicted graphically in figure 10.1. The top part of this figure repeats our distinction between indirect and direct effects from the preceding chapter. We use this model as a theoretical basis, assuming its validity for the moment, for analyzing both laypeople's and scientists' perspectives on leadership and performance. In this chapter we will keep this theoretical model simple, separating tactics only into direct and indirect groupings and ignoring differences pertaining to specific tactics (for example, changing culture).

In the preceding chapter (see table 9.1) we discussed the problems perceivers (both leaders and observers alike) have in assessing the causal impact of both direct and indirect activities performed by top-level leaders like CEOs. Our main argument was that indirect tactics are difficult to link to *specific* leadership behaviors and that both direct and indirect tactics are difficult to link to performance. These difficulties occur because both tactics and their effects are distributed over time, rather than being focused in a narrow period of time. Further, cognitive changes, while more important at upper than at lower levels, are also difficult to observe. The net result of such

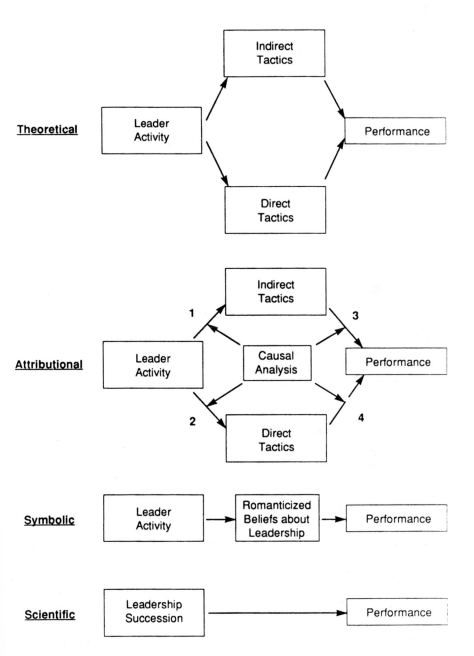

Figure 10.1
Alternative Models of the Leader-Performance Relationship

difficulties is that simple attributional processes based on limited-capacity models do not work well in accurately perceiving leaders' effects. In addition, rational attributional analyses are generally precluded by the complexity of the phenomena, lack of relevant information, time delays between causes and effects, and other cognitive demands on perceivers trying to assess the effects of top-level leadership. Therefore, perceivers will have great difficulty discerning causal chains linking *specific* leader activities to specific performance outcomes. In other words, they will have great difficulty applying the attributional model shown in the second panel of figure 10.1. It is in this sense that Meindl and his colleagues (1985) are correct in stating that direct, unambiguous information for rationally assessing the effects of leadership is absent for most perceivers. We assert that in most situations, perceivers simply cannot perform the required causal analysis. This assertion does not mean that leaders have no causal impact; rather, it simply means that the causal impact of top-level leaders cannot be analyzed using the typical procedures laypeople apply to normal social perceptions.

The alternative for most perceivers is to substitute general information about leadership for a detailed, empirical analysis. It is this process that we depict in the third panel of figure 10.1 and that corresponds to a symbolic or romanticized model of leadership. Here the activities of top leaders make them salient symbols, but the linkage to performance is supplied by perceivers' beliefs or implicit theories, colorfully labeled "romanticized beliefs" by Meindl, Ehrlich, and Dukerich (1985). In this model, the mediating linkage between leadership and performance is not empirical, since it is difficult for perceivers to establish ties to any specific activity or tactic through causal analysis. Instead, performance and leadership are linked by the cumulative knowledge and experience a perceiver has about leadership, reflecting limited-capacity (or in some cases expert) models of information processing.

Meindl et al. (1985) suggest that leadership attributions are especially likely to occur for extremely good or extremely poor performance, because extreme performance requires a causal explanation, and it is reassuring for perceivers who are dependent on favorable outcomes to attribute causality to top leaders. The work of Meindl and his colleagues is based on students' evaluations of short written scenarios about business performance, discussions of leadership by the business media (*Wall Street Journal* and other business periodicals), and scholarly interest in leadership as indicated by the number of dissertations on this topic. All these sources provide support for Meindl et al.'s predicted curvilinear relationship between attributions to (or coverage of) leadership and performance, with leadership receiving more emphasis as performance became very good or very poor. It should be stressed, however, that though such explanations may reflect general "romanticized beliefs" about leadership, *these explanations are not necessarily inaccurate*. In fact, it would be quite surprising if there was not substantial validity to the widely held belief that top-level leaders affect the performance of an organization (or a nation). Further, extremes in performance may very well be associated with exceptional actions by top leaders.

The key issue is how we can develop a more insightful substitute for romanticized beliefs about leadership. There are two possibilities. First, we can carefully apply a theoretical or analytic perspective (as we do in this book). Second, we can collect empirical data and use statistical techniques to analyze relationships that otherwise could not be clearly perceived. This second approach is precisely the one represented in the bottom panel of figure 10.1, where researchers have sought to link empirically one important leadership event—the succession of an organization's CEO—to changes in an organization's performance. Such empirical analyses help us see effects *associated* with leadership but, as noted by Day and Lord (1988), do not help us see what tactics produced these effects or whether the effects were caused by leaders or some external factor. Succession studies, however, are a first step in moving from romance to science in relation to executive-level leadership. For this reason, the findings from studies of executive succession are covered in some detail in the next section.

Leadership Succession

Reinterpretation of Classic Succession Studies. Leadership succession is defined as any change in the formal leader of a group or organization. Successions may be planned or unplanned, or forced or unforced, and the nature of these contextual variables may be important in understanding the effects of succession (Friedman and Singh 1989). Studies of leadership succession are a popular method for analyzing the effect of leadership on performance. The outcome variables typically incorporated in succession studies include winning percentages for athletic teams and such indices of financial health as profit, income, or revenue for other kinds of organizations. The usual approach is to analyze the performance changes associated with succession by means of multiple regression. Several prominent studies (Lieberson and O'Connor 1972; Salancik and Pfeffer 1977; Weiner and Mahoney 1981) use regression analysis to estimate the amount of variance in performance associated with succession, which indicates the *maximum potential* effect of leadership. Many factors change when top leaders do, but if succession has no impact on performance, then, researchers have reasoned, it is implausible for leaders to have much of an impact.

Two of the most widely cited succession studies are those by Lieberson and O'Connor (1972) and Salancik and Pfeffer (1977). Since these are the principal sources of empirical support cited by organizational researchers claiming that leaders do not affect organizational performance, we will briefly summarize their approach and findings (Day and Lord [1988] provide a more detailed analysis). In a study of 167 corporations in 13 industries over a period of 20 years, Lieberson and O'Connor analyzed changes in sales, earnings, and profit margin associated with the succession of the president or chairperson of the board. They compared succession effects with year, industry, and company influences by apportioning performance variance to these sources. They found that leader succession accounted for far less of the performance variance than either industry (which explained 19 to 29 percent of the variance, depending on the performance measures) or company (which explained 23 to 65 percent of the variance for the different performance measures). These results contrasted with the variance explained by leadership succession, which was 6.5 percent for sales, 7.5 percent for net income, and 15.2 percent for profit margin, *with an assumption of no time lag between succession and its effects on performance*. But while the effects of succession on sales and net income did not vary with different lags, the percentage of variance in profit margin that was explained by succession increased dramatically, to 32 percent, when lags of 2 or 3 years were used. Profit margin is actually the more important variable for examining leadership effects, because it is unconfounded with the size of a company. Much of the company effects on sales and net income simply reflect the fact that larger companies had higher sales and income, which has very little to do with leadership succession effects. For performance as measured by profit margin 2 or 3 years after succession, leadership (32 percent) actually explained more variance than either industry (27 percent) or company (22 percent) (Lieberson and O'Connor 1972, 124). Thus, what Lieberson and O'Connor actually showed is that new leaders can have substantial effects on profits (perhaps by reducing costs), even though they have less effect on sales or net income. Nevertheless, even the smallest effect associated with succession (6.5 percent of the variance in sales) can be very important. Further, there was no control for the ability of the leader involved. Although replacing a leader with another person of similar ability and orientation should not be expected to have much effect, replacing a leader with someone of much different ability or orientation should have more impact (Pfeffer and Davis-Blake 1986; Smith, Carson, and Alexander 1984).

In another widely cited succession study, Salancik and Pfeffer (1977) examined political rather than business leadership by analyzing the effects of mayoral succession. They looked at mayoral succession for 30 U.S. cities for the years 1951–68, with a total of 172 different mayors. They examined the relative effects of city, year, and mayor on the dependent variables of property tax revenues, general debt, and eight expenditure variables (police, fire, highways, and so on). When the budget variables were computed in *total dollars*, the effects of the mayor variable was limited to about 10 percent of the variance; however, these effects are misleading, because of the large but theoretically trivial effect of city size. (Larger cities spend more money in all budget categories.) When budget variables were computed as *proportions of the total city budget* to control for size effects, the variance explained by mayors was still about 5 percent for property tax revenues (which are usually constrained by voters), but it increased to 24 percent for general debt and to 19 percent for the median for all expenditures. (Comparable effects on median expenditures were 3 percent for year and 59 percent for city.) In other words, different mayors were associated with dramatic differences in debt levels and expenditures when city size was controlled, but city was still an important variable.

In summary, what these two classic succession studies show is that when business or city size is controlled and when sufficient time lags are used, succession can have a dramatic impact on key performance indices. This conclusion is supported by other, more methodologically sophisticated studies. Weiner and Mahoney (1981) examined the effects of CEO changes in a sample of 193 manufacturing companies over a 19-year period. By effectively controlling for size and order effects, they found that the CEO had a substantial impact on some organizational variables. For example, stewardship (that is, leadership succession) explained 43.9 percent of the profitability (profits/assets) variance and also accounted for 47 percent of the variance in stock prices.

Leadership Succession and Ability. Thomas (1988) interprets analyses of succession effects somewhat differently. He argues that variance due to such variables as company are largely irrelevant in estimating a leader's effect; they should be controlled before investigating the potential effects of leadership succession. Following this logic, Thomas argues that the key analysis is the extent to which succession explains the unexplained variance that remains after discounting the effects of nonleadership variables. Using this approach in a study of 12 United Kingdom retailing firms over a 20-year period, Thomas found that the unexplained performance variance attributable to leadership was 61.4 percent for profit, 66 percent for sales, and 51.2 percent for profit margin. He also reports very similar results for two other studies of leadership succession when the same analyses are used.

These substantial effects of succession occurred in spite of the fact that neither Weiner and Mahoney (1981) nor Thomas (1988) controlled for leader ability. Two more recent studies that did control for ability found it to be an important variable. In a study using a sample of Methodist ministers, Smith, Carson, and Alexander (1984) assessed the impact of leaders on organizational performance. They found no effect of succession *by itself* on dependent variables of attendance, membership, property value, operating budget, or total tithing. They also, however, identified high-performing ministers, based on prior salaries, and found that this distinction had a significant incremental effect on organizational performance for all five dependent variables, despite the large amount of variance accounted for by the control variable of the church's performance in the minister's first year of service (Median $R^2 = .701$). While significant, the effects of high-performing ministers versus other ministers were generally small, explaining less than 4 percent of the variance for every dependent variable.

In a study of basketball coaches' influence on team performance, Pfeffer and Davis-Blake (1986) reported similar findings. They found that succession had no effect on performance when the prior performance of the team and the number of new players were controlled. But when the competence of the new coach (as indicated by several measures of prior performance or experience) was included in the analysis, succession significantly affected subsequent performance. Succession by coaches who had previous professional coaching experience and by coaches who performed well with prior teams resulted in improved performance compared with that of coaches who lacked experience or had poorer performance with prior teams. Again, however, these effects were not large. The incremental variance explained by the combined ability/succession variable was less than 2 percent for all equations. Pfeffer and Davis-Blake argue that whether leaders affect performance cannot be answered merely by looking at organizational performance before and after succession; instead, investigators must examine the conditions that occur around succession (such as changes in team or organizational personnel) and the characteristics of successors, particularly ability and experience.

In short, studies by Smith and his colleagues (1984) and Pfeffer and Davis-Blake (1986) show that talented leaders can make a difference, even in such highly constrained situations as churches or basketball games. The effects found in these two studies do not, however, appear to be nearly as large as those from the prior three studies of succession.

Upper- versus Middle-level Succession.   Part of the difference between the succession studies conducted by Smith et al. (1984) and Pfeffer and Davis-Blake (1986) and the first three succession studies we discussed (Lieberson and O'Connor 1972; Salancik and Pfeffer 1977; Weiner and Mahoney 1981) pertains to the organizational level of the leaders investigated. The first three studies investigated the effects of top-level administrators (CEOs and mayors), whereas the latter two investigated the effects of leaders who represent more middle levels in an organizational hierarchy (church ministers and basketball coaches). Both studies of middle-level leaders reported no succession effects when the ability of the successor was ignored, and small but significant effects when such ability was used as a predictor. The studies of top-level leaders, when analyzed appropriately, reported much larger effects. This difference suggests that the effects of leader succession would be much less for middle- than for upper-level leaders. This conclusion is precisely what Day and Lord (1988) reached in their review of the succession literature.

Day and Lord (1988) have noted that many studies of succession have investigated athletic managers or coaches. They argue that such leaders are actually middle- rather than top-level management. These middle-level managers make decisions that affect performance on a day-to-day basis, and they may also have an impact on the motivation and development of their players. These managers do not, however, create the underlying conditions that differentiate exceptional athletic franchises from mediocre ones. Such long-term factors as the organization's overall atmosphere, the quality of players, the strength of the organization's scouting staff and farm system, and, in modern athletics, the salary levels paid are influenced more by the owners and general managers of athletic teams. Thus, Day and Lord argue that athletic coaches (and other middle-level managers) have much smaller effects on performance than top-level officers do.

In reviewing many succession studies in the area of athletics, Day and Lord (1988) found very clear and consistent results. Changing field leaders does not significantly affect performance. These effects held for major league baseball team managers (Allen, Panian, and Lotz 1979; Gamson and Scotch 1964; Grusky 1963), for head coaches of basketball teams (Eitzen and Yetman 1972; Pfeffer and Davis-Blake 1986), and for head coaches of National Football League teams (Brown 1982). The only qualification of these effects is the Pfeffer and Davis-Blake study, which found small but significant effects of succession only when the ability of the new coach was considered.

Some additional comments on this work are warranted. It is unfortunate that such a large proportion of the succession studies involves athletic performance. We think these types of organizations are overemphasized because they have such clear and readily available performance indices such as winning performance. Athletics are also highly salient in this society. Yet they are not very good arenas for studying the effects of leadership, because they involve middle- rather than upper-level leaders. Moreover, in athletics, performance is largely a function of the quality of personnel available (Jones 1974), which factor is generally beyond the control of coaches. It should also be noted that many of these studies have investigated only brief time frames, typically examining succession effects in the season in which succession occurred; longer lag times may be required for all the effects of managerial succession to occur. Although short time frames may be appropriate for effects involving player morale, long-term efforts at rebuilding a ball club and player development involve lag times of perhaps several years.

For these reasons, we do not believe the results from studies of coach or field manager succession should be generalized to more typical public or private organizations. If future researchers want to continue to investigate succession effects in athletics, they should use longer time lags and look at the effects of general managers and owners, not just coaches. To use a salient example, we believe that George Steinbrenner has had more effect on the performance of the New York Yankees than Billy Martin or Lew Pinella.

Utility and Leadership

Utility analysis provides a quantitative technique for assessing the financial contribution to an organization of a particular action--buying a new plant or a piece of equipment, instituting a training program, or hiring a new leader. Thus, when applied to the effects of leadership, utility analysis can provide a complement to the studies of succession in terms of gauging such effects. One recent study by Barrick, Day, Lord, and Alexander (1989) took this approach, yielding interesting results. Their study combined archival data from 132 industrial organizations from the Fortune 500 group for a 15-year period (1971-85) with survey data from a sample of 41 financial analysts. These data were used to estimate a number of parameters, which, when combined, provided a point estimate for the utility of hiring an effective leader. Two parameters are of particular interest. The first is an estimate of the value of one performance standard deviation (SD_y), which can be directly estimated (Schmidt, Hunter, McKenzie, and Muldrow 1979). The study by Barrick et al. had the financial analysts estimate this parameter in terms of the percentage impact of an average executive on the net income of a Fortune 500 industrial company. The average estimate for this parameter was 15 percent. This average was then converted into a dollar-value estimate by applying the percentage to actual net income values from the sample of 132 industrial firms. The second noteworthy parameter is an estimate of effect size (d_t) associated with having a good as compared with a mediocre leader.

This estimate was obtained by differentiating executives for these 132 firms into "effective" and "mediocre" groups according to their salary (after adjusting for the size of the assets under a leader's control). This grouping was based on the reasoning that higher-performing executives would command a higher salary. The effect size then, is simply the standardized difference in performance for the firms of these two groups of executives. In the study by Barrick and his colleagues, effect sizes for different dependent variables and different subgrouping procedures converged on a value of .21.

To estimate utility, these two parameters are multiplied and are adjusted by a number of accounting factors, such as the discount rate (cost of capital), average tenure of executive leaders, and recruiting costs, using standard utility estimating procedures (Alexander and Barrick 1987). Barrick et al. found that the utility of having a good rather than mediocre executive was about $24 million for a Fortune 500 industrial firm, with a 95 percent confidence interval from about $8 million to $40 million. This effect was significantly above zero, and it illustrates the substantial impact executives can have on the performance of their firms.

To interpret these results properly, some methodological factors should be considered. First, utility is not the effect of a leader in a single year; rather, it is the discounted effect of executives on their firms' performance over an average of 10.33 years' tenure with their firm. Second, financial analysts' estimates of the effect of executive leaders on the net income of firms are subjective. Nevertheless, the financial analysts' estimate of 15 percent agrees quite closely with the average effects of succession studies that are derived from objective data. For example, Lieberson and O'Connor's (1972) data show an average effect size of .148 for leadership succession with 3-year time lags. Salancik and Pfeffer's (1977) data yield an average effect size of .161 across all budget categories when computed as proportions of the total city budget. Third, these firms were quite large. The dollar value would, of course, be smaller for executives with smaller firms. The percentage effect, however, may be even larger for small firms. Since there are fewer constraints on executives in small as compared with large firms, CEOs at small firms may have larger effects on key variables (Miller and Droge 1986).

When all these factors are considered, there appears to be substantial utility in dollar terms of having a good as compared with a mediocre chief executive. Though based on just one study, this conclusion is consistent with the results of succession studies of upper-level corporate and political leaders. This approach to understanding executive utility does, however, require further examination.

There is also an alternative possibility that the effect size (d_t) used in estimating utility reflects something other than an executive's ability. For example, differences in executive compensation may merely reflect the fact that successful firms pay executives more, regardless of the CEO's contribution, an idea that contrasts with Barrick et al.'s interpretation of differential compensation as a reward for the executive's actual effect on a firm's performance. One way to address this possibility is to estimate utility for a subsample of firms in which the salaries of executives are closely related to these individuals' effect on an organization's performance. According to Tosi and Gomez-Mejia (1989), if a firm is owner controlled (if a single individual or an institution like a bank owns at least 5 percent of its stock), performance and executive salary are more strongly related than in management-controlled firms, in which no single party or institution owns at least 5 percent of the stock. Thus, utility analysis based on owner-controlled firms should be less susceptible to this alternative interpretation. Our current research is examining this issue.

To summarize the chapter to this point, we have explained the nature of the "leadership paradox." Some authors argue that executive leadership has a tremendous impact on organizational performance. Others, however, argue for a more perceptual perspective: leadership is a construct by which causality for outcomes is inferred. This paradox can be explained by the difficulty we have in linking specific leader behaviors (both direct and indirect means) to organizational outcomes. It is argued in this book that this link is often supplied by perceivers' implicit theories or "romanticized beliefs" of leadership. Others have approached this paradox empirically, through leadership succession studies, with the assumption that changes in executive leadership will be associated with measurable changes in organizational performance.

A few widely cited leadership succession studies are often interpreted as demonstrating that leaders do not affect organizational outcomes. Yet if properly interpreted, these studies show that succession has a substantial impact on performance. One factor that must be considered is the hierarchical level of the organization in which succession occurs. In some studies that show small succession effects, the leaders investigated were actually middle- rather than upper-level leaders. We argue that most middle-level managers do not make decisions or engage in activities that create conditions for organizationwide performance; therefore, strong succession effects should not be expected at this level. Utility analyses also suggest that there is considerable utility in dollars of having a good executive leader. Such research provides additional support for the impact of top leaders on organizational performance.

In short, we have illustrated that executive leaders do have substantial effects on organizational performance. In the next section of this chapter, we will identify specific factors that can affect (moderate) the impact a leader has on organizational outcomes.

DETERMINANTS OF A CEO'S IMPACT ON PERFORMANCE

Having established that top-level leaders can affect the performance of an organization, we can now examine the question of what explains the variability in their impact. That is, why do some leaders have a dramatic effect on their organization's performance, while others seemingly have no effect at all? Part of the answer to this question involves issues already discussed—top-level leaders like CEOs probably have more of an impact than leaders one step lower in the hierarchy, and the delayed or cumulative effect of leadership may be greater than its short-run effects. Moreover, leaders with exceptionally high ability (or very low ability) may have more of an impact than typical leaders. Nevertheless, one must also consider the power of an executive leader to influence both the internal and the external environments, along with the environmental factors and historical context of an organization.

Power and Managerial Discretion

Power, which is defined in terms of the capacity to influence others, is a natural outgrowth of perceptual processes (French and Raven 1959; Lord 1977). Thus, the power of a CEO depends in part on the way he or she is perceived by others in an organization. Particularly important are perceptions in terms of leadership, because as a romantic view of leadership implies, leaders are thought to have the capacity to create favorable organizational outcomes. Power and perceived leadership provide a type of leverage for executives that allows them increased influence. Such influence is particularly crucial for gaining the acceptance of relevant constituencies (other top executives, the board of directors) for nontraditional actions. These actions are likely to have the most impact on an organization's performance. In short, we are arguing that to have a significant impact, top executives often have to deviate from a steady course and initiate internal and/or external changes. To gain acceptance of such changes, executives must be perceived as being powerful and also as having leadership ability. Ironically, perceivers also infer power and leadership from successful influence attempts, creating a cyclical process that amplifies perceived power as influence is repeatedly exercised (Stein, Hoffman, Cooley, and Pearse 1979). Thus, perceived leadership may be most crucial for new CEOs when other bases for influence have not yet been developed (a situation that is most likely when new CEOs come from outside an organization) and a CEO lacks a history of salient successes. (Fredrickson, Hambrick, and Baumrin's [1988] model of CEO dismissal supports this assertion.)

A similar argument has been made by Hambrick and Finkelstein (1987), who focus on managerial discretion (the discretion of CEOs) as a bridge between strategic choice theorists and population ecologists. Strategic choice theorists argue that organizations can proactively shape their own fate; population ecologists assert that survival is best explained by environmental selection rather than adaption. Hambrick and Finkelstein conceive of managerial discretion as varying both across and within organizations over time, with discretion being very high in some organizations or time periods and being very low in other organizations or time frames. CEOs act in many substantive domains (securing resources, resource allocation, product market selection, competitive initiatives, administrative choices, and staffing) and in many symbolic domains (language, demeanor, and personal actions) that affect values and standards (Hambrick and Finkelstein 1987, 371–72). Hambrick and Finkelstein's main argument is that chief executives vary substantially in the number of domains in which they have discretion. These researchers assert that lack of discretion in significant domains will often give rise to the accentuation of decision-making choices in trivial domains. We think that when executives have discretion in important domains, their impact on an organization's performance can be accentuated; when they lack discretion in significant domains, their impact is greatly reduced.

Hambrick and Finkelstein (1987) elaborate their position by conceiving of three determinants of discretion—factors determined by the manager or CEO, those determined by the organizational context, and those arising from the external environment. *Managerial determinants* include factors that affect the awareness of potential actions (experience, scanning, and insight). This component is particularly important given that CEOs, like everyone else, often operate as limited-capacity information processors. Discretion also involves the capacity of a manager to sell or stage his or her actions. Here, fit with the prototypes of relevant constituencies and familiarity with an organizational culture would be crucial factors, as would the ability to disaggregate complex objectives into sequences of more concrete steps. Managerial characteristics that increase discretion include aspiration level, cognitive processing ability, tolerance for ambiguity, an internal locus of control, ability to use personal bases of power, and political acumen. *Organizational determinants* of discretion are primarily socio-political. Large organizations and established organizations constrain CEOs. Strong organizational cultures and internal political conditions (degree of ownership in a firm, relationship with the board of directors) can limit discretion. Discretion can also be limited by capital intensity and by the extent of resource availability. *External limitations on discretion* involve product factors, such as degree of product differentiation; industry factors, such as the amount of concentration (monopolies or oligopolies have more discretion); and the stability of demand for a product. In short, certain types of CEOs create more discretion, some organizations allow more discretion, and some external environments afford more discretion.

Time, however, is also likely to be a crucial factor. Organizational and environmental factors that may be relatively fixed in the short run may be more malleable in the long run for a CEO whose personal qualities enhance discretion. Internal sociopolitical factors can be changed, new products and technologies can be introduced, and even industries can be restructured, as is shown by Bower's (1986) in-depth study of the petrochemical industry in the 1980s. Thus, we argue that a primary requirement for effective leadership is the ability to create discretion in key domains. Top-level executives who cannot create discretion may be very competent managers or administrators who fulfill important functions, but they may not have a large impact on the performance of an organization. We would not define them as leaders, given the perspective of this book. Further, creating discretion may involve much more than the mere application of personal or organizational power. It may involve proactive changes in organizations or environments that may take years or even decades to materialize fully. Thus, we posit that one major determinant of managerial discretion is an ability to develop visions that extend far into the future. Jaques (1989) makes a similar point, arguing that top leaders need a higher level of cognitive development to conceptualize and develop plans with a time span of up to 10 years for typical leaders and up to 20 years for visionary leaders. How such long-range vision can be accomplished given people's limited-information processing capacity is an issue we address in chapter 13.

Convergent and Reorientation Periods

Another factor moderating the influence of a CEO on organizational performance is the evolutionary period of an organization. Tushman and Romanelli (1985) developed a theory that integrated divergent models of organizational evolution (adaption, transformational, and ecological models). They explained that organizations evolve through convergent periods punctuated by reorientations (or recreations) that structure the subsequent convergent period. In this punctuated equilibrium model, convergent periods are relatively long time spans in which incremental change occurs. In convergent periods,

CEOs engage in mainly *symbolic activities* to legitimize the core values, strategic orientation, power distribution, structure, and control systems of an organization. Further, many decision-making and administrative activities are performed by middle-level leaders during convergent periods. Reorientations, on the other hand, are relatively short periods of discontinuous change wherein strategy, power, structure, or controls are fundamentally transformed largely through the actions of top-level leaders. The outcome of such reorientations often has a lasting and powerful effect on organizational performance. If core values are also dramatically changed during this period, Tushman and Romanelli describe this situation as a re-creation rather than a reorientation. A key argument of Tushman and Romanelli is that executive-level leadership is the main process that mediates between (a) internal and institutional forces for inertia and (b) competitive/ technological pressures for fundamental change. During reorientations or re-creations, the role of executive leadership is greatly expanded to include both *substantive and symbolic* activities. Executives are also pivotal forces for or against change. Thus, the ability to foster or effectively guide reorientations is a crucial means by which CEOs influence organizational performance.

During long convergent periods, several factors develop that create a source of inertia that impedes discontinuous change. For example, inertia increases as organizations age and grow in size, encounter periods of sustained performance, develop a strong internal culture, devise procedures for internally training managers, and stabilize internal power structures. Opposing these sources of stability are dramatic environmental changes in technology, products, industry structures, or internal shifts in power. These latter forces may produce large misalignments between an organization and the environment, misalignments that cannot be remedied by the type of incremental change likely to occur in convergent periods. Such factors typically produce an accelerating decline in performance and a period of crisis that precedes a reorientation.

Evolutionary Periods, Leadership, and Organizational Effectiveness

The process implied by the Tushman and Romanelli (1985) model is depicted graphically in figure 10.2, which shows a response surface representing the performance of an organization. The response surface can be folded to represent both incremental (back face) and discontinuous (front face) change. This surface is part of a cusp catastrophe mathematical model, which will be developed in more detail in the next chapter. Its value in understanding evolution is that it fits very well with the effects described by Tushman and Romanelli, because it

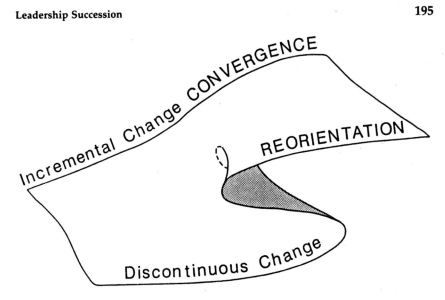

Figure 10.2
A Cusp Catastrophe Model of Leadership and Organizational Performance

can represent both incremental and discontinuous change. We posit
that the back face of figure 10.2 corresponds to the convergent period
in Tushman and Romanelli's model. During this phase, executives'
activities are primarily symbolic and change is gradual. Convergent
periods fit with relatively stable environments. The front face of the
figure represents discontinuous change, characteristic of reorientation
or re-creation periods. Here, executives engage in substantive activities
that can dramatically affect organizational performance. Through such
substantive actions (for example, strategic planning), it is possible for
leaders to guide the organization through the cusp to a drastically
lower (or higher) level of performance. In short, the back face of figure
10.2 represents convergent periods, whereas the front face of the figure
represents periods of reorientation or re-creation.

The front surface is interesting in another respect. The fold or
pleated surface shows that performance may depend on the direction
from which an area on this surface is approached. In other words, the
historical path followed by a firm (how it moves around the surface
shown in figure 10.2), as well as the position it occupies, affects
organizational performance. For example, Tushman and Anderson
(1986) found that early adopters of new technology reaped much
greater benefits than firms that were slow to adopt technological
advances. Early adopters would be on the upper-right side of the
figure (the high performance plane, since they lead their industry),
while late adopters would be on the lower performance plane shown in

the left part of this figure. We expect that even if, over time, early and late adopters approached the same level of environmental fit shown by the folded region, early adopters would still exhibit substantially better performance, both because they would be more skilled at applying the new technology (they had advanced farther on organizational learning curves) and because they would have developed stable ties with required suppliers or customers that consumed the technologically advanced product. In other words, late adopters of a technology cannot "catch up" to early adopters by simple imitation; they have to perform better than early adopters before they can increase their performance and market share relative to early adopters. This disadvantage of late adopters is depicted by the low-performing surface folding under the high-performing surface on the front of figure 10.2.

This model of evolution and executive leadership is interesting in several respects. One is that it essentially answers the leadership paradox raised at the outset of the chapter. During periods of convergence, executives have only a small impact on performance, effects associated with their administrative capabilities and their symbolic activities. Further, because convergent periods are of long duration, most unforced successions (deaths, retirements) will occur during these periods. During periods of reorientation, however, leaders' activities and their impact on an organization can be radically different. Here, leaders have both symbolic and substantive functions and their impact on an organization's performance can be quite dramatic.

In short, the convergent face of figure 10.2 is consistent with the arguments of Pfeffer (1977) and others who posit that leadership is largely symbolic, and the reorientation face is consistent with the dramatic effects suggested by the work of Meindl et al. (1985). Meindl and his colleagues found that leaders are seen as increasingly important causes for large variances in organizational performance (very poor or very good performance), variance that would occur on the front face of figure 10.2. Interestingly, this model makes some statistical predictions that go beyond the insights of Meindl et al. That is, where convergence is common (either in stable industries or in stable time periods) executive leaders should have little impact; where reorientations are common, leaders should have very large impacts on performance. Thus, succession studies should find different amounts of variance depending on where they examine succession: stable industries or time periods would show little effects; turbulent industries or time periods should show dramatic effects.

We will examine Tushman and Romanelli's (1985) theory and the cusp catastrophe model shown in figure 10.2 in more detail in succeeding chapters (particularly chapter 11). We introduce the model in this chapter only to note that it also helps us resolve the leadership paradox, by showing that evolutionary processes can substantially affect the impact a top-level leader has on organizational performance.

SUMMARY

In the first half of this chapter we discussed the problems perceivers have in trying to assess accurately a leader's effect on organizational performance. We noted that researchers have relied on succession studies to answer this question of leaders' influence on performance. Further, we noted that the effects of leadership successions depend on leaders' hierarchical level, time lags, how variables are ordered in regression procedures, and leaders' relative ability.

In the second half of this chapter we identified several additional determinants of a leader's impact on organizational outcomes. One such determinant is amount of discretion (Hambrick and Finkelstein 1987). Executives can have discretion in a variety of substantive and symbolic domains. When executives have discretion in a particular domain, their influence on organizational performance may be enhanced.

A second major determinant of executives' impact on performance is the evolutionary period of the organization. According to Tushman and Romanelli (1985), organizations evolve through periods of convergence and reorientation. During reorientation periods, executives perform both substantive and symbolic activities, and the impact that leaders have on organizational performance often has direct linkages to executive activities and decisions. During periods of convergence, however, executives are engaged in primarily symbolic activities, which are difficult to link to specific activities.

With respect to the leadership paradox discussed at the beginning of this chapter, lack of discretion in some domains and the evolutionary period of an organization may affect whether leaders are causally linked to organizational outcomes. In domains of little discretion, leaders will probably not have much influence on organizational performance. Leaders, however, may have a substantial impact in other domains. The salience of the domain of activity in which leaders have discretion, then, may govern whether leaders are perceived as having an effect on outcomes. This issue further complicates the problem of perceivers trying to assess how direct and indirect leadership activities affect organizational outcomes.

In the final section, we posited that both the convergent and the reorientation phases discussed by Tushman and Romanelli (1985) fit a folded performance plane from a cusp catastrophe model. This model's advantages are that the folded front surface represents the directional (historical) effects needed to understand evolution and market dynamics. Moreover, the difference between the front and the back faces graphically contrasts convergent periods, in which change is slow and leadership succession should have minimal effects, with reorientation periods, in which change is rapid and discontinuous and leadership succession should have dramatic effects on organizational performance. This model is more fully developed in chapter 11.

Chapter 11

A Cusp Catastrophe Model of Organizational Performance

*I*n this chapter we develop the cusp catastrophe model of leadership and organizational evolution in more detail. The model will serve as an integrating framework for much of the material in the remainder of this book. Our purpose is not to give a detailed account of the catastrophe theory model. For a thorough explanation of the mathematical representations involved in the theory, the reader is referred to Guastello (1987) or Stewart and Peregoy (1983). Catastrophe theory has been used by other researchers in organizational theory to demonstrate both the continuous and the discontinuous aspects of change. Oliva, Day, and MacMillan (1988) present a catastrophe model of competitive dynamics that integrates both industry inertia and relative competitive force components of the market. Sheridan (1985) describes employee withdrawal in catastrophe theory terms; in this model, behavioral outcomes of withdrawal, such as declining job performance, absenteeism, and turnover, can be explained as discontinuous changes in behavior rather than as continuous linear responses. Guastello (1987) also applies catastrophe theory to a broader model of motivation. We apply catastrophe theory to leadership, evolution, and organizational performance.

From the previous chapter, figure 10.2 depicts the response surface of a *cusp catastrophe* mathematical model (Guastello 1987; Stewart and Peregoy 1983). This model is extended in figure 11.1 through the addition of the normal (environmental fit) and bifurcating (nature of organizational change processes) control variables. These control variables are estimated as latent variables (variables that are linear functions of several empirical indicators) that need not be completely independent (Cobb 1980). What the use of latent variables means theoretically is that several variables may be used to represent a single dimension, or control variable. For example, *the nature of organizational change processes* (our front-to-back control variable) may be determined by multiple factors, such as leadership activities, power distributions, latitude of discretion, organizational culture, and labeling processes. Similarly, *environmental fit* can be determined by such factors as the

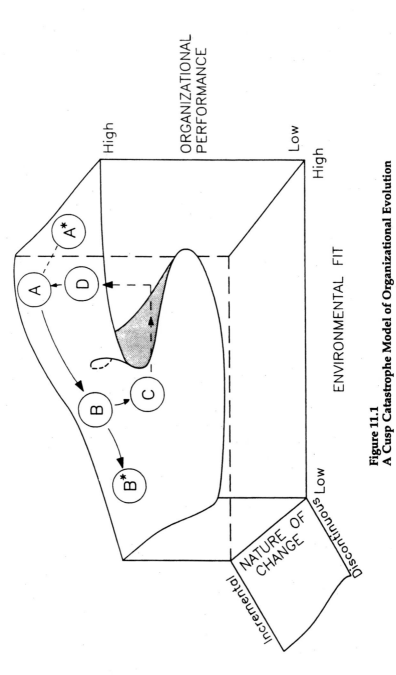

Figure 11.1
A Cusp Catastrophe Model of Organizational Evolution

strategic decision making of an organization, the behavior of key competitors, changes in government regulations, and technological change. Thus, fairly rich theoretical explanations can all be related to the same basic figure. For the sake of simplicity, we represent the two dimensions or control variables as being orthogonal, though in reality they can be correlated.

NORMAL AND BIFURCATING CONTROL VARIABLES

The two control variables shown in figure 11.1 represent our extension of the ideas originally proposed by Tushman and Romanelli (1985), who saw the fit of an organization with its environment as being a key determinant of organizational performance. In our model, environmental fit is the normal control variable, the side-to-side dimension in figure 11.1. Environmental fit has a monotonic increasing relationship to performance on the back face and a discontinuous relationship on the front. The relationship between environmental fit and performance changes as a function of the second control variable, called a bifurcating variable—the front-to-back control variable in figure 11.1. This variable is labeled the nature of organizational change processes.

The major difference between our model and that of Tushman and Romanelli (1985) concerns this bifurcating control variable. Tushman and Romanelli's punctuated equilibrium theory emphasizes executive leadership activities in distinguishing between convergent and re-orientation periods. We extend their thinking in two ways. First, we provide a more encompassing label for this bifurcating control variable: nature of organizational change processes. Second, we develop a broader conceptualization of the factors underlying the nature of change processes. Like Tushman and Romanelli, we view leadership, political factors, and prior history as influencing organizational change processes. But we also think there is a critical cognitive component those researchers have ignored. As we explain in detail in chapter 13, during convergent periods gradual changes in environmental fit are produced by minor organizational adjustments that take place within the overarching perspective provided by a common set of organizational schemas—a uniform organizational culture. We posit, however, that a major component of discontinuous change involves shifts in schemas that guide top executives' categorization of key environments and responses to environmental perceptions. Thus, we show by the front face of figure 11.1 that discontinuous change is produced in part by switching from one schema to another. This assertion parallels our explanation in chapter 5 of discontinuities in social perceptions.

Further, we expect that shifts from convergent to reorientation periods are associated with decreased performance (for the same level of environmental fit), since this shift requires movement to less familiar political structures and less efficient modes of information processing. Therefore, the nature of internal processes associated with change directly affects organizational performance. Performance declines as one moves from the back to the front of figure 11.1.

The nature of processes associated with change includes both political and cognitive factors. Both political structures and cognitive processes can change in incremental ways. Single individuals gain or lose power or people engage in cybernetic information processing on the back face. Political and cognitive processes also change in discontinuous ways on the front face, where entire power structures are realigned or people change to more effortful, intendedly rational information processing. During transition periods, people use more effortful processes because information no longer fits with existing schemas and people have not yet developed new schemas that can assimilate this information.

Advantages of the Cusp Catastrophe Model

This representation shows how context, history, and leadership activities can all be integrated visually on the response surface. This treatment actually subsumes contingency models, which have been common in the leadership literature. For example, the strategic decision-making activities of top executives may move an organization along the "environmental fit" dimension, whereas changes in organizational culture may move organizations along the "nature of change" dimension. But the effect of these actions on performance depends on a number of contingency factors—competitor response to changed strategy, or whether the new culture produces a unique competitive advantage. Our model allows a more dynamic treatment of such contingency factors by including the direction of movement on the response surface. Direction is important because it allows one to link explicit paths or types of movement around the performance surface in figure 11.1 with underlying organizational or market processes. These processes can be proactive, whereby changes initiated within the firm move it around the response surface, or passive, showing how changes in the environment affect a firm that fails to adapt. More realistically, the model shows that changes in a firm and changes in the environment can occur simultaneously, as many firms enact their environment (Smircich and Stubbart 1985).

The value of this approach can best be seen by focusing on the folded area on the front surface of figure 11.1. The fold actually reflects a catastrophe theory principle called *hysteresis*, which means that the value on the dependent variable (organizational performance) depends on the direction from which the fold is approached. Firms that lead technological change have an advantage over firms that lag technological change (Tushman and Anderson 1986). Although a leading and a lagging firm may end up with the same level of environmental fit (some middle value in figure 11.1), the leading firm would approach this fit from the upper-right surface, whereas the lagging firm would approach it from the lower-left surface—resulting in very different levels of performance for firms that may ultimately use identical technologies. If we attempted to predict performance without taking history into account, we would mistakenly predict identical performance for leading and lagging firms that use the same technology. Barney (1986) makes a similar point with respect to organizational culture, arguing that those firms which attempt to imitate another firm's culture will not achieve the same competitive advantage.

Direction of movement on the surface also represents history of evolution or organizational change. History is crucial in understanding evolutionary processes. For example, firms that approach the folded area from the lower-left surface run the risk of being selected out of their market through such processes as bankruptcy because of their poor performance. Firms approaching the same degree of fit from the upper surface perform very differently and run different risks: they may be attractive takeover targets because of their advanced technology or large cash flow.

A related notion is the idea of *divergence*, another key principle of catastrophe theory. Divergence describes the fact that firms that are very close together in one period of time may diverge substantially as one firm moves across the performance surface. For example, two firms on the back of the performance surface near the cusp region may diverge over time if one firm follows a path that moves it to the upper surface, while the other firm follows a path that moves it to the lower surface (for example, the leading and lagging firms in our example of technological innovation). Thus, history often determines whether similar initial decisions turn out to be good or poor choices. As we saw with the literature on succession, lags of two or three years may be required to see the full effect of successions that affect strategic decisions.

Organizational Change Cycles

In the remainder of this chapter we explain in some detail how organizational decline and rebirth can be understood in terms of movement around the performance surface shown in figure 11.1. This figure can organize our thinking about how organizational change cycles operate.

On the back face of figure 11.1, the activities of lower- and middle-level leaders are crucial in creating incremental adjustments that keep an organization on the flat, back-right response surface (region A), which represents a stable area of relatively high performance. This stability in performance can be seen by moving over to the vertical axis and noting the fairly small differences in performance associated with the different points in region A. Here the impact of executive-level leadership is small, serving mainly to legitimize the activities of others. This area is also where cybernetic information processing may work well because of the smooth linear relationship between environmental fit and performance. This fairly constant relationship should facilitate learning and adjustment. Minor adjustments to established standards or small shifts in standards may be all that are required to maintain performance. Further, dynamic homeostasis suggested by systems theorists (Katz and Kahn 1978) can be attained by cognitively simple adjustment processes managed by middle-level leaders. The phrase *dynamic homeostasis* refers to imprecise adjustments that work because small errors can be corrected over time through additional feedback. Executive leaders' activities are mainly symbolic and in fact may be constrained by inertial forces.

Figure 11.1 illustrates graphically why high-performing firms constrain executives during convergent periods. Fundamental substantive changes initiated by executive leadership could easily produce large changes in environmental fit, moving an organization over the fold and through the cusp region (the shaded part of figure 11.1) to a dramatically lower level of performance. That is, executive leadership activities that were ill conceived could produce an extremely rapid decline in performance. There is high instability associated with executive leadership when organizations are on the upper surface of figure 11.1 and are near the fold region. For this reason, most organizations try to operate on the back face of figure 11.1 during convergent periods. Eventually, however, environmental turbulence will produce accelerating misalignments between the environment and an organization, along with accelerating declines in performance—organizations move from region A, sliding toward region B, then region C.

Region C is often aptly characterized as a crisis situation, both because there is an immediate history of performance below traditional standards and because traditional responses cannot produce adjustments of sufficient magnitude to realign the organization with its environment. Moreover, during such crisis periods the internal dynamics of organizations often change. Forces for change often disrupt political stability and/or efficient internal functioning. People must cope with both political and cognitive uncertainty as organizations reevaluate such core factors as technology, structures, or control systems. That such uncertainty can have a negative impact on performance is reflected in the downhill slope moving from the back to the front of the performance surface of figure 11.1. Decreased efficiency also results from a shift in the type of cognitive processes emphasized. Incremental change on the back face of figure 11.1 fits quite well with cybernetic information processing and with minor adjustments in well-learned social or task schemas, which, as we have already argued, can be very effective. Still, reevaluation of basic organizational factors during periods of low performance requires a more effortful, rational form of information processing, along with increased communication requirements in organizations.

At such points, the role of executive leadership must shift, resolving uncertainty and creating a fundamental transformation if the organization is to remain viable. The alternative is for organizations to remain rigid (to move to region B* of figure 11.1), with fit being produced by the birth and death of alternative organizational forms, as suggested by a population ecology model of evolution. Thus, top-level leaders of an organization must produce discontinuous and fundamental shifts in such key areas as strategy, power distributions, organizational structures, and control systems in order for organizations to regain successful performance. Favorable outcomes of such shifts are shown on the front face of figure 11.1 as movement from region C through the cusp region to region D, reflecting a discontinuous jump in performance. But as noted by Oliva, Day, and Macmillian's (1988) application of catastrophe theory to competitive dynamics, movement from region C to region D requires a substantial change, a *heroic* effort, and and extensive commitment of resources—"competitive force," in these authors' terms. In our terms, it requires a major change in the degree of environmental fit. The cycle is then completed by movement from region D to region A as people adjust to a new convergent period (for example, new political and/or cognitive structures become familiar), efficiency increases, and top-level leaders return to mainly symbolic activities and normal administration. In addition, executives are again able to function with primarily cybernetic processing.

As shown in figure 11.1, movement from region C to region D is associated with a dramatic increase in performance resulting from realignment with the environment. This instance is the classic turnaround scenario common in the business literature, wherein dynamic executive leadership reverses rapidly declining performance. Not shown in this figure is the possibility that executives will make a major mistake, which increases misalignment, rather than producing realignment, and which moves an organization to a level of performance far below that of region C. Rather than reflecting heroic turnarounds, such mistakes may result in the demise of an organization—takeover, withdrawal from a market, or bankruptcy.

The model in figure 11.1 is of interest in a second respect, as it has implications for how perceptions of leadership and information processing are related to reorientations. Consider the situation of a CEO in region C of this figure. The immediately preceding period is one of a dramatic decrease in performance. The size of this decrease would foster attributions of causality to a CEO, and a dramatic decline would seriously shake perceivers' beliefs in the leadership capacity of this individual. Concurrent with this shrinking basis of perceptual power, the CEO must overcome inertia and precipitate dramatic change. This task is formidable, requiring a firm grounding of power in other sources—recognition based, as well as inferential power or ownership of key resources like stock or patents. It may also require effective management of attributional processes to prevent blame for poor performance. Alternatively, what is perhaps more likely is that the CEO will be removed and replaced with an individual not associated with performance declines. In fact, Tushman, Newman, and Romanelli (1986) report that 80 percent of the reorientations they investigated involved replacement of top management teams with new leaders. We expect that this type of succession attracts more attention, enhancing leaders' perceived causal impact on performance. Such successions send clear signals to others, such as stockholders, that change is forthcoming, and they produce greater stock market reactions (Friedman and Singh 1989). In other words, forced succession and outside succession would be most likely to occur with firms in region C. Unforced successions (caused by retirement or death) and internal successions would be most likely to occur with firms in region A.

Cognitive/information processing problems may also accompany the crisis situation of region C in figure 11.1; these problems are discussed in more detail in chapter 13. As suggested by Staw, Sandelands, and Dutton (1981), crisis may be accompanied by a restriction of communications, centralization of power and authority, and more conservative approaches to problem solving. Such threat-rigidity effects reflect inertial factors rather than forces for change. These effects also reflect limited-capacity information processing based on familiar categorizations of environments and familiar scripts. To counter such factors, symbolic activities associated with labeling and imagery may be important (Dutton and Jackson 1987; Sapienza 1987). Conceptualizing crises as opportunities rather than threats may elicit different types of thinking and communications and may spur a willingness to take risks rather than avoid them. To foster appropriate labeling, executives must have visions that extend beyond stereotypical organizational thinking. They must also be able to communicate these visions through more rational forms of information processing. The ability of CEOs to create an alternative cognitive perspective through the use of appropriate imagery or metaphors is also crucial.

In short, both the power and the cognitive/information processing problems associated with the crisis region suggest an extreme challenge for executive leaders. Though this turnaround model of leadership shown by the A-B-C-D path is common, it is unlikely to result in sustained excellence in organizational performance, because of the attributional and information processing problems just mentioned. This model also reflects the mainly reactive and internally oriented nature of Tushman and Romanelli's (1985) theory; we suggest, instead, two alternatives that are more proactive and externally oriented.

One alternative is for executives to anticipate or lead rather than lag significant changes. Visionary executive teams may be able to reorient before performance declines reach dramatic proportions. This proactive response results in a higher degree of environmental fit, characterized by the upper-right response surface of figure 11.1. (It also results in reorientations that do not always have a discontinuous impact on performance, a factor absent from Tushman and Romanelli's [1985] model.) In other words, executives make strategic changes that move their firms from the back to the front of figure 11.1, while staying on or near the upper-right surface (movement from region A to region A*). To do so, executives must have the external connections, knowledge, and insight to recognize fundamental changes in the environment in early stages. We expect that only certain types of executives with high tolerance for uncertainty are capable of such flexibility. They must also have the internal power to react to such changes without crises developing. That is, they must already have expanded their latitude of actions in key domains. This point suggests that such executives create a strategic orientation and an organizational culture attuned to change. Miles and Snow's (1978) prospector strategic type provides a good metaphor for organizations that are amenable to change. Interestingly, Tushman and Anderson (1986, 459) found that companies that made early adoptions of discontinuous technological changes had much higher subsequent growth than other firms did.

Our second alternative may be even more effective, because it is both proactive and externally oriented. In other words, rather than reacting to a changed environment or making proactive strategic choices, executives have a vision of the environment they would like to create. These exceptional CEOs may be effective operators in both the internal *and the external* environment to alter fundamental factors. They are likely to pursue competence-enhancing technological change

(Tushman and Anderson 1986) internally, and they are likely to try to operate externally in order to alter environmental forces. Such changes require the *collective actions* of parties (other firms, the government) outside organizations. These changes cannot be shown in figure 11.1, because they alter the nature of the response surface itself (the plane representing organizational performance), rather than merely reflecting alternative paths on the response surface. Such changes will be discussed in more detail in the last sections of chapters 12 and 15.

Because this type of response requires external influence, it may be quite difficult to implement. We expect that how the executive is perceived in terms of leadership potential is crucial for garnering the power for external as well as internal change. Operating in the political-government-market environment may, however, require an executive to fit a different prototype in order to be recognized as a leader. Typical business activities may not be recognized as leadership when they occur in the political rather than the business realm. (Recall from chapter 3 that prototypes of political and business leaders are not that similar.) Thus, attempts to invoke leadership perceptions in unfamiliar domains could create a substantial problem for some leaders. We also expect that the time perspective associated with such changes would be longer than that associated with either of the two previously mentioned types of leadership. Despite such problems, this last type of leadership may be highly effective, though it is difficult to implement (Hirsch 1975).

SUMMARY

In this chapter we have presented a cusp catastrophe model of leadership to represent continuous and discontinuous changes in organizational performance. We specified the nature of organizational change processes and environmental fit as the two control variables. Discontinuous (catastrophic) change is represented on the front surface of the cusp; continuous (linear) change is represented on the back face. Discontinuous change involves shifts in schemas that guide leaders' perceptions of the environment; continuous change reflects incremental shifts within an existing schema. The type of change affects organizational performance.

The degree of fit with the environment is also a factor incorporated into this model. Thus, the degree of environmental fit and the nature of organizational change processes (convergence or reorientation) affect organizational performance. The model also accounts for the history of evolutionary processes within an organization. Organizations at the same level of environmental fit but approaching it from different directions can have different levels of performance, based on their history. The impact of leadership is also different, depending on the location of the organization on the performance surface. On the back face, lower- and middle-level managers can maintain the organization's performance. Similarly, symbolic activities on the part of top leaders also serve to keep the organization operating on the back surface. Organizations on the front, or discontinuous, face of the cusp model (the crisis region) may require substantive activities on the part of top leaders to yield considerable improvements in an organization's performance. In chapter 12, we extend the catastrophe model by identifying some specific activities of executive leaders that affect organizational performance.

Chapter 12

Executive Leadership and Organizational Performance

*W*hat leadership activities of top executives have an impact on organizational performance? To answer this question, we will rely heavily on the concepts developed in the preceding three chapters and on the typology developed by Day and Lord (1988). More specifically, we will be concerned with both the direct and the indirect effects that executives have on organizational performance, topics that were discussed in chapter 9. Tushman and Romanelli's (1985) theory of organizational evolution, which we explained in chapters 10 and 11, will also be used to help understand how leaders affect organizational performance. We cast that model into cusp catastrophe mathematical terms to represent the differential impact of convergent and reorientation evolutionary periods on performance. As suggested by Day and Lord, the alternative means by which executives affect performance can be equated with different paths of movement on the cusp surface and, in exceptional instances, with changes in the nature of the cusp surface itself.

Two preliminary issues must be addressed. First is whether the construct of leadership is necessary to understand how executives change determinants of organizational performance, such as corporate strategy or production technology. We believe that leadership is crucial to understanding such changes because they are not made by single individuals. Rather, decisions to make major changes involve top executives from many different areas in an organization, and often the active support of an entire organization is needed to implement changes. Thus, changing such fundamental factors as corporate strategy requires that top executives influence many other individuals in ways that often go beyond the formal authority of their position. Such influence falls within common definitions of leadership as an influence increment extending beyond the formal powers associated with one's office (Katz and Kahn 1978), particularly when the focus of influence is external rather than internal to an organization. Further, as we have explained, the ability to exert dramatic and widespread influence depends on whether an individual is perceived as a leader by others—which is the definition of leadership used in this book.

Second is whether we should be concerned more with leadership style (for example, characteristic leader behaviors, participative decision making) or with substantive decisions (strategy, organizational design, capital spending, or personnel policies). Behavioral style has been a principal concern of researchers interested in lower-level leadership, wherein subordinates and superiors generally interact face to face. Day and Lord (1988), however, argue that substantive factors are more important for understanding the impact a CEO has on the performance of an organization, because effective (or ineffective) decisions can be made using many different styles. Style may be important to the extent that it connotes fit or lack of fit with salient prototypes—decisiveness and aggressiveness are prototypical of leaders. But as we have already seen, leadership prototypes involve many trait assessments that are not closely related to behavioral styles—intelligence, honesty, verbal skill, and understanding. Further, we think that organizational members emphasize inferential processes rather than recognition-based processes in perceiving upper-level leaders (see chapter 4). Hence, our emphasis in this chapter is on the substantive actions of leaders and how those actions relate to organizational performance. To explain performance, we will borrow from organizational and management theory, integrating these topics with our coverage of leadership as a perceptual and cognitive process.

Day and Lord's (1988) typology involves three main foci of executive actions: (a) actions that are internally directed and attempt to increase efficiency or product quality, (b) actions that affect an organization's adaptation to external environments, and (c) actions that change the nature of external environments. This typology is based on an open-systems approach to understanding organizations (Katz and Kahn 1978), a view recognizing that organizations exist through a continual dynamic exchange with a variety of environments. A basic requirement of executive leaders is to manage these exchanges through both internal and external actions.

Table 12.1, which is adapted from Day and Lord (1988), shows many of the potential means by which top-level leaders can affect organizational performance. We will discuss most of these means, using the table as an organizing framework for this chapter. In table 12.1, the means to influence organizational performance are analyzed in terms of the targets and objectives of influence attempts. These influence tactics involve both direct and indirect approaches. Most direct tactics have been discussed extensively in the management literature and will be familiar to many readers. The importance of indirect tactics, however, should not be underestimated. Indirect tactics affect such target criteria as productivity and also interact with direct tactics, enhancing or diminishing their effects. For example, developing a product-oriented, engineering-based organizational culture through indirect approaches may strengthen quality norms, thereby improving product quality, and also enhance the impact of more direct approaches to improving quality control, such as quality circles.

INTERNAL INFLUENCE AND ADAPTION

When problems in organizational performance occur, we expect that leaders first look at internal factors, because these are more salient and more familiar and are often thought to be more controllable. This expectation is consistent with Cyert and March's (1963, 121–22) assertion that a search for solutions to organizational problems is "simple-minded." An internally focused search can also be simplified by existing schemas that help executives understand internal problems and suggest ways to solve them. Further, knowledge of an organization's culture permits realistic appraisals of the acceptability of internally directed actions. As shown in table 12.1, there are several kinds of internal factors that executive leaders can influence to change organizational performance.

Subsystem Organization and Management

Katz and Kahn (1978) conceptualize an organization as being composed of several important subsystems—production, maintenance, boundary, adaptive, and management—that must be appropriately organized and managed for organizations to operate efficiently. Rationalizing and integrating these subsystems is a fairly typical focus of executive leadership. As shown in table 12.1, one means by which top-level leaders can affect organizational performance is to change the functioning of these key subsystems. *Maintaining* the normal, day-to-day functioning of these subsystems involves administration, not leadership; however, *changing* the organization or integration of subsystems is a much more dramatic and far-reaching activity, one requiring leadership on the part of top executives.

Coordination and appraisal systems are also widely recognized as being chief aspects of modern management. Changing these systems also requires top-level leadership and can have a dramatic impact on performance. To illustrate, as recounted by Chandler (1962, 145–61), one of the most important changes Alfred Sloan made at General Motors in the mid-1920s was to develop cost accounting and budgeting systems to coordinate and appraise the performance of different

TABLE 12.1
Potential Means by Which Top-level Leaders Can Affect Organizational Performance

Target	Objective	Tactics Direct	Indirect
A. Adapting to and Influencing Internal Environments			
1. Subsystem organization and management	Rationalization and integration	Define and specify function of roles	Shape top management's schemas; organizing; select those with similar schemas
			Use information as sign and symbol
	Coordination and appraisal	Design and implement management information systems	Strengthen productivity norms
		Reduce capital or personnel costs	
2. Productivity	Increased organizational efficiency		
3. Quality	Increased product quality	Increase quality control	Strengthen quality norms
4. Organizational climate and culture	Increased employee motivation and commitment	Determine or influence organizational politics	Enhance participative decision-making norms; symbolism of CEO
B. Adapting to External Environments			
1. Choice of markets or environments	Increased stability and munificence	Improve strategic planning	Influence top management's schemas; select those with similar schemas
2. Management and production system	Fit with environment and strategy	Improve organizational design	Guide top management's labeling of environments
C. Influencing External Environments			
1. Acquisition of resources and maintenance of boundaries	Increased stability and reduced competition	Integrate horizontally or vertically; promote entry barriers and noncompetitive pricing	Create favorable public opinion; enhance image of organization or product
2. Government policy (e.g., regulation, taxation, trade)	Policy change to reduce uncertainty or increase resources	Exercise direct political influence	Exercise political influence via other groups (e.g., unions, suppliers)

Note: For each objective there are additional tactics; however, space limitations prohibit their inclusion in this table.
Source: Adapted from Day and Lord (1988).

divisions. Use of quantitative data (ten-day sales reports) that allowed timely production adjustments to changes in car sales were also developed. These changes, coupled with rationalization of the internal organizational structure, quickly made GM a much more efficient producer of automobiles than its competitors.

Both direct and indirect leadership tactics can help organize and manage subsystems. Top executives can directly influence the functional specifications or design of information systems. Alternatively, they can affect these types of systems through indirect actions. For example, emphasizing a very careful rational information processing approach may lead to the development of management information systems that are quite different from those developed by emphasizing intuition (judgments based on expert schemas) or cybernetic processes. In his history of Ford Motor Company, Halberstam (1986) notes that Henry Ford's recruitment and empowerment of highly methodical, Harvard Business School–trained "whiz kids" (Robert McNamara, Arjay Miller, Edward Lundy, and, much later, Philip Caldwell), who emphasized financial analysis as the primary basis of decisions, had a lasting impact on management. Further, their methodical, analytic, data-oriented approach was a continual source of frustration for individuals who preferred more intuitive, action-oriented approaches based on product-oriented considerations (for example, Lee Iacocca and Hal Sperlich). Empirical work by Miller, Droge, and Toulouse (1988) illustrates a similar process. In a study of 77 small firms (firms with fewer than 500 employees), these investigators found that CEOs rated high in need for achievement created intendedly rational strategy-making processes that emphasized formalized, centralized, and integrated structures. Further, the researchers found that decision-making rationality was reciprocally related to product innovation. Their LISREL analysis showed that CEOs indirectly affected such organizational variables as structure and strategy through the nature of the information processing they supported in organizations.

Productivity

Productivity, which involves the amount of goods or services produced with a given level of resource inputs, is closely tied to the technology of an organization. Productivity is crucial for organizations, since it relates directly to cost per unit and profitability. It is a particularly critical concern when resources are fixed or unit volume is declining. Thus, deteriorating national business conditions, increased competition, or downsizing to fit new market conditions often results in an emphasis on productivity. In periods of decline and uncertainty, effective executive leadership is required to resolve uncertainty and make the large-scale changes needed to increase productivity. The need for such changes is particularly acute during retrenchment periods, when a key political issue is how to allocate a shrinking pool of resources (Greenhalgh 1983). During such periods, organizations often make large reductions in capital or personnel costs. For example, in response to dramatic declines in auto sales in the late 1970s, Philip Caldwell, who became CEO of Ford Motor Company in October 1979, cut $2.5 billion out of the company's fixed costs during an 18-month period in 1980–81 (Halberstam 1986). Such reductions in the resources consumed by an organization are often coupled with indirect actions aimed at strengthening productivity norms and with reorganization of key systems to achieve greater efficiency.

An important requirement of an organization is to keep its cost structure in line with that of competitors and with market conditions. This need is especially crucial in industries with high fixed costs or declining demand. Those conditions often produce severe price competition, whereby products are sold at prices above marginal costs but below average total costs (Scherer 1970, 64–78). Such pricing may still be profitable for low-cost producers, while higher-cost producers sustain large losses. As noted by Scherer (1970) in his work on oligopolistic pricing, lowest-cost producers also have considerable power to punish competitors, helping to set profitable market prices and to avoid price competition. General Motors used to have this power in the American auto industry, and Saudi Arabia currently has this power in the international oil market.

Costs in relationship to those of competitors are particularly important in markets with undifferentiated products and stable environments, wherein cost leadership is the dominant strategy (Miller 1988). Cost can be conceptualized as one aspect of environmental fit, a key dimension of the cusp catastrophe model discussed in chapter 11. Thus, the general punctuated equilibrium model of chapter 11 can be recast in terms of costs, as shown in figure 12.1. Here, the typical adjustments that occur on a continual basis can be thought of as the convergent phase of a punctuated equilibrium model and probably require little in the way of executive leadership in order to be implemented. But the large-scale change needed to adjust to new market conditions requires both substantive and symbolic leadership from top executives. This type of change fits best with the reorientation phase on the front face of this figure.

Consider, as an example, the automobile industry. Capital expenditures are routinely made in conjunction with the development of new models, and numbers of production personnel are adjusted periodically to match changes in demand. Similarly, many management activities are directed at maintaining productivity norms. These actions can be conceptualized as working within the narrow region A

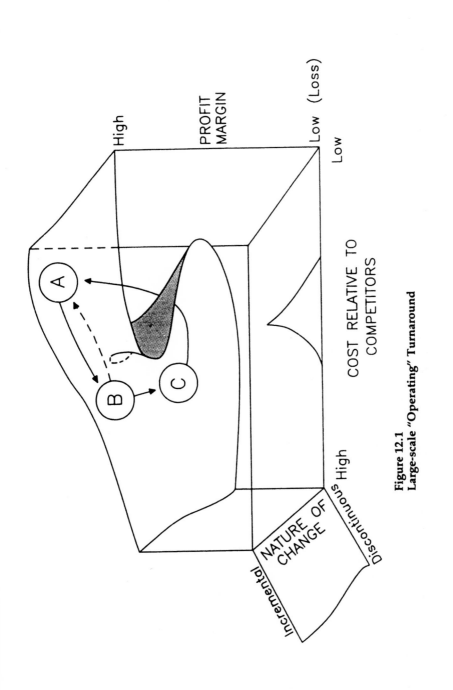

Figure 12.1
Large-scale "Operating" Turnaround

in figure 12.1, which represents the convergent phase of a punctuated equilibrium model. However, with the oil crisis and increased competition from Japanese automakers in the late 1970s, the cost structures (as well as the type of product) of the three leading American producers became quickly out of line with market conditions. This situation is conceptualized as a fairly rapid movement to region B of figure 12.1. It required radical change in personnel and output targets (as well as in the type of product) for these three American automakers in the late 1970s and early 1980s to adjust to this changed environment. These large-scale changes are qualitatively different from routine adjustments, as are the fundamental shifts in worker and union values that may be required to gain acceptance of and commitment to new norms for productivity. Both require effective executive-level leadership and reorientation phases of organizational evolution. Consistent with the punctuated equilibrium model, turn-arounds at both Chrysler and Ford were preceded by periods of large declines in performance and by internal crises (region C in figure 12.1), and they required fundamental metamorphoses in terms of organizational size, products, and market share. During these crisis periods, uncertainty about appropriate actions was high, and resolution of this uncertainty required leadership (*new* leadership, in two of the three major American automobile manufacturers), rather than the application of typical administrative procedures.

Chrysler's turnaround under Iacocca is perhaps the most widely discussed "resuscitation" of a dying company. This turnaround involved a number of internally focused, direct and indirect actions by Iacocca and his management team. Iacocca's leadership and reputation (and expanded latitude of action) were essential in gaining commitment to needed actions, but many of the substantive decisions themselves were not that different from those made in other turnarounds wherein costs are radically reduced. Such "operating" rather than "strategic" turnarounds are common to many companies in retrenchment modes. Here, actions taken by key executives are often very familiar (reduce personnel and capital expenditures), but some of these actions may be dramatic; Iacocca fired thousands of employees at Chrysler. Interestingly, these actions often represent a reactive rather than a proactive response. Iacocca's explanation is insightful: "Everybody talks about 'strategy,' but all we knew was survival. Survival was simple. Close the plants that are hurting us the most. Fire the people who aren't absolutely necessary or who don't know what's going on" (Iacocca and Novak 1984, 186).

If such turnarounds required only large-scale cuts, they could probably be best conceptualized simply as heroic movements up the back face of figure 12.1, along the dashed line to a region of better fit with the environment and improved performance. Large cost reductions, however, are not all that is required to turn a company around. As noted by Weick (1988), the way such actions are interpreted by people who remain in an organization can be crucial. If resource reductions and layoffs are seen as signifying lack of concern with a plant or area of a company, these interpretations can negatively affect productivity, quality, or morale. For example, one of General Motors' key problems has been its focus on technological responses while neglecting the human resource aspects of large-scale change.

Though such operating turnarounds included actions characteristic of convergent periods, the scope of actions, the degree of associated ambiguity, and the need to create an acceptable interpretation for the actions indicate that reorientations and metamorphoses were involved. In many ways Chrysler was a different company after the turnaround led by Iacocca. So was Ford, after Philip Caldwell's less publicized rescue. These turnarounds are better conceptualized as movement from the crisis region (C) of figure 12.1, through the cusp surface, and to the upper region on the right front face of this figure.

There are alternative approaches to managing costs and productivity that do not follow the turnaround pattern shown in figure 12.1. One approach that is more visionary and proactive is the early adoption of new productive technologies (Tushman and Anderson 1986). When such changes involve the core technology of organizations, they require successful executive leadership. The result is often a metamorphosis of an organization (or an entire industry). Such proactive changes would be characterized by back-to-front movement (from convergence to reorientation) in figure 12.1 but this movement would be likely to occur on the upper-right (high-performance) surface of the cusp. Such changes can occur in response to performance downturns, following the A-B-C path in figure 12.1. But changes in technology often require large capital expenditures, which are more difficult to make during periods of decline. Technological change during periods of poor performance is likely to occur only when an organization is following competitors that have already demonstrated that such a technology is productive. Reactive companies that lag, rather than lead, technological changes often are less successful, however, in gaining the full benefits of the new technology (Tushman and Anderson 1986).

Quality

The ability to market products is often directly related to their perceived quality. But objectives for high quality often conflict with those for high productivity; resources devoted to quality control reduce those available for production, and quality-related adjustments often produce downtime in both machines and people. Consequently, quality is often sacrificed to maintain productivity. Such trade-offs between quality and productivity are particularly severe in such industries as auto manufacturing, because quality reflects both production and design components, with each component requiring a major capital expense. (Bringing a completely new model to market often costs well over a billion dollars in design and tooling, before production is even started.) Achieving both high quality and high productivity therefore becomes very difficult and requires both direct and indirect aspects of leadership.

The productivity-quality trade-off can be resolved in a number of ways. One means of resolution is through the values and philosophies communicated by chief executives. CEOs can create an underlying premise that defines an organization, and CEOs can empower certain factions in organizations at the expense of others. For example, if a CEO's emphasis is on the bottom line rather than product quality, financial managers may have much greater influence than product development people or applied engineers. Further, as suggested by our discussion in chapter 8, these different "orientations" can develop an impact that extends beyond specific individuals when such orientations become incorporated into schemas that define the culture of an organization. Cost and product orientations provide two dominant criteria for many organizational tasks. Thus, the actions of CEOs can directly translate the productivity-quality issue into the power, politics, and culture of an organization.

An alternative means of resolving the productivity-quality trade-off is through adopting new technology (for example, robotics or other forms of automation) that increases both productivity and quality. The cost of new technology, however, can be very high. For example, Kellogg recently completed a fully automated cereal production plant to achieve higher quality and gain manufacturing efficiency; the cost—$1.2 billion—made it the most expensive food-processing facility ever built (Sellers 1988). Such large expenditures require the support and initiative of top-level executives, as well as a willingness to take substantial risks.

Achieving high quality also requires that top management strengthen quality-control norms through indirect, symbolic activities. Such actions are required to communicate clearly the importance of quality. For example, William LaMothe, the chairman of Kellogg, emphasized quality both directly and symbolically by instituting, for top executives, a Monday-morning breakfast at which samples of cereals from Kellogg's domestic and foreign plants are taste tested, using very stringent standards (Sellers 1988). Although such taste tests could be performed by other, less costly personnel, the use of top executives has symbolic value that communicates the importance of quality throughout the organization.

Perhaps one of the most popular approaches to achieving increased quality is through quality circles, arrangements in which lower-level workers are given an increased role and responsibility for quality decisions. Quality circles may not seem, on the surface, to require top-level leadership, yet they do represent nontraditional approaches to both manufacturing and management-worker interactions. Thus, both the management style and the dual emphasis on quality and productivity must be supported by the actions of executive-level leaders. (Van Fleet and Griffin [1989] document the fact that management support of quality circles was an issue very early in the history of quality circles.) Top-level support is needed to overcome resistance to such changes from both unions and middle-level management, as well as to communicate a genuine commitment to quality. Otherwise, such innovations in production are likely to be viewed as just a fad that warrants only superficial compliance. Minimal compliance is unlikely to produce the full benefit of such innovations. In fact, one could argue that quality circle approaches work best when coupled with changes in organizational climates or cultures (Pascarella 1982).

Culture

As noted by Weiner (1988, 534), organizational culture has not always been defined carefully. We define culture as the shared values, schemas, and types of information processing that apply to organizations as a whole and to distinct subunits of an organization. These shared elements distinguish one organization from another and provide a social and normative "glue" that holds an organization together.

Weiner (1988) identifies two sources (and anchors) for culture: organizational traditions and charismatic leadership. Organizational traditions produce a stable culture that is transmitted from one generation of organizational members to another and that is relatively independent of specific individuals. General Motors' management culture provides a good example of a tradition-based culture (Yates 1983). On the other hand, cultures anchored through members' identification with charismatic leaders are highly dependent on the specific values and activities of those leaders. Moreover, these effects may not last beyond the tenure of a specific leader.

Returning to the punctuated equilibrium model, traditionally anchored culture corresponds to the convergent period and would be a source of inertia, whereas culture anchored in identification with a charismatic leader could be either a source of inertia or a force for change, depending on the values, schemas, and information processing activities of the particular leader. Weiner's (1988) typology of culture has two important implications for the impact that leaders have on organizational evolution: it implies that reorientations will be more common when culture is maintained primarily through leadership activities, and it implies that rebirths of organizations, where fundamental change occurs, can be created only by charismatic leadership. We expect, however, that charismatic leadership is of primary significance when perceivers are relying on general stereotypes and on limited-capacity processing in evaluating leaders through automatic processes. When more controlled processes are emphasized, as they often are during reorientation periods, the analytic skills of a leader and his or her perceived ability to produce good performance may be just as important. In either case, this perspective on culture helps explain why executive leadership is so critical in reorientation phases of organizational evolution.

Culture is also important in ordering competing objectives in an organization. As noted by Weiner (1988), many values are functional in nature, pertaining to appropriate modes of conduct or to particular goals that should be pursued. Such values deal with issues like product quality, productivity, customer service, and innovation. Thus, the emphasis of some goals at the expense of others can be traced back to the cultural values of an organization. Priorities are also contained in organizational members' schemas, which are another key component of culture (see chapter 8). Empirical research by Porac, Thomas, and Baden-Fuller (1989) also suggests that these cultural effects can occur at a supraorganization level. Their study of the Scottish knitwear industry found that a common culture strongly affected the values and schemas of an entire competitive group of organizations. The common culture emphasized consumer value rather than production efficiencies, and it limited price competition within the industry while emphasizing flexibility in serving individual customers. The link from a common culture to top managers' cognitive schemas and to their strategic responses is well captured in the descriptive phrase *cognitive oligopolies* that Porac et al. applied to this industry.

Interestingly, culture need not operate through controlled, rational processing to affect decisions and behavior. Rather, through its tie to limited-capacity models of information processing, culture can have a more automatic impact on decisions and behavior. Recall that limited-capacity processors often conceptualize a problem or issue from a narrow perspective, using heuristic procedures and minimal processing to generate decisions or behavior. This type of processing is possible because of fairly general knowledge structures stored in long-term memory. Such schemas may involve categorical structures used to interpret and organize information, or they may involve scripts that can be used to solve problems or generate behaviors with minimal thought. For example, Porac and his colleagues (1989) note that it is the mental models of top executives (learned through interaction with their culturally homogenous competitive group) that guide their interpretation of environmental conditions and enactment of strategic responses. Culture can also be equated with expert information processing when the knowledge structures of organizational members become more highly developed. In such cases, schemas can both guide environmental perceptions and evoke acceptable responses with very little controlled processing.

We propose that these knowledge structures provide cognitive repositories of acculturation experiences that exist on individual, subunit, organizational, or even supraorganizational levels. In fact, as we noted in chapter 8, these knowledge structures can be used to define culture. Moreover, we posit that these structures can be evoked, or primed, through reference to key cultural values or central aspects of these structures. Thus, when a CEO emphasizes quality in communications to workers and quality is an integral part of a corporate culture, a subset of workers' knowledge structures are made more salient. This increased salience of quality-related schemas in turn primes workers to interpret familiar situations in terms of quality and also to enact scripts that are related to quality. Because limited-capacity processors operate from a narrow rather than a comprehensive perspective, such priming of knowledge structures by a CEO can change the perspective they use to interpret events and guide behaviors. If all schemas were always available or were always considered, such priming activities would have little effect on the schema used to guide processing.

This view of culture has two significant practical implications. First is that culture can be a vehicle for executive control of workers. This interpretation of culture has been a central aspect of its popularity in practitioner-oriented publications (Barley, Meyer, and Gash 1988). Culture is also thought to be a means of controlling employees' emotions when a major component of the organization's product is providing a pleasant experience for consumers (Van Maanen and Kunda 1989). Control can arise from a leader's selective emphasis on certain existing knowledge structures, or new knowledge structures can be created through socialization and selection procedures (George 1990; Schneider 1987). The first means of control, emphasizing existing knowledge structures and values, is most easily used by top-level leaders to refocus an organization; the second means, based on socialization and selection, is more likely to be associated with traditional sources of culture. Nevertheless, the second means could be used by top leaders to change the culture of their small group of top executives. As we will see in chapter 13, this instance is particularly likely to occur during reorientations, when new management teams are brought in to create a fresh approach. Here, however, the process sometimes works in reverse, with new top-level executives being socialized into values and ways of thinking that are more in line with the existing organizational culture. Managing rewards is another common means of controlling workers, but Kerr and Slocum (1987) suggest that rewards can be used to manage culture as well.

The second practical implication is that, as with other simplification schemas used by limited-capacity processors, culture can be a source of error and bias as well as a means of efficiently processing information or coordinating activities. Thus, the very processes that can make an organization (or an individual) operate effectively can also lead to mistakes when schema-based expectations or interpretations are inaccurate. Yates (1983) clearly described how the "Detroit mind" in general and the General Motors culture in particular—which had produced years of sustained high profits—limited the ability of the American auto industry to recognize and respond to the competitive challenge of Japanese auto manufacturers. Similarly, the unique features making some corporations excellent performers at one period may make them mediocre performers later on. For example, Peters and Waterman (1982) identified 21 "excellent" corporations that had eight common cultural traits, but two years later these firms were not classified as being excellent ("Who's Excellent" 1984); nor were they found to be consistently excellent when rigorous statistical criteria were applied (Aupperle et al. 1986). Taking a longer time perspective, we expect that an organizational culture that produces excellence during one phase of the organization's life cycle may limit its ability to manage transformations to subsequent life-cycle stages. Hunt, Baliga, and Peterson (1988) make a similar argument, asserting that those schemas which are beneficial during one stage of an organization's life cycle may limit top management's ability to make strategic adjustments in other stages of that life cycle.

In short, the challenge for executive leadership is to manage cultures without being limited by either the values they espouse or the knowledge structures and types of information processing they elicit. It is only recently (see chapter 8) that leadership researchers have paid much attention to this indirect means by which leaders can affect an organization.

ADAPTING TO EXTERNAL ENVIRONMENTS

We have seen that internally focused, efficiency-oriented leadership is vulnerable to changes in important environments. Maintaining a fit with the environment is necessary, since organizations depend for survival on a continual flow of resources from the external environment. Outputs from the organization (products) must be exchanged for resources, and it is generally the environment, not the organization, that determines the acceptability of these outputs (Berrien 1976). Two major areas of organizational theory—strategic planning and organizational design—are concerned with the issue of adjustment to environments. These areas are represented in the middle portion of table 12.1, which depicts the primary focus of leadership tactics as adapting to external environments; such adaptation is often only a secondary consequence of the internally focused tactics discussed previously.

Choice of Markets or Environments
A factor with significant consequences for environmental adaptation is the choice of markets or environments. At various times in their histories, most organizations face key choices (for example, whether to devote more resources to a business, whether to sell a business). These and other types of strategic decisions can have tremendous impact on the types of environments organizations encounter. The degree of stability and the carrying capacity (munificence) of a firm's environment are largely determined by the strategic choices made in the past. One of the principal responsibilities of top-level executives is to formulate and implement appropriate strategies. Because of its obvious implications for the future, strategic planning is an area in which substantive leadership actions are crucial.

Strategic planning can be idealized as a rational process in which highly developed management information systems are used to scan and interpret relevant environments and in which decisions are made using analytic processes (for example, Porter 1980). Here, consistent with a rational information processing model, strategic decisions result from a process of conscious choice, extensive information processing precedes decisions, and decisions are based on normative principles, such as microeconomic theories. Under such circumstances, a key role of top management is to contribute to the rationality of such strategic decision-making systems. The symbolic activities of chief executives can support rationality (for example, their insistence on having all the facts prior to making decisions). Also crucial is the ability of chief executives to assimilate relevant information and to understand or apply analytic procedures. In such systems, top executives must be good rational processors (or rely on other rational processors) if strategic decisions are to be effective. (Chapters 13 and 14 elaborate on this point.)

Strategic processes are not always rational, however. Consider, for example, the actions of Pan American Airways, which made a series of questionable divestitures while struggling to meet its debt obligation. Specifically, Pan Am sold most of its *profitable* ventures (real estate and hotels) and its most profitable Pacific airline routes to concentrate on the competitive and marginally profitable airline business. Staw and Ross (1987, 62) suggest that the possibility of selling all the airline routes and concentrating on the profitable subsidiaries never occurred, because Pan Am defined itself as being in the airline, not the hotel or real estate, business.

Consistent with the bounded rationality exemplified by Pan Am's actions, much recent work on strategic decision making (Dutton and Jackson 1987; Hambrick and Mason 1984; Jackson and Dutton 1988; Porac and Thomas 1990; Schwenk 1984, 1988; Walsh 1989; Walsh and Fahey 1986) emphasizes limited-capacity processing or processing guided by more elaborate (expert) knowledge structures. Other work emphasizes what we have described as expert (Day and Lord 1990; Walsh 1989) or cybernetic (Daft and Weick 1984; Schreyogg and Steinmann 1987) processes in making strategic decisions. For example, Hambrick and Mason (1984) view top management's values and cognitive processes as having a large impact on strategic choice through limited attention, selective perceptions, and idiosyncratic interpretations of environmental information. Such processes can lead to poor decisions, as the above example illustrates; however, as Schwenk (1984) notes, limited-capacity processes can be functional in many ways. As we note in table 12.1, one important method by which CEOs affect strategic decision making is to select individuals with a particular type of cognitive schema or information processing approach. For example, when Lee Iacocca went to Chrysler, he built a management team of many former Ford executives who shared his product and quality orientation as well as his more action-oriented approach to strategy (Halberstam 1986, 565). Selecting individuals with the same types of schemas or ways of processing information provides a cognitive means of influence that is in many ways analogous to the hereditary influence of genes—the influence is indirect, pervasive, and enduring.

The cognitive structures of executives can provide a basis for specific strategy decisions, or perhaps more importantly, they can define a general approach to strategic decision making. These "metastrategies" for strategic decision making can be thought of as the "implicit theories" of top executives. Miles and Snow (1978) identified four different strategic types—Defenders, Prospectors, Analyzers, and

Reactors—that reflect different metastrategies. As we will show in chapter 13, these different strategic types also can be related to different ways of processing information when making strategic decisions.

Defenders excel at manufacturing efficiency and maintenance of traditional markets. They emphasize cost leadership, which is a commonly discussed strategy (Kim and Lim 1988; Miller 1988). Prospectors stress product development and marketing effectiveness, differentiating themselves from other firms by product innovation (Kim and Lim 1988) or by creating a favorable image through unique marketing practices (Miller 1988). According to Miles and Snow (1978), Analyzers blend these two approaches in producing and selling products. These new products are generally first developed by others, with Analyzers making minor refinements and being both efficient producers and effective marketers of these products. Reactors, thought to be the least effective strategic type, are generally late adopters of new products or production approaches. They develop neither product market niches to exploit nor large-volume production efficiencies. Reactors are not thought to be a viable strategic type in the long run, but this type may characterize firms in transition (for example, moving from being a Prospector to a Defender).

Interestingly, we think these strategic types would occupy different areas on the cusp model shown in figure 12.2. Defenders have a rather mechanistic, hierarchical structure that is oriented toward achieving production efficiencies. They minimize use of expensive technocrats (well-trained experts such as scientists and engineers) and emphasize formal controls (Miller 1988). Such firms would be on the back face of this figure and would normally operate on the upper-right surface, assuming they were in a relatively stable environment. They would not, however, be perfectly adjusted to their environment, since they are slow to change. Further, change would occur mainly through cybernetic processes, and so they would have to wait for indications of poor performance before they would attempt adjustment. Nevertheless, the small-scale incremental adjustments would normally keep them within the Defender region in figure 12.2. But because of their internal focus, mechanistic structure, and reluctance to change, Defenders would be susceptible to the slide around the cusp region that we previously characterized as a classic turnaround scenario. This pattern is shown in figure 12.3 (Path D_1–D_2–D_3–D_4–D_1). Though this type of movement was previously illustrated with respect to production cost problems, we posit that cost-related turnarounds would occur for Defenders only when newer, more efficient production technologies surfaced or when oligopolistic market structures removed incentives for efficient production. A more likely slide for Defenders

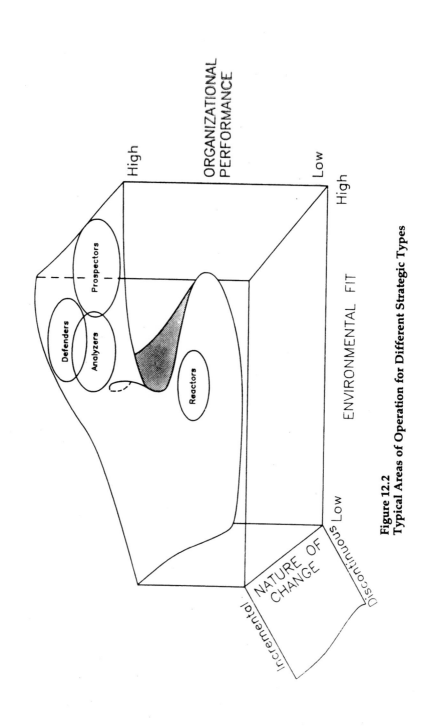

Figure 12.2
Typical Areas of Operation for Different Strategic Types

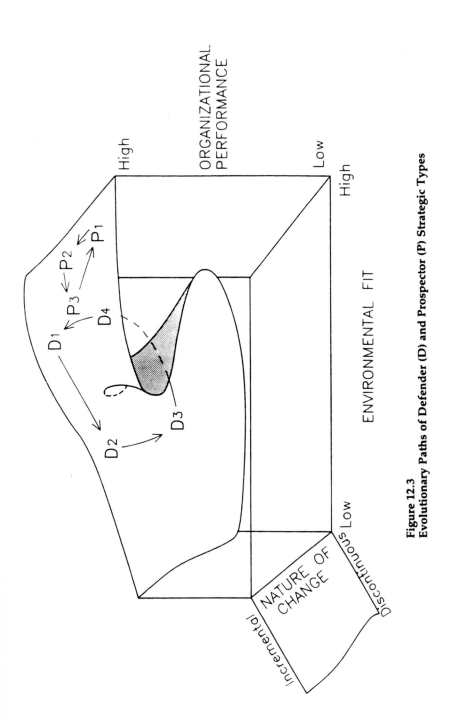

Figure 12.3
Evolutionary Paths of Defender (D) and Prospector (P) Strategic Types

would be in terms of product obsolescence or markets drying up, both of which require "strategic" rather than operating turnarounds.

Prospectors would occupy a different region in figure 12.2. Since Prospector organizations are geared toward product development and market research, they should excel at fitting their current market. They should be far to the right in figure 12.2. Prospector organizations are not very effective, though, at developing well worked out production technologies or administration systems (Miles and Snow 1978), which result in cost and production quality problems. Organizations emphasizing product innovation must also support expensive scientific and engineering personnel, and these organizations require costly liaison mechanisms to manage the need for integration in uncertain environments (Miller 1988). Thus, we expect that such firms would be at the front of figure 12.2. Over time, Prospectors would move toward the back surface, gaining greater internal efficiencies, but as their products began to drift away from the leading edge of the market, they would quickly adjust, moving back toward the front-right surface (Path P_1–P_2–P_3–P_1 in figure 12.3).

Consistent with the findings of Snow and Hrebiniak (1980), both Defenders and Prospectors are viable strategic types, generally being on the upper-right surface of figure 12.2. Each performs well because of different strengths, and each has different weaknesses. According to Miles and Snow's (1978) theory, Analyzers would occupy a region between Defenders and Prospectors, but they, too, should be viable performers. In our model Analyzers would be quite close to the beginning of the fold in the cusp surface in figure 12.2, suggesting that small errors might produce fairly large decrements in performance. Thus, we doubt whether Analyzers would be consistently good performers. Supporting this caution, Snow and Hrebiniak's (1980) study of plastics, semiconductors, automotive, and air transportation industries found that Analyzers were usually not good performers. Finally, we expect that Reactors would be on the front surface of figure 12.2, because their consistent changes keep them from gaining internal efficiencies. Because Reactors lag rather than lead environmental changes and lack a coherent overall strategy, however, they would lie toward the center left on the dimension of environmental fit, operating mainly on the lower-performance plane. The low performance associated with this position occurs because Reactors cannot exploit the marketing potential of a new product, since they exist in markets with many prior entrants (probably Prospectors and Analyzers). Reactors also cannot compete on a cost basis, since they are not large-volume, low-cost producers, as Defenders are.

In summary, this section has emphasized that the actions of executive leaders alter an organization's ability to adjust to its environment. Further, each of the types of actions we have discussed can be related to the cusp model shown in figure 12.2. Actions having a short-run impact, such as labeling a particular environmental event, may result only in a single shift along the environmental fit axis of figure 12.2; however, actions that change the capacity of an organization to adjust to new environments can be thought of as enduring movement to a different region on the cusp surface. For example, we might expect that organizations matched to their environment in terms of strategy and capacity for adjustment (organic organizations in unstable environments; mechanistic organizations in stable environments) would be on the back-right (high-performance) surface; mismatched organizations would tend to be on the left (low-performance) surface. Consistent with this assertion, Miller (1988) has found high-performing firms to be better than low-performing firms at matching strategies to complementary environments and structures.

As illustrated by our discussion of Miles and Snow's (1978) strategic types, different strategic types can be equated with different regions and paths of movement on the cusp surface of figures 12.2 and 12.3. Effective executive leadership can be crucial in differentiating successful from unsuccessful scenarios. Finally, the choice of markets has implications for the nature of the cusp surface itself: choosing a munificent environment would be equivalent to raising the level of performance for each point on the cusp surface, in comparison with choosing an environment that otherwise was similar but had fewer resources. Such effects can be conceptualized as up or down movements of the entire performance plane in figure 12.2.

Management and Production Systems

Many aspects of organizational design are concerned with an organization's ability to adapt to external environments. To reduce the impact of environmental variations, organizations can create buffers (backlogs of orders or supplies are good examples) and can assign specific people the role of managing boundaries with important environments (Adams 1976). Nonetheless, in highly differentiated organizations, such as most large manufacturing organizations, adjustments to changes in environments pose special problems. Differentiated organizations often develop complex systems to integrate their differentiated subsystems (Lawrence and Lorsch 1969; Galbraith 1973), and some of these integration mechanisms break down during adjustments to environmental changes. A key question in organizational design, then, centers on the trade-off between internal efficiency and the ability to adjust to changing environments (Miller 1988). We assert that top leaders are a major determinant of how organizations resolve this trade-off. They largely determine the strategic orientation and type of management structure that will exist in an organization, and they thereby influence an organization's ability to adjust to changing environments. Further, change in management structures is almost always initiated by top management. In this section we discuss two design issues that illustrate the importance of leadership activities. A more complete coverage of organizational design can be found in many excellent texts (for instance, Daft 1989).

The first crucial design issue is whether to have a more organic or mechanistic organization. Organic types of management structures—those involving less hierarchical control, more lateral communication, and more dependence on the judgment and motivation of lower-level employees—are capable of closer adjustments to changing environments than are more mechanistic organizations—those relying more heavily on formal, centralized, hierarchical control and communication. But if environments are complex and uncertain, the adjustment capacities of organic organizations must also be coupled with many integrating mechanisms (Daft 1989, 58). Strategic decisions must also be incorporated into attempts to match structures to environments (Miller 1988). The mechanistic/organic dimension is part of the front-to-back dimension—the nature of internal change processes—in the cusp catastrophe model of figure 12.1.

The contingency notion that the right type of organizational structure depends on the nature of the environment involves more than just the fit between structure and environment. Mechanistic organizations are more consistent with different strategies (Miller 1988) and different types of organizational cultures (as well as with different leadership styles for lower-level managers) than organic organizations are. These contrasting types of organizations also differ on such basic values as how much autonomy, responsibility, and initiative individuals should have. This aspect of organizational design must also be integrated with the technology of an organization. Thus, a key function of top-level leaders is to appraise these requirements and create a structure that best fits the combined requirements of various aspects of an organization. This task is not easy. In managing these trade-offs, leaders can find little help from organizational theory, which has only recently recognized that contingency theories need to incorporate a multidimensional notion of fit (Van de Ven and Drazin 1985, 347–57).

The second design issue concerns how various components of diversified organizations are to be structured. Key structural decisions, such as whether to have a functional or a divisional organizational form, also affect the ability of an organization to adjust to environments. The multi-divisional, or M-form, organization, which has partially diversified divisions with separate profit and loss responsibility, has become increasingly common in the past 50 years. A chief advantage of this organizational form is that it allows top management to allocate resources effectively across divisions, as opposed to allowing each division to use resources most efficiently (Barney and Ouchi 1986, 178). Accurate allocation is needed to adjust to environmental changes that affect divisions differentially. The M-form organization is also helpful in separating strategic and operating decision making, with divisional executives being responsible for operating decisions and corporate-level executives formulating strategy, thereby keeping top executives from being overwhelmed by operating decisions.

Under the leadership of Alfred Sloan in the 1920s, General Motors was one of the first major organizations to adopt an M-form structure; currently, though, it is the predominant form for major organizations. Thus, at some point in the past 70 years, top executives for most large organizations switched from a functional organization (wherein organizational units were based on specialties, such as finance, marketing, or applied engineering) to an M-form. This development shows that executive decision making, rather than natural selection, was the prime mechanism affecting the diffusion of this new organizational form.

Consistent with our explanation for the fold in the front performance surface of figure 12.2, the timing of such changes in organizational design can affect performance. When more appropriate organizational forms are beginning to diffuse through populations of organizations, early adoption of a newer form can result in superior performance. Armour and Teece (1978) studied the adoption of M-form structures in the petroleum industry, finding that the structure was associated with superior performance during the period 1955–68, when diffusion of this form was taking place, but not in later periods (1969–73), when most petroleum organizations had adopted this organizational form. (Only 18 percent of the firms in these investigators' sample had an M-form organization in 1958; by contrast, 78 percent had this form by 1972.) The role of executive leadership in adopting new organizational forms is clear, because *existing* organizations have changed form as they evolved. Population ecology models, which deny the metamorphic qualities of organizations, would predict that inappropriate forms would be selected out. We expect that such changes in organizational design would involve reorientations in terms of a punctuated equilibrium model and would require changes in leadership activities, strategies, and control systems (Tushman and Romanelli 1985), as well as in how information is processed (see chapter 13). Further, since restructuring reflects a major change in strategic and operating activities, it is likely to be resisted by management. Thus, an expanded latitude of action is needed to effect this change. Key personnel may also be replaced as a means of expanding latitude and effecting these changes (Tushman et al. 1986). Accurate perceptions of environmental trends would also be required for executives making early, as compared with late, shifts in a particular industry.

Less dramatic actions of top executives can also affect the ability of an organization to adjust to environmental changes. Organizations must collectively interpret the environment while they are adjusting to it (Daft and Weick 1984), and the kind of interpretations used by top leaders can have powerful effects (Walsh and Fahey 1986; Walsh 1989). One key process is the labels top managers give to environmental events. The work of Dutton and Jackson (1987) addresses this issue. These researchers posit that the meanings associated with strategic issues are often ambiguous and that this ambiguity is resolved in part through the categorization and labeling processes of decision makers. These processes affect the information that is attended to, remembered, inferred, and communicated to others. According to Dutton and Jackson, a crucial distinction is whether an event is labeled as a threat or an opportunity. Besides being an important label in its own right, threat can induce threat-rigidity effects in which information processing is restricted and hierarchical control is increased (Staw et al. 1981).

Empirical work by Jackson and Dutton (1988) indicates that threats involve the likelihood of loss without gain, low feelings of control, and perceptions of being unqualified in the presence of a threat. Opportunities, on the other hand, suggest a high potential for gain without loss, strong feelings of control, and personal competence to take needed actions. Interestingly, when characterizing a series of hypothetical but ambiguous scenarios, respondents in Jackson and Dutton's sample of MBA alumni were biased toward interpreting issues as threats. The investigators note that this finding is consistent with other work suggesting that managers operate on the basis of problemistic search (Cyert and March 1963) and find themselves responding to "problems" more often than to opportunities (Nutt 1984). When, however, the elements of scenarios are more consistent with opportunities (such as expected gain and high personal control), they are labeled as such; when scenarios indicated expected loss and lack of control, they are labeled as threats (Jackson and Dutton 1988). Since these distinguishing factors are often ambiguous in real situations, we expect that top executives could affect the interpretations of others by emphasizing certain factors (for instance, the potential for gain) as well as by labeling situations in terms of threats and opportunities.

The importance of such symbolic actions is also illustrated by the work of Sapienza (1987). She extensively studied the communications of top-management groups in two teaching hospitals that were responding to a similar environmental event concerning changed state regulations for cost containment pertinent to hospital cost inflation. She found that the CEOs and top executives in each hospital created very different images for these environmental events. One hospital communicated that the changes in operating cost regulations were "putting us in a box" (Sapienza 1987, 449), with assured loss of resources; the other hospital emphasized that the changes in regulations would cause employee suffering, leading the hospital to search for alternative sources of funding. The images of the respective hospitals then partially constrained subsequent strategic decisions made by top management.

In short, the capacity of an organization to adjust to environmental changes depends on the organization's design and on how key organizational members perceive, label, and interpret environmental events. Although organizational design is relatively fixed in the short run, it reflects previous leadership activities and can be changed. Perceptions and labels for environmental events are much more fluid and responsive to the immediate actions of top executives, though there may be persistent biases in certain organizations that favor one interpretation over another. Thus, actions of top-level leaders can permanently or temporarily move an organization along the front-to-back dimension (the nature of organizational change processes) of figure 12.2.

INFLUENCING EXTERNAL ENVIRONMENTS

Acquiring Resources and Maintaining Boundaries
To this point, we have been concerned with the role of executive leadership in promoting adjustment to external environments. But another crucial requirement is to use both direct and indirect tactics to change environments themselves, as is shown in the bottom section of table 12.1. Rather than guiding their organizations to adjust to environmental changes, successful executives often help to change their environments. Such actions have a critical impact on the capacity of an organization to acquire resources and maintain boundaries. Many strategic actions (for example, mergers, joint ventures, and long-term contracts) have an important consequence of promoting less price competition on an industrywide basis. As the work of Scherer (1970) has shown, directing competition to nonprice aspects can have a favorable impact on profits. The positive effect of nonprice competition was demonstrated by the American auto industry in the 1950s and 1960s, when Ford, Chrysler, and American Motors operated under the umbrella of General Motors' price leadership. Managing price competi-

tion is often important when overcapacity in industries would otherwise produce pricing near marginal (rather than average total) costs (Bower 1986).

Consistent with our earlier treatment, we think maintaining existing external environments involves mainly traditional symbolic activities. Still, creating new market structures or restabilizing markets that have been altered by worldwide forces represents a dramatic change, one requiring executive leadership to create new shared interpretations and to make substantive strategic decisions. But in this instance the focus is external (creating new market conditions), rather than being primarily internal (bringing costs in line with competitors). Hirsch (1975) provides an interesting comparison of the pharmaceutical and record industries, explaining the greater profits of the former by its more successful actions at controlling its market. Interestingly, in both industries, attempts were made to control "gatekeepers" (doctors and pharmacists, in the case of drugs; disc jockeys, in the case of records), but Hirsch notes that the strategies of the pharmaceutical industry were effective, while those of the record industry were not. Effective decision making by top executives and sophisticated use of institutional structures (such as the American Medical Association) distinguish between the actions of the two industries.

In the area of acquiring resources and maintaining boundaries, the actions of Lee Iacocca at Chrysler provide a prototypical and more familiar example. Iacocca's reputation as a leader and his ability to persuade outsiders (the federal government, the state of Michigan, the United Auto Workers, and suppliers, as well as key financial institutions) were essential factors in assembling the financial resources needed to keep Chrysler solvent from 1979 through 1981 (Halberstam 1986, 564). Iacocca's indirect actions also proved to be important. His role in marketing Chrysler products communicated both an improved emphasis on quality and an enhanced image of the Chrysler corporation. These activities created a better context for exchange with the environment—selling cars, in this case.

Interestingly, if we return to the cusp catastrophe model we find that externally directed changes have effects that are qualitatively different from those discussed so far. Rather than moving a firm's position on the cusp surface to a new region or creating a characteristically different path, successful external actions would *change the shape of the cusp surface itself*. For example, reducing competition can be thought of as creating a larger high-performance surface to the right of the fold and a smaller surface to the left of it. Such effects pertain to the cusp surface encountered by an *entire industry*, not just a single firm, and in fact they are created by the collective enactment activities of all members of a competitive group

(Smircich and Stubbart 1985). Increasing the competitiveness in a market has just the opposite effect. These two states of an industry are shown in figures 12.4a and 12.4b. Consider again the American automobile industry. In the 1960s, a company that had a moderately good fit with the environment in terms of costs and products (for example, Ford) would be on the upper-performance surface in figure 12.4b, but the same fit would be to the left of the fold on the lower-performance surface (figure 12.4a) in the market of the late 1970s, when competition was much greater in terms of costs and products. In other words, the same degree of environmental fit (shown by the arrows in figures 12.4a and 12.4b) could result in different levels of performance when the leadership activities of other firms (Japanese automakers) change the nature of the environment.

An alternative type of executive action is to focus on increasing stability in critical environments. Stability is particularly crucial for organizations that require a long lead time to adjust to changes, such as in oil production, or manufacturing new types of autos or airplanes. Vertical integration, wherein sources of supply or distribution are incorporated into an organization, is a key strategy for stabilizing relevant markets. Stability also allows for different types of information processing as guides to decisions, as we discuss in chapter 13.

We represent executive actions that affect environmental stability in terms of the front-to-back dimensions in figure 12.4. Stabilizing an industry would move the start of the fold toward the front, as shown in figure 12.4c, producing a larger area behind the fold in which firms can operate using conventional administration activities. To see the importance of such actions, consider the problem of an Analyzer—one of the strategic types discussed earlier. There may be a sufficient region for such a firm to operate in an industry that corresponds to figure 12.4c, but not in the less stable environment represented in figure 12.4d, where the start of the fold is very close to the back surface.

Where stability concerns are paramount, organizations often act collectively to reduce uncertainty. Alternatively, they may cooperate with the government to develop institutions (the FAA, FCC, and so on) that regulate the environment. Leblebici and Salancik's (1982) analysis of the Chicago Board of Trade, which regulates many important commodity futures markets, shows that changes in the working rules are used to reestablish stability when environmental change increases uncertainty. Though it may seem as if such institutions operate by themselves, which rules are changed and how they are changed are influenced by the environmental interpretations created by commodity traders and by their exercise of political influence.

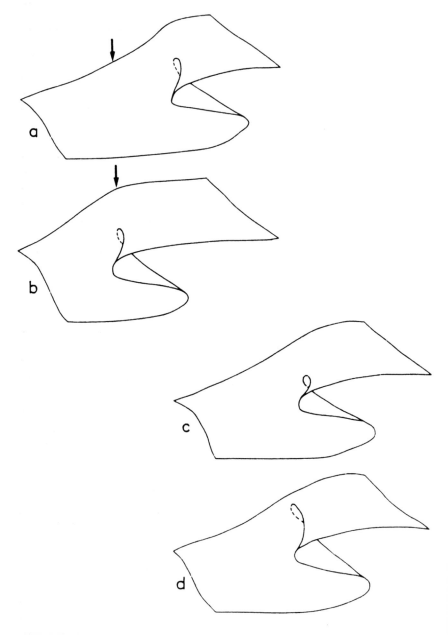

Figure 12.4
Reduced High-performance Plane for Competitive Industry (a); Expanded
High-performance Plane in Noncompetitive Industry (b); More Stable
Environment with Reduced Cusp Region (c); and Less Stable
Environment with Enhanced Cusp Region (d)

Rule changes often create groups of winners and losers, and these groups are not passive reactors to such changes. This process is aptly illustrated by Abolafia and Kilduff's (1988) analysis of the cause and resolution of speculation in the silver market in the late 1970s. Fueled largely by the actions of Nelson Bunker Hunt and his associates, who clandestinely accumulated enormous futures contracts for silver and then adopted the highly unusual strategy of requiring *actual delivery* of silver bullion, the price of silver futures rose dramatically, from $8.97 in August 1979 to panic levels of $50.00 per ounce on January 20, 1980. But the Hunt brothers and their trading partners had misperceived the nature of the commodities exchange market, believing it was a free market, when in reality it, like any social organization, was subject to a set of formal and informal rules. The Hunts had violated these rules, and those violations triggered a response that reaffirmed the interest of the established members. On January 21, 1980, COMEX changed the rules, declaring an unprecedented "liquidation only" order for silver futures. After this change, the price of silver immediately began to drop, reaching a bottom of $10.80 an ounce on March 28, 1980, and the Hunts and their associates lost several billion dollars.

The Hunts borrowed extensively to cover their speculative losses (accounting for 12.9 percent of all business loans in the United States in February and March 1980, when credit and interest rates were already high) but failed to meet a margin call of $100 million on March 28, 1980, creating a second crisis. This second crisis was resolved when the chairman of the Federal Reserve Board, Paul Volcker, fearing a dominolike collapse of large banks and brokerage houses, organized a consortium of banks to float a $1.1 billion loan to the Hunts (Abolafia and Kilduff 1988, 188).

As this example dramatically illustrates, the leadership of a few top executives can radically alter markets: the Hunts created a self-serving rise in prices, the COMEX directors reestablished stability in the chaotic silver futures market, and Federal Reserve chairman Volcker prevented destabilization of financial institutions. The example also illustrates an important requirement of top executives: in addition to being perceived as leaders, executives must also be able to perceive accurately external environments (which the Hunt brothers failed to do) and be resourceful in finding ways to change them (as were both the COMEX directors and Paul Volcker). More systematic evidence of this requirement of top executives is provided by Bourgeois's (1985) study of 20 nondiversified public corporations. He reports that the accuracy with which CEOs perceived environmental uncertainty explained more than 30 percent of the variance in their firm's economic performance (Bourgeois 1985, 560).

Changing Government Policy

Table 12.1's final category of executive action concerns changing government policy through either direct or indirect actions. Governments can provide resources through several means—specialized funding, tax credits for capital investment—and they also affect stability for some industries through regulatory or antitrust actions. Moreover, many large industries operate in global markets in which trade restrictions, variable exchange rates, and government subsidies are common. Therefore, important changes in environments may often require the actions of national governments. To illustrate, Halberstam (1986, 731) places the dollar value to Detroit auto producers of the temporary export restraints of the Japanese auto manufactures at about $1,000 per car. Clearly, these "voluntary" restraints, negotiated through the U.S. government, alter the nature of the competitive environment facing auto producers, in many instances making the difference between reasonable profits and losses. Similarly, the change in the value of the yen in the winter and early spring of 1986 (from 250 to 200 yen per dollar), created by the decisions of Japan's Western trading partners to bring about fairer trade, had a substantial impact on the Japanese auto companies, virtually eliminating the cost advantage of Japanese (as compared with American-produced) cars (Halberstam 1986, 743–44.)

The role of governments in changing environmental conditions is not always so clear, as is shown by Bower's (1986) in-depth analysis of the restructuring of the worldwide petrochemical industry. Plagued with overcapacity and increasing costs from the dramatic increases in raw material costs (petroleum) in the 1970s, the key problem faced in these industries was how to collectively manage a reduction in worldwide capacities. Bower's analysis indicates that downsizing was as much a political as a strategic activity that involved both companies (for example, Du Pont, Dow) and nations (Germany, Britain, Italy, France, Japan, and the United States). A principal factor in restructuring was the recognition by executives that solutions required the actions of the entire industry, not merely the actions of individual firms, which typically focus on cost reduction. Moreover, this recognition had to be persuasively communicated to the respective governments.

Such executive actions involved leadership in the sense that we have defined it, for the restructuring of the petrochemical industry was as much a political as a business problem. Organizations had first to greatly reduce their costs in order to become efficient producers of petrochemicals. They then had to adopt modern means of financial (portfolio) analysis to evaluate the comparative rates of returns on investments in different markets. But Bower (1986) argues that ultimately, the only viable strategy was political, requiring a restructuring of the industry to reduce overcapacity that cut across national boundaries and allowed companies to focus their competitive activities in market segments in which they had special competencies. The most startling strategic problem was that without coordinated actions, it was difficult for any individual company to find a strategy other than withdrawal from a market that returned profits on investments that were higher than the cost of capital (Bower 1986, 49).

CONCLUSIONS

There are several concluding points we would like to make. First, we have used real-world examples to illustrate the processes described, and we have tied our perspective to economic and organizational theories where possible. Yet it should be stressed that the typology and theoretical perspective we propose have not been systematically tested by leadership researchers, who have generally ignored how top-level leaders affect performance. We have based our arguments on empirical research when available, yet further development and empirical research are clearly needed.

Second, the means by which executive-level leaders can have an impact on organizational performance have been covered independently. In reality, however, they must all be dealt with simultaneously by a CEO. During reorientations, he or she must integrate actions that affect organizational systems, production processes, quality and design, organizational culture, strategy, and sometimes the external environment. This multidimensional aspect of top-level management creates a cognitive demand on executive leaders that is as important as the way these leaders are perceived and how well they are able to muster internal political support for key programs. Thus, understanding how top executives process information is crucial to understanding the difference between effective and ineffective CEOs. (This issue will be covered in more detail in the following chapter.)

One final point concerning the relationship of our perspective to current debates in organizational theory is worth mentioning. Astley and Van de Ven (1983) suggest that four alternative perspectives on organizational theory can be classified along two axes—a micro-macro axis and a reactive-proactive axis. We can relate the leadership activities we have discussed to Astley and Van den Ven's fourfold typology, which is shown in table 12.2. Their natural selection view, which is macro and reactive, corresponds to our description of failed executive leadership. Such organizations, locked into threat-rigidity effects or inflexible cultures, are unable to change to meet new

TABLE 12.2
Correspondence among Organizational Paradigms, Executive Leadership, and the Cusp Catastrophe Theory Model

Organizational Paradigm	Type of Executive Leadership	Correspondence to Cusp Catastrophe Model
Natural selection	Failed leadership	1. Back-left area
System-structural	Internally focused leadership	1. Back-right area 2. Turnaround path
Strategic choice	Integrative, internal-external leadership	1. Front-right area 2. Vertical movement of performance plane
Collective action	External leadership	1. Changes in shape of cusp surface

environmental demands and are selected out of environments. This type of response corresponds to region B* region of figure 11.1.

Astley and Van de Ven's (1983) two micro-level views—system-structural and strategic-choice—correspond roughly to the first two classes of leadership activities we discussed in this chapter. Internally focused actions, as well as some organizational design issues, would fall within a systems-structural viewpoint, being mainly reactive to external environmental changes. Here, reactions still require executive leadership, but the impetus is change in external environments. Such actions fit best with the turnaround scenarios depicted by a Defender's slide around the cusp catastrophe surface shown in figure 12.3. Astley and Van de Ven's strategic-choice viewpoint is more proactive, being based on a leadership team's collective visions of the future and the view that organizations enact their environments. It corresponds best to our depiction of Prospector-type strategies that move firms from back to front on the cusp surface (see figure 12.3), or in the choice of new markets with different performance surfaces on which to operate.

Finally, Astley and Van de Ven's (1983) collective action view corresponds best to our last class of leadership means, those that change the very nature of environments. We conceptualize such activities as changes in the cusp surface that represent organizational performance (see figure 12.4). We have two objectives in drawing out these parallels: (a) to note that alternative views on executive leadership correspond to alternative views of organizational theory and (b) to note that our catastrophe theory framework also integrates these alternative views on organizational theory.

SUMMARY

In this chapter we have systematically illustrated a number of means by which top-level executives can affect organizational perform-ance through actions that go well beyond traditional administration. Both direct and indirect effects of executives were discussed, based on Day and Lord's theoretical framework (1988). There are three main arenas for executive action: internally directed activities, actions that affect adaption to external environments, and actions that change the nature of external environments. Executives can have an impact on several internal factors, including subsystem organization, productivity, quality, and culture.

There are also several ways in which leaders can affect an organization's ability to adapt to external environments. Executives can create mechanisms to buffer key systems (such as production), they can institute more organic or mechanistic organizational designs, and they can choose relevant or appropriate markets and environments. Further, executives can also directly alter the nature of the environment through the acquisition of resources and the maintenance of boundaries. Leaders can, moreover, directly affect government policy that is related to the operating environment. Each of these domains can be influenced through both direct and indirect leadership tactics. We tie all the actions in our typology to a common analytic framework provided by cusp catastrophe theory, which gives structure and precision to our typology of executive actions.

Our set of actions is not exhaustive, but it does systematically organize the types of issues leadership researchers need to address to understand the impact of top-level leaders. These actions (a) require an expanded latitude of discretion that is closely tied to the perception that executives have leadership ability, (b) may be internally or externally directed, and (c) may focus on a single company, an industry, or interrelations among nations.

Part IV ———————————————————
Stability, Change, and Information Processing

Chapter 13 ─────────────────────────────

Executive Leadership, Information Processing, and Change

───

*I*n prior chapters we have focused on whether executives have an impact on organizational performance, and we have proposed a model for the effects of executive leadership on performance. In this chapter we will address several issues pertaining to the cognitive, emotional, and structural factors that underlie executive actions. Here we directly address the question of how executives process information in making key organizational decisions, and we relate our coverage of this issue to understanding change processes at both the organizational and the individual levels. In doing so, we integrate many of the ideas that have been developed in previous chapters and show how this approach helps organize some of the existing research on leadership and organizational decline.

INFORMATION PROCESSING AND EXECUTIVE ACTIONS

Descriptive Information

To understand how top executives manage the cognitive demands of their job, we need to begin with a synopsis of the descriptive information on executive decision making. Chapter 12 laid out some of the requirements of top leaders in terms of decision making—such leaders must function effectively as organizational engineers, developing appropriate internal systems, and they must at times also be environmental architects, designing new types of external environments in which they can operate more effectively. Such tasks seem to require reflective, logical processing that is firmly grounded in comprehensive, up-to-date information: rational information processing.

Yet descriptions of management decision making contradict this type of processing (Mintzberg 1973). Managers' tasks are fragmented; much activity is reactive rather than proactive; decision processes are disorderly and political; most communication is oral rather than written; and planning, if it occurs at all, is informal, incremental, and intuitive (Yukl 1989, 55–61). Managers typically spend less than nine minutes on any one task (Mintzberg 1973), are interrupted frequently, must make decisions before adequate data are available, and usually do not have refined analytic techniques to assimilate information and generate appropriate solutions. In short, they must use intuition, hunches, and guesses. They must also be able to cope with uncertainty, ambiguity, and the considerable risk that decisions will turn out wrong. Finally, they must accomplish this feat while constrained by normal human information processing limitations: a severely limited short-term or working memory and a fallible long-term memory.

Models of Information Processing Revisited

The inconsistency between what seems to be required of top executives and what they actually do can be partially resolved by referring to the information processing perspective identified in chapter 2. That chapter developed an information processing perspective and identified four alternative models of information processing—rational, limited-capacity, expert, and cybernetic. These models are briefly summarized in table 13.1.

Rather than being purely rational information processors, top executives often rely extensively on limited-capacity or expert processing models. Actions generated by these procedures are adjusted in a cybernetic fashion by both task and social feedback. We should stress, however, that executives use all four of these types of processes at

TABLE 13.1
Summary of Alternative Information Processing Perspectives

Model	Characteristics
Rational	Assumes extensive use of information and optimizing procedures prior to behavior. High long- and short-term memory demands make its descriptive value questionable.
Limited-capacity	Emphasizes use of limited amounts of information and general heuristic processes. Moderate memory demands make it feasible in most situations.
Expert	Emphasizes recognition processes based on elaborate knowledge structures in long-term memory and automatic linkages to appropriate responses. Low short-term memory demands, but high long-term memory demands make this model appropriate only for very experienced individuals.
Cybernetic	Emphasizes processing information while performing actions. Feedback is interpreted through comparison with standards and produces corrective actions. Very low memory demands make this type of processing easy to use.

different times. Similarly, at any one time, all these types of information processing will be in use in different parts of an organization. Further, at different periods in an organization's history, different models of information processing may predominate. Thus, the key to understanding executive information processing lies in understanding how individuals—and organizations—shift from emphasizing one type of information processing to another. We address this issue in terms of individual information processing by discussing Anderson's (1987) work on skill acquisition. At the organizational level, shifts in information processing are discussed within the context of incremental and discontinuous evolutionary changes.

Skill and Executive Information Processing

Anderson's (1987) ACT* theory of skill acquisition pertains directly to the transition from limited-capacity to expert processing. We will extend this line of thinking to suggest an ordering from rational to limited-capacity to expert modes of information processing. Further, we will suggest that cybernetic processes precipitate movement along this ordinal dimension.

Anderson's (1987) ACT* theory asserts that people solve problems in a new domain by applying weak problem-solving procedures to declarative knowledge they have about this domain. Weak problem-solving procedures are such general heuristics as analogies, means-end analysis, working backward, hill climbing, and pure forward search (Anderson 1987, 196). These procedures are weak because they fail to take advantage of domain characteristics—that is, the same problem-solving procedures are used across domains. *Declarative knowledge* is the store of domain-relevant facts held in long-term memory. This knowledge is distinct from *procedural knowledge*, which concerns rules about how to do things and which is also contained in long-term memory. Initial problem solving involves the application of weak problem-solving procedures to declarative knowledge about a problem domain. This problem-solving activity is accomplished using short-term memory as a work space for applying heuristics to information retrieved from long-term memory. Because of high dependence on this working memory, many errors in initial problem solving will be failures of working memory.

Several aspects about initial problem solving are important. Declarative information is not directly incorporated into familiar problem-solving routines; rather, it must first be "proceduralized" through active use and practice. Proceduralization involves encoding information into elementary units called productions, which are based on if-then relationships. Productions, in turn, can be organized into larger productions systems, which are hierarchically organized goal structures (Anderson 1987, 196). Such systems have many features in common with scripts (Lord and Kernan 1987). Interestingly, Anderson (1987) argues that proceduralization into production systems affects the transfer of skills. He asserts that transfer will be positive among skills only to the extent that they involve the same productions.

Initial problem solving fits closely with our description of limited-capacity processing. It involves the application of general processes to limited amounts of problem-relevant information. Even though it is heavily dependent on working memory and involves primarily controlled processing, it is not a rational mode of processing, because of its heuristic nature and limited data base. Rational processing uses optimal procedures and more comprehensive knowledge.

As experience develops with a particular solution and problem area, procedures are compiled. *Compilation* involves the development of more efficient domain-specific productions from the memory trace of a problem-solving episode. Thus, the process of knowledge compilation critically depends on the goal structures generated in the initial problem solving. These goal structures indicate how to chunk the sequences of events into new productions. As new problems are encountered that require the same combination of productions, sequences of productions are combined into single operators, and the productions in these sequences are strengthened. Thus, vicarious learning from leaders or culturally based tendencies to approach problems in a particular manner may have a pervasive and enduring effect on the type of problem-solving approaches that are developed, because each affects which approaches are proceduralized.

This compilation process reduces the demands that problem solving places on working memory, permitting more automatic processing. But it also reduces the extent to which minor changes can be easily incorporated into a productions system, thereby increasing the domain specificity of a skill and reducing the potential for transfer. New information cannot be incorporated into compiled productions without costs associated with disrupting this more efficient processing.

Anderson's (1987) notion of experienced problem solving corresponds to what most people would call skill development. It also fits well with our description of expert problem-solving models. Experts have compiled knowledge in many areas, and they also have refined categorical systems for determining the fit between stimulus environments and these efficient problem-solving procedures. We can now see how managers handle the many brief tasks they encounter: the tasks are familiar or routine, and compiled problem-solving procedures can be applied to produce quick and seemingly effortless solutions.

We can also see, however, what types of tasks would be

problematic for managers. Tasks in which the initial conditions fit closely but were not identical with prior problems would be difficult for managers to address. Here, routine problem-solving procedures would probably not work well, or they might produce unexpected outcomes. To solve such problems, managers might have to shift out of expert problem-solving modes and rely on more general limited-capacity procedures (weak problem-solving procedures and declarative knowledge, in Anderson's [1987] terms). Such shifts are likely to occur only after feedback, indicating that more routinized approaches would not work, and these shifts are costly in terms of increased processing time.

We also expect that repeated failure of limited-capacity approaches would: (a) motivate a search for more information, (b) reduce reliance on existing context-specific declarative knowledge, and (c) motivate people to find more effective problem-solving procedures. People would shift to more rational procedures that use extensive information and analytic processes to produce more optimal outcomes. In short, the search for new information and new ways to use that information (new heuristics) would characterize movement toward more rational modes of information processing.

Anderson's (1987) ACT* model of problem solving can be easily conceptualized as applying to the technical tasks normally encountered in many organizations—preparing a stockholder's report, designing a new product, handling a customer complaint, formulating a new strategic initiative. We should stress, however, that the same processes can also be applied to the social aspects of organizations. We learn appropriate ways of interacting with classes of individuals (for example, individuals of our own or the opposite gender) based on models existing in organizations. Once "compiled," this knowledge does not transfer well to new organizations or to individuals who do not fit existing social classifications. Reprogramming our responses to certain types of individuals requires that we move first to less efficient ways of processing, and it may interfere with already-compiled social knowledge. It may be much easier to use alternative social categories to handle individuals who do not fit well with familiar classes. For example, we may differentiate female executives from female secretaries, developing new ways to interact with the executives while retaining old patterns of activities with respect to the secretaries. Similarly, reclassification of a specific individual, such as a subordinate moving from in-group to out-group status, may require a dramatic change in compiled knowledge. Thus, compiled productions may be important sources of cognitive inertia that inhibit change at both individual and organizational levels.

In summary, we argue that through experience, leaders acquire task and social domains in which they can apply expert problem-solving procedures. Expert processing allows them to manage their job efficiently, but somewhat inflexibly. Flexibility can be achieved only at greater information processing costs associated with moving first to more limited-capacity processes and perhaps eventually to more rational modes of processing. We should also note that problem-solving activity occurs within the constraints of an existing culture, limiting the degree of movement away from current problem-solving approaches. Since organizations involve many interdependent individuals, movement away from compiled problem-solving procedures may disrupt the efficient work activities of many other individuals. Novel problem-solving approaches make the skills (compiled, proceduralized knowledge) of many individuals obsolete, as do new reclassifications of social groups or individuals.

ORGANIZATIONAL CHANGE

In this section we assert that many of the processes we just described at the individual level have analogues at the organizational level. Further, we posit that organizational change can be classified in terms of the kind of problem solving and information processes required. These aspects of change are relevant to understanding how leaders can facilitate or retard change. They are also helpful in understanding the difference between the incremental change that occurs during convergent evolutionary periods and the discontinuous change that occurs during radical reorientations. Important evolutionary changes will correspond to shifts in the type of information processing that predominates in an organization, particularly with respect to strategic decision making.

Organizations as Collective Information Processors
We can link individual, group, and organizational levels of analysis by viewing groups and organizations as collective information processors. This linkage is appropriate for several reasons. First, as we have explained, how one person processes information may be interrelated with the information processing activities of another. Novelty and innovation on the part of one person may require a qualitative shift in the type of information processing used by others. Second, our coverage of organizational culture stresses its link with information processing. The schemas underlying culture, as well as the types of information processing emphasized, may be crucial factors in defining culture. Third, we suggest that organizations provide salient models that guide initial problem solving and consequently affect the nature of the proceduralized knowledge that is developed. Fourth,

Morgan (1986) sketches a useful analogy between organizations and the human mind. He notes that both are hierarchically organized cybernetic systems that have the "holographic" capacity to reassemble coherent patterns and images from many separate pieces of information. Further, such issues as understanding cybernetics, learning, and learning to learn can be studied equally well as individual and organizational problems.

There is also a notable precedent for conceptualizing change as involving collective cognitive systems. Kuhn (1962) provides a penetrating analysis of scientific revolutions in which he depicts fundamental changes as involving the paradigms that guide normal science. According to Kuhn, paradigms define the dominant historical traditions and provide the rules and standards for scientific practice. In our terms, paradigms are the schemas that define "scientific culture." They also include the "domain-specific problems" and the "compiled knowledge" used by scientists in everyday activities. Kuhn argues that normal science occurs within the overarching guidance of dominant paradigms. Scientific revolutions and major advances in science, however, correspond to shifts in paradigms that make old science obsolete. They also undermine the reputations and skills of scientists attached to old paradigms. Therefore, they are resisted vigorously by such individuals. Paradigm shifts usually occur through the ascendance of younger, more flexible individuals to positions of power and prestige.

Kuhn's (1962) description of normal and revolutionary science is quite similar to the punctuated equilibrium model of Tushman and Romanelli (1985) that was discussed in chapters 10 and 11. The most obvious parallel between these two theories is that convergent periods correspond to normal science, while reorientations correspond to scientific revolutions. In much of the remainder of this chapter, we examine this similarity at a more detailed level. We argue that the paradigms that define normal science are similar to the schemas, information processing, and compiled knowledge that define a culture. Incremental change involves solving minor "organizational puzzles" within these existing schematic orientations. Reorientations, however, involve changes in the dominant schemas that define the culture of an organization; they function as a paradigm shift.

Another point is that often some information processing models are used in combination. Experts may define a situation and select actions based largely on existing schematic representations, but these responses may be implemented through reliance on cybernetic processes. Moreover, we suggest that movement around the cusp surface of figure 11.1 can be related to the models of information processing that predominate in an organization. The advantage of this perspective is that it helps us to understand the nature of change processes and it also helps specify the appropriate role for executive leadership.

INFORMATION PROCESSING AND INCREMENTAL CHANGE

Our central thesis is that different information processing models are used to generate incremental and discontinuous change. We posit that incremental change involves elaborations and adjustments based on common organizational schemas and compiled procedural knowledge, whereas discontinuous change involves shifts to alternative schemas. These alternative schemas make new information salient, leading to the development of new problem-solving approaches that are eventually compiled for easier use. When occurring on an individual level, such changes may take place automatically, in a manner that parallels our model of changed social perceptions in figure 5.5; inconsistencies and problems with old schematic approaches accumulate until new, more appropriate schemas are suddenly *recognized* as being appropriate. But when applied at the organizational level, the process is different. At this level, schema change involves changed cultures. Cultures do not change with a flash of insight; instead, cultural change requires executive-level leadership to identify, communicate, and support a new culture. In other words, it requires symbolic leadership.

We stress the information processing differences associated with incremental and discontinuous change; however, we should also emphasize that very different types of leadership, administration, politics, and economic factors are also associated with incremental and discontinuous change (Greenhalgh 1983; Tushman et al. 1986). Neither formal systems (planning, control, reward, or human resource management) nor informal systems (core values, beliefs, norms, communication patterns, decision-making practices, or conflict resolution patterns) require revamping to accommodate incremental change (Tushman et al. 1986, 33). On the other hand, discontinuous change also *requires* simultaneous changes in strategies, structures, power, and controls (Tushman et al. 1986). These changes compound the cognitive difficulties involved in shifting from one schema to another. Thus, discontinuous change is much more difficult for executive leaders to manage effectively.

We expect that incremental change works best with those information processing approaches which are based on a common underlying schema (or a collection of schemas). Incremental changes can be produced by minor elaborations of such schemas or by decision processes that are schematically based. Moreover, incremental change can operate within existing formal and informal management systems. When a common schematic framework exists, middle- and lower-level leaders can provide the elaborations and adjustments needed to align an organization with minor changes in its environments, because widely shared schemas provide a basis for acceptance and understanding of action, thereby reducing the need for top-level leadership. Walsh and Fahey (1986) also emphasize the effects of cognitive schemas shared by groups of people in organizations. They argue that the information processing and political aspects of strategic decisions coalesce into "negotiated belief structures"—configurations of power and beliefs that establish the decision premises within strategy-making groups. This negotiated belief structure reduces the political and power requirements of incremental adjustments, allowing the relatively fast responses (Walsh and Fahey 1986) that are needed for an incremental approach to be effective. Porac, Thomas, and Baden-Fuller (1989) developed a similar argument to explain strategic decision making in "cognitive oligopolies," which are groups of competitive firms linked by a shared culture.

Interestingly, much work on strategic decision making argues for a schematically based view (Hambrick and Mason 1984; Porac and Thomas 1990; Schwenk 1984; Walsh 1989). This work conceptualizes strategic decision making as more of an implicit, intuitive process that reflects the cognitive biases and values of decision makers. Building on earlier research on bounded rationality, Hambrick and Mason (1984) view top management's values and cognitive processes as having a large impact on strategic choice through limited attention, selective perceptions, and idiosyncratic interpretations of environmental information. Porac and Thomas (1990) assert that the cognitive taxonomies of top managers define potential competitors, often focusing strategic response in a narrow area, as we saw in our earlier summary of the work by Porac et al. (1989) on the Scottish knitwear industry. Similarly, Schwenk (1984) discusses several heuristic processes that simplify strategic decision making. Though such processes can result in poor decisions, Schwenk notes that they can also be functional in terms of reducing complexity, providing consistency, or enhancing political feasibility. We think such processes also allow organizations to use simplified, incremental approaches to strategic decision making.

Because incremental change is schema based, it depends on the extensive use of expert and limited-capacity models of information processing. Yet for an organization to adjust to minor environmental changes also requires some means of altering existing schemas or combining their use with other forms of information processing. We expect that one combination of information processing models, an expert-cybernetic model, would work well in producing incremental change.

Expert-Cybernetic Processing

Expert and cybernetic processes can be combined effectively if the three basic requirements for cybernetic processes to work well—meaningful standards, relevant feedback, and a repertoire of effective responses—are integrated by the knowledge structures of experts. Meaningful standards should develop from historical trends (Pound 1969) and should be part of the well-defined knowledge structures experts can use to classify environments. Moreover, given relevant feedback, faulty or outdated standards should be identified. We expect that the schemas of experts incorporate processes that seek feedback on relevant dimensions, although this aspect of expert processing has been given little theoretical or empirical attention. We posit that a combination of expert and cybernetic processing would be most effective. Cybernetic processing is oriented toward seeking and using feedback. Further, others suggest that problems are often recognized because cybernetic processes show discrepancies from desired states or standards (Billings, Milburn, and Schaalman 1980; Cowan 1986; Kiesler and Sproull 1982), supporting our suggested linkage of meaningful standards with feedback processes. The third requirement, a repertoire of effective responses, is a key distinguishing feature of expert knowledge structures. Further, these responses are linked to appropriate classifications of environments by experts' knowledge structures. In fact, Glaser (1988) has argued that experts' categorical systems are organized in a manner that facilitates appropriate responses. Thus, experts can move from problem recognition to knowledge of appropriate responses relatively automatically. For this reason, experts may be particularly effective at generating relatively fast responses to indications of problems, and effective use of cybernetic processes requires timely responses.

Research on strategic decision making by CEOs in the tool-and-die industry adds empirical support to our description of how experts process information. Day and Lord (1990) showed that the categories of experts (CEOs in the tool-and-die industry) incorporated information both on surface features of problems and on the underlying meaning or response implications of a problem. Further, they found that experts could make categorizations and decisions much faster than novices, suggesting that experts could move relatively *automatically* from stimulus categorizations to appropriate responses because highly familiar categories were organized to facilitate such linkages. These researchers' model of expert problem solving is contrasted to that of novice problem solving in figure 13.1. In addition to experts being faster than novices, Day and Lord found that experts made decisions that were more normatively correct, illustrating that the content-specific knowledge structures were both effective and easy for experts to use.

Extending these ideas to an organizational level, we expect that when organizations (or groups of top managers) share a common well-developed perspective, they can operate collectively much as expert processors do individually. That is, strategic problem solving occurs within the problem space defined by common schemas or negotiated belief structures (Walsh and Fahey 1986). Top managers can move from shared interpretations of environments to responses that are generally viewed as being correct without having to engage in extensive analysis or evaluation of alternative possible actions. Moreover, the need to manage internal conflict and build a common basis for accepting actions would be lower when expert schemas are widely shared in an organization. Further, as noted previously, incremental change can occur within formal and informal management systems that already exist within an organization. This capacity for efficient, coordinated actions by many people or many parts of an organization can be further increased when the common schemas are so widespread and linked to key values that they define the culture of an organization. In these cases, the major role of leaders may be the maintenance of a common culture and the core values to which it is linked.

We should note, however, that for expert-cybernetic processes to work on an organizational level, the collective capacity to understand meaningful patterns and generate appropriate responses must be coupled with the capacity to seek and transmit feedback, particularly negative feedback, to relevant parts of an organization. The normal tendency of people to avoid or delay communicating negative feedback (Larson 1989; Tesser and Rosen 1975) must be counteracted by cultural norms and management systems. Further, organizations must allow leaders to experiment, rather than encouraging consistency in actions (Staw and Ross 1980). In addition, retrospective cognitions must emphasize learning from mistakes, as opposed to rationalizing past actions.

The expert-cybernetic information processing model corresponds to the back face of the cusp catastrophe model, where change is incremental but is bound to an existing conceptualization of the environment and appropriate actions. The expert-cybernetic model fits nicely with Tushman and Romanelli's (1985) definition of convergent periods of organizational evolution. It also helps explain why the activities of top-level leaders are mainly symbolic during convergent periods. Where environments are stable so that the overall schematic

Novice (Panel A)

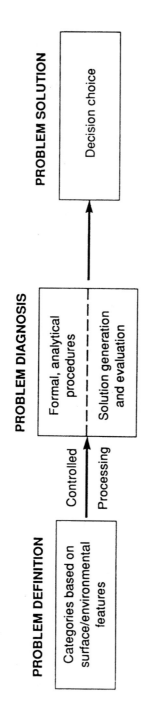

Expert (Panel B)

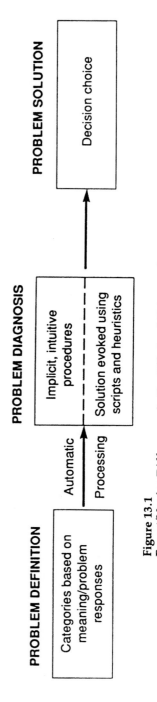

Figure 13.1
Expert/Novice Differences in the Effects of Category Structure and
Information Processing on Organizational Decision Making

representations of expert processors are fairly accurate, high levels of fit between an organization and an environment could be maintained by expert-cybernetic processes and extant organizational structures and processes.

Common expert schemas can facilitate organizational responses in both a cognitive and a political sense (Walsh and Fahey 1986). Then too, expert knowledge structures represent a repository of prior experience and learning for an organization. We think that because of these properties, organizations relying on expert-cybernetic processes would be very efficient, operating on the back-right region of the cusp model, an area of very high organizational performance. It should be stressed, however, that this degree of performance is gained at the risk of being unable to adjust quickly to drastic changes in organizational environments.

Interestingly, Eisenhardt (1989) provides a description of strategic decision making in high-velocity environments that is quite consistent with our discussion of expert-cybernetic processing. She found that in such environments, successful firms were able to use more information yet still make decisions more quickly than unsuccessful firms. Successful firms, she argues, relied on intuitive patterns developed through continual exposure to actual situations to assimilate information and make decisions. As we described previously, expert processors develop rich classification schemas and proceduralized knowledge through experience. Thus, expert processing provides a more precise definition of how the intuition described by Eisenhardt may operate. Eisenhardt also notes that successful firms relied on the advice of "experienced counselors" to speed strategic decision making, a factor that is also suggestive of expert-cybernetic processing.

Alternative Processing Models

It is instructive to contrast briefly the widespread use of expert-cybernetic processes with alternative information processing models for incremental change. Organizations emphasizing expert-cybernetic information processing would be more stable and efficient than organizations using limited-capacity processing (which involves more general but less optimal categorical systems, partial information, and satisficing decision rules) or intendedly rational processing (which is often slow and costly to use). But limited-capacity and rational processing may produce greater ability to adjust to dramatic changes in environments. Since these two types of information processing emphasize more explicit, controlled *choice processes* than expert information processing models do (see figure 13.1), albeit with different amounts of information processing, they should both be associated with organizational learning. Rational processing, since it is not as closely tied to existing schemas, has a greater capacity to facilitate long-term change, but it may also be slower in the short run, since it takes more time to gather and process the additional information.

Expert-cybernetic processing has advantages over expert processing in terms of having a greater capacity to adjust to changed environments. Predominantly expert processing corresponds to organizations that operate in convergent periods but do not continually fine-tune their structures and processes to minor shifts in their environments. Such organizations should either drift out of fit with the environment or quickly become misaligned when environments change dramatically. Finally, organizations emphasizing expert-cybernetic processing should be much more consistent and efficient than those using predominantly cybernetic processing. Purely cybernetic processing provides no accepted basis for choosing among alternative courses of action other than experimentation and learning, which lack political legitimacy (Campbell 1969; Staw and Ross 1980), and may be too slow when applied on an organizational level.

These brief comparisons are summarized graphically in figure 13.2a, which shows that region of the cusp catastrophe model which corresponds to each of the information processing models discussed above. We doubt whether the types of organizations on the bottom left in this figure are viable in the long run.

In this discussion of alternative information processing models, we have not addressed the extent to which the schematic or value basis for decision making is consistent throughout an organization. For all models, we expect that, to the extent that there is a common basis for applying any of these models (for example, a common organizational culture exists), the need for top-level leaders to be involved in substantive decisions would be reduced. Further, organizations should operate more efficiently but should also be less receptive to change. Therefore, they should be more toward the back-left surface of our cusp model, trading adaptability for increased efficiency. In short, the location of an organization within each region in figure 13.2a depends largely on the degree of diversity that exists within an organization. It also depends on how well top-level leaders manage relevant information processing and political processes when cultures are heterogeneous.

It is interesting to compare the location of these information processing types on the cusp surface with the location of the different strategic types that were identified by Miles and Snow (1978) and discussed in chapter 11. To facilitate this comparison, the cusp surface of figure 12.2 is shown as figure 13.2b. Several strategic types align with our characterization of types of information processing. We have already suggested that Defenders would be characterized by expert-

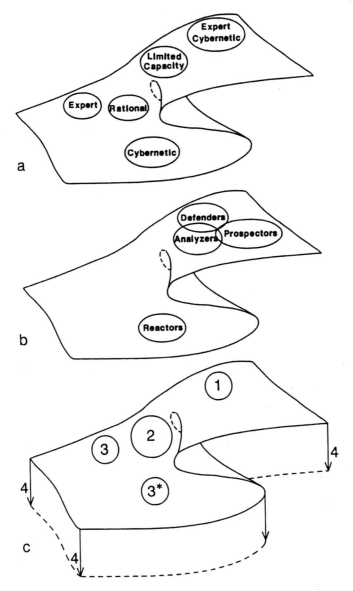

Figure 13.2
Comparison of Information Processing Types (a), Strategic Types (b), and
Phases of Bankruptcy (c)

cybernetic processing, and so this alignment requires no further comment. The Analyzer area is quite close to both the limited-capacity and the rational processing regions. We have argued elsewhere (Lord and Maher 1990b) that these two types of information processing have opposite strengths and weaknesses. Perhaps the low viability of Analyzers that was found by Snow and Hrebiniak (1980) partly reflects unsuccessful attempts to use both these styles of processing information in making strategic decisions. The Reactor strategic type corresponds to that area which would be occupied by cybernetic information processing. We posit that this type of information processing by itself provides little inherent logic or legitimacy for actions within an organization. Thus, while cybernetic processors may be receptive to change, they may have a poor environmental fit because changes are difficult to implement politically. Figure 13.2 shows that Prospector strategic types do not correspond to any type of information processing we have discussed; they are geared to handle routinely the discontinuous type of change discussed in the next section of this chapter.

INFORMATION PROCESSING AND DISCONTINUOUS CHANGE

As shown in figure 13.2, the more efficient forms of information processing are schematically based, but this type of processing hinders rather than facilitates *substantial* change. Substantial change requires sensitivity to new types of information and the capacity to use both new information *and different types of information processing* in order to develop new problem solutions and organizational responses. This type of change also requires dramatic shifts in many formal and informal organizational systems. In addition, it often destroys schema-based organizational competencies that may support existing power strutures and be a major source of an organization's competitive advantage (Reed and DeFillippi 1990). Thus, major changes are often resisted until performance declines are extensive. All these factors combine to place exceptional demands on executive leadership and other management systems when discontinuous change is required.

The cusp catastrophe model indicates that substantial change can be risky for organizations: the wrong change can produce considerably lower performance, which can threaten the very existence of an organization. This possibility often combines with the efficiency, cognitive, political, leadership, and competitive concerns to prevent discontinuous change from occurring until performance declines precipitously. Thus, to understand how discontinuous change occurs, we need first to understand the initial stages of decline that serve as a catalyst for discontinuous change.

Organizational Decline and Discontinuous Change

When environments change dramatically, actions based on an outdated schematic interpretation are likely to produce increasingly poorer fits with an environment. This tendency is particularly strong when schemas are well practiced and widely shared, that is, when they engender expert information processing within a consistent culture. If such schemas are also supported by a centralized source of power, they produce an even more inflexible negotiated belief structure (Walsh and Fahey 1986). Thus, the very types of processes that allow for efficiency and implicit coordination in stable environments limit an organization's ability to detect and respond to dramatic shifts in environments. Consistent with this viewpoint, Weitzel and Jonsson's (1989) research on organizational decline notes that the first stage of decline involves a failure to recognize important changes that have taken place in an organization's environment. Schemas can "blind" perceivers to environmental information that cannot readily be incorporated into these knowledge structures.

Weitzel and Jonsson's (1989) second stage of organizational decline involves inaction in the face of deteriorating performance. We argue that this development can be explained in part by the cognitive, administrative, and political consequences associated with shifts away from more schematic bases of information processing and extant organizational structures and practices. Initial decline may induce an organization to collect more and more varied information about the environment and also to consider changing strategic orientation, technology, control systems, or even core values. Such information is often processed in an intendedly rational manner by top-management groups, but uncertainty, differing perspectives, and narrow political interests may make any substantial change difficult to agree on. Such processes as threat-rigidity effects (Staw et al. 1981) and escalation of commitment to prior approaches that no longer work (Staw and Ross 1987) may limit the capacity of an organization to change substantially. Nevertheless, in addition to the psychological determinants of escalation, Staw and Ross (1987) also discuss social, structural, and project determinants of the escalation phenomenon. Thus, multiple factors limit an organization's capacity to respond appropriately to decline.

Meyer and Zucker (1989) describe precisely these problems in their attempt to explain why some organizations are characterized by permanent failure (sustained low performance) rather than effective adjustment to change. For example, powerful constituencies both within and external to the organization can exert considerable pressure to maintain organizational functioning even in the face of decline or inefficiency. D'Aveni (1989) describes a similar process, whereby organizations with a poor fit and poor performance "linger" for several year before changed environmental conditions force them into bankruptcy. During this period, such organizations consume their slack resources and sell vital components to generate cash flow. They also shift the emphasis of key personnel away from efficient throughput and instead focus on managing problems unique to poor performance (for instance, becoming skilled at dealing with creditors) (D'Aveni, 1989). Such changes, however, further limit an organization's ability to transform itself into a better performer. Greenhalgh (1983) makes a similar point by noting that during periods of decline, the slack capital or human resources required to support fundamental organizational change may not be available within an organization. Moreover, major changes take time to work through. Thus, shifts to more change-oriented internal processes may result in initial periods of inaction or in delayed action, which can further erode the fit between an organization and its environment. Interestingly, a combination of Weitzel and Jonsson's (1989) first two stages—the "blinded" and "inaction" stages—seems to describe aptly the drift from phase 1 to phase 2 that characterize the initial stages of bankruptcy in Hambrick and D'Aveni's (1988) study (see figure 13.2c).

Several factors directly associated with executive leadership may also delay needed actions. While prior periods of substantial decline in performance marshal forces for fundamental change, poor organizational performance can also undercut the inferential basis for leadership perceptions, often resulting in the replacement of top-level leaders (Schwartz and Menon 1985). Thus, changed leadership perceptions reduce the power of top-level leaders, and their ability to manage internal conflict may be diminished. Prior failure and the increased uncertainty associated with considering new perspectives may also make leaders more cautious. Finally, at this time the information processing demands placed on top-level leaders are especially high. Such leaders must carefully consider new alternatives in basic aspects of the organization, they must help manage the associated internal conflict, and they must communicate effectively both internally and externally. Each of these tasks is made more difficult when leaders cannot rely on intuitive, schematically based understanding. More information must be gathered, it must be interpreted more carefully, and communications must be more detailed and explicit to be fully understood.

In short, movement away from reliance on established schemas and heuristics places extreme demands on executive-level leaders. To facilitate change, top leaders must make increased use of more demanding rational models of information processing as a means of breaking away from the limits of prior schemas. Overlaid on this information processing problem is the emotional problem of operating during times of increased uncertainty when recent failures are still salient and when one's personal reputation for effective leadership is increasingly questioned. Finally, internal politics may be very hard to manage, because groups that stand to lose from proposed changes perceive high stakes and because slack resources with which to ameliorate conflict may be few (Greenhalgh 1983). How to manage such crises is a key question for leadership research. One danger is that leaders will spend so much time managing internal processes and leadership perceptions that accurate assessments of the environment are less likely to occur.

Frame-breaking, or discontinuous, changes are also difficult for other members of an organization, who must rely much less on familiar ways of interpreting and reacting to task and social stimuli. Instead, these individuals must think carefully about issues that previously had not been considered, and often they must learn new ways of performing important tasks. Such learning occurs, moreover, in the context of dramatic and widespread organizational change. Moving away from familiar interpretations, heuristics, and known responses neutralizes the schematically based individual and organizational learning that has accumulated over time. Thus, while more rational information processing increases the capacity to detect and respond to changed environments, it also reflects competence-destroying change that parallels the destruction in competence sometimes associated with the adoption of very different technologies (Tushman and Anderson 1986). Such changes are naturally resisted by individuals whose competence is destroyed or whose power is reduced. A key function of top-level leadership is to devise policies to minimize the negative consequences of such changes for both the organization and the individuals involved. Also important is a leader's role in devising ways of returning to schematically based modes of processing when fit with the environment is reestablished. The development of new schemas reflects movement up organizational learning curves, re-creating the competencies destroyed by change.

As this discussion illustrates, cognitive and organizational processes that facilitate change also have costs to an organization. Information processing becomes much more effortful for top leaders and other organizational members, organizational processes work less efficiently, and accumulated organizational learning becomes less relevant. Therefore, we think movement from the back to the front surface in figure 13.2 would be associated with a decrease (albeit a temporary one) in organizational performance. This decrease is reflected in the downward slope of performance from the front to the back surface. It is analogous to an organizationwide extension of Tushman and Anderson's (1986) idea of competence-destroying change (which they applied only to technology). Such changes involve more than decreased organizational efficiency; they may also create substantial risk if, in the process, organizations give up key areas of distinctive competence that are tied to causally ambiguous internal processes (Reed and DeFillippi 1990). These ambiguous internal processes as discussed by Reed and DeFillippi (1990) are very similar to expert processing as we view it. Reed and DeFillippi assert that these internal processes are a principal source of a firm's unique competitive advantage. Thus, the front surface of the cusp model is both less efficient and more competitively risky for organizations.

Times of change are inherently unstable, and there are strong pressures for movement to a new period of stability that will again be guided by widely accepted schematic orientations and consistent organizational structures and practices. Sometimes old schemas or values will be reestablished, perhaps resulting in further misalignment with the environment. At other times, new, more accurate schemas will be developed that fit better with the changed environment. In terms of the cusp catastrophe model, the crisis period near the center of the performance surface can be resolved either by movement toward the back left, an area of poorer fit with the environment and very low performance (which corresponds best with the assertion of population ecology theorists that organizations cannot adjust to dramatic environmental changes), or by reorientations that produce much better fits with new environments (a response consistent with views of strategic-choice theorists). The way such crisis periods are labeled helps determine which of these outcomes will occur. Dutton and Jackson (1987) propose that organizations label strategic issues in terms of "threats" or "opportunities." Such labels have a pervasive impact, affecting the meaning of strategic issues to many organizational members, the potential responses that are considered, and many intraorganizational processes related to communications and decision processes. Threat labels can elicit threat-rigidity syndromes (Staw et al. 1981), in which communication is restricted and control becomes more centralized in top administrative levels. Threat seems to be an appropriate label for the increased cognitive and emotional stress associated with movement away from familiar schemas and patterns of organizational relations. Change is also threatening to interest groups, which stand to lose power and prestige. Yet this label can also reduce the capability of an organization to change effectively. Conceptualizing change as an opportunity may produce much more effective strategic decision making; it also enhances an organization's capacity for substantial change. Because leaders have considerable power to affect the way others in an organization interpret key environmental events (see Sapienza 1987), they can foster either threat or opportunity labels. Such symbolic activities of leaders can be crucial in resisting or enhancing change, which steps move an organization toward the back or the front face, respectively, in figure 13.2.

We have depicted the transition from outmoded to more appropriate schemas as being difficult for organizations generally, and for top-level leaders in particular. Such transitions, however, can be critical to organizations, for they represent the major means by which the degree of fit with an environment can be significantly improved (Tushman et al. 1986). Sometimes incremental approaches simply cannot produce change that is rapid enough to reestablish high levels of fit with crucial environments (products, markets, technologies). For these reasons, changed organizational schemas can be a major source of discontinuous change. We posit that changes in schemas are a primary component of the frame-breaking transformations that permit significant evolutionary changes in organizations.

Yet it should be recognized as well that this change in underlying schemas occurs in the sociopolitical context of an organization. Frame-breaking change requires dramatic and nearly simultaneous shifts in organizational missions; power and status; structures, systems, and procedures; interaction patterns; and new executives (Tushman et al. 1986, 37–38). Thus, it is not surprising that innovation is resisted by a large part of an organization and that leaders must have considerable power to manage transformations.

Discontinuous Change and Leadership Succession

Leaders can have important effects in managing the labeling processes that facilitate or retard change (for example, threats versus opportunities). As we explained in chapters 3 and 4, leadership perceptions are also labels, and serve symbolic roles in organizations. It is ironic that when many key aspects of an organization are changed simultaneously, there may be substantial advantages in changing top leaders as well. In fact, Tushman and his colleagues (1986) note that CEO succession and frame-breaking change were coupled in more than 80 percent of the cases they examined. Further, when CEO succession and frame-breaking change both occurred, performance was higher than it was when former executives remained (Tushman et al. 1986, 42). New top executives can bring different skills, fresh perspectives, and greater energy, and they are also unfettered by prior commitments linked to the status quo (Tushman et al. 1986). Nevertheless, succession processes often function to maintain consistency in strategic orientation and in the cognitive orientation of departing CEOs (Smith and White 1987). To facilitate frame-breaking changes, organizations must select top executives who have different kinds of specialized training and different institutional experiences, that is, top executives who have different cognitive schemas.

Changing top-level leadership teams can symbolize substantial change. Leadership succession can be a signal that internal changes are needed, and it can also communicate to key external constituencies that substantial change will occur (Friedman and Singh 1989). Changed leadership may also reflect shifts in power, as individuals disassociate themselves from failed leaders and align themselves with competitive individuals and viewpoints. Thus, in failing firms, top leaders are often forced out of office and successors are more likely to be outsiders than is the case when succession occurs in successful firms (Schwartz and Menon 1985), although this tendency may be limited by the availability of outsiders who are willing to lead firms having extremely low performance (Dalton and Kesner 1985). Often, it may be easier to communicate change symbolically than by a detailed explanation of how each aspect of an organization has been changed. Thus, the scapegoating often associated with leadership succession may be functional when viewed in the contexts of signaling and implementing change. Still, leadership succession may also be merely symbol manipulation, as when new leaders are quite similar to departing ones and no real change in key policies occurs (Pfeffer 1977).

A final consideration is the possibility of using leadership change to manage both the symbolic and the competence-destroying aspects of dramatic change. If leadership change is used to bring in new leadership teams that have considerable experience with a new schematic orientation, then leadership change can facilitate reorienta-tion in both a symbolic and a substantive way. As discussed by Dalton and Kesner (1985), outside succession is one possible means of facilitating major change. Inside succession, however, can often have similar results. For example, when Ford Motor Company promoted Philip Caldwell to president, the company gained the benefit of his experience in operating in the much more competitive and consumer-oriented European car market. (Caldwell had headed Ford of Europe in 1972 and managed Ford's international operations for several more years.) Rather than having to learn new ways of designing, producing, and marketing cars, Ford could make use of the European experience of Caldwell and other key executives, thereby reducing the normal "start-up costs" of adopting new organizational strategies. Thus, leadership change can be "competence enhancing" as well as symbolic. It can be an important part of the process of moving from the left-front toward the back-right surface of the catastrophe model.

To summarize, we have asserted that discontinuous change can be understood in information processing terms as a movement from schematic to more rational to schematic (albeit new schemas) types of processing. This kind of change also reflects simultaneous shifts in many formal and informal structures. Top-level leaders play a crucial role in facilitating such change but, ironically, are often the most salient victims of change. Also explained has been how such changes can be conceptualized as movement around the cusp catastrophe surface we use to represent organizational performance.

EXAMPLES OF DISCONTINUOUS CHANGE

Defender Strategic Type
To see how difficult it is to move from the back face of the cusp surface, characterized by expert-cybernetic processing and incremental change, to the front face, reflecting discontinuous change, let us take a closer look at the turnaround cycle for two Defender-type organizations in the same industry—General Motors and Ford. These firms experienced the same changing environment in the late 1970s and early 1980s, but whereas GM maintained its basic approach, Ford was radically transformed.

Defenders have distinctive competencies (expert knowledge structures and information processing) in general management, financial management, applied engineering, and production (Snow and Hrebiniak 1980). GM provides a familiar example of a Defender organization, with a heavy investment in state-of-the-art production technology and a corporate philosophy geared to high-volume production. We assert that the specialized competencies of Defenders require the development of well-understood knowledge structures that are widely shared and perpetuated by the organizational culture (which, as Yates [1983] notes, is quite strong at GM). These knowledge structures are tied to a basic assumption about how a firm like GM will compete in the auto market, what kinds of approaches to issues like product design and marketing will be acceptable within the culture, and what types of management structures and control processes will be needed. A Defender approach can work well in a stable environment. But when dramatic changes occur, such firms will be slow to recognize that change has taken place and will be very likely to attempt adjustments that reassert the dominant schematic orientation. In other words, there will be a strong tendency to rely on expert-cybernetic processing.

Consider the strategic decision making at GM in the mid-1980s. After almost a decade of declining market share and poor product quality, GM attempted to increase its market share dramatically. This strategy, however, was incompatible with the changed and more internationally competitive environment faced (but not accurately perceived) by GM, though it was consistent with GM's prior competitive capability. The actual effect of this strategy was an accelerated decline and dramatic losses, necessitating many plant closings and a streamlining of the organization so as to be profitable with a much smaller market share. This reversal of GM's previous strategic response (contraction rather than expansion), based on new feedback from the marketplace, was another cybernetic adjustment. But it remains to be seen whether this type of incremental adjustment will be sufficient in the long run. Basic philosophies do not appear to have changed, and GM still seems to be locked within a dominant strategic approach and cybernetic adjustments to major changes in environments. Interestingly, these adjustments have taken place under the continuous leadership of Roger Smith, GM's CEO.

An analysis in 1988 of Lee Iacocca, head of Chrysler, also reveals cybernetic adjustments at GM taking place within an overarching expert schema. In his comments, Iacocca shows how GM has had to adjust its conceptualization of an acceptable market share over a ten-year period of increased competition:

> When imports went from 15% of the market to 30%, somebody had to lose. GM had about half the market then, and it gave up ten points to imports. GM has a 37% market share now, and it will never get back to 40%, any more than imports are going under 30% [they are now at 32%]. The problem all of us—GM, Ford, and Chrysler—have with foreign cars, both imports and ones made in the U.S., is to make sure the imports don't get to 40%. That would leave only 60% of the market for us, and that would be slim pickings. GM has to decide on its own, but I would think a third of the market is ambitious for it. . . . But will the imports stay at only 30% and will GM be content with 33%? GM executives say they're determined to get back to 40%; I don't think they really believe that. But I'll bet you that internally they believe anything under 35% will be a disaster. So everybody will go nuts over that last 5%. (Bellis 1988, 41)

What this analysis suggests is that despite hard times, GM has not made a successful reorientation, but its financial strength and vast resources still allow it to dominate the American automotive market. In contrast, Ford appears to have made this change successfully under the new leadership of Caldwell and Peterson. Although we have already discussed this reorientation extensively, it is worth noting that the changes at Ford came after a period of much poorer performance, when the survival of the company was maintained only by extensive profits from its European division (Halberstam 1986, 604). Further, the new leadership literally "bet the company" on a new product line and a new way of doing things at Ford (Doody and Bingaman 1988). To manage this change, Ford had to develop new "distinctive competencies" in such areas as product design, in which "driver friendliness," aerodynamics, and functionality became key constructs; product development, in which the prior "sequential and uncoordinated" approach to decisions was replaced with "concurrent, integrated, team oriented procedures"; quality control, in which new union-management relations and different incentive systems were developed; and marketing research, in which mechanisms for increased information on market trends were developed and integrated with production decisions (Doody and Bingaman 1988). Interestingly, these new competencies fit well with those which Snow and Hrebiniak (1980) found to characterize Prospector-type organizations—competencies in general management, product research and development, marketing research, and basic engineering.

Following Anderson's (1987) model of skill acquisition, developing such competencies should first involve new declarative knowledge and new ways of solving problems combined through the application of controlled processes. With time, however, such competencies should be proceduralized through "compilation" of these problem-solving routines as many individuals develop skill with new approaches. Such compilation makes new skills easier to apply but also limits their generalizability and capacity for further adjustment.

Of course, these dramatic and widespread changes had to be supported by changes in the corporate culture and management systems, yet they also necessitated an initial shift from more schema-guided to rational information processing. As Donald Peterson said, "Maybe we'd better do it right for a change, and do the research before making the decisions" (Doody and Bingaman 1988, 47).

In short, this contrast between two large manufacturers in the same industry suggests that GM has maintained traditional approaches and continued to operate within a dominant culture and negotiated belief structure by applying expert-cybernetic processes in strategic decision making. Ford, in contrast, has turned a much steeper decline into a successful reorientation. As stated by Doody and Bingaman (1988, 131), "GM has been *company*-focused; Ford has been *customer*-focused. GM has been *internally* oriented and preoccupied with reducing costs; Ford has been *externally* oriented and intent on increasing customer values." In our terms, Ford seems to have evolved into a new type of company, while GM has not.

Prospector Strategic Type

As our contrast of Ford and GM shows, we expect Defenders to operate on the back and lower left of the cusp surface and Prospectors to operate on the front and upper right. Miles and Snow (1978) note that Prospectors are almost the opposite of Defenders. Prospectors' prime capability is that of finding and exploiting new product and market opportunities. This type of organization is almost immune from the pressures of a changing environment, since it continually keeps pace with change and since it also frequently creates change itself (Miles and Snow 1978, 57). It has distinctive competencies in general management, product research and development, marketing research, and basic engineering (Snow and Hrebiniak 1980) that are geared to change.

Creating Prospectors out of Defenders—as Ford seems to have done—is a formidable task for leaders, and it is likely that not all aspects of such transitions will be handled equally well. Prospectors can be so externally focused that internal factors are neglected. The experience of Richard Mahoney as CEO at Monsanto illustrates such a problem.

Beginning in 1981, Monsanto sold businesses worth $4 billion in annual sales, including many of the businesses that made Monsanto strong: petrochemicals, paper chemicals, oil, and gas (Reiff 1989). Mahoney took over as CEO of Monsanto in 1983 and continued selling off businesses, while at the same time pumping considerable sums of money into research and development, particularly in biotechnology and pharmaceuticals (Chakravarty 1986). Mahoney's leadership was instrumental in moving the company to a Prospector-oriented strategy with a strong emphasis on research and development.

From an information processing perspective, it is unlikely that such a change at Monsanto would have been enabled without the alternative schemas provided by Mahoney. He was able to utilize alternative schemas that were more congruent with the environment, reflecting a rational model of processing. Since Mahoney took over as CEO, he has effectively managed the change effort, as profits have increased steadily (Nulty 1989; Reiff 1989). Alternative schemas (that is, redirecting the company toward biotechnology) served as a source of discontinuous change for Monsanto.

Interestingly, though financial reports show that Mahoney has successfully managed the transition in terms of performance, there is evidence that he has not effectively managed a similar shift in schemas among Monsanto's work force. Many members of the work force may have been locked into outdated notions of Monsanto's distinctive competencies, identity, and culture. Thousands of workers left Monsanto with the sold businesses, and many others accepted early retirement options (Mahoney 1988). *Fortune* magazine calls Mahoney one of America's toughest bosses (Nulty 1989), because he places a new emphasis on performance at Monsanto. As Mahoney himself reports, there is no longer a semipaternalistic culture at Monsanto based on forgiveness; now, employees are judged and rewarded on performance (Mahoney 1988). Many of those employees remaining at Monsanto are unwilling to accept this change in the work environment, as evidenced by the dissemination among some of Monsanto's employees of bumper stickers reading "Dick Mahoney before he dicks you" (Nulty 1989). In an effort to communicate the changes at Monsanto to the employees, Mahoney wrote a book, *A Commitment to Greatness*, available free to Monsanto's 50,000 employees. Interestingly, only 7,000 employees picked up their free copy ("Yeah, the guy's name rings a bell, but . . ." [1989]). In short, Mahoney has been less successful at generating organizationwide support for his actions. Although he has increased Monsanto's ability to detect and respond to changes in the environment, Mahoney has been ineffective at generating support from Monsanto's employees.

INCREMENTAL CHANGE, DISCONTINUOUS CHANGE, AND BANKRUPTCY

We think the framework we have developed for conceptualizing change agrees with current theories of information processing concerning skill acquisition. It also corresponds to theories about how science progresses (Kuhn 1962). In addition, it is consistent with historical examples from the business literature and with the empirical work of several researchers (Porac et al. 1989; Tushman and Anderson 1986; Tushman et al. 1986), but it also requires more systematic investigation. In this section, we seek to draw parallels between the perspective on change we have developed and studies of firms that have failed to manage transitions adequately. Some of this literature has already been presented (D'Aveni 1989; Greenhalgh 1983; Meyer and Zucker 1989), in our discussion of organizational decline. In this section, we make some more detailed comparisons with a specific empirical study by Hambrick and D'Aveni (1988).

Hambrick and D'Aveni (1988) compared 57 large firms that went bankrupt with a matched sample of 57 successful firms that closely resembled each of the bankrupt firms five years prior to bankruptcy. It is instructive to compare the two representations in figures 13.2a and 13.2b with Hambrick and D'Aveni's framework. Compared with the surviving firms' experiences, bankruptcies were preceded by a relatively long downward spiral of several years. Early in this process, available slack resources and performance declined. This situation can be conceptualized as movement out of region 1 in figure 13.2c to region 2. Region 1 should include mainly effective Defenders and Prospectors, but region 2 would probably include all four strategic types. The period of decline was followed by a period in which amounts of working capital were satisfactory but in which extreme vacillation in strategy took place within a relatively supportive environment. In this latter period, some strategic approaches were extremely conservative, with no changes in product markets occurring in the three to five years before bankruptcy (region 3 in figure 13.2c); other strategies were very risky, engaging in many new product or market initiatives (region 3*). The conservative strategic approach may characterize those weak Defenders or Analyzers which cannot break free of dominant schematic orientations that have outlived their usefulness. As we have described, such intransigence often reflects a combination of leadership, cultural, and labeling processes. The more inconsistent approach moves firms to the front face, very near the folded surface region 3*, a region in which we would expect to find Reactors, cybernetic processing, and a lack of effective leadership.

The final phase of bankruptcy described by Hambrick and D'Aveni (1988) was the "death struggle," which spanned the two years preceding bankruptcy. In this phase, sudden declines in demand produced sharp deteriorations in working capital (slack) and performance from which the organizations lacked the resources to recover. This situation can be thought of as an environmental shock that lowered the cusp surface itself, moving firms in regions 3 and 3* below the level of profitability needed to remain viable. That is, the entire performance plane moves to a lower level of performance, which we show as path 4 in figure 13.2c. Bankruptcy, or natural selection processes, can then be thought of as a truncation of this plane by a horizontal surface that defines an acceptable level of performance. Performance below this level does not provide sufficient resources, the organization's financial resources are consumed, and the firm is forced by creditors to file for bankruptcy. The final phase may be viewed as externally caused by an unfortunate turn of environmental events. But the prior phase—movement from region 2 to 3—has internal origins that correspond to the type of information processing used and to the nature of executive leadership processes. It reflects a failure to manage the discontinuous changes periodically required by organizations in the evolutional process we have discussed.

This study provides some support for the framework we have developed; however, more research is clearly needed. Managing discontinuous change is a challenging problem for top-level leadership. We need both better theory and better understanding of applied techniques that can help organizations and leaders traverse these difficult transitions. We conclude by offering a few general observations of continuous and discontinuous change at both individual and organizational levels.

GENERAL MODEL OF CHANGE

There are many parallels between our coverage of changes in social perceptions in chapter 5 and our coverage of organizational changes in this chapter. Though we do not suggest that the processes are identical, we do think it useful briefly to note these parallels. Effective leaders must be concerned with change at both levels, and scientists concerned with leadership might benefit from this dual focus as well.

The most obvious parallel is that changes in social perceptions and such organizational factors as strategy can be either incremental or discontinuous. This parallel can be easily seen by comparing figure 5.5 and figure 11.1, which shows that a cusp catastrophe model fits both individual-level changes in perceptions and change at an organizational level.

A second area of similarity is that change is generally the result of a combination of cybernetic and other forms of information processing. Discontinuous change may involve attempts to use more effortful types of processing so as to make sense of large or persistent discrepancies. For example, at an organizational level, strategic decision making may shift from expert processing using compiled and familiar approaches to more general weak problem-solving approaches, in order to make sense of new data or discrepant results–limited-capacity processing. Similarly, at an individual level, the simple tagging of inconsistent behaviors onto existing schemas may be replaced by more effortful attempts to understand the causal basis of inconsistent behaviors. The heuristics involved in attributional analyses may be general procedures that reflect either limited-capacity (relying on salience or script consistency) or more rational approaches (for example, using Kelley's [1973] consensus, consistency, and distinctiveness information).

A third area of similarity is that discontinuous change requires many more cognitive, emotional, and social adjustments than incremental change does. If our focus is on social perceptions, changing the classifications we have applied to other persons requires more effortful (less automatic) processing to make sense of their behavior and also to generate appropriate responses to an individual. Compiled knowledge that formerly could be used to facilitate interactions with that person may no longer be relevant. For example, consider how the promotion of a colleague may immediately alter our relationship with that person. Similar processes occur at an organizational level, wherein frame-breaking changes can destroy previous competencies and require much more effortful forms of cognitive processing.

When social perceptions change, emotion is involved in both the reconciling of new and old classifications and in the greater uncertainty inherent in new interactions with the person, particularly if reclassifications involve affective responses as well. When we must interact in a novel fashion with respect to an individual, we do not know how he or she will respond, and at the same time we are more likely to be held personally responsible than we would be for more routine actions. We have already discussed how threatening frame-breaking change can be at an organizational level. The risk and uncertainty are greatly compounded, since many more relationships can be involved and since many organizational rewards (power, prestige, employment) may change with reorientations.

Finally, certain social factors resist change in both social classifications and organizational reorientations. Social classifications can provide a basis for dyadic interactions, as we suggested in chapter 7 in our discussion of dyadic leadership. When classifications change, so does the established pattern of interactions. Such changes may be resisted by the reclassified member of a dyad who seeks to restore the prior, more comfortable relationship. Similarly, at an organizational level schematic changes produce winners and losers on many dimensions. Losers naturally resist such changes. Discontinuous change also requires simultaneous shifts—in power, organizational structures, strategies, and control processes—that may be resisted by many individuals.

An information processing approach can also be used to develop general principles that explain stability and change at multiple levels. We think the following five principles are fairly general, but this issue obviously requires additional research. First, information processing, social and organizational activities occur within hierarchical structures, albeit different types of structures. For example, at the level of individual cognitions, both goals and categories are organized hierarchically (Lord and Foti 1986).

Second, stability in these hierarchical systems can be maintained by movement up and down those hierarchies, as long as this movement stays within the same schematic structure (type of category or script, specific management strategic frame, or organizational subculture). Movement downward within these schemas generally relies on automatic processes.

Third, downward movement reflects attempts to maintain fit with a relevant environment through schema-guided adjustments (such as a search for problem solutions within the limited set of alternatives suggested by a script; the fit of person features with prior labels; or a search for a better-fitting organizational strategy within a threat or an opportunity decision-making frame).

Fourth, dramatic change results from *horizontal movement* in hierarchical systems (for example, use of contrasting categories in person perception, alternative scripts in task activities, or relabeling of environments as opportunities rather than threats in strategic decision making). Nevertheless, whether change is viewed as continuous or discontinuous also depends on the level at which change is measured.

Fifth, horizontal movement at any level of the hierarchical system will be seen as discontinuous for measures directly related to that level but as more continuous change for measures related to higher levels. For example, working within high-level goal-related schema may produce continuous changes in task performance but discontinuous changes in lower-level measures related to task strategies or behaviors.

SUMMARY

In this chapter, we have discussed the importance of using alternative information processing models at both individual and organizational levels of analysis, and we have related these alternative models to change processes. At the individual level, executives may use either declarative knowledge, which corresponds to limited-capacity processing, or compiled knowledge, which corresponds to expert processing, to solve problems. Over time, declarative knowledge and "weak" but general problem-solving heuristics become compiled into specific, domain-relevant problem-solving procedures. Declarative knowledge can be applied to many domains but may be less efficient than compiled, proceduralized knowledge. Compiled knowledge, on the other hand, is highly efficient but may lead to inflexible, inappropriate responses because of its domain-specific nature. Thus, individuals can move from rational to limited-capacity to expert processing to achieve greater efficiency, and they can move back to rational processing to achieve greater flexibility of response.

At the organizational level, evolutionary changes correspond to changes in type of information processing. Different types of information processing are associated with incremental and discontinuous change. Incremental change works best with information processing that is schematically based, particularly when there are common sets of organizational schemas, reflecting limited-capacity or expert processing. Incremental change implies slight modifications within schemas, which can be accomplished by a combination of expert and cybernetic processing. The type of leadership required during incremental change is mainly symbolic, because no dramatic change is needed. These types of information processing work well only in stable environments.

Discontinuous change is inhibited by the very processes that make incremental change efficient. Such types of information processing may render an organization inflexible and limit the ability to detect or respond to shifts in the environment, thereby leading to organizational decline. Information processing demands on leaders during discontinuous change are high. Thus, during these periods, executives should make use of rational processing, which increases the ability to detect and respond to change. Leaders are required not only to detect change but to devote considerable energy to minimizing the deleterious effects of change on organization members. Therefore, a shift to rational processing is likely to produce a temporary decline in performance. This chapter used a study of organizational bankruptcy (Hambrick and D'Aveni 1988) to illustrate the change framework.

Also presented were examples of discontinuous change in two types of organizations: Defenders and Prospectors (Miles and Snow 1978). Defenders function quite well in stable environments because they can rely on commonly understood schemas to maintain functioning. If, however, the environment is unstable, Defenders may be slow to react to these changes and may find it difficult to break away from the dominant schema. Here, expert-cybernetic processing is likely to predominate. Comparing performance with existing standards will result only in incremental change. Prospectors, on the other hand, tend to seek out change by continually identifying new markets, technologies, and other opportunities. Thus, unstable environments may pose little threat to these latter types of organizations.

In the last section of this chapter, we outlined a general model of change, noting four similarities between organizational change and change in social perceptions (chapter 5). First, in both cases change can be either incremental or discontinuous, and these two types of change can be represented on a cusp catastrophe surface. Second, change in both situations usually involves some form of cybernetic processing in combination with other forms of information processing. Third, discontinuous change at both levels requires much more adjustment, in cognitive, emotional, and social realms. Fourth, there are social factors that resist change in both social classifications and organizational reorientations. Concluding the chapter was a description of five general principles that explain stability and change.

Relationships among Power, Leader Traits, and Change

─────────────────────────────────

The coverage of leadership in this book is quite different from traditional leadership theories. Yet as shown in this chapter, several recent works concerning leadership are relevant to the perspective we have developed. We relate this work on leadership to four main issues: (a) how leaders can increase their power and expand their latitude of discretion, (b) what traits or characteristics may be relevant to effective leadership during convergent and reorientation periods, (c) how experience and intuition reduce information processing demands, and (d) how leaders can effectively manage organizational change. We also suggest several areas of future research that are needed to provide additional empirical support for our perspective.

RELATED VIEWS OF LEADERSHIP

Latitude of Discretion
Hambrick and Finkelstein (1987) identify three determinants of a leader's latitude of discretion—factors in the environment, the organization, and the chief executive's own attributes. We suggested in chapter 12 that collective actions directed at the external environment can change key aspects of markets or environments, expanding the latitude of action for an organization. Certain strategic decisions (choice of products or markets) also have this effect. In this section, however, we focus mainly on the latter two determinants of discretion—the organization and the attributes of a CEO.

Organizational Factors. Chief executives' latitude of action is limited by organizational factors that make change more difficult (size, age, culture, and capital intensity), insufficient resources, and powerful inside forces besides the CEO. These limitations can be particularly severe during periods of extreme decline, when slack resources are scarce and when powerful others engage in political actions aimed at protecting their slice of a shrinking pie. Although little can be done to change these factors in the short run, a farsighted executive should realize that such periods will occur from time to time in organizations. Thus, he or she should attempt to expand the latitude of discretion during convergent periods. Here, two approaches seem likely to succeed, each of them corresponding to topics already covered by leadership researchers.

The first of these approaches is to build political support of key constituencies in organizations during convergent periods in order to enhance one's ability to exert influence at a later time. This idea corresponds directly to Hollander's (1958) notion that leaders build up "idiosyncratic credit" by demonstrating contributions to a group and loyalty to a group's norms. Such credits exist only in the perceptions of followers, but they allow a leader to take innovative actions in the direction of needed change (Hollander 1978, 40–42). In other words, by conforming to group norms, leaders may gain increased latitude for innovative actions when those actions are seen as needed and within the role of leadership activities.

While much of the support for Hollander's theory comes from group-level studies of leadership (for example, Bray, Johnson and Chilstrom 1982), there seems to be an obvious analogue at the organizational level: symbolic activities during convergent periods and a history of contribution to an organization may provide a basis for exceptional actions during reorientation periods. This idea is perhaps the best explanation for Philip Caldwell's exceptional actions at Ford. When he assumed the role of CEO, he had a long history of contribution to the company, and it was widely recognized by others that dramatic actions on the part of a CEO were needed. We think top leaders, particularly female executives, should be aware of the notion of idiosyncratic credit. Moreover, they should realize that it is primarily a perceptual process and that such perceptions can be managed.

The second approach to expanding discretion is through creating a culture that is more receptive to change. Many of the ways culture can be changed were covered in chapter 8, in which we noted the numerous recent works on leadership that focus on culture. Here we wish only to stress three points. One is that building a more heterogeneous culture creates an array of alternative schemas and sources of information that can be called on in times of crisis. These alternatives facilitate change as follows: (a) alternative schemas serve as new sources of information and promote different interpretations of existing information, and (b) alternative ways of processing information become practiced in more heterogeneous cultures, so that the type of information processing modes needed to support dramatic changes are familiar and socially accepted.

Our second point is that there are advantages to developing a culture capable of dramatic change *prior* to the need for such change. These advantages can be illustrated by the distinction between declarative and proceduralized or compiled knowledge discussed in chapter 13. Since change itself is unsettling and demands increased attention and controlled processing, we posit that organizations need to "proceduralize" the processes that facilitate change. Otherwise, these supportive processes will compete for attention with the substantive issues associated with change. In other words, organizationwide "coping skills" need to be proceduralized through experience so that they can be applied quickly and effortlessly during times when dramatic change is considered and implemented. For example, Linville and Clark (1989) indicate that stress management techniques can be proceduralized, which might make it easier to manage change.

The need for proceduralized change processes pertains to CEOs as well as other top managers. Declarative knowledge pertaining to managing stress, uncertainty, or political factions is probably insufficient during times of reorientation. As we explained in chapter 13, periods of change are already demanding in a cognitive and emotional sense. Key people cannot spend the time or emotion to determine how to manage stress or organizational processes. Instead, they must rely on already-practiced routines. We think managing heterogeneous cultures provides some opportunity for practicing such routines. Having experience with managing reorientations also helps proceduralize needed skills. Thus, Prospector-type organizations may have a repertoire of practiced skills that gives them a competitive advantage when reorientation is needed. For example, experience may proceduralize many of the aspects associated with threat versus opportunity labeling (Dutton and Jackson 1987; Jackson and Dutton 1988), such as expanded versus contracted information use or centralization versus decentralization of power and decision making.

Our third point is that the culture relevant to change may extend beyond an organization. Competitors can serve as key models that suggest alternative ways to address competitive issues. Where competitive groups reflect a diversity of schemas, they can be a source that facilitates change. Still, as Porac and his colleagues' (1989) work on the Scottish knitwear industry shows, when a consistent culture links competitors, "cognitive oligopolies" can restrict alternative approaches. In such situations, external scanning provides no new models of how a firm can approach strategic issues, and social comparison processes can reinforce current approaches. We expect that these tendencies could be especially severe when competitors share a long, common history and are geographically clustered (autos in Detroit, steel in Pittsburgh, tires in Akron, or computers in the Silicon Valley). In such situations, international perspectives might need to be developed to facilitate substantial change.

CEO Characteristics. Hambrick and Finkelstein (1987) assert that several characteristics increase leaders' latitude of discretion. Such factors include high aspiration levels, tolerance for ambiguity, cognitive complexity, internal locus of control, and political acumen. Many of these same characteristics (for instance, cognitive complexity) pertain to the capacity of top executives to make effective decisions. Three factors not cited by Hambrick and Finkelstein will be discussed briefly in this section: need for achievement, power, and charisma.

Traditional research on need for achievement relates this personality variable to aspiration levels (Jackson 1974; McClelland 1961), particularly when goals are self-set (Hollenbeck, Williams, and Klein 1989; Kernan and Lord 1988). On the basis of this work, we would expect that CEOs high in the need for achievement have aspiration levels that are upwardly biased, or much more likely to be raised than lowered. Recall our example of Richard J. Mahoney of Monsanto: he continually raised goals as soon as previous goals were almost achieved (Nulty 1989). Such executives would be highly sensitive to cybernetic processes used to define problems and make adjustments; that is, they would be highly sensitive to standards and relevant feedback. They would probably also be proactive sources of change, since "problems" would be defined by increases in their aspiration levels, rather than by performance below historical levels. Thus, the initiative of these executives may increase their latitude of action.

Need for achievement is also of interest because at least in small firms, it has been related to the type of information processing that we suggest is required for fundamental or radical change. Miller, Droge, and Toulouse (1988) found that *in small firms*, CEOs with a higher need for achievement emphasized more rational analytic processes for making strategic decisions. Further, rational strategic decision-making processes were found to be reciprocally related to product innovation. Rational decision-making procedures tended to be required for innovation because many nonroutine problems in design and implementation arise in the process of commercializing new products. These problems also require extensive interactions among decision makers. These very processes of analysis and interaction, however, also produce further innovation. Thus, in the study by Miller and his colleagues, the personality of CEOs affected the processes and structures that in turn produced product innovation. This example illustrates how the need for achievement can increase the latitude of action of CEOs.

Power and influence have been studied frequently in the context of leadership (Lord 1977; Yukl 1989). The power bases used by leaders (French and Raven 1959) also pertain to their latitude of action. Some types of power—legitimate, reward, and coercive—depend on a leader's position, while expert and referent types of power depend on the personal qualities of an influencing agent, *as perceived by others.* Expertise must be perceived by others and must be demonstrated through such actions as effective problem solving in order to be a continual source of power. Referent power depends on the leader's developing the deep friendship and loyalty of others, which action can lead others to identify with a leader and adopt attitudes and values that are similar to the leader's. Thus, referent power may serve as a source of cultural change in addition to serving as basis for short-term influence. Several aspects of these two sources of power should be noted. First, they can be used for upward, lateral, or downward influence (Yukl 1989). Second, they depend on the perceptions of others as built up over a period of time, through recognition and inferential processes. Third, these sources of power supplement the position power of leadership roles and may also be the basis of developing extensive networks of relationships that provide timely information and political support during crises. Finally, expert power may be closely related to task contributions (Lord 1977), whereas referent power is related to emotional attachment to a leader.

Emotional attraction to the leader is also an important aspect of charismatic leadership, which has been discussed extensively in the recent leadership literature (Bass 1981; Conger and Kanungo 1988; House, 1977). Charisma is a form of influence based not on position but on followers' perception that a leader has exceptional qualities. Charisma is not strictly dependent on the leader but instead depends on the interactions among leaders, followers, and their situation (Hollander and Offermann 1990; Yukl 1989). Charisma is important in business settings, particularly during times of crisis, but it has been studied mostly in the area of political leadership. According to House's (1977) theory, charisma involves followers' affection, trust, willing obedience, and unquestioned acceptance of the leader. Followers also have beliefs similar to those of charismatic leaders, heightened performance goals, and certainty that they can contribute to the success of the group's mission. Charismatic leaders elicit these perceptions by clearly articulating their deeply rooted values, ideals, and aspirations to followers. Charismatic leaders are also extremely confident and may engage in impression management activities to bolster the trust of followers (Yukl 1989). Bass (1981) notes that charismatic leaders are more likely to emerge in periods of transition and stress. Thus, we would expect charismatic leadership to be particularly significant in reorientation evolutionary periods.

Conger and Kanungo (1987) emphasize the attributional aspects of charismatic leadership. They describe charismatic leadership as involving a pattern of (a) future goals that are extremely discrepant from the status quo, (b) the use of innovative and unconventional means to achieve these goals, (c) realistic assessment of environmental constraints and resources relevant to such goals, and (d) clear articulation of leaders' future vision and their own motivation to achieve that vision. Interestingly, this description sounds much like the processes that would be required to overcome inertia and produce successful change during the fundamental reorientations noted by Tushman and Romanelli (1985). We argue that although leadership perceptions based on recognition and inferential processes are important during reorientations, successful reorientation also involves cognitive, structural, political, and social factors that go beyond charismatic leadership. Perhaps charisma entails an oversimplification by followers of all these factors into a "mysterious leadership process."

In short, there are many ways a leader can expand his or her latitude of action. Some of these ways correspond to actions that must be taken in advance to build a basis for influence and change; others pertain to qualities of specific leaders *as perceived by others*. The image management activities of leaders may be especially crucial to convey these personal qualities accurately. Many of these qualities have been discussed by prior work in the leadership field.

Traits and CEO Effectiveness

Neither the management literature nor the leadership literature identifies traits that successfully distinguish effective from ineffective leaders (or CEOs) in most contexts. There are several general problems with trait approaches to leadership. We suggested in chapter 3 that leadership traits are related to leadership categories by a family resemblance, rather than a critical feature, structure. This idea suggests that no traits are associated with leaders in all contexts. Moreover, differences from study to study may often reflect mere sampling error, rather than the need for substantive theories to account for such differences (Lord et al. 1986). Finally, our description of convergent and reorientation periods illustrates that different leadership activities may be required in each period. Hence, different traits may also be associated with effective leadership. For these reasons, it makes sense to consider some of the personal characteristics that one might expect to be associated with effective leadership. Such a discussion helps clarify the relationship between our perspective and other work on leadership or administrative science; it may also help indicate areas in which future research would be useful.

Many critical decisions must be made by teams of executive

leaders, particularly during times of crisis and reorientation. Further, the need for both an environmental and an organizational focus creates additional demands on the cognitive capacities and abilities of executive leaders. Thus, we think leadership research should be concerned with the cognitive aspects of executive leadership. Until recently, this area has not been a focus of leadership research, which has been more concerned with personality variables.

A number of theorists and researchers have recently discussed cognitive factors associated with leadership (Fiedler and Garcia 1987; Jaques 1989; Kotter 1988; Lord et al. 1986). For example, Kotter (1988) argues that environmental changes have increased competitive pressures—competition has become more international, markets have been deregulated and have matured, and technology now develops at an increasing rate. Coupled with these changes, organizations are more complex—firms are larger and multinational, products are more diversified, and organizations use more sophisticated technology. According to Kotter, increased competition and complexity require more effective leadership, which in turn requires visionary strategies on the part of leaders. Kotter asserts that vision comes from a combination of broad knowledge of one's industry and company (expert or schema-guided knowledge, in our terms); effective cognitive skills (analytic ability, good judgment, flexibility, and the aptitude to think strategically and multidimensionally); a network of internal and external relationships that provides timely information; and strong interpersonal skills. The cognitive skills allow top-level leaders to combine flexibly both schema-based and more rational types of information processing. The more interpersonally oriented factors allow leaders to manage reorientations.

Research that takes a broader perspective in looking at the effects of cognitive abilities also shows that cognitive ability becomes increasingly important as job complexity increases. Hunter, Schmidt, and Judiesch (1990) performed a meta-analysis of managerial jobs and found that both cognitive demands and variance in performance increase dramatically with a manager's level in the organizational hierarchy. Thus, these results also demonstrate the importance of cognitive ability for executive performance.

Interestingly, Fiedler and Garcia's (1987) cognitive resource theory also emphasizes experience (expert or schematically guided knowledge) and intelligence as being crucial determinants of performance, but the impact of these elements varies with degree of stress. Intelligence has a strong positive correlation with performance ratings under situations of low stress, but not when stress is high; experience shows just the opposite relationship, being highly correlated with performance when stress is high but not when stress is low.

Interpreted from the perspective of this book, intelligence may affect one's capacity to use declarative knowledge and the more rational processes associated with learning and solving novel problems. These procedures place high demands on working memory. That the capacity of working memory is often reduced by the cognitive and emotional aspects of stress may explain why intelligence is not correlated with performance under situations of high stress. Experience, on the other hand, permits the compilation of situation-specific knowledge into easily applied procedures. Compiled knowledge can produce quick but appropriate actions with little cognitive load, permitting effective functioning under stressful situations. Experience can also develop proceduralized skills at coping with stress (Linville and Clark 1989). Thus, experience permits expert processing in task, social, and self-management domains.

Jaques (1989) makes a similar point in arguing for the importance of experience. The time span a leader must consider increases with organizational level, being up to 20 years for visionary executive-level leaders. Therefore, leaders need greater levels of experience and intelligence to recognize environmental trends and put together strategic plans with time spans of 10 to 20 years. Consistent with this viewpoint, some researchers argue that the cognitive demands on leaders increase as a leader moves up the organizational hierarchy (Day and Lord 1988; Katz and Kahn 1978).

Further, as discussed in chapter 3, a meta-analysis of prior studies (Lord et al. 1986) found intelligence to be the trait with the strongest relationship to leadership emergence, and studies of implicit theories (Lord et al. 1984) showed that intelligence characterizes leaders in most situations. Interestingly, the recent work of Baumgardner and her colleagues (1989) on implicit leadership theories found that although intelligence was still the most commonly mentioned trait in different contexts, expert subjects (those with experience in a specific work context) did not mention intelligence as a leadership characteristic as often as novices (college students) did. Experts were also more likely to mention factors that could be expected to develop through experience, such as communication skills, than novices were. Both experts and novices frequently mentioned experience as an important leadership trait.

In short, this work emphasizes top leaders' intelligence, which we think pertains to their capacity to use rational-analytic processes where appropriate. The research also emphasizes experience, and it is through extensive experience that task-relevant schemas and proceduralized knowledge develop. That researchers (Fiedler and Garcia 1987; Jaques 1989; Kotter 1988) assert top-level leaders need both intelligence and experience is understandable from our framework, because these capacities enable the different types of information processing that characterize convergent and reorientation evolutionary phases.

It should also be recognized that top-level leaders have to be able not only to make complex decisions but to communicate those decisions to diverse constituencies, using both direct and symbolic means of communication. This point is consistent with the frequent mention of communication skills by the expert sample in Baumgardner et al. (1989). Moreover, work on charismatic leadership stresses the ability of such leaders to articulate a clear and convincing vision of the goals they are trying to achieve, a quality that seems essential to manage reorientation periods effectively. The capacity of top-level leaders to communicate effectively is also important during convergent periods, but here communication can be mainly symbolic. During convergent periods, leaders need only maintain support for goals and visions that are already well understood. During reorientation periods, however, they must explain and gain acceptance for new organizational missions or goals.

Intuition and Leadership

Experience and intelligence are closely related to a topic that is currently receiving attention in the management area—intuition. Agor (1989), who has extensively investigated this topic in applied settings, finds that top executives frequently rely on intuition in making important decisions and that intuitive abilities are higher for executive-level than for middle- or lower-level managers. Interestingly, Agor's results also indicate that the average degree of intuitive ability is greater for women than for men, and greater for Asian as compared with American samples.

Agor (1989) defines intuition as insight or understanding that comes from unconscious, nonanalytical forms of information processing. Some researchers (Harper 1989) contrast intuition and quantitative analysis, asserting that intuition involves the right hemisphere of the brain and analytic activities the left side of the brain. We think it is more useful to understand intuition in terms of the type of information processing involved. Agor (1989) supports the position developed by Herbert Simon (1987) that intuition is developed through long periods of experience that allow one to recognize instantly the patterns and consequences of alternative actions. In other words, it corresponds to the type of processing we have labeled expert information processing.

This parallel is more obvious in Isenberg's (1989, 97–98) description of intuition. In describing how senior managers think, he notes five distinct ways intuition is used. These ways of using intuition correspond to reliance on specific knowledge structures that are well developed for experts. In the following list, we include in parentheses the expert knowledge structures that correspond to Isenberg's description of how senior managers use intuition: (a) it is used to sense when a problem exists (comparison of feedback with categories or goals); (b) it is used to perform well-learned behavioral patterns rapidly and automatically (scripts); (c) it permits the synthesis of isolated bits of data and experience into an integrated picture, often in an "Aha!" experience (category-based recognition); (d) it is used as a check on the results of more rational analysis (category confirmation); and (e) it is used to bypass in-depth analysis in order rapidly to generate plausible solutions to problems (links of categories to scripts).

The gap-filling and judgmental aspects of intuition also fit our model of expert information processing; however, researchers also describe an alternative aspect of intuition. Goldberg (1989), for example, emphasizes the role of intuition in discovery and creativity. We think his description of these processes corresponds quite closely to the automatic shift from one organizing schema to another, a shift that we believe corresponds to the folded surface in our model of discontinuous individual- or organizational-level changes (see figures 5.5 and 11.1). This shift can occur automatically, suddenly, and with considerable surprise, as is often the case when people view the sequence of pictures we showed in figure 5.4. Inconsistencies with old schemas are noticed and gradually accumulate until they form sufficient associations with alternative categories or scripts to access these schemas automatically. Insight occurs with the recognition that these alternative schemas fit better with noted inconsistencies. Thus, this type of creative insight often requires an antecedent period of effortful, conscious processing in which the person attempts to resolve inconsistencies through analytic means. The creative resolution, however, often occurs automatically, either while working on these problems or at a later time when attention is focused elsewhere. For example, the Nobel laureate Melvin Calvin resolved a perplexing inconsistency in his research on photosynthesis while waiting in the car for his wife:

> One day I was waiting in my car while my wife was on an errand. I had had for some months some basic information from the laboratory which was *incompatible* with everything which, up until then, I knew about the photosynthetic processs. I was waiting, sitting at the wheel, most likely parked in the red zone, when the *recognition* of the missing compound occurred. It occurred just like that—quite suddenly—and suddenly, also, in a matter of seconds, the cyclic character of the path of carbon became apparent to me, not in the detail which ultimately was elucidated, but the original recognition of phosphoglyceric acid, and how it got there, and how the acceptor might be regenerated, all occurred in a matter of 30 seconds. (Agor 1989, 54–55; emphasis added)

Implications for Effective Change in Organizations

Our coverage of leadership emphasizes the role of top executives as originators and managers of organizationwide change. Many of the factors related to initiating and managing change were mentioned in chapter 8, in which we took a detailed look at changing cultures, and again in chapter 13, in which we looked at change from an information processing perspective. We mention two additional factors below: transformational leadership and personal characteristics related to change.

Transformational Leadership. This aspect of leadership pertains to the nature of the exchange between leaders and followers. As noted earlier, transformational leadership involves an abstract type of exchange that "ultimately becomes *moral* in that it raises the level of human conduct and ethical aspiration of both leader and led, and thus has a transforming effect on both" (Burns 1978, 20). It is a *process* that can be viewed on both a microlevel, where individuals are transformed, and a macrolevel, where collective transformations mobilize the power to change social systems and reform institutions (Yukl 1989, 210). Transformational leadership depends on the charismatic qualities of a leader, on follower identification with the leader, and on the arousal of strong emotions (Hollander and Offermann 1990). Yet it can also have aspects that increase skill development in followers. For example, Bass (1985) notes that leaders can transform followers by serving as coach, teacher, or mentor. Kuhnert and Lewis (1987) propose that the capacity for transformational leadership is rooted in stages of cognitive and personality development; they suggest that transformational leadership involves the development by leaders of a subjective frame of reference based on internal values and standards. This process is a cognitively demanding one, much like the development of culture, that ultimately transcends the leader as a source of motivation and commitment.

Transformational leadership, then, seems to be an ideal basis for sustained change. It describes a process capable of changing groups or whole cultures. But transformational leadership may not create the type of change that produces an enduring adjustment of an organization to its environment. Change localized in underlying values, particularly moral values, may develop fairly rigid perspectives that limit long-term adjustment. For example, Westley and Mintzberg (1988) note that the strategic vision of Rene Levesque, creator of the Parti Quebecois, which sought to create an independent Quebec, was self-limiting, producing the eventual collapse of the movement for independence. These authors explain the demise of the movement in terms of Levesque's commitment to a value-based, ideological perspective. His strategy flowed from this ideological perspective and was consistent with it; however, his perspective ultimately became too constraining, preventing the compromises and strategic adjustments required to sustain the movement.

This example suggests that transformational leaders may indeed radically transform organizations, perhaps creating greater levels of adjustment and environmental fit, but that such transformations may sow the seeds of misalignment with future environmental changes. In many ways, such transformations are similar to the dramatic turn-arounds of organizations that reestablish fit with a changed environment but create no fundamental changes in their adaptive capacities. In these instances, one constraining system simply becomes another type of constraining system. Radically changed organizations (or individuals) also need to develop the capacity for future adjustments. This assertion is similar to Argyris's (1976) perspective on leadership that was discussed earlier. He asserted that double-loop learning, or learning to learn, is as important as single-loop learning, involving simply learning new information. We think a danger of transformational leadership is the capacity for single- rather than double-loop learning.

Although the notion of transformational leadership is fascinating, in our view transformational leadership results from the application by perceivers of the processes that have been presented in this book. Transformational leadership clearly represents a combination of the recognition-based and inferential modes of leadership perception discussed earlier. Many researchers describe transformational leaders as conforming to the notions of followers—recognition-based processes. It is also clear that transformational leadership involves the perception by followers that leaders have an agenda for producing favorable performance outcomes—inferential processes. Critical evaluation of the construct should ask whether transformational leadership is anything more than categorizing someone as an effective leader. Bass and Avolio (1989) found descriptions of leaders on dimensions of transformational leadership to be highly related to the extent to which those leaders were described in prototypical terms. Further, controlling for proto-typicality of leader descriptions was found to reduce substantially or eliminate the correlation between transformational leadership dimensions and satisfaction with the leader and perceived effectiveness of the leader. We would caution researchers interested in the topic to keep in mind the lessons learned from prior research on questionnaires and leadership perception. Like other "behavioral" measures, transformational leadership scales may tell us as much about how leaders are integrated with subordinates' implicit theories as they do about the actual behaviors of transformational leaders.

Personal Qualities and Change. Leadership theories have not directly addressed those personal qualities of leaders which help them manage change. We think several possibilities should be investigated. As already mentioned, one topic pertains to compiled knowledge that relates to intra- and interindividual coping skills. Such skills minimize the cognitive demands of managing such factors as the leader's own stress, conflict among others, or political disruption created by change. More traditional personality variables, such as tolerance for ambiguity and cognitive complexity (Streufert and Swezey 1986), may also be associated with effective change.

Interpersonal factors, such as the capacity to develop the trust and commitment of followers or the ability to manage group processes effectively, have also been related to change. For example, Eisenberger, Fasolo, and Davis-LaMastro (1990) found that support from a leader increased organizational commitment and the creativity of subordinates' responses. In contrast, leadership can also be a source of self-limiting behavior, such as groupthink (Janis 1982). Yukl (1989) suggests three main clusters of attributes associated with effective leadership—interpersonal skills, technical skills, and conceptual skills. All three areas pertain to the capacity of leaders to facilitate effective change.

FUTURE RESEARCH

This book's analysis of executive leadership covers many areas not commonly addressed by leadership researchers. We hope this treatment redirects the attention of leadership researchers and theorists to leadership at the executive level of organizations. In this brief section we identify particular areas that we think are in need of further empirical work.

Situational Theories of Executive Leadership

Contingency theories are quite common in the literature on leadership (for example, Fiedler 1964; Vroom and Yetton 1973). Our coverage of leadership suggests three general contingency factors related to leadership perceptions. The first, context, stems from our work on categorization theories of leadership. We suggest that prototypes of leaders are different in most contexts. Context may be a key determinant of what types of leadership traits or activities are accepted and produce effective performance. Culture is a second contingency factor. Although problems with culturally bound definitions of leadership may become increasingly important as multinational corporations become more and more common, we currently know very little about cultural differences in the way perceivers recognize leadership. A third contingency factor is the evolutionary period of an organization. We think that very different types of leadership are required during convergent and reorientation periods and, further, that the construct of leadership may have differential significance during these two periods. A comparison of leadership succession during convergent and reorientation periods would be particularly informative.

Our coverage of executive leadership suggests another form of contingency theory for explaining organizational performance. We have shown that a number of key factors related to executive leadership can be organized in terms of a cusp catastrophe model in which environmental fit and the nature of change processes are the two control variables and in which organizational performance is the response surface. We depicted these dimensions as latent variables that reflect many organizational factors, including executive leadership. In empirically estimating these latent control variables, it should be possible to gauge the relative importance of executive leadership in comparison with other organizational or situational variables. Further, this representation can itself be considered a contingency theory of leadership. It suggests that different types of leadership are needed in convergent and reorientation periods, that leadership will have a much different impact in such periods, and that paths around the perform-ance surface partly reflect the effects of executive leadership. What this form of contingency theory actually does is to integrate leadership with other aspects of organizational theory, thereby providing a much more comprehensive contingency view than prior theories have done.

Leadership Perceptions

Though our coverage of leadership perceptions has been thorough and empirically based, some areas clearly need more work. Foremost is the notion that leadership perceptions, like other social judgments, are frequently updated. We discussed this issue in chapter 5; nonetheless, empirical work on "on-line" leadership perceptions is needed. Theor-etical work should also explore alternative conceptualizations of leadership categorization processes. For example, classification may often be based on exemplar- rather than prototype-based categories (Day 1989), or categories may be refined by general world knowledge, as has been proposed by Medin (1989). Practical considerations also suggest a need for increased concern for external validity. Research needs to examine categorization processes with real leaders, not just "paper" or "tape" (videotaped) people. Research also needs to use more perceivers who are familiar with leaders in a given context. It seems to us that assessment centers provide an ideal area for research not limited by artificial stimuli and inexperienced assessors. Finally, as we discussed in chapter 6, future work should examine the effects of gender on leadership perceptions. Here, the most crucial issue is the potential for gender to provide an alternative category to "leadership" that can be used to interpret the traits and behaviors of women, thereby affecting future expectations and career opportunities for these individuals.

Leadership Prototypes in Other Countries

Our discussion of culture has focused on the organizational level; however, the ideas can be extended to national or societal cultures as well. One intriguing possibility is to use our perspective to examine cultural differences in leadership perceptions. This type of research can be done by comparing the content of cognitive categories that guide leadership perceptions for different cultures. O'Connell, Lord, and O'Connell (1990) followed this approach in comparing Japanese and American leadership categories. They found that the family resemblance values of leadership traits provided by Japanese students were virtually unrelated (r = .08) to those same kinds of values as described by American students. For example, a prototypical Japanese leader might be fair, flexible, a good listener, outgoing, and responsible, as all these traits had family resemblance values of .875 in the Japanese sample. In contrast, the family resemblance values for these same traits found in Lord and his colleagues' (1984) study using an American sample were 0, 0, 0, .5, and 0, respectively. Moreover, cluster analysis comparing basic-level American and Japanese leadership categories (business, finance, education, and media leaders, as described in each culture) showed that all the basic-level categories clustered first within a culture, rather than linking the same types of leaders across cultures (for example, a Japanese business leader and an American business leader).

These findings illustrate the importance of investigating leadership within cultural contexts. The results also suggest that understanding cultural differences in leadership prototypes may be necessary in order for managers in foreign countries to perform usefully. That effective cross-cultural training of managers has traditionally been problematic (Black and Mendenhall 1990) demonstrates a need to understand automatic, schema-based components of perceptions and behavior that may be specific to a particular culture. Prototypes associated with different national cultures may also be significant for multinational firms (for example, Honda): individuals who fit leadership prototypes of Japanese workers may not be evaluated favorably in an American organization and vice versa. Such problems can cause misperceptions and underutilization of managerial talent. We have argued that being perceived as a leader is crucial to effective top-level leadership, and this process can be limited by culturally bound definitions of leadership.

Leadership and Organizational Performance

Much of our coverage of executive leadership and organizational performance is tentative; it requires empirical support and theoretical elaboration. A general area for research is the comparison of direct and indirect effects of executive leaders. One possibility worth considering is that direct effects generally relate to the environmental fit control variable in the cusp catastrophe model, while indirect effects relate to the nature of change control variable. More work is also needed on two theoretical ideas that strongly influenced our organization of this section of the book—Tushman and Romanelli's (1985) punctuated equilibrium model and our representation of this process in cusp catastrophe terms. Needed are historical studies that investigate the punctuated equilibrium model, as well as research that determines whether performance during evolutionary cycles coincides with a catastrophe mathematical model. Finally, research is needed on the cognitive capacities of executive leaders and on how these capacities relate to organizational performance during different evolutionary periods. Such research should examine (perhaps through specially developed assessment center exercises) the ability of leaders to switch processing modes and the relationship between different types of information processing and organizational performance during different evolutionary periods.

Leadership and Change Processes

We assert that a crucial requirement of top-level executives is to manage both short- and long-run changes effectively. This area needs thorough investigation, and two realms seem especially worthy of research. First is the development of a general model of incremental as compared with discontinuous change. Parallels between micro- and macrolevel change should be investigated (see the final section of chapter 13), as should the activities of top-level executives in managing such change processes. Second is an exploration of the need for top executives to manage both incremental and discontinuous change. We have argued that such changes require different types of information processing on the part of executives. They may also require different types of personality or cognitive capacities. Incremental change may involve experience, a need for precision and structure, or risk aversion; discontinuous change may require more conceptual/analytic ability, tolerance for ambiguity, or willingness to take risks.

Leadership Training

Executive training programs may take on different emphases, given our contingency framework. Training programs might be made more effective by taking into consideration the different evolutionary periods of an organization and the different demands of leaders during these periods. Many existing training programs may be relevant, with their focus on training people in new ways of thinking and on expanding cognitive skills. In particular, Argyris's (1976) double-loop learning places an emphasis on encouraging the confrontation of views, the sharing of information, and the minimizing of defensiveness. These elements can increase leaders' ability to engage in more rational forms of processing, thus facilitating change efforts. Janis's (1989) notion of "vigilant problem solving" also underscores more rational information processing; however, this type of training may be inappropriate during stable convergent periods, because more appropriate, schematically based means of dealing with environments may be unnecessarily questioned. Finally, earlier in this chapter we identified the importance to executive performance of a high need for achievement. Here, McClelland's (1961) approach may be especially useful in order for managers to increase initiative and expand latitude of discretion. High levels of the need for achievement may increase leaders' tendency to seek change, rather than avoid it.

The point we wish to make, however—and an area for future research—is that a contingency approach should be taken with executive training. Specifically, different types of training may be required for managing convergent and reorientation periods. Training to manage convergent periods should focus on symbolic activities and the use of expert-cybernetic processes that can help maintain the organization in stable periods through incremental change. Executive training for periods of reorientation should accentuate the identification of inflexible schemas, and the use of more rational processing to facilitate change.

SUMMARY

This chapter has highlighted some key qualities that effective leaders should possess. It is important for leaders to develop latitude of discretion in various organizational domains (Hambrick and Finkelstein 1987). Environmental factors, organizational factors, and a leader's personal attributes can all affect the degree of discretion a leader has. Environmental factors were discussed at length in chapter 12.

Organizational factors include culture, size, age of an organization, and scarcity of resources. Because these factors are especially limiting in reorientation periods, we think it is vital that leaders build up discretion during times of convergence. One way to do so is to increase political support from key actors during stable periods so that greater influence can be exerted during unstable times. Another way to expand discretion is to create a culture that is change oriented. By doing so, change during reorientations will proceed more smoothly and will thereby be less stressful for organizational members.

Several personal characteristics of leaders can expand latitude of discretion. Those with a high need for achievement are likely to be proactive agents in the change process. Moreover, they are likely to engage in more rational processing, which is required for innovation. Executives may therefore be perceived as being high in initiative, thereby increasing their discretionary levels. The type of power base used by leaders can also affect the amount of discretion afforded to them. To the extent that power is perceived to be related to the personal characteristics of a leader (for example, expert power), latitude may be increased. A leader who is perceived to be charismatic is also likely to have more discretionary influence. Image management can increase perceptions of the qualities outlined above.

Other personal attributes can also characterize effective leaders. Effective leaders must be highly skilled decision makers, a factor that places emphasis on leaders' cognitive abilities. Leaders should have both intelligence and experience in their relevant domains, for intelligent leaders can make use of rational processes when change is required and experienced leaders can develop proceduralized knowledge in various domains. Finally, effective leaders must have considerable communication skills to convey information to organization members in both direct and symbolic ways.

We identify one additional factor that is important in order for executives to implement change in organizations: transformational leadership. Transformational leadership pertains to the nature of exchanges between a leader and others, wherein followers identify with the values of the leader. This type of leadership can be particularly useful for organizational change because it acknowledges the ways in which leaders can transform followers to conform to new values or assumptions. Such transformations, however, may result in new, inflexible systems that lead to misalignment in the future. Moreover, as currently operationalized, transformational leadership may be little more than the perception that someone is an effective leader.

We concluded this chapter with ideas for future research in the leadership field. Most importantly, we identified a need for a contingency theory of leadership that is based on the context of leaders and on the evolutionary period of the organization. More research should be conducted in the area of leadership perceptions that addresses external validity concerns through means other than those entailing artificial stimuli and naive raters. Cross-cultural comparisons in leadership perceptions may be an interesting area for additional research. Studies comparing the direct and indirect effects of leaders and the cognitive capacities of leaders, as well as research comparing the management of both short- and long-term change efforts, would also be useful. Finally, a new area for leadership training may be teaching leaders to consider the evolutionary period of organizations based on the contingency model presented in this book.

Chapter 15

Extensions and Conclusions

The whole distinction of real and unreal, the whole psychology of belief,
disbelief, and doubt, is thus grounded on two mental facts—first, that we are
liable to think differently of the same; and second, that when we have done so,
we can choose which way of thinking to adhere to and which to disregard.
—William James, 1890

One hundred years ago, William James contemplated how people change their thinking over time when encountering new ideas. Today, social scientists are still interested in this topic. Anderson (1989, 176) asserts that "life is on-line" and involves the continuous updating of perceptions, values, goals, and strategies. Knowledge of information processing and knowledge of leadership are central to this issue. Individual cognitions, social perceptions, dyadic relations, group functioning, and organizational processes are all on-line activities that involve the interplay between leadership and information processing. In this book, we have tied those two topics together, asserting that leadership is largely a perceptual phenomenon that occurs in the context of ongoing cognitive, social, and task-related activities. Leadership both affects and is constrained by cognitive and social processes at all levels of human systems: individual, dyadic, group, organizational, and societal institutions. It also affects and is constrained by task performance at each of these levels.

ADVANTAGES TO THIS APPROACH

We think there are four advantages to the approach this book takes to understanding leadership. First, we have provided an information processing perspective and shown that it can be applied at multiple levels of analysis. The four alternative information processing models described in chapter 2 help in understanding both individual- and organizational-level information processing. Second, it links perceptions and performance and in so doing resolves the "paradox" of executive leadership and offers insights into the difficulties women and minority members may experience in achieving leadership roles. Third, our coverage of executive leadership and organizational performance integrates leadership with current thinking on organizational evolution, power, executive decision-making processes, culture, and change. Fourth, we show how both stability and change can relate to organizational performance, albeit at different time periods. Each of these advantages is briefly discussed below.

Multiple and Multilevel Perspectives

The four alternative models of information processing—limited-capacity, expert, rational, and cybernetic—are different in their emphasis on automatic and controlled processing and in their reliance on information stored in long-term memory versus contemporaneous processing in working memory. These models provide alternative interpretations of leadership processes at all levels of analysis. At the individual level, we have shown how limited-capacity and expert models of information processing can determine leadership perceptions using recognition-based processes based on perceivers' leadership categories. Perceivers also use either limited-capacity or rational attributional analyses to form leadership perceptions through inferential processes. Updating of leadership perceptions can occur through cybernetic processes that integrate feedback on performance or changed behavioral responses.

Perceptions are also a critical aspect of dyadic-level leader-subordinate interactions. The cognitive processes that produce these perceptions, however, are not integrated with most extant leadership theories. Because people often rely on limited-capacity processing in social interactions, initial impressions or categorizations of others can powerfully affect subsequent interactions. Moreover, the use of limited-capacity processes can be highly resistant to change, even in the face of disconfirming evidence. In addition, the fact that limited-capacity processing often occurs for both members of a dyad makes its effects even more complex. Limited-capacity processes can explain subordinates' categorizations of leaders, subordinates' script-based responses, leaders' categorization-based interpretations of subordinates, and leaders' script-based responses to their classifications of subordinates. The interweaving of these schema-based, limited-capacity processes in dyads makes perceptions difficult to change. Perceptions based on rational processes are more amenable to frequent updating and accurate social perceptions, but research suggests they may be too difficult to use in most situations in which other issues deplete available attentional resources.

At the organizational level, schema-based processing, which we define as organizational culture, is important in the maintenance of stable patterns of thinking and behavior. We have recast into information processing terms Schein's (1985) insight that one must move beyond artifacts to assess culture. A schema-based approach to culture can also help explain why culture may be resistant to change, and it suggests means by which leaders can change culture through priming alternative schemas or by shifting the ways members process information. Leaders can also be constrained by culture, however. Schemas shared by organizational members can limit leadership perceptions; they can also limit discretion by making only a narrow set of problem-solving approaches acceptable to members. Expert processing that may automatically link culturally based categories to familiar responses may be particularly resistant to change; in chapter 13 we linked this pattern to organizational decline.

In sum, the type of information processing that is used can have very real effects on leadership perceptions and outcomes at all levels of analysis. Leadership and other issues can be understood more fully by considering the alternative processing explanations provided by these four information processing models.

Linking Perceptions and Performance

A paradox is an entity or phenomenon that seems to have contradictory qualities. At the beginning of chapter 10 we described the "leadership paradox", which poses the simple question, Do leaders make a difference? The source of the paradox lies in the fact that some researchers have argued that leaders have no impact on organizational performance, while others have asserted that leaders can be quite influential in determining organizational outcomes. The resolution of this paradox comprises much of the latter portions of this book. Poole and Van de Ven (1989) provide a useful framework that outlines four means of resolving paradoxes: accept the paradox and use it constructively; clarify levels of analysis; temporally separate the two aspects of the paradox; and introduce new terms to resolve the paradox. We have used each of these means to resolve the leadership paradox.

Much of the research in the field of leadership has revolved around the paradox of whether leaders can affect performance. Scholars have used this paradox constructively to generate research and theorizing, illustrating Poole and Van de Ven's (1989) first means for resolving paradoxes. Some have argued that the leadership phenomenon is mostly perceptual (Calder 1977; Pfeffer 1977), while contingency theorists (for example, Kerr and Jermier 1978) have suggested that leadership is sometimes effective and sometimes not, depending on situational constraints. At the opposite extreme from the perceptual viewpoint is the focus of the many popular books on leadership and biographies of specific leaders. This work documents the specific activities and attributes of leaders that affect performance. Population ecologists also subscribe to the view that leadership is constrained by environmental forces. Thus, the two sides of this paradox have generated considerable theory and research in attempts to resolve the issue. In this book, we have acknowledged this paradox and tried to resolve inconsistencies through the other three means outlined by Poole and Van de Ven (1989).

Paradoxes can sometimes be better understood by clarifying levels of analysis (Poole and Van de Ven's [1989] second means of paradox resolution); one side of the issue may operate at a certain level of analysis, while the other view may operate at another level of analysis. Much of this book is devoted to showing how leaders can affect performance in certain situations, while being more constrained in other situations. For example, Day and Lord (1988) have argued that many of the studies interpreted as showing that leaders do not affect performance have actually pertained to middle-level, rather than executive-level, leaders. These authors argue that studies of executive-level leaders would more clearly demonstrate the effects of leadership on organizational performance. Further, Thomas (1988) has suggested that analyses that span levels of analysis (for example, partition variance into industry, firm, and leadership factors) must consider the degree of variability that exists at each of these levels. If the variance is low across leaders but high across firms, then leadership will not explain much variance in performance; if there is little variance at the industry or firm level, leadership can be critical.

Poole and Van de Ven's (1989) third means of resolving paradoxes is to consider temporal relationships—leadership may be more important at certain times than at others. Our analysis and integration of Tushman and Romanelli's (1985) evolutionary perspectives resolve the paradox in this manner, by showing how leaders' substantive activities may be more important in periods of reorientation, while symbolic activities are all that is necessary in periods of convergence. Symbolic activities do not provide as clear a link to performance as substantive activities do. Thus, it may be difficult to assess the effects of leadership on organizational performance during some periods of an organization's growth cycle.

Finally, Poole and Van de Ven (1989) suggest that one can introduce new terms to resolve the paradox. We think this approach is one of the primary advantages of this book. The synthesis of information processing and leadership can help to explain the effects of leadership in a unique way, and can show how leadership's effects on subordinate or organizational performance are partly the products of perceivers' responses. Leadership is influenced by followers' schemas of leaders. Leadership also depends in part on the amount of discretion afforded to leaders (Hambrick and Finkelstein 1987), which is largely a perceptual process. Thus, the influence of perceptions may determine whether leaders actually have an impact on performance. Leaders' own schemas and models of information processing can also affect organizational performance. We have noted, for example, that expert-cybernetic processing is appropriate during times of environmental stability, whereas rational and limited-capacity processing is more appropriate for organizational learning in turbulent times. In short, a synthesis of leadership and information processing allows us to explain why leaders have effects on performance in some situations and not in others.

Such an integration also allows us to posit the precise mechanisms that underlie some of the problems women may have in being perceived as leaders, and the associated problems with the effect of female leaders on performance. In chapter 6 we suggested that to the extent that the majority of individual interactions in which a female executive is involved are characterized by stereotypical notions, she is less likely to be firmly connected to relevant constituencies. Brass (1985) provides some support for the assertion that a lack of connections in relevant constituencies is tied to the perception of less influence. Exclusion from relevant constituent groups could have substantial consequences for latitude of discretion and effects on organizational performance (Hambrick and Finkelstein 1987). The unfortunate implication is that women, by virtue of having less influence, may therefore have less of an impact on organizational performance.

For top-level female leaders, symbolic activities in periods of convergence may be particularly difficult, depending on cultural assumptions (both internal and external) related to female executives. The ability to foster or effectively guide reorientations may also be especially difficult for top-level female leaders, as they may lack the discretion to engage in substantive activities. Even during convergent periods, female top executives should attempt to expand their latitude of discretion by concentrating on gaining "idiosyncratic credit" (Hollander and Julian 1969). Here the added complexity of managing both organizational-environmental fit and stereotypical perceptions of females may increase the probability of error. The challenge for leadership researchers—and for society in general—is to help female leaders manage these difficulties. Otherwise, society will underutilize this source of leadership talent and alternative schematic perspectives.

Leadership and Context

An underlying theme in this book is that leadership can best be understood by considering its role in context. First, in understanding leadership perceptions, context can be conceptualized as being equivalent to basic-level categories, for example, business leaders versus military leaders. As shown by Baumgardner and her colleagues (1990), prototypes of effective leaders vary by these contexts.

Second, at an organizational level, the effect of leadership activities depends on the historical context in which they occur. As the cusp model graphically illustrates, the performance consequences of a particular movement (side to side or front to back) on the organizational response surface is highly dependent on the initial location of an organization, which, in turn, may be dependent on its evolutionary period. Minor decreases in environmental fit for organizations on the front face may move them over the fold in the cusp region, dramatically reducing performance, whereas analogous movement on the more linear back face may have very little effect on performance.

Third, and most importantly, context can be conceptualized as the net effect of many external factors on organizational performance. One particularly important external factor is the concurrent response of other competing organizations. In reality, organizations do not face static environments; instead, the environments they are adjusting to are continually changing. Organizations "enact" (Smircich and Stubbart 1985) their environment based on the interpretations they create (Daft and Weick 1984). In this sense, the very activities a firm undertakes to respond to a perceived environment can create the environment it encounters; this process occurs not just for one firm but for multiple firms, which collectively interpret and enact their environment (Porac et al. 1989). If firms expect an industry to be competitive, their competitive strategies may create a competitive marketplace; if firms expect stability, conventional strategies may create stability.

A parallel of the enactment process at the dyadic level is the idea of self-fulfilling prophecy, wherein mutual expectations can create and reinforce behaviors. As we discussed in chapter 7, the operation of expectations can lead to in-group or out-group status for group members. Similarly, expectations about the behavior of females and minority members in leadership roles can create a cognitive and behavioral context that is consistent with those expectations.

The notion of mutual enactment processes is fascinating. We think our perspective can aid further understanding in two respects. First is that enactment can be seen as resulting from common schemas that are widely shared, a point that corresponds directly to our discussion of culture. Second is that a cusp catastrophe framework can be extended to incorporate the notion that the environment itself is changing, a point that is very similar to our observation in chapter 12 that some externally focused leadership strategies could change the shape of the cusp surface itself. In terms of catastrophe theory, changing the cusp surface corresponds to the addition of a third control variable, a biasing variable, that predicts such changes (Alexander 1990). Thus, higher-order catastrophe models can be used to represent enactment processes. To adjust successfully in changing environments, strategists not only must incorporate knowledge of the type of response surface confronting a firm but also need to reflect accurate assessments of how that surface itself changes while strategies are being implemented. Since strategic change generally takes several years, it is not surprising that work on executive-level leadership emphasizes vision and accurate environmental perceptions.

In short, at all levels we have tied leadership to context. We have done so by relating leadership activities to the underlying cognitive schemas that generate interpretations in responses to perceived environments, whether task, social, organizational, or market. Where contextual interpretations are widely shared, they can be a powerful force in creating environments. Finally, we have suggested how this process might be conceptualized graphically in terms of catastrophe theory and have noted its implications for leadership theory.

Stability, Change, and Performance

Based on the amount of attention given to change processes in this book, it is clear that we think the study of change processes is important. We do not necessarily, however, advocate change in a practical sense. Moreover, there are also clear linkages of stability to performance. Dramatic change is disruptive and risky, and it is not appropriate in all situations. Most organizations should encounter long periods of convergence that may be both efficient and comfortable. Still, the same processes that facilitate adjustment in stable periods may limit an organization's capability to adjust to environmental shocks or natural evolutionary trends. The ability of social systems to transcend natural selection processes through collective activity depends on their ability to understand and use change. Though organizations and decision makers should respond flexibly if the culture is change oriented, change is also hazardous. This meta-morphic ability may be required only infrequently; however, we assert that it is directly tied to the leadership process explained in this book.

LIMITATIONS

There are also several limitations of some of the research presented in this book. The limitations are related to methodology and empirical support and to the comprehensiveness of our perspective. While these limitations may be seen as threats to the adequacy of the perspective we have developed, work on labeling (Dutton and Jackson 1987) indicates that they can also be viewed as opportunities for future research.

Methodology and Empirical Support

We acknowledge several methodological limitations of some of the research presented herein. First, a large segment of the work on recognition-based and inferential processes discussed in the first and second parts of this book was conducted in the laboratory. This aspect raises obvious concerns about generalizability: the stimuli are simple, stimulus persons may not be real leaders, and subjects never interact with the people they are rating. Moreover, perceptions are neither revised over time nor interrupted for long periods of time while attention is focused on other tasks or people. The very nature of laboratory settings often precludes subjects from engaging in cybernetic processing to revise perceptions over time. Further, laboratory situations may have implicit norms for rational processing. And laboratory studies often rely on novices rather than experts, although some of the empirical research cited herein attempts to examine that difference (Baumgardner et al. 1990; Day and Lord 1990).

The methodological limitations of the research discussed in the third and fourth parts of this book are different. For example, naturally occurring events like leadership succession are confounded with many other factors (company or industry). This aspect produces concerns related to internal validity; that is, how do researchers separate the effects of succession from the effects associated with companies or industries? Even though succession studies involve real leaders and organizations, they have external validity problems as well. Succession that involves changes in leader ability should produce effects different from those pertaining to succession in which ability does not change. Similarly, succession during convergent periods may be different from succession during reorientations. Issues related to a leader's ability may also create concerns about construct validity. For example, Barrick and his colleagues (1989) used past salary levels to distinguish high- from average-ability leaders, but this operationalization of ability may also reflect differences among leaders in control over compensation.

At the organizational level, the theory of decline and adaption we have developed may be difficult to test empirically, in that the theory encompasses a larger population of organizations than researchers are likely to encounter in a single industry or time frame. Organizations having an extremely poor fit are likely to have succumbed to environmental pressures very quickly in competitive environments or declining industries. In growing environments or noncompetitive industries, however, organizations having a poor fit may linger (Meyer and Zucker 1989). Thus, to test this theory, researchers may be looking for a type of organization that is unlikely to exist. This problem is particularly severe when examining early stages of organizational growth. Some emerging organizations, because of selection pressures or limited market niches, never become large enough to be studied (Katz and Gartner 1988). Similarly, strategic mistakes may be fatal in those small organizations which lack sufficient resources to recover and move through a turnaround cycle (Romanelli 1989). These issues are particularly relevant to attempts at testing the cusp catastrophe model. The model may serve as a reasonable explanation of evolutionary processes, yet a single study could easily include a sample of firms that were operating only on the back face of the performance surface instead of at the cusp region. Such a sample would show no advantage for a cusp model as compared with a linear model of organizational performance.

While these limitations are substantial, they suggest areas and topics that require future research. It should also be stressed that by attempting to develop an information processing perspective that spans multiple levels, we have not restricted our empirical base to any one type of study. Thus, the limitations of one type of study are offset by the strengths of alternative types of research.

Comprehensiveness

In developing our model of leadership, we have focused extensively on the individual, dyadic, and organizational levels. Other levels should also be integrated with our framework. For example, leadership is critical in understanding small-group performance, but we have not incorporated this area of the literature. Similarly, leadership is important at the supraorganizational level. In fact, industries are often thought of as competitive groups. Our approach could be expanded to include these other levels of analysis.

Much of our discussion of executive leadership has centered on organizations with declining performance and the change in response to such decline. But change may also be crucial to organizational growth. The same types of cognitive processes may operate in growth, yet because resources are expanding, political processes and leadership perceptions may be easier to manage. The manner in which leaders can facilitate the changes required for growth provides an interesting topic for extending our approach to leadership.

The model has also emphasized particular substantive areas, while excluding others. Our focus on cognitive processes should not be interpreted to mean that these are the only processes necessary to understand leadership. For example, power, political processes, influence, and conflict are significant elements in understanding leadership during periods of stability and change. Though we underemphasize those processes in our model, we recognize they are needed for a more comprehensive understanding of leadership.

APPLIED VALUE

Our bias has been to stress theoretical and conceptual development and to ground ideas in the extant scientific literature. We think, however, the theory has applied value as well. Throughout this book, we discuss many practical issues, such as why females may not be perceived as leaders, how to expand discretion, and how context may limit leadership perceptions, to name just a few. We think that understanding such issues from a theoretical perspective is valuable. In addition, we have extended thinking about leadership by integrating it with theories of information processing and organizational evolution; such extensions are of practical value because they go beyond the experience and perspectives of most individual leaders or organizations.

A widespread pragmatic issue is that real leaders address problems from a perspective that is too narrow. Our approach suggests ways of expanding leaders' perspectives by considering alternative types of information processing. We recommended that researchers consider these alternative perspectives as ways of developing richer theories (Lord and Maher 1990b). Nevertheless, the four information processing models presented in this book may also be useful as practical tools for leaders, since they suggest alternative ways to approach problems. No single way of processing information is always appropriate. A key strategy for leaders to consider is first to diagnose the type of information processing they typically apply to problems and then to consider how the problems might be approached using alternative types of information processing. In doing so, leaders should focus both on processes related to social perceptions and on processes related to performance. As shown by the example that began this book, people like Philip Caldwell, who perform very well but ignore the perceptual component of leadership, may be misperceived, may have limited discretion, may lose power, and, ultimately, may lose their position of leadership.

Bibliography ——————————————————————

Abolafia, M. Y., and M. Kilduff 1988. Enacting market crisis: The social construction of a speculative bubble. *Administrative Science Quarterly* 33: 177–93.

Ackerman, P. L. 1987. Individual differences in skill learning: An integration of psychometric and information processing perspectives. *Psychological Bulletin* 102: 3–27.

Adams, J. S. 1976. The structure and dynamics of behavior in organization boundary roles. In *Handbook of industrial and organizational psychology,* edited by M. D. Dunnette, 1175–99. Chicago: Rand McNally.

Agor, W. H., ed. 1989. *Intuition in organizations: Leading and managing productively.* Newbury Park, Calif.: Sage.

Alba, J. W., W. Chromiak, L. Hasher, and M. S. Attig 1980. Automatic encoding of category size information. *Journal of Experimental Psychology* 6: 370–78.

Alexander, R. A. 1990. Personal communication, 19 Feb.

Alexander, R. A., G. M. Alliger, K. P. Carson, and G. V. Barrett 1985. The empirical performance of measures of association in the 2 × 2 table. *Educational and Psychological Measurement* 45: 79–87.

Alexander, R. A., and M. R. Barrick 1987. Estimating the standard error of projected dollar gains in utility analysis. *Journal of Applied Psychology* 72: 475–79.

Allen, M. P., S. Panian, and R. Lotz 1979. Managerial succession and organizational performance: A recalcitrant problem revisited. *Administrative Science Quarterly* 24: 167–80.

American Psychological Association. 1988. Brief of amicus curiae in support of respondent. *Labor Law Series* (1988–89 term of Court) 22: 233–74.

Anderson, J. R. 1987. Skill acquisition: Compilation of weak-method problem solutions. *Psychological Review* 94: 192–210.

———. 1990. *Cognitive psychology and its implications.* New York: Freeman.

Anderson, N. H. 1989. Functional memory and on-line attribution. In *On-line cognition in person perception,* edited by J. Bassili, 175–220. Hillsdale, N.J.: Erlbaum.

Argyris, C. 1976. *Increasing leadership effectiveness.* New York: Wiley.

Armour, H. O., and D. J. Teece 1978. Organizational structure and economic performance: A test of the multidivisional hypothesis. *Bell Journal of Economics* 9: 106–22.

Ashmore, R. D. 1981. Sex stereotypes and implicit personality theory. In *Cognitive processes in stereotyping and intergroup behavior,* edited by D. L.

Hamilton. Hillsdale, N.J.: Erlbaum.

Ashour, A. S. 1982. A framework of a cognitive-behavioral theory of leader influence and effectiveness. *Organizational Behavior and Human Performance* 32: 407–30.

Astley, W. G., and A. H. Van de Ven 1983. Central perspectives and debates in organization theory. *Administrative Science Quarterly* 28: 245–73.

Aupperle, K. E., W. Acar, and D. E. Booth 1986. An empirical critique of *In Search of Excellence*: How excellent are the excellent companies? *Journal of Management* 12: 499–512.

Bales, J. 1988. Sex stereotyping data valid, brief says. *APA Monitor*, Aug., 23.

Barley, S. R., G. W. Meyer, and D. C. Gash 1988. Cultures of culture: Academics, practitioners, and the pragmatics of normative control. *Administrative Science Quarterly* 33: 24–60.

Barney, J. B. 1986. Organizational culture: Can it be a source of sustained competitive advantage? *Academy of Management Review* 11: 656–65.

Barney, J. B., and W. G. Ouchi 1986. *Organizational economics*. San Francisco: Jossey-Bass.

Barrick, M. R., D. V. Day, R. G. Lord, and R. A. Alexander 1989. *Assessing the utility of executive leadership*. Unpublished manuscript, University of Akron.

Bass, B. M. 1981. *Stogdill's handbook of leadership*. New York: Free Press.

———. 1985. *Leadership and performance beyond expectations*. New York: Free Press.

Bass, B. M., and B. J. Avolio 1989. Potential biases in leadership measures: How prototypes, leniency, and general satisfaction relate to ratings and rankings of transformational and transactional leadership constructs. *Educational and Psychological Measurement* 49: 509–27.

Bass, B. M., B. J. Avolio, and L. Goodheim 1987. Biography and the assessment of transformational leadership at the world-class level. *Journal of Management* 13: 7–19.

Baumgardner, T. L., R. G. Lord, and J. C. Forti 1990. *A prescription for aspiring leaders: Implications of expert-novice schema differences and alternative leadership categorization models*. Manuscript submitted for publication.

Bellis, W. 1988. Iacocca. *Fortune*, 29 Aug., 38–43.

Berrien, F. K. 1976. A general systems approach to organizations. In *Handbook of industrial and organizational psychology*, edited by M. D. Dunnette, 41–62. Chicago: Rand McNally.

Billings, R. S., T. W. Milburn, and M. L. Schaalman 1980. A model of crisis perception: A theoretical and empirical analysis. *Administrative Science Quarterly* 25: 300–16.

Binning, J. F., and R. G. Lord 1980. Boundary conditions for performance cue effects on group process ratings: Familiarity versus type of feedback. *Organization Behavior and Human Performance* 26: 115–30.

Binning, J. F., A. J. Zaba, and J. C. Whattam 1986. Explaining the biasing effects of performance cues in terms of cognitive categorization. *Academy of Management Journal* 29: 521–35.

Black, J. S., and M. Mendenhall 1990. Cross-cultural training effectiveness: A review and a theoretical framework for future research. *Academy of*

Management Review 15: 113–36.

Boal, K. B., J. G. Hunt, and R. L. Sorenson 1988. *Strategic leadership: Inside the black box.* Manuscript submitted for publication.

Borman, W. C. 1987. Personal constructs, performance schemata, and "folk theories" of subordinate effectiveness: Explorations in an army officer sample. *Organizational Behavior and Human Decision Processes* 40: 307–22.

Bourgeois, L. J., III. 1985. Strategic goals, perceived uncertainty, and economic performance in volatile environments. *Academy of Management Journal* 3: 548–73.

Bourne, L. E., R. L. Dominowski, and E. F. Loftus 1979. *Cognitive processes.* Englewood Cliffs, N.J.: Prentice Hall.

Bower, G. H. 1981. Emotional mood and memory. *American Psychologist* 36: 129–48.

Bower, J. L. 1986. *When markets quake: The management challenge of restructuring industry.* Boston, Mass.: Harvard Business School Press.

Brass, D. J. 1985. Men's and women's networks: A study of interaction patterns and influence in an organization. *Academy of Management Journal* 28: 327–43.

Bray, R. M., D. Johnson, and J. T. Chilstrom, Jr. 1982. Social influence by group members with minority opinions: A comparison of Hollander and Moscovici. *Journal of Personality and Social Psychology* 43: 78–88.

Brenner, O. C., J. Tomkiewicz, and V. E. Schein 1989. The relationship between sex role stereotypes and requisite management characteristics revisited. *Academy of Management Journal* 32: 662–69.

Brewer, M. B. 1988. A dual process model of impression formation. In *Advances in social cognition, vol. 1*, edited by T. K. Srull and R. S. Wyer, Jr., 1–36. Hillsdale, N.J.: Erlbaum.

Brickner, M. A. 1989. *The role of the working self-concept in motivated behavior.* Manuscript submitted for publication.

Brief, A. P., and H. K. Downey 1983. Cognitive and organizational structures: A conceptual analysis of implicit organizing theories. *Human Relations* 36: 1065–90.

Broverman, I. K., S. R. Vogel, D. M. Broverman, F. E. Clarkson, and P. S. Rosenkrantz 1972. Sex role stereotypes: A current appraisal. *Journal of Social Issues* 28: 59–78.

Brown, C. K. 1979. Women and business management. *Signs* 5: 266–88.

———. 1981. *The woman manager in the United States: A research analysis and bibliography.* Washington, D.C.: Women's Foundation.

Brown, M. C. 1982. Administrative succession and organizational performance: The succession effect. *Administrative Science Quarterly* 27: 1–16.

Bureau of Labor Statistics. 1988. Employment and earnings report, May edition.

Burns, J. M. 1978. *Leadership.* New York: Harper & Row.

Calder, B. J. 1977. An attribution theory of leadership. In *New directions in organizational behavior,* edited by B. M. Staw and G. R. Salancik. Chicago: St Clair Press.

Campbell, D. T. 1969. Reforms as experiments. *American Psychologist* 24: 409–29.

Cantor, N., and W. Mischel. 1979. Prototypes in person perception. In *Advances in experimental social psychology*, edited by L. Berkowitz. New York: Academic Press.

Cantor, N., W. Mischel, and J. C. Schwartz. 1982. A prototype analysis of psychological situations. *Cognitive Psychology* 14: 45–77.

Carver, C. S. 1979. A cybernetic model of self-attention processes. *Journal of Personality and Social Psychology* 37: 1251–71.

Chakravarty, S. N. 1986. Taking risks is what they pay you for. *Forbes*, 10 Feb., 45–46.

Chandler, A. D., Jr. 1962. *Strategy and structure: Chapters in the history of the industrial enterprise*. Cambridge, Mass.: The MIT Press.

Chi, M. T. H., R. Glaser, and E. Rees. 1982. Expertise in problem solving. In *Advances in the psychology of human intelligence, vol. 1*, edited by R. J. Sternberg. Hillsdale, N.J.: Erlbaum.

Chi, M. T. H., R. Glaser, and M. J. Farr. eds. 1988. *The nature of expertise*. Hillsdale, N.J.: Erlbaum.

Cobb, L. 1980. Estimation theory for the cusp catastrophe theory model. *Proceedings of the Section on Survey Research Methods*. Washington, D.C.: American Statistical Association.

Conger, J. A., and R. N. Kanungo. 1987. Toward a behavioral theory of charismatic leadership in organizational settings. *Academy of Management Review* 12: 637–47.

———. 1988. *Charismatic leadership: The elusive factor in organizational effectiveness*. San Francisco: Jossey-Bass.

Corporate culture. 1980. *Business Week*, 27 Oct., 148–60.

Cowan, D. A. 1986. Developing a process model of problem solving. *Academy of Management Review* 11: 763–76.

Crocker, J., D. B. Hannah, and R. Weber. 1983. Person memory and causal attributions. *Journal of Personality and Social Psychology* 44: 55–66.

Cronshaw, S. F., and R. G. Lord. 1987. Effects of categorization, attribution, and encoding processes on leadership perceptions. *Journal of Applied Psychology* 72: 97–106.

Cyert, R. M., and J. G. March. 1963. *A behavioral theory of the firm*. Englewood Cliffs, N.J.: Prentice Hall.

Daft, R. L. 1989. *Organization theory and design*. St. Paul, Minn.: West.

Daft, R. L., and K. E. Weick. 1984. Toward a model of organizations as interpretation systems. *Academy of Management Review* 9: 284–95.

Dalton, D. R., and I. F. Kesner. 1985. Organizational performance as an antecedent of inside/outside chief executive succession: An empirical assessment. *Academy of Management Journal* 28: 749–62.

Dandridge, T. C. 1985. The life stages of a symbol: When symbols work and when they can't. In *Organizational culture*, edited by P. Frost, L. Moore, M. R. Louis, C. Lundberg, and J. Martin, 141–53. Beverly Hills, Calif.: Sage.

Dansereau, F., G. Graen, and W. J. Haga. 1975. A vertical dyad linkage approach to leadership within formal organizations: A longitudinal investigation of the role making process. *Organizational Behavior and Human Performance* 13: 46–78.

Darley, J. M. and R. H. Fazio. 1980. Expectancy confirmation process arising in the social interaction sequence. *American Psychologist* 35: 867–81.

D'Aveni, R. A. 1989. The aftermath of organizational decline: A longitudinal study of the strategic and managerial characteristics of declining firms. *Academy of Management Journal* 32: 577–605.

Day, D. R., and R. M. Stogdill. 1972. Leader behavior of male and female supervisors: A comparative study. *Personnel Psychology* 25: 353–60.

Day, D. V. 1989. *Further examination of the nature of leader categories.* Unpublished manuscript, Louisiana State University.

Day, D. V., and R. G. Lord. 1988. Executive leadership and organizational performance: Suggestions for a new theory and methodology. *Journal of Management* 14: 111–22.

———. 1990. *Expertise and problem categorization: The role of expert processing in organizational sense-making.* Manuscript submitted for publication.

Deal, T. E., and A. A. Kennedy. 1982. *Corporate cultures: The rites and rituals of corporate life.* Reading, Mass.: Addison-Wesley.

DeVanna, M. A. 1984. *Male/female careers: The first decade.* New York: Center for Research in Career Development, Columbia University Graduate School of Business.

———. 1987. Women in management: Progress and promise. *Human Resource Management* 26: 469–81.

Dienesch, R. M., and R. C. Liden. 1986. Leader-member exchange model of leadership: A critique and further development. *Academy of Management Review* 11: 618–34.

Dipboye, R. L. 1985. Some neglected variables in research on discrimination in appraisals. *Academy of Management Review* 10: 116–27.

———. 1987. Problems and progress of women in management. In *Working women: Past, present, and future,* edited by K. S. Koziara, M. H. Moskow, and L. P. Tanner. Washington, D.C.: Bureau of National Affairs.

Doody, A. F., and R. Bingaman. 1988. *Reinventing the wheels: Ford's spectacular comeback.* Cambridge, Mass.: Ballinger.

Dubno, P. 1985. Attitudes toward women executives: A longitudinal approach. *Academy of Management Journal* 28: 235–39.

Duchon, D., S. G. Green, and T. D. Taber. 1986. Vertical dyad linkage: A longitudinal assessment of antecedents, measures, and consequences. *Journal of Applied Psychology* 71: 56–60.

Dugan, K. W. 1989. Ability and effort attributions: Do they affect how managers communicate performance feedback information? *Academy of Management Journal* 32: 87–114.

Dutton, J. E., and S. E. Jackson. 1987. Categorizing strategic issues: Links to organizational action. *Academy of Management Review* 12: 76–90.

Dyer, W. G., Jr. 1985. The cycle of cultural evolution in organizations. In *Gaining control of the corporate culture,* edited by R. Kilmann, M. Saxton, and R. Serpa, 200–29. San Francisco: Jossey-Bass.

Eden, D. 1984. Self-fulfilling prophecy as a management tool: Harnessing Pygmalion. *Academy of Management Review* 9: 64–73.

Eden, D., and U. Leviatan. 1975. Implicit leadership theory as a determinant of the factor structure underlying supervisory behavior scales. *Journal of*

Applied Psychology 60: 736–41.

Eden, D., and G. Ravid. 1982. Pygmalion versus self-expectancy: Effects of instructor- and self-expectancy on trainee performance. *Organizational Behavior and Human Performance* 30: 351–64.

Eden, D., and A. B. Shani. 1982. Pygmalion goes to boot camp: Expectancy, leadership, and trainee performance. *Journal of Applied Psychology* 67: 194–99.

Eisenberger, R., P. Fasolo, and V. Davis-LaMastro. 1990. Perceived organizational support and employee diligence, commitment, and innovation. *Journal of Applied Psychology* 75: 51–59.

Eisenhardt, K. M. 1989. Making fast strategic decisions in high-velocity environments. *Academy of Management Journal* 32: 543–76.

Eitzen, S. D., and N. R. Yetman. 1972. Managerial change, longevity, and organizational effectiveness. *Administrative Science Quarterly* 17: 110–26.

Elliott, E. S., and C. S. Dweck. 1988. Goals: An approach to motivation and achievement. *Journal of Personality and Social Psychology* 54: 5–12.

Farris, G. F., and F. G. Lim, Jr. 1969. Effects of performance on leadership, cohesiveness, influence, satisfaction, and subsequent performance. *Journal of Applied Psychology* 53: 490–97.

Farris, R. and L. Ragan. 1981. Importance of mentor-protégé relationships to the upward mobility of the female executive. *Mid South Business Journal* 1: 24–28.

Feldman, J. M. 1981. Beyond attribution theory: Cognitive processes in performance appraisal. *Journal of Applied Psychology* 66: 127–48.

———. 1986. A note on the statistical correction of halo error. *Journal of Applied Psychology* 71: 173–76.

Fernandez, P. 1981. The plight of women in management. *Signs* 7: 304–11.

Fiedler, F. E. 1964. A contingency model of leadership effectiveness. In *Advances in experimental social psychology, vol. 1,* edited by L. Berkowitz, 149–90. New York: Academic Press.

Fiedler, F. E., and J. E. Garcia. 1987. New approaches to effective leadership: Cognitive resources and organizational performance. New York: Wiley.

Fiske, S. T., D. R. Kinder, and W. M. Larter. 1983. The novice and the expert: Knowledge based strategies in political cognition. *Journal of Experimental Social Psychology* 19: 381–400.

Fiske, S. T., and S. L. Neuberg. 1990. A continuum model of impression formation from category-based to individuating processes: Influences of information and motivation on attention and interpretation. In *Advances in experimental social psychology, vol. 23,* edited by M. P. Zanna. San Diego, Calif.: Academic Press.

Fiske, S. T., and S. E. Taylor. 1984. Social cognition. Reading, Mass.: Addison-Wesley.

Foti, R. J., S. L. Fraser, and R. G. Lord. 1982. Effects of leadership labels and prototypes on perceptions of political leaders. *Journal of Applied Psychology* 67: 326–33.

Foti, R. J., and R. G. Lord. 1987. Prototypes and scripts: The effects of alternative methods of processing information. *Organizational Behavior and Human Decision Processes* 39: 318–41.

Foti, R. J., R. G. Lord, and F. Dambrot. In press. The effects of election outcomes on descriptions of political leaders. *Journal of Applied Social Psychology*.

Fraser, S. L., and R. G. Lord. 1988. Stimulus prototypicality and general leadership impressions: Their role in leadership and behavioral ratings. *Journal of Psychology* 122: 291–303.

Fredrickson, J. W., D. C. Hambrick, and S. Baumrin. 1988. A model of CEO dismissal. *Academy of Management Review* 13: 255–70.

French, J. R. P., and B. Raven. 1959. The bases of social power. In *Studies in social power*, edited by D. H. Cartwright. Ann Arbor: University of Michigan, Research Center for Group Dynamics, Institute of Social Research.

Friedman, S. D. and H. Singh. 1989. CEO succession and stockholder reaction: The influence of organizational context and event content. *Academy of Management Journal* 32: 718–44.

Galambos, J. A., R. P. Abelson, and J. B. Black. 1986. *Knowledge structures*. Hillsdale, N.J.: Erlbaum.

Galbraith, J. 1973. *Designing complex organizations*. Reading, Mass.: Addison-Wesley.

Gamson, W. A., and N. A. Scotch. 1964. Scapegoating in baseball. *American Journal of Sociology* 70: 69–72.

George, J. M. 1990. Personality, affect, and behavior in groups. *Journal of Applied Psychology* 75: 107–116.

Georgopoulos, B. S., G. M. Mahoney, and N. W. Jones. 1957. A path-goal approach to productivity. *Journal of Applied Psychology* 41: 345–53.

Gilbert, D. T., and D. S. Krull. 1988. Seeing less and knowing more: The benefits of perceptual ignorance. *Journal of Personality and Social Psychology* 54: 193–202.

Gilbert, D. T., D. S. Krull, and B. W. Pelham. 1988. Of thoughts unspoken: Social inference and the self-regulation of behavior. *Journal of Personality and Social Psychology* 55: 685–94.

Gilbert, D. T., and R. E. Osborne. 1989. Thinking backward: Some curable and incurable consequences of cognitive busyness. *Journal of Personality and Social Psychology* 57: 940–49.

Gilbert, D. T., B. W. Pelham, and D. S. Krull. 1988. On cognitive busyness: When person perceivers meet persons perceived. *Journal of Personality and Social Psychology* 54: 733–40.

Gioia, D. A., and P. P. Poole. 1984. Scripts in organizational behavior. *Academy of Management Review* 9: 449–59.

Gioia, D. A., and H. P. Sims, Jr. 1986. Cognition-behavior connections: Attribution and verbal behavior in leader-subordinate interactions. *Organizational Behavior and Human Decision Processes* 37: 197–227.

Glaser, R. 1982. Instructional psychology: Past, present, and future. *American Psychologist* 37: 292–305.

———. 1988. Expertise and learning: How do we think about instructional processes now that we have discovered knowledge structures? In *Complex information processing: The impact of Herbert Simon*, edited by D. Klahr and K. Kotovsky. Hillsdale, N.J.: Erlbaum.

Goldberg, P. 1989. The many faces of intuition. In *Intuition in Organizations: Leading and Managing Productively*, edited by W. M. Agor: 62–77. Newbury Park, Calif.: Sage.

Gordon, G. G. 1985. The relationship of corporate culture to industry sector and corporate performance. In *Gaining control of the corporate culture*, edited by R. Kilmann, M. Saxton, and R. Serpa, 103–25. San Francisco: Jossey-Bass.

Graen, G., and J. F. Cashman. 1975. A role-making model of leadership in formal organizations: A developmental approach. In *Leadership frontiers*, edited by J. G. Hunt and L. L. Larson, 143–65. Kent, Ohio: Kent State University Press.

Graen, G., J. F. Cashman, S. Ginsburg, and W. Schiemann. 1977. Effects of linking-pin quality on the quality of working life of lower participants. *Administrative Science Quarterly* 22: 491–504.

Graen, G., R. C. Liden, and W. Hoel. 1982. Role of leadership in the employee withdrawal process. *Journal of Applied Psychology* 67: 868–72.

Graen, G., and T. A. Scandura. 1987. Toward a psychology of dyadic organizing. In *Research in organizational behavior, vol. 9*, edited by B. M. Staw and L. L. Cummings, 175–208. Greenwich, Conn.: JAI Press.

Graen, G., and W. Schiemann. 1978. Leader-member agreement: A vertical dyad linkage approach. *Journal of Applied Psychology* 63: 206–12.

Green, S. G., and T. R. Mitchell. 1979. Attributional processes of leaders in leader-member interactions. *Organizational Behavior and Human Performance* 23: 429–58.

Greenhalgh, L. 1983. Organizational decline. In *Research in the sociology of organizations, vol. 2*, edited by S. B. Bacharach, 231–76. London: JAI Press.

Greenhouse, L. 1989. Court, 6-3, eases task of plaintiffs in job-bias suits. *New York Times*, 2 May, 1.

Grusky, O. 1963. Managerial succession. *American Journal of Sociology* 69: 72–76.

Guastello, S. J. 1987. A butterfly catastrophe model of motivation in organizations: Academic performance. *Journal of Applied Psychology* 72: 165–82.

Halberstam, D. 1986. *The reckoning*. New York: Avon.

Hambrick, D. C., and R. A. D'Aveni. 1988. Large corporate failures as downward spirals. *Administrative Science Quarterly* 33: 1–23.

Hambrick, D. C., and S. Finkelstein. 1987. Managerial discretion: A bridge between polar views of organizational outcomes. In *Research in organizational behavior, vol. 9*, edited by B. M. Staw and L. L. Cummings. Greenwich, Conn.: JAI Press.

Hambrick, D. C., and P. A. Mason. 1984. Upper echelons: The organization as a reflection of its top managers. *Academy of Management Review* 9: 193–206.

Hamilton, D. L., D. M. Driscoll, and L. T. Worth. 1989. Cognitive organization of impressions: Effects of incongruency in complex representations. *Journal of Personality and Social Psychology* 57: 925–39.

Hanges, P. J., E. P. Braverman, and J. R. Rentsch. 1989. *Changes in raters' impressions of subordinates: A catastrophe model*. Manuscript submitted for publication.

Harlan, A., and C. L. Weiss. 1982. Sex differences in factors affecting managerial career advancement. In *Women in the workplace*, edited by P. A. Wallace. Boston, Mass.: Auburn House.

Harper, S. C. 1989. Intuition: What separates executives from managers. In *Intuition in organizations: Leading and managing productively*, edited by W. H. Agor, 111–24. Newbury Park, Calif.: Sage.

Hasher, L., and R. T. Zacks. 1979. Automatic and effortful processes in memory. *Journal of Experimental Psychology* 108: 356–88.

Hastie, R., and B. Park. 1986. The relationship between memory and judgment depends on whether the judgment task is memory-based or on-line. *Psychological Review* 93: 258–68.

Hauenstein, N. 1987. *A process approach to ratings: The effects of ability and level of processing on encoding, retrieval, and rating outcomes*. Doctoral diss., University of Akron.

Hauenstein, N. M. A., and R. J. Foti. 1989. From laboratory to practice: Neglected issues in implementing frame-of-reference training. *Personnel Psychology* 42: 359–78.

Heilman, M. E. 1983. Sex bias in work settings: The lack of fit model. *Research in Organizational Behavior* 5: 269–98.

———. 1984. Information as a deterrent against sex discrimination: The effects of applicant sex and information type on preliminary decisions. *Organizational Behavior and Human Decision Processes* 33: 174–86.

Heilman, M. E., C. J. Block, R. F. Martell, and M. C. Simon. 1989. Has anything changed? Current characterizations of men, women, and managers. *Journal of Applied Psychology* 74: 935–42.

Heilman, M. E., and R. F. Martell. 1986. Exposure to successful women: Antidote to sex discrimination in applicant screening decisions? *Organizational Behavior and Human Decision Processes* 37: 376–90.

Heneman, R. L., D. B. Greenberger, and C. Anonyuo. 1989. Attributions and exchanges: The effects of interpersonal factors on the diagnosis of employee performance. *Academy of Management Journal* 32: 466–76.

Hennig, M., and A. Jardim. 1977. *The managerial women*. New York: Pocket Books.

Herold, D. M. 1977. Two-way influence processes in leader-follower dyads. *Academy of Management Journal* 20: 224–37.

Hirsch, P. M. 1975. Organizational effectiveness and the institutional environment. *Administrative Science Quarterly* 20: 327–44.

Hogan, E. A. 1987. Effects of prior expectations on performance ratings: A longitudinal study. *Academy of Management Journal* 30: 354–68.

Hollander, E. P. 1958. Conformity, status, and idiosyncrasy credit. *Psychological Review* 65: 117–27.

———. 1964. *Leaders, groups, and influence*. New York: Oxford University Press.

———. 1978. *Leadership dynamics: A practical guide to effective relationships*. New York: Free Press.

———. 1985. Leadership and power. In *The handbook of social psychology*, edited by G. Lindzey and E. Aronson. New York: Random House.

Hollander, E. P., and J. W. Julian. 1969. Contemporary trends in the analysis of leadership perceptions. *Psychological Bulletin* 71: 387–97.

Hollander, E. P., and L. R. Offermann. 1990. Power and leadership in organizations: Relationships in transition. *American Psychologist* 45: 179–89.

Hollenbeck, J. R., C. R. Williams, and H. J. Klein. 1989. An empirical examination of the antecedents of commitment to difficult goals. *Journal of Applied Psychology* 74: 18–23.

House, R. J. 1971. A path goal theory of leader effectiveness. *Administrative Science Quarterly* 16: 321–38.

———. 1977. A 1976 theory of charismatic leadership. In *Leadership: The cutting edge*, edited by J. G. Hunt and L. L. Larson. Carbondale: Southern Illinois University Press.

Hunt, J. G., B. R. Baliga, and M. F. Peterson. 1988. Strategic apex leader scripts and an organizational life cycle approach to leadership and excellence. *Journal of Management Development* 7.

Hunt, J. G., K. B. Boal, and R. L. Sorenson. In press. Top management leadership: Inside the black box. *Leadership Quarterly*.

Hunter, J. E., F. L. Schmidt, and G. B. Jackson. 1982. *Advanced meta-analysis: Quantitative methods for cumulating research findings across studies.* Beverly Hills, Calif.: Sage.

Hunter, J. E., F. L. Schmidt, and M. K. Judiesch. 1990. Individual differences in output variability as a function of job complexity. *Journal of Applied Psychology* 75: 28–42.

Iacocca, L., and S. Kleinfield. 1988. *Talking straight.* New York: Bantam.

Iacocca, L., and W. Novak. 1984. *Iacocca: An autobiography.* New York: Bantam.

Ilgen, D. R., and W. A. Knowlton, Jr. 1980. Performance attributional effects on feedback from superiors. *Organizational Behavior and Human Performance* 25: 441–56.

Isenberg, D. J. 1989. How senior managers think. In *Intuition in organizations: Leading and managing productively*, edited by W. H. Agor, 91–110. Newbury Park, Calif.: Sage.

Jackson, D. N. 1974. *Personality research form manual.* Port Huron, Mich.: Research Psychologist Press.

Jackson, S. E., and J. E. Dutton. 1988. Discerning threats and opportunities. *Administrative Science Quarterly* 33: 370–87.

Jago, A. G., and V. H. Vroom. 1982. Sex differences in the incidence and evaluation of participative leader behavior. *Journal of Applied Psychology* 67: 776–83.

James, W. 1890. *Principles of psychology.* New York: Holt.

Janis, I. L. 1982. *Groupthink: Psychological studies of policy decisions and fiascoes.* Boston: Houghton Mifflin.

———. 1989. *Crucial decisions: Leadership in policy making and crisis management.* New York: Free Press.

Jaques, E. 1989. Requisite organization: *The CEO'S guide to effective structure and leadership.* Arlington, Va.: Cason Hall.

Jones, E. E., and K. E. Davis. 1965. From acts to dispositions. In *Advances in experimental social psychology, vol. 2*, edited by L. Berkowitz. New York: Academic Press.

Jones, M. B. 1974. Regressing group on individual effectiveness. *Organizational Behavior and Human Performance* 11: 426–51.

Kahneman, D. 1973. *Attention and effort.* Englewood Cliffs, N.J.: Prentice Hall.

Kanter, R. M. 1977. *Men and women in the corporation*. New York: Basic Books.

———. 1982. The impact of hierarchical structures on the work behavior of men and women. In *Women and work: Problems and perspectives*, edited by R. Kahn-Hut, A. K. Daniels, and R. Colvard. New York: Oxford University Press.

Kaplowitz, S. A. 1978. Towards a systematic theory of power attribution. *Social Psychology* 41: 131–48.

Katz, D., and R. L. Kahn. 1978. *The social psychology of organizations*. 2nd edn. New York: Wiley.

Katz, J., and W. B. Gartner. 1988. Properties of emerging organizations. *Academy of Management Review* 13: 429–41.

Kelley, H. H. 1973. The processes of causal attribution. *American Psychologist* 28: 107–27.

Kernan, M. C., and R. G. Lord. 1988. The effects of participative versus assigned goals and feedback in a multi-trial task. *Motivation and Emotion* 12: 75–86.

Kerr, J., and J. W. Slocum, Jr. 1987. Managing corporate culture through reward systems. *Academy of Management Executive* 1: 99–107.

Kerr, S., and J. M. Jermier. 1978. Substitutes for leadership: Their meaning and measurement. *Organizational Behavior and Human Performance* 22: 375–403.

Kiesler, S., and L. Sproull, 1982 Managerial responses to changing environments: Perspectives on problem sensing from social cognition. *Administrative Science Quarterly* 27: 548–70.

Kim, L., and Y. Lim. 1988. Environment, generic strategies, and performance in a rapidly developing country: A taxonomic approach. *Academy of Management Journal* 31: 802–27.

Kipnis, D., P. J. Castell, M. Gergen, and D. Mauch. 1976. Metamorphic effects of power. *Journal of Applied Psychology* 61: 127–35.

Kleinmuntz, D. N., and J. B. Thomas. 1987. The value of action and inference in dynamic decision making. *Organizational Behavior and Human Decision Processes* 39: 341–46.

Komaki, J. L. 1986. Toward effective supervision: An operant analysis and comparison of managers at work. *Journal of Applied Psychology* 71: 270–79.

Kotter, J. P. 1988. *The leadership factor*. New York: Free Press.

Kozlowski, S. W. J., and M. L. Doherty. 1989. Integration of climate and leadership: Examination of a neglected issue. Journal of Applied Psychology 74: 546–53.

Kuhn, T. S. 1962. *The structure of scientific revolutions*. Chicago: University of Chicago Press.

Kuhnert, K. W., and P. Lewis. 1987. Transactional and transformational leadership: A constructive/developmental analysis. *Academy of Management Review* 12: 648–57.

Lachman, R., J. L. Lachman, and E. C. Butterfield. 1979 *Cognitive psychology and information processing: An introduction*. Hillsdale, N.J.: Erlbaum.

Larson, J. R., Jr. 1984. The performance feedback process: A preliminary model. *Organizational Behavior and Human Performance* 33: 42–76.

———. 1986. Supervisor's performance feedback to subordinates: The impact of subordinate performance valence and outcome dependence. *Organiza-*

tional Behavior and Human Decision Processes 37: 391–408.

———. 1989. The dynamic interplay between employees' feedback-seeking strategies and supervisors' delivery of performance feedback. *Academy of Management Review* 14: 408–22.

Lawrence, P. R., and J. W. Lorsch. 1969. *Organization and environment.* Homewood, Ill.: Irwin.

Leblebici, H., and G. R. Salancik. 1982. Stability in interorganizational performance: Rulemaking processes of the Chicago Board of Trade. *Administrative Science Quarterly* 27: 227–42.

Leiberson, S., and J. F. O'Connor. 1972. Leadership and organizational performance: A study of large corporations. *American Sociological Review* 37: 117–30.

Lingle, J. H., J. M. Dukerich, and T. M. Ostrom. 1983. Accessing information in memory-based impression judgments: Incongruity versus negativity in retrieval selectivity. *Journal of Personality and Social Psychology* 44: 262–72.

Lingle, J. H., and T. M. Ostrom. 1979. Retrieval selectivity in memory-based impression judgments. *Journal of Personality and Social Psychology* 37: 180–94.

Linville, P. W., and L. F. Clark. 1989. Can production systems cope with coping? *Social Cognition* 7: 195–236.

Lord, R. G. 1977. Functional leadership behavior: Measurement and relation to social power and leadership perceptions. *Administrative Science Quarterly* 22: 114–33.

———. 1981. *Heuristic social information processing and its implications for behavioral measurement: An example based on leadership categorization.* Paper presented at the American Psychological Convention, Los Angeles, Aug.

———. 1985. An information processing approach to social perceptions, leadership, and behavioral measurement in organizations. In *Research in organizational behavior, vol. 7,* edited by B. M. Staw and L. L. Cummings, 87–128. Greenwich, Conn.: JAI Press.

Lord, R. G., and G. M. Alliger. 1985. A comparison of four information processing models of leadership and social perceptions. *Human Relations* 38: 47–65.

Lord, R. G., J. F. Binning, M. C. Rush, and J. C. Thomas. 1978. The effect of performance cues and leader behavior on questionnaire ratings of leadership behavior. *Organizational Behavior and Human Performance* 21: 27–39.

Lord, R. G., C. De Vader, and G. Alliger. 1986. A meta-analysis of the relation between personality traits and leadership perceptions: An application of validity generalization procedures. *Journal of Applied Psychology* 71: 402–10.

Lord, R. G., and R. J. Foti. 1986. Schema theories, information processing, and organizational behavior. In *The thinking organization,* edited by H. P. Sims, Jr., and D. A. Gioia, 20–48. San Francisco: Jossey-Bass.

Lord, R. G., R. Foti, and C. De Vader. 1984. A test of leadership categorization theory: Internal structure, information processing, and leadership perceptions. *Organizational Behavior and Human Performance* 34: 343–78.

Lord, R. G., R. J. Foti, and J. S. Phillips. 1982. A theory of leadership categorization. In *Leadership: Beyond establishment views,* edited by J. G.

Hunt, U. Sekaran, and C. Schriesheim, 104–21. Carbondale: Southern Illinois University Press.

Lord, R. G., and M. C. Kernan. 1987. Scripts as determinants of purposeful behavior in organizations. *Academy of Management Review* 12: 265–77.

Lord, R. G., and K. J. Maher. 1990a. Leadership perceptions and leadership performance: Two distinct but interdependent processes. In *Applied social psychology and organizational settings*, edited by J. Carroll, 129–54. Hillsdale, N.J.: Erlbaum.

———. 1990b. Alternative information processing models and their implications for theory, research, and practice. *Academy of Management Review* 15: 9–28.

Lord, R. G., J. S. Phillips, and M. C. Rush. 1980. Effects of sex and personality on perceptions of emergent leadership, influence, and social power. *Journal of Applied Psychology* 65: 176–82.

Lord, R. G., and J. E. Smith. 1983. Theoretical, information processing, and situational factors affecting attribution theory models of organizational behavior. *Academy of Management Review* 8: 50–60.

Louis, M. R. 1985. An investigator's guide to workplace culture. In *Organizational culture*, edited by P. Frost, L. Moore, M. R. Louis, C. Lundberg, and J. Martin, 73–93. Beverly Hills, Calif.: Sage.

Lowe, C. A., and S. M. Kassin. 1980. A perceptual view of attribution: theoretical and methodological implications. *Personality and Social Psychology Bulletin* 6: 532–42.

Lowin, A., and J. R. Craig. 1968. The influence of level of performance on managerial style: An experimental object-lesson in the ambiguity of correlational data. *Organizational Behavior and Human Performance* 3: 440–58.

Lundberg, C. C. 1985. On the feasibility of cultural intervention in organizations. In *Organizational culture*, edited by P. Frost, L. Moore, M. R. Louis, C. Lundberg, and J. Martin, 169–85. Beverly Hills, Calif.: Sage.

Lurigio, A. J., and J. S. Carroll. 1985. Probation officers' schemata of offenders: Content, development and impact on treatment decisions. *Journal of Personality and Social Psychology* 48: 1112–26.

McClelland, D. C. 1961. *The achieving society*. New York: Van Nostrand.

McElroy, J. C., and H. K. Downey. 1982. Observation in organizational research: Panacea to the performance-attribution effect? *Academy of Management Journal* 25: 822–35.

McKeithan, K. B., J. S. Reitman, H. H. Rueter, and S. C. Hirtle. 1981. Knowledge organization and skill differences in computer programmers. *Cognitive Psychology* 13: 307–25.

Maher, K. J., R. G. Lord, and T. L. Scheiwe. 1990. *Alternative memory search models of rating bias and accuracy*. Paper presented at the meeting of the Society for Industrial and Organizational Psychology, Miami Beach, Fla., Apr.

Mahoney, R. J. 1988. *A commitment to greatness*. St. Louis: Monsanto.

Mann, R. D. 1959. A review of the relationships between personality and performance in small groups. *Psychological Bulletin* 56: 241–70.

Manz, C. C. 1986. Self-leadership: Toward an expanded theory of self-influence processes in organizations. *Academy of Management Review* 11: 585–600.

Manz, C. C., and H. P. Sims, Jr. 1980. Self-management as a substitute for leadership: A social learning theory perspective. *Academy of Management Review* 5: 361–67.

———. 1987. Leading workers to lead themselves: The external leadership of self-managing work teams. *Administrative Science Quarterly* 32: 106–29.

March, J. G., and H. A. Simon. 1958. *Organizations*. New York: Wiley.

Martin, H. J. 1985. Managing specialized corporate cultures. In *Gaining control of the corporate culture*, edited by R. Kilmann, M. Saxton, and R. Serpa, 148–62. San Francisco: Jossey-Bass.

Martin, J., S. B. Sitkin, and M. Boehm. 1985. Founders and the elusiveness of a cultural legacy. In *Organizational culture*, edited by P. Frost, L. Moore, M. R. Louis, C. Lundberg, and J. Martin, 99–124. Beverly Hills, Calif.: Sage.

Martinko, M. J., and W. L. Gardner. 1987. The leader/member attribution process. *Academy of Management Review* 12: 235–49.

Matthews, A. M., R. G. Lord, and J. B. Walker. 1990. *The development of leadership perceptions in children.* Unpublished manuscript, University of Akron.

Maurer, T. J., and R. G. Lord. 1988. IP variables in leadership perception: Is cognitive demand a moderator? Paper presented at the annual conference of the American Psychological Association (Div. 14), Atlanta, Ga., Aug.

Medin, D. L. 1989. Concepts and conceptual structure. *American Psychologist* 44: 1469–81.

Meglino, B. M., E. C. Ravlin, and C. L. Adkins. 1989. A work values approach to corporate culture: A field test of the value congruence process and its relationship to individual outcomes. *Journal of Applied Psychology* 74: 424–32.

Meindl, J. R., and S. B. Ehrlich. 1987. The romance of leadership and the evaluation of organizational performance. *Academy of Management Journal* 30: 91–109.

Meindl, J. R., S. B. Ehrlich, and J. M. Dukerich. 1985. The romance of leadership. *Administrative Science Quarterly* 30: 78–102.

Meyer, M. W., and L. G. Zucker. 1989. *Permanently failing organizations.* Newbury Park, Calif.: Sage.

Miles, R. E., and C. C. Snow. 1978. *Organizational strategy, structure, and process.* New York: McGraw-Hill.

Miller, D. 1988. Relating Porter's business strategies to environment and structure: Analysis and performance implications. *Academy of Management Journal* 31: 280–308.

Miller, D., and C. Droge. 1986. Psychological and traditional determinants of structure. *Administrative Science Quarterly* 31: 539–60.

Miller, D., C. Droge, and J. Toulouse. 1988. Strategic process and content as mediators between organizational context and structure. *Academy of Management Journal* 31: 544–89.

Miller, G. A. 1978. Practical and lexical knowledge. In *Cognition and categorization*, edited by E. Rosch and B. B. Lloyd, 305–19. Hillsdale, N.J.: Erlbaum.

Mintzberg, H. 1973. *The nature of managerial work.* New York: Harper and Row.

Mischel, W. 1973. Toward a cognitive social learning reconceptualization of personality. *Psychological Review* 80: 252–83.

Mitchell, T. R., and L. S. Kalb. 1982. Effects of job experience on supervisor attributions for a subordinate's poor performance. *Journal of Applied Psychology* 67: 181–88.

Mitchell, T. R., and R. E. Wood. 1980. Supervisor's responses to subordinate poor performance: A test of an attribution model. *Organizational Behavior and Human Performance* 25: 123–38.

Morgan, G. 1986. *Images of organization* (77–109). Beverly Hills, Calif.: Sage.

Morrison, A. M., and M. A. Von Glinow. 1990. Women and minorities in management. *American Psychologist* 45: 200–8.

Morrison, A. M., R. P. White, E. V. Van Velsor, and the Center for Creative Leadership. 1987. *Breaking the glass ceiling: Can women reach the top of America's largest corporations?* Reading, Mass.: Addison-Wesley.

Nieva, V. F., and B. A. Gutek. 1980. Sex effects on evaluation. *Academy of Management Review* 5: 267–76.

Nisbett, R., and L. Ross. 1980. *Human inference: Strategies and shortcomings of social judgment.* Englewood Cliffs, N.J.: Prentice Hall.

Noseworthy, C. M., and A. J. Lott. 1984. The cognitive organization of gender stereotypic categories. *Personality and Social Psychology Bulletin* 10: 474–81.

Nulty, P. 1989. America's toughest bosses. *Fortune*, 27 Feb., 43.

Nutt, P. C. 1984. Types of organizational decision processes. *Administrative Science Quarterly* 29: 414–50.

O'Connell, M. S., R. G. Lord, and M. K. O'Connell. 1990. *An empirical comparison of Japanese and American leadership prototypes: Implications for overseas assignment of managers.* Unpublished manuscript.

Offermann, L. R., J. K. Kennedy, Jr., and P. W. Wirtz. 1989. *Implicit leadership theories: Content, structure, and generalizability.* Unpublished manuscript.

Oliva, T. A., D. L. Day, and I. C. MacMillan. 1988. A generic model of competitive dynamics. *Academy of Management Review* 13: 374–89.

Olson, C. A., and B. E. Becker. 1983. Sex discrimination in the promotion process. *Industrial and Labor Relations Review* 36: 624–41.

Ostrom T. M. 1984. The sovereignty of social cognition. In *Handbook of social cognition*, edited by R. S. Wyer, Jr., and T. K. Srull. Hillsdale, N.J.: Erlbaum.

Ott, J. S. 1989. *The organizational culture perspective.* Pacific Grove, Calif.: Brooks/Cole.

Pascarella, P. 1982. Quality circles: Just another management headache? *Industry Week*, 28 June, 50–55.

Pazy, A. 1986. The persistence of pro-male bias despite identical information regarding causes of success. *Organizational Behavior and Human Decision Processes* 38: 366–77.

Peters, T. J., and A. Austin. 1985. *A passion for excellence: The leadership difference.* New York: Random House.

Peters, T. J., and R. H. Waterman, Jr. 1982. *In search of excellence: Lessons from America's best-run companies.* New York: Harper and Row.

Pfeffer, J. 1977. The ambiguity of leadership. *Academy of Management Review* 2: 104–12.

Pfeffer, J., and A. Davis-Blake. 1986. Administrative succession and organizational performance: How administrator experience mediates the succession effect. *Academy of Management Journal* 29: 72–83.

Phillips, J. S. 1984. The accuracy of leadership ratings: A cognitive categorization perspective. *Organizational Behavior and Human Performance* 33: 125–38.

Phillips, J. S., and R. G. Lord. 1981. Causal attributions and perceptions of leadership. *Organizational Behavior and Human Performance* 28: 143–63.

———. 1982. Schematic information processing and perceptions of leadership in problem-solving groups. *Journal of Applied Psychology* 67: 486–92.

Podsakoff, P. M. 1982. Determinants of a supervisor's use of rewards and punishments: A literature review and suggestions for further research. *Organizational Behavior and Human Performance* 29: 58–83.

Poole, M. S., and A. H. Van de Ven. 1989. Using paradox to build management and organization theories. *Academy of Management Review* 14: 562–78.

Porac, J., and H. Thomas. 1990. Taxonomic mental models in competitor definition. *Academy of Management Review* 15: 224–40.

Porac, J., H. Thomas, and C. Baden-Fuller. 1989. Competitive groups as cognitive communities: The case of Scottish knitwear manufacturers. *Journal of Management Studies* 26: 397–416.

Porter, M. E. 1980. *Competitive strategy.* New York: Free Press.

Potter, M. C. 1990. Remembering. In *Thinking: An invitation to cognitive science,* edited by D. N. Osherson and E. E. Smith, 3–32. Cambridge, Mass.: MIT Press.

Powell, G. N., and D. A. Butterfield. 1979. The "good manager": Masculine or androgynous. *Academy of Management Journal* 22: 395–403.

———. 1988. The "good manager": Does androgyny fare better in the 1980's? *Group and Organizational Studies* 14: 216–33.

Pound, W. 1969. The process of problem finding. *Industrial Management Review* 11: 1–19.

Pulakos, E. D., and K. N. Wexley. 1983. The relationship among perceptual similarity, sex, and performance ratings in manager-subordinate dyads. *Academy of Management Journal* 26: 129–39.

Ragan, L. 1984. Women and mentors. *Signs* 5: 289–94.

Raynolds, E. H. 1987. Management women in the corporate workplace: Possibilities for the year 2000. *Human Resource Management* 26: 265–76.

Read, S. J. 1987. Constructing causal scenarios: A knowledge structure approach to causal reasoning. *Journal of Personality and Social Psychology* 52: 288–302.

Reed, R., and R. J. DeFillippi. 1990. Causal ambiguity, barriers to imitation, and sustainable competitive advantage. *Academy of Management Review* 15: 88–102.

Reiff, R. 1989. Blood, sweat, and profits. *Forbes,* Mar., 110–12.

Romanelli, E. 1989. Environments and strategies of organization start-up: Effects on early survival. *Administrative Science Quarterly* 34: 369–87.

Rosch, E. 1978. Principles of categorization. In *Cognition and categorization,* edited by E. Rosch and B. B. Lloyd. Hillsdale, N.J.: Erlbaum.

Rosen, B., L. Templeton, and A. Kechline. 1981. Top-level women executives.

Business Horizons 5: 233–41.

Rosenkrantz, P., S. Vogel, H. Bee, I. Broverman, and D. M. Broverman. 1968. Sex role stereotypes and self-concepts in college students. *Journal of Consulting and Clinical Psychology* 32: 287–95.

Rush, M. C., and L. L. Beauvais. 1981. A critical analysis of format-induced versus subject-induced bias in leadership ratings. *Journal of Applied Psychology* 66: 722–27.

Rush, M. C., J. S. Phillips, and R. G. Lord. 1981. Effects of a temporal delay in rating on leader behavior descriptions: A laboratory investigation. *Journal of Applied Psychology* 66: 442–50.

Rush, M. C., J. C. Thomas, and R. G. Lord. 1977. Implicit leadership theory: A potential threat to the internal validity of leader behavior questionnaires. *Organizational Behavior and Human Performance* 20: 93–110.

Saffold, G. S., III. 1988. Culture traits, strength, and organizational performance: Moving beyond "strong" culture. *Academy of Management Review* 13: 546–58.

Salancik, G. R., and J. Pfeffer. 1977. Constraints on administrator discretion: The limited influence of mayors on city budgets. *Urban Affairs Quarterly* 12: 475–98.

Sapienza, A. M. 1985. Believing is seeing: How culture influences the decisions top managers make. In *Gaining control of the corporate culture*, edited by R. Kilmann, M. Saxton, and R. Serpa, 66–83. San Francisco: Jossey-Bass.

——. 1987. Imagery and strategy. *Journal of Management* 13: 543–55.

Schank, R. C., and R. P. Abelson. 1977. *Scripts, plans, goals, and understanding.* Hillsdale, N.J.: Erlbaum.

Schein, E. H. 1985. *Organizational culture and leadership.* San Francisco: Jossey-Bass.

Schein, V. E. 1973. The relationship between sex role stereotypes and requisite management characteristics. *Journal of Applied Psychology* 57: 95–100.

——. 1975. Relationship between sex role stereotypes and requisite management characteristics among female managers. *Journal of Applied Psychology* 60: 340–44.

Schein, V. E., R. Mueller, and C. Jacobson. 1989. The relationship between sex role stereotypes and requisite management characteristics among college students. *Sex Roles.*

Scherer, F. M. 1970. *Industrial pricing: Theory and evidence.* Chicago: Rand McNally.

Schmidt, F. L., J. E. Hunter, R. C. McKenzie, and T. W. Muldrow. 1979. Impact of valid selection procedures on work-force productivity. *Journal of Applied Psychology* 64: 609–26.

Schneider, B. 1987. The people make the place. *Personnel Psychology* 40: 437–53.

Schreyogg, G., and H. Steinmann. 1987. Strategic control: A new perspective. *Academy of Management Review* 12: 91–103.

Schwartz, E. B., and W. B. Waetjen. 1976. Improving the self-concepts of women managers. *Business Quarterly* 41: 20–27.

Schwartz, K. B., and K. Menon. 1985. Executive succession in failing firms. *Academy of Management Journal* 28: 680–86.

Schwenk, C. R. 1984. Cognitive simplification processes in strategic decision-making. *Strategic Management Journal* 5: 111–28.

———. 1988. The cognitive perspective on strategic decision making. *Journal of Management Studies* 25: 41–55.

Sellers, P. 1988. How king Kellogg beat the blahs. *Fortune*, 29 Aug., 54–55, 58, 60, 64.

Sheridan, J. E. 1985. A catastrophe model of employee withdrawal leading to low job performance, high absenteeism, and job turnover during the first year of employment. *Academy of Management Journal* 28: 88–109.

Shiffrin, R. M., and W. Schneider. 1977. Controlled and automatic human information processing: Perceptual learning, automatic attending, and a general theory. *Psychological Review* 84: 127–90.

Siehl, C. 1985. After the founder: An opportunity to manage culture. In *Organizational culture*, edited by P. Frost, L. Moore, M. R. Louis, C. Lundberg, and J. Martin, 125–40. Beverly Hills, Calif.: Sage.

Simon, H. A. 1987. Making management decisions: The role of intuition and emotion. *Academy of Management Executive* 1: 57–64.

Sims, H. P., Jr. 1977. The leader as a manager of reinforcement contingencies: An empirical example and a model. In *Leadership: The cutting edge*, edited by J. G. Hunt and L. L. Larson. Carbondale: Southern Illinois University Press.

Sims, H. P., Jr., and C. C. Manz, 1984. Observing leader verbal behavior: Toward reciprocal determinism in leadership theory. *Journal of Applied Psychology* 69: 222–32.

Smircich, L., and C. Stubbart. 1985. Strategic management in an enacted world. *Academy of Management Review* 10: 724–36.

Smith, E. R., and F. D. Miller. 1983. Mediation among attributional inferences and comprehension processes: Initial findings and a general method. *Journal of Personality and Social Psychology* 44: 492–505.

Smith, J. E., K. P. Carson, and R. A. Alexander. 1984. Leadership: It can make a difference. *Academy of Management Journal* 27: 765–76.

Smith, M., and M. C. White. 1987. Strategy, CEO specialization, and succession. *Administrative Science Quarterly* 32: 263–80.

Smith, P. C., and L. M. Kendall. 1963. Retranslation of expectations: An approach to the construction of unambiguous anchors for rating scales. *Journal of Applied Psychology* 47: 149–55.

Smith, R. E. 1979. *The subtle revolution*. Washington, D.C.: Urban Institute.

Snow, C. C., and L. G. Hrebiniak. 1980. Strategy, distinctive competence, and organizational performance. *Administrative Science Quarterly* 25: 317–36.

Snyder, M. 1984. When belief creates reality. In *Advances in experimental social psychology, vol. 18*, edited by L. Berkowitz, 247–305. Orlando, Fla.: Academic Press.

Srull, T. K., and R. S. Wyer, Jr. 1989. Person memory and judgment. *Psychological Review* 96: 58–83.

Staw, B. M. 1975. Attribution of the "causes" of performance: A general alternative interpretation of cross-sectional research on organizations. *Organizational Behavior and Human Performance* 13: 414–32.

Staw, B. M., P. I. McKechnie, and S. M. Puffer. 1983. The justification of organizational performance. *Administrative Science Quarterly* 28: 582–600.

Staw, B. M., and J. Ross. 1980. Commitment in an experimenting society: A study of the attribution of leadership from administrative scenarios. *Journal of Applied Psychology* 65: 249–60.

———. 1987. Behavior in escalation situations: Antecedents, prototypes, and solutions. In *Research in organizational behavior, vol. 9*, edited by B. M. Staw and L. L. Cummings, 39–78. Greenwich, Conn.: JAI Press.

Staw, B. M., L. E. Sandelands, and J. E. Dutton. 1981. Threat-rigidity effects in organizational behavior: A multilevel analysis. *Administrative Science Quarterly* 26: 501–25.

Stein, R. T., and T. Heller. 1979. An empirical analysis of the correlations between leadership status and participation rates reported in the literature. *Journal of Personality and Social Psychology* 11: 1993–2002.

Stein, R. T., L. R. Hoffman, S. J. Cooley, and R. W. Pearse. 1979. Leadership valence: Modeling and measuring the process of emergent leadership. In *Crosscurrents in leadership*, edited by J. G. Hunt and L. L. Larson, 126–47. Carbondale: Southern Illinois University Press.

Stewart, I. N., and P. L. Peregoy. 1983. Catastrophe theory modeling in psychology. *Psychological Bulletin* 94: 336–62.

Stewart, L. P., and W. B. Gudykunst. 1982. Differential factors influencing the hierarchical level and number of promotions of males and females within an organization. *Academy of Management Journal* 2: 586–97.

Stogdill, R. M. 1948. Personal factors associated with leadership: A survey of the literature. *Journal of Psychology* 25: 35–71.

———. 1963. *Manual for the Leader Behavior Description Questionnaire—Form XII.* Columbus: Bureau of Business Research, Ohio State University.

———. 1974. *Handbook of leadership: A survey of theory and research.* New York: Free Press.

Streufert, S., and R. W. Swezey. 1986. *Complexity, managers, and organizations.* Orlando, Fla.: Academic Press.

Strickland, L. H. 1958. Surveillance and trust. *Journal of Personality* 26: 201–15.

Sutton, R. I., and A. L. Callahan. 1987. The stigma of bankruptcy: Spoiled organizational image and its management. *Academy of Management Journal* 30: 405–36.

Sutton, C. D., and R. W. Woodman. 1990. Pygmalion goes to work: The effects of supervisor expectations in a retail setting. *Journal of Applied Psychology* 74: 943–50.

Taylor, S. E., and S. T. Fiske. 1978. Salience, attention, and attribution: Top of the head phenomena. In *Advances in experimental social psychology*, edited by L. Berkowitz. New York: Academic Press.

Terborg, J. R. 1977. Women in management: A research review. *Journal of Applied Psychology* 62: 647–64.

Terborg, J. R., and D. R. Ilgen. 1975. A theoretical approach to sex discrimination in traditionally masculine occupations. *Organizational behavior and human performance* 13: 352–76.

Tesser, A., and S. Rosen. 1975. The reluctance to transmit bad news. In *Advances in experimental social psychology, vol.8*, edited by L. Berkowitz, 193–232. New York: Academic Press.

Thom, R. 1975. *Structural stability and morphogenesis.* New York: Benjamin-

Addison-Wesley.

Thomas, A. B. 1988. Does leadership make a difference to organizational performance? *Administrative Science Quarterly* 33: 388–400.

Tosi, H. L., Jr., and S. W. Einbender. 1985. The effects of type and amount of information in sex discrimination research: A meta-analysis. *Academy of Management Journal* 28: 712–23.

Tosi, H. L., Jr., and L. R. Gomez-Mejia. 1989. The decoupling of CEO pay and performance: An agency theory perspective. *Administrative Science Quarterly* 34: 169–89.

Tsui, A. S., and B. A. Gutek. 1984. A role set analysis of gender differences in performance, affective relationships, and career success of industrial middle managers. *Academy of Management Journal* 27: 614–35.

Tsui, A. S., and C. A. O'Reilly, III. 1989. Beyond simple demographic effects: the importance of relational demography in superior-subordinate dyads. *Academy of Management Journal* 32: 402–23.

Tulving, E., and D. M. Thompson. 1973. Encoding specificity and retrieval processes in episodic memory. *Psychological Review* 80: 352–73.

Turban, D. B., and A. P. Jones. 1988. Supervisor-subordinate similarity: Types, effects, and mechanisms. *Journal of Applied Psychology* 73: 228–34.

Tushman, M. L., and P. Anderson. 1986. Technological discontinuities and organizational environments. *Administrative Science Quarterly* 31: 439–65.

Tushman, M. L., W. H. Newman, and E. Romanelli. 1986. Convergence and upheaval: Managing the unsteady pace of organizational evolution. *California Management Review* 29: 29–44.

Tushman, M. L., and E. Romanelli. 1985. Organizational evolution: A metamorphosis model of convergence and reorientation. In *Research in organizational behavior, vol. 7*, edited by B. M. Staw and L. L. Cummings. Greenwich, Conn.: JAI Press.

U.S. Department of Commerce, Bureau of the Census. 1984. We, the American women of the 80's. Washington, D.C.: Government Printing Office.

Van de Ven, A. H., and R. Drazin. 1985. The concept of fit in contingency theory. In *Research in organizational behavior, vol. 7*, edited by B. M. Staw and L. L. Cummings, 333–65. Greenwich, Conn.: JAI Press.

Van Fleet, D. D., and R. W. Griffin. 1989. Quality circles: A review and suggested future directions. In *International review of industrial and organizational psychology*, edited by C. L. Cooper and I. T. Robertson, 213–33. Chichester, England: Wiley.

Van Maanen, J., and S. R. Barley. 1984. Occupational communities: Culture and control in organizations. In *Research in organizational behavior, vol. 6*, edited by B. M. Staw and L. L. Cummings, 287–365. Greenwich, Conn.: JAI Press.

Van Maanen, J., and G. Kunda. 1989. "Real feelings": Emotional expression and organizational culture. In *Research in organizational behavior, vol. 11*, edited by B. M. Staw and L. L. Cummings, 43–103. Greenwich, Conn.: JAI Press.

Vroom, V. H. 1964. *Work and motivation.* New York: Wiley.

Vroom, V. H., and A. Jago. 1988. *The new leadership: Managing participation in organizations.* Englewood Cliffs, N.J.: Prentice Hall.

Vroom, V. H., and P. W. Yetton. 1973. *Leadership and decision-making*. Pittsburgh: University of Pittsburgh Press.

Walsh, J. P. 1989. *Knowledge structures and the management of organization: A research review and agenda*. Manuscript submitted for publication.

Walsh, J. P., and L. Fahey. 1986. The role of negotiated belief structures in strategy making. *Journal of Management* 12: 325–38.

Wayne, S. J., and G. R. Ferris. 1989. *Influence tactics, affect, and exchange quality in supervisor-subordinate dyads*. Manuscript submitted for publication.

Weick, K. E. 1979. *The social psychology of organizing*. Reading, Mass.: Addison-Wesley.

———. 1985. The significance of corporate culture. In *Organizational culture*, edited by P. Frost, L. Moore, M. R. Louis, C. Lundberg, and J. Martin, 381–89. Beverly Hills, Calif.: Sage.

———. 1988. Enacted sensemaking in crisis situations. *Journal of Management Studies* 25: 305–17.

Weiner, N. 1988. Forms of value systems: A focus on organizational effectiveness and cultural change and maintenance. *Academy of Management Review* 13: 534–45.

Weiner, N., and T. A. Mahoney. 1981. A model of corporate performance as a function of environmental, organizational, and leadership influence. *Academy of Management Journal* 24: 453–70.

Weiss, H. M., and S. Adler. 1981. Cognitive complexity and the structure of implicit leadership theories. *Journal of Applied Psychology* 66: 69–78.

Weitzel, W., and E. Jonsson. 1989. Decline in organizations: A literature integration and extension. *Administrative Science Quarterly* 34: 91–109.

Westley, F. R., and H. Mintzberg. 1988. Profiles of strategic vision: Levesque and Iacocca. In *Charismatic leadership: The elusive factor in organizational effectiveness*, edited by J. A. Conger and R. N. Kanungo. San Francisco: Jossey-Bass.

White, M. C., G. De Sanctis, and M. D. Crino. 1981. Achievement, self-confidence, personality traits, and leadership ability: A review of the literature on sex differences. *Psychological Reports* 48: 547–69.

Who's excellent now? 1984. *Business Week*, 5 Nov., 76–86.

Wilkins, A. L., and W. G. Dyer, Jr. 1988. Toward culturally sensitive theories of culture change. *Academy of Management Review* 13: 522–33.

Wilkins, A. L., and W. G. Ouchi. 1983. Efficient cultures: Exploring the relationship between culture and organizational performance. *Administrative Science Quarterly* 28: 468–81.

Winter, L., and J. S. Uleman. 1984. When are social judgments made? Evidence for the spontaneousness of trait inferences. *Journal of Personality and Social Psychology* 47: 237–52.

Woll, S. B., and A. C. Graesser. 1982. Memory discrimination for information typical or atypical of person schemata. *Social Cognition* 1: 287–310.

Wong, P. T. P., and B. Weiner. 1981. When people ask "why" questions, and the heuristics of attributional search. *Journal of Personality and Social Psychology* 40: 650–63.

Yates, B. 1983. *The decline and fall of the American automobile industry*. New York: Empire.

Yeah, the guy's name rings a bell, but . . . *St. Louis Post-Dispatch.*
Yukl, G. A. 1989. *Leadership in organizations.* 2nd ed. Englewood Cliffs, N.J.: Prentice Hall.
Zalesny, M. D., and S. Highhouse. In press. Accuracy in performance evaluations. *Organizational Behavior and Human Decision Processes.*

About the Authors ———————————————

Robert G. Lord is Professor of Industrial/Organizational Psychology at the University of Akron. He is a fellow of the Society for Industrial and Organizational Psychology, American Psychological Association, and is a member of the Academy of Management and the American Psychological Society. Professor Lord received his Ph.D. in industrial/organizational psychology from Carnegie-Mellon University, and he received a B.A. in economics from the University of Michigan. He is an associate editor of the *Journal of Applied Psychology* and serves on the editorial boards for *Organizational Behavior and Human Decision Processes*, the *Leadership Quarterly* and the *Journal of Applied Social Psychology*. Professor Lord has published over 50 articles in the areas of leadership perceptions, information processing and social cognition, group problem solving behavior, and motivation.

Karen J. Maher is Assistant Professor of Management at the University of Missouri, St. Louis. She received a Ph.D. in industrial/organizational psychology from the University of Akron. Maher is a member of the Academy of Management, the American Psychological Association, and the American Psychological Society. She has co-authored several book chapters on information processing and leadership, and has published work on information processing in the *Academy of Management Review*.

Author Index

Subject Index ———————————————